Brush Management

Brush Management

Past, Present, Future

Edited by
Wayne T. Hamilton
Allan McGinty
Darrell N. Ueckert
C. Wayne Hanselka
and
Michelle R. Lee

Texas A&M
University Press
College Station

A grant from the Texas Agricultural Experiment Station,
Texas A&M University, helped make this book possible.

Library of Congress Cataloging-in-Publication Data

Brush management: past, present, future / edited by Wayne T. Hamilton
...[et al.].—1st ed.
p. cm.—(Texas A&M University agriculture series; no. 7)
Includes index.
ISBN 1-58544-355-7 (cloth: alk. paper)—ISBN 1-58544-357-3 (pbk.: alk. paper)
1. Brush–Control–Texas. 2. Rangelands–Weed control–Texas. 3. Range
management–Texas. 4. Prescribed burning–Texas. I. Hamilton, W. T. (Wayne T.), 1933–
II. Series.
SB612.T4B78 2004
636.0'845–dc22
2004007213

Dedicated to Dr. Charles J. Scifres (1941–2003) for his outstanding contributions to the field of brush and weed management

Contents

Brush Management

1 Introduction

Rangeland Woody Plant and Weed Management—Past, Present, and Future

Wayne T. Hamilton
and
Darrell N. Ueckert

Management of woody plants and weeds has been at or near the top of every survey we have seen that asked rangeland producers to identify top priority issues affecting their operations. Although we have changed the way we view brush and weeds with respect to the best composition of plants for a variety of purposes, the fact remains that they are of as much or greater concern to us today than they have been at any time during the past century. Indeed, this is a pervasive issue that has not gone away. 3

Although several of the chapters in this book will reflect on the origin of the Texas brush and weed problem, we felt it would be appropriate to offer a historical overview in the introduction. We cannot give full measure to solving the problem unless we understand how it came about. Without this understanding, we will likely continue to repeat past mistakes that we now regret.

Vegetation Changes on Texas Rangelands

Many of the changes in rangeland ecosystems in Texas are the direct influence of human activity, but some are not. As recently as 8,000 years ago, most of our current Chihuahuan Desert and semiarid grasslands were woodlands, dominated by pinyon pines (*Pinus* spp.), junipers (*Juniperus* spp.), and oaks (*Quercus* spp.). Beginning about this time, the climate of the region became drier and warmer, and over a few thousand years the vegetation changed from mesic forests and woodlands to xeric (desertlike) grasslands and savannas. A cooling period from about 600 to 150 years ago may have reversed some of the earlier vegetation changes, but since about 1850 the earth has been in a warming mode. When the first European ranchers visited Texas they were probably seeing a vegetation type persisting from a previous set of environmental conditions. Many plant species and plant communities present then may have been in a state of flux, and subject to elimination by one or two severe droughts, especially if coupled with unwise rangeland management practices. Therefore, present vegetation reflects long-term changes in climate as well as influences of relatively recent disturbances (Robinson 1979, Hester 1980). The changing human influence, an alteration in the role of fire, the elevation of atmospheric carbon dioxide, and the interactions of these factors appear to be the most important recent disturbances impacting vegetation in the state (Scifres and Hamilton 1993). Consequently, changes during the last 100 to 350 years may be the most germane to the current vegetative composition of Texas rangelands (Bogush 1952, Inglis 1964, York and Dick-Peddie 1969, Jones 1975, Archer et al. 1988).

A key point must be made about grazing in the pre-European time period. Rangelands were used, often heavily, by large herbivores that included a variety of species, most notable of which were bison. Extensive herds of wild horses and cattle, introduced into Texas by the Spanish, roamed free across much of the state. These herds followed fresh forage supplies brought on by rainfall and/or fires, and generally stayed within close proximity to available surface water. Their grazing behavior is probably best described as periodically intensive, but interspersed with periods of no grazing that provided ample time for the vegetation to recover.

Because the focus on brush as a problem is relatively recent, some have deduced illogically that woody plants only recently became part of the landscape. Humans have inhabited Texas for at least 11,000 years, and the now omnipresent mesquite (*Prosopis* spp.) was here as early as 3000 B.P. (before present time) and likely even longer (Hester 1980). Oak was observed in biosilica analyses of samples from the Choke Canyon areas of South Texas radiocarbon dated to approximately 5300 B.P. There is no reason to believe that the many other species now present on Texas rangelands were not also prehistoric, with notable exceptions, such as Macartney rose (*Rosa bracteata*), salt cedar (*Tamarix* spp.), and others that were introduced.

In the mid-nineteenth century, Europeans eliminated the vast herds of free-roaming wild horses, cattle, bison, bear, prairie dogs, and even deer (from parts of the state) and their influences on rangeland vegetation. People became sedentary and proprietary in the 1870s with the advent of barbed wire, which could limit livestock to a specific property and prevent ingress of livestock from adjacent lands. A secondary effect of these activities, the increase in woody plants, changed wildlife habitat that once favored prairie or savanna species. For example, Hester found remains of antelope and prairie dogs in archeological sites in what has long been known as the "brush country" of South Texas, an undesirable habitat for either species in the memory of living humans (*The Discourse* 1974). Berlandier, cited by Ohlendorf et al. (1980:364), traveled from Matamoros to Goliad in 1834 across an area between Santa Gertrudis Creek and the Nueces River and encountered, among other wildlife, "a species of antelope without doubt unknown to natural history called berrendo, the pronghorn." Pronghorn antelope have not been seen in this region of Texas for at least 100 years.

In the early 1500s, Cabeza de Vaca traveled through South Texas. His journal accounts provide the earliest descriptions of the inhabitants and vegetation of the state. Early travelers across Texas generally referred to the rangelands they traversed as grasslands. Although these landscapes were characterized as open prairies or savannas, woody plants did occur along drainages, ridges, escarpments, and in other areas (Bogush 1952, Malin 1953, Inglis 1964). Young woody plants were likely present even when early travelers described only expanses of prairie; they simply were not evident in the heavy swards of dominating grasses (Scifres and Hamilton 1993). As the disturbance regime changed with settlement, stands of woody plants began to replace grasslands. While the speed of this change obviously varied within the state, it was apparently very dramatic during the years between 1820 and the late part of the nineteenth century. For example, around 1821, the area near Goliad, Texas was described by travelers as "rolling prairie." Subsequent descriptions shifted to "alternate prairie and woodland" followed by "mesquite prairie." By 1866, travelers described this area as "country covered with mesquite and cactus" (Inglis 1964, McConnell 1889).

There is ample evidence to document a dramatic shift in the relative proportions of the different types of vegetation, grasses and grasslike species, forbs, succulents, shrubs, and trees in other areas of the state between the first quarter and the end of the nineteenth century. For example, there is little doubt that juniper on the Edwards Plateau and contiguous areas and honey mesquite (*Prosopis glandulosa*) in the Rolling Plains encroached on grassland prairies or open savannas, perhaps paralleling encroachment of mixed-brush species in South Texas.

Early Texas ranchers assumed that the rangelands were capable of supplying unlimited amounts of forage for their grazing livestock. This is not surprising, considering the lush swards of forage resources that they saw. There is evidence at the turn of the nineteenth century in the Edwards Plateau region that ranges were stocked at 150 or more animal units per section (Taylor and Kothmann 1993). These early ranchers preceded development of proper grazing management based on plant physiology and ecological principles. Concepts such as proper forage utilization, carrying capacity of the range, plant succession, plant and animal interactions, or grazing management were not part of their understanding.

Heavy, continuous grazing by livestock, which rapidly reduced the abundance of mulch, litter, and standing vegetation, coupled with fire suppression efforts, essentially eliminated fire as an ecological factor on the rangelands. While woody plants and cactus (*Opuntia* spp.) were present when Europeans arrived in Texas, they were restricted to certain sites and, under pristine conditions with recurring, intense fires, only rarely moved out into the grasslands and savannas. Continuous excessive grazing killed out or greatly reduced the abundance of the more palatable, productive, and deeprooted grasses and reduced the soil protective layers of mulch and standing vegetation. The amount of bare ground greatly increased, as did the loss of topsoil to erosion.

Scifres (1980) and Scifres and Hamilton (1993) summarized the influence of human activity on rangeland vegetation change in Texas by identifying the following factors: (1) continual and excessive grazing pressure on grasslands by an increase in the number of grazing animals, (2) reduction of naturally occurring fires, (3) intentional and severe restrictions in the movements of grazing animals by fencing, (4) cultivation and abandonment of grassland soils, (5) the increased mobility of people and their animals which augmented the dispersion of woody plant propagules, (6) introduction of woody plants such as Macartney rose which escaped cultivation to become serious problems, and (7) the increase in competitive advantage of woody plants over warm-season perennial grasses associated with the elevation of atmospheric carbon dioxide.

Impact of the Changing Rangelands

Vegetation changes on Texas rangelands led to the very serious deterioration of several ecological processes that must be maintained in a healthy state to sustain productive rangelands. These processes include energy flow, the hydrological cycle, and mineral cycling. Continuous, excessive grazing left too little photosynthetic tissue (green leaves) for the desirable forage plants to capture sufficient energy from sunlight to nourish both the plants and the animals that grazed them. The larger, most palatable, deep-rooted grasses, which had previously been able to effectively utilize moisture and nutrients from deep within the soil profile, decreased in abundance and were replaced by less efficient, short-rooted species. Removal of the mulch component, along with the deep-rooted species, coupled with soil compaction from too many hooves, exposed the surface soil to the full energy of rain, wind, and the direct rays of the sun. This resulted in decreased soil porosity, less organic matter within the soil, decreased rainfall infiltration, and a reduction in water-holding capacity. The rangelands rapidly became more xeric, rainfall was less effective, and the nitrogen-rich surface soil was moved elsewhere by the forces of wind and water.

The environment rapidly became less and less amenable to the growth and reproduction of desirable forage plants, but more and more suitable for the establishment, growth, and reproduction of plant species that were well adapted to nitrogen-poor soils and desertlike conditions. Many of these plants had adaptations that protected them from heavy use by herbivores, such as the spines, thorns, and secondary plant compounds in mesquite, juniper, and pricklypear (*Opuntia engelmannii*). As these invader or increaser plants became abundant and matured, they competed with the remaining forage plants for moisture, nutrients, and light and caused further declines in production, cover, density, and diversity of the desirable forage species. This process created an environment very suitable for the establishment of the seedlings of the xeric plants but less and less conducive for intense fires. This desertification cycle, once begun, is a dynamic, self-perpetuating process (Thurow 1991).

Rangelands that have been converted to brush-dominated woodlands become "steady states," just as the original grasslands and savannas were steady states (Archer et al. 1988, Dye 1995). Brush-dominated rangelands will not revert to productive grasslands or savannas if livestock grazing is reduced or even totally eliminated. The conversion of woodlands back to grasslands requires sustained human intervention, including brush removal (with reseeding in many cases), maintenance or follow-up control practices, and proper livestock grazing management.

Dealing with the Brush Problem

Our attempts to deal with brush have evolved through several eras and different philosophies. In the post–World War II era of the 1940s and 1950s, the pervasive philosophy was to eradicate brush to grow grass and make money from livestock production. Brush control replaced eradication as the philosophical approach in the 1960s and 1970s when it became obvious that eradication was an economic, if not a biological, impossibility. During this period, we learned that most woody species could not be controlled economically on target areas with single treatments and begrudgingly accepted the persistence of brush species as part of most posttreatment plant composition. In the late 1970s and early 1980s, we began to recognize the value of some woody plants in the range environment, primarily because of the increasing economic importance of wildlife. Therefore, we began to leave some brush in patterns and designs for wildlife. Unfortunately, as during the earlier periods, the benefits of brush treatments often diminished before economic returns could outweigh costs.

By the mid-1980s, integrated brush management systems defined a new commitment to long-term, strategic, and systematic planning for brush control over the 15 to 20 years required to economically reduce and hold stands at maintenance levels.

Integrated brush and weed management implies the application of an array of carefully selected control or management practices in a planned sequence and with proper timing so that the characteristic weaknesses of one treatment are offset by the unique strengths of subsequent treatments. Follow-up or maintenance practices must be selected and properly timed and applied so that the effective life of expensive, initial reclamation treatments will be extended long enough for costs to be recovered. Sound grazing management is an integral component of all integrated brush or weed management systems on rangeland or improved pastures.

Tactical brush management, exemplified by the "Brush Busters" program that evolved during the mid-1990s, has proven the success of individual plant treatments for long-term suppression of stand densities of 400 plants per acre or less. Probably one of the most significant realizations that has evolved in rangeland brush and weed management is that we should utilize all available knowledge on the biology and ecology of the target species in our weed management programs. All weed and brush species have a vulnerable spot, or a weak link, in their life cycle. This is the life stage when they can most easily and effectively be killed or managed, and usually at the least cost. Still, brush, and how to best manage it, remains a pervasive question for range producers, as well as the industries, organizations, and institutions that serve them.

Why Do We Need to Manage Brush?

The reasons for renewed interest in brush and weed management in Texas are discussed throughout this book but may be briefly summarized here.

Livestock Production. The presence of brush and weeds, as every livestock producer knows, results in competition for water, light, nutrients, and space, and thus reduces herbaceous forage production for livestock. Even when they are fairly palatable, woody plants may offer little accessible forage for livestock. Dense spines or thorns prevent livestock from getting to the nutritional parts of many woody and succulent plants. Another problem with woody plants and some forbs is the presence of secondary compounds that reduce palatability and digestibility of the plant material.

Yet, woody plants have value on the range, even for cattle, when animals are able to select for them among an ample supply of herbaceous forage, as opposed to being forced to eat them on depleted rangelands or pastures. Goats, either Spanish or angora, can make better use of woody plants, preferring a substantial component of browse in their diets, and, in fact, may be part of the solution for managing some woody species.

Water Yield. The relationship between rangeland brush and potential water yield continues to be studied and debated by scientists. However, the appropriation of millions of taxpayer dollars for brush control by the Texas legislature in 1999 and 2002 clearly demonstrates the widely held belief that excessive densities of woody plants waste water that is urgently needed by urban Texans and that billions of gallons of water can be conserved by the management of woody vegetation. While there may be no scientific proof that watershed-scale manipulation of brush increases downstream water yield, the concern of policy makers and the general public about the vegetation on Texas rangelands is at an unprecedented level and concern will undoubtedly increase in the future, particularly during droughts.

Carbon Sequestration and Global Climate Change. Several organizations and entities in the world are proposing financial contracts or subsidies to landowners who will plant or keep vegetation on their land to sequester carbon. Carbon sequestration is important in mediating global climate change and, in some areas, woody plants may provide greater carbon sequestration than other forms of rangeland vegetation (Archer et al. 2001). Research has indicated that increasing concentrations of carbon dioxide (CO_2) in the atmosphere confers a physiological advantage, manifested as increased growth and competitive ability, to plants with a C_3 carbon pathway (most woody plants) over C_4 species (warm-season perennial grasses). Carbon dioxide concentrations in the atmosphere have increased from about 265 parts per million (ppm) only about 135 years ago to about 350 ppm in 1991 (Mayeux et al. 1991). As CO_2 levels in the atmosphere increase, it is hypothesized that there will be concomitant shifts in terrestrial vegetation. For example, Emanuel et al. (1985) simulated climate for elevated CO_2 levels and predicted substantial increases in thorn woodlands and desert brush within Life Zones that would include parts of Texas. Subsidizing landowners for establishing or maintaining vegetation with high potential for carbon sequestration is another example of public interest in rangeland vegetation. Someday, we may have people wanting to pay us to remove brush for water yield and another group wanting to pay us to grow brush to sequester carbon! This futuristic possibility is something that should be of interest to landowners contemplating brush control.

Wildlife, Nature-based Tourism, and Real Estate Value. The relationships between rangeland vegetation and wildlife species have long been recognized and often integrated into brush management plans. However, there has been an evolution in the level of attention paid to "specific blueprints" for meeting multiple habitat requirements in brush manipulation designs. As noted earlier, we have moved from the simple brush strip designs of 40 years ago to designs that accommodate not only the amount of woody vegetation appropriate for key wildlife species, but also the relationship between ecological sites and habitat. This has led us to the era of brush sculpting, which takes the habitat requirements of target wildlife species into full consideration during the planning and implementation of brush management programs. It embraces not only where, what, and how much brush to control but also how it is arranged to optimize edge areas, create corridors for travel, provide structural amenities (deep shade and cover) and mast, and encourage nature-based tourism. At least two of the very large ranches in South Texas have established brush management criteria that incorporate all of the above. Brush control contractors can currently use Global Positioning Systems to precisely re-create on-the-ground brush sculpting designs that have been developed with aerial photographs and computers by resource managers and consultants. In certain areas of the state, rangeland is more attractive to potential real estate investors and developers if woody plants have not been removed. Old-growth stands of large trees are of special significance and value.

Better Results. Many of us have realized less-than-expected results from our attempts to control woody vegetation, cactus, and herbaceous weeds on rangeland. Shortly after Neil Armstrong stepped onto the surface of the moon, a commonly heard statement among brush control optimists was: If we can put a person on the moon, we can surely find a way to solve the brush problem. The truth is, there is not a silver bullet—not yet anyway—and I would not hold my breath in anticipation of its appearance. The complexity of brush infestations, especially in South Texas where the brush "problem" is a combination of many, rather than one or two species, results in uneven susceptibility to brush control treatments, particularly herbicides. Even combinations of herbicides, while helpful, may not deliver acceptable control to more than one or two species. Additional complexities arise from the combination of plant growth stages and environmental conditions necessary to optimize treatment results. Across entire populations of woody plants in a field environment, there are different soil factors, including texture and moisture, that affect plant physiological activity. These factors relate to herbicide susceptibility and even to efficacy of some mechanical control technologies. The Brush Busters program has been successful, in large part, because the technologies provide high mortality levels of the target species and concomitant high levels of landowner satisfaction. High levels of control can similarly be achieved with other brush and weed management methods if the users are adequately knowledgeable, select the appropriate treatments for their brush problem, and apply these treatments correctly.

Cost Effectiveness and Aesthetic Consideration. The changes in land ownership patterns during the past 20 years have brought on a new generation of landholders with a nontraditional concern for the economic feasibility of range improvements. Many of these new landowners have sufficient income and a reduced interest in livestock production. The return on their investment in brush control is no longer measured by increased livestock products, such as cattle and wool or mohair yields. For many landowners, managing brush may provide improved habitat for nongame wildlife and increased visibility of wildlife and the desirable native plants, which adds aesthetic value to their property. For most ranchers, however, good business practices dictate economic analysis in the planning process to show the potential net present value and internal rate of return on their brush control investments. It is often difficult to show returns on investments for brush control that are competitive with off-ranch investment alternatives. This is particularly true when benefits from initial, high-cost treatments are allowed to deteriorate before maintenance treatments are applied. The value of brush control treatments can also include a particular aesthetic amenity or wildlife habitat improvement that may or may not be recoverable in added lease benefits.

Brush Management Methods

The largest part of this book deals with the four major methods for manipulating brush and weeds on rangeland and the individual technologies contained within those methods.

Mechanical. Mechanical brush control includes a multitude of technologies and has some unique advantages over other methods. Several mechanical practices provide soil disturbance that can effectively reduce compaction and promote infiltration and retention of rainfall. A signal advantage is seedbed preparation, which is not achieved with other methods. Mechanical alternatives offer the opportunity to maximize edge effect, sculpt the landscape with appropriate amounts and locations of brush to enhance wildlife habitat, and modify the structural arrangement of woody plants. As a component of integrated brush management systems, mechanical practices provide technologies for both initial broadcast treatments to reduce plant density and maintenance practices for individual plant treatments (IPT). Mechanical treatments remain some of the most effective for manipulating woody plants, especially as a component of integrated systems that include a combination of treatments.

Chemical. With the exception of the use of coal oil or kerosene for individual plant treatment (primarily for mesquite) in the pre-World War II era, serious use of chemicals for brush and weed control in rangeland environments began in the postwar period with introduction of the hormone herbicides. Needed information about rates of application, plant physiology and growing conditions related to application timing, and appropriate application techniques lagged behind the first commercial use of these chemicals and reduced their effectiveness. New herbicides, along with research and demonstrations by state and federal agencies and industries, have vastly improved the overall performance of herbicides. However, escalating costs, environmental concerns, and urbanization of rangelands have placed economic, ecological, and societal constraints on their use. While environmental considerations and costs will continue to be important to this method, IPT application techniques through the Brush Busters program are fostering a widespread renewed interest in herbicides by producers.

Biological. Second only to the purposeful use of fire to manipulate wildlife vegetation, biological control of plants with animals has been an effective agent for change in many ecosystems. Just as the unwise use of biological agents (grazing livestock) contributed to the degradation of pristine grasslands, grazing animals and insects can be used to suppress undesirable vegetation and facilitate range recovery through selective feeding, shifting the competitive advantage, and secondary plant succession. The classical success story of biological control, the use of the imported moth (*Cactoblastis cactorum*) in Australia for control of pricklypear in the 1920s, actually predated any widespread use of mechanical or chemical brush control in the United States or other parts of the world. The potential for natural, long-term, economical reduction of problem plant species via the use of biological organisms is of great interest worldwide and has been successful in several instances.

Prescribed Fire. Stewart (1956) stated that Peking Man burned vegetation for specific purposes at least a quarter of a million years ago. The evolutionary success of aboriginal cultures depended largely upon their ability to harness the potentials of fire and the discovery of a method to ignite vegetable matter looms as one of humanity's greatest accomplishments. Then, as our ancestors became increasingly sedentary, the awesome destructiveness of wildfires caused them to progressively restrict the uses of fire. By the late nineteenth century, many land managers had profound misgivings concerning burning as a tool for management of forests and rangelands. This attitude has mediated substantially in more recent times, beginning with an understanding of the need for fire to keep forest ecosystems healthy for multiple uses. The use of prescribed fire to meet management objectives for woody plant populations, such as Ashe juniper (*Juniperus ashei*) and eastern red cedar (*Juniperus virginiana*), has proven highly successful. Legislation in Texas is addressing landowner liability in the use of prescribed fire, a significant step in opening the door for its wider use. Prescribed fire, as both a reclamation and maintenance tool for brush management, should be, and is, a significant element of this book.

You Can Beat the Statistics!

Some will read this book because they feel that efforts over the past 50 years have been largely ineffective in dealing with the brush and weed problem in the state. Statistics available on acreage and canopy cover of brush species in Texas generally show an increase in influence of major problem species, such as juniper and honey mesquite on rangeland landscapes. Decades of concern for the negative influence of brush on rangeland productivity and the application of control practices on tens of millions of acres have had, at best, a minimal effect on the statewide problem. This being said, two important points should be made. First, changing attitudes about the presence of brush in certain proportions to enhance wildlife habitat, real estate value, nature-based tourism, and aesthetics have reduced the amount of brush control being implemented. Second, landowners and managers have been more willing to accept control technologies that "manage" brush rather than those that eliminate it. Even considering these points, many people still believe that control technologies, when weighed against overall progress in reducing brush in the state, fall short in both technical and economic adequacy. However, there is no question that individual land operators, using these same technologies, have had successes in managing rangeland vegetation effectively when initial treatments are followed by maintenance treatments to stretch benefits over long periods of time.

Individuals who plan brush management in an integrated, systematic way, apply the treatment correctly, and follow up with good grazing management and maintenance of regrowth can "beat the odds" and have both technically and economically successful results. Many landowners have often looked for that one-shot, miracle cure rather than accepting the fact that the technologies we have today, when used in an integrated, systematic, long-term planning approach are capable of meeting many of our objectives.

Literature Cited

Archer, S. R., T. W. Boutton, and K. A. Hibbard. 2001. Trees in grassland: biogeochemical consequences of woody plant expansion. Pages 115–37 *in* E. D. Schulze, S. P. Harrison, M. Heimann, E. A. Holland, J. Lloyd, I. C. Prentice, and D. Schimel, editors. Global biogeochemical cycles in the climate system. Academic Press, San Diego, California.

———, C. J. Scifres, C. R. Bassham, and R. C. Maggio. 1988. Autogenic succession in a subtropical savanna: conversion of grassland to thorn woodland. Ecological Monographs 58:111–27.

Bogush, E. R. 1952. Brush invasion in the Rio Grande Plain of Texas. Texas Journal of Science 4:85–91.

Dye, K. L., III, D. N. Ueckert, and S. G. Whisenant. 1995. Redberry juniper-herbaceous understory interactions. Journal of Range Management 48:100–107.

Emanuel, W. R., H. H. Shugart, and M. P. Stevenson. 1985. Climate change and the broad-scale distribution of terrestrial ecosystem complexes. Climatic Change 7:29–43.

Hester, T. R. 1980. Digging into South Texas prehistory. Corona Publishing Co., San Antonio, Texas.

Inglis, J. M. 1964. A history of the vegetation on the Rio Grande Plains. Texas Parks and Wildlife Department Bulletin 45.

Jones, F. B. 1975. Flora of the Texas Coastal Bend. Contribution B-6. Welder Wildlife Foundation. Mission Press, Corpus Christi, Texas.

Malin, J. C. 1953. Soil, animal, and plant relations of the grassland, historically reconsidered. Scientific Monthly, April:207–20.

Mayeux, H. S., Jr., H. B. Johnson, and H. W. Polley. 1991. Global change and vegetation dynamics. Pages 62–74, Chapter 7 *in* L. F. James, J. D. Evans,

H. H. Ralphs, and R. D. Childs, editors. Noxious range weeds. Westview Press, Boulder, Colorado.

McConnell, H. H. 1889. Five years a cavalryman; or, sketches of regular army life on the Texas frontier, twenty odd years ago. J. N. Rogers and Co. Printers, Jacksboro, Texas.

Ohlendorf, S. M., J. M. Bigelow, and M. M. Standifer. 1980. John Louis Berlandier, journey to Mexico during the years 1826 and 1834. Texas State Historical Association and Center for Studies in Texas History, University of Texas, Austin.

Robinson, R. L. 1979. Biosilica and climatic change at 41 GD 21 and 41 GD 21A. Pages 102–13, Appendix IV *in* D. E. Fox, editor. Archaeological investigations of two prehistoric sites on the Coleto Creek drainage, Goliad County, Texas. Archaeological Survey Report 69. Center for Archaeological Research, University of Texas, San Antonio.

Scifres, C. J. 1980. Brush management: principles and practices for Texas and the Southwest. Texas A&M University Press, College Station.

———, and W. T. Hamilton. 1993. Prescribed burning for brushland management: the South Texas example. Texas A&M University Press, College Station.

Stewart, O. C. 1956. Fire as the first great force employed by man. Pages 115–33 *in* W. L. Thomas, editor. Man's role in changing the face of the earth. University of Chicago Press.

Taylor, C. A., Jr., and M. M. Kothmann. 1993. Managing stocking rates to achieve livestock production goals on the Edwards Plateau. Pages 42–52 *in* J. R. Cox and J. F. Cadenhead, editors. Proceedings managing livestock stocking rates on rangeland. Texas Agricultural Extension Service Unnumbered Publication.

The Discourse. 1974. South Texas shares its archaeological secrets. Volume 2, Number 8. The University of Texas, San Antonio.

Thurow, T. L. 1991. Hydrology and erosion. Pages 141–59 *in* R. K. Heitschmidt and J. W. Stuth, editors. Grazing management: an ecological perspective. Timber Press, Portland, Oregon.

York, J. C., and W. A. Dick-Peddie. 1969. Vegetation changes in southern New Mexico during the past 100 years. Pages 155–66 *in* W. G. McDinnies and B. J. Goldman, editors. Arid lands in perspective. University of Arizona Press, Tucson.

Mechanical Brush Management

2   Mechanical Practices prior to 1975

Wayne T. Hamilton
and
C. Wayne Hanselka

A variety of mechanical tools and procedures were developed to combat   17
brush problems throughout the eradication and control eras. Extensive
mechanized brush control has a history beginning in the early 1930s that
has developed through concurrent and distinct phases involving the use of
plows, saws, steel cables, heavy chains, large rolling choppers, large rootplows, and other equipment. This chapter reviews the early efforts at mechanical brush manipulation until 1975, the beginning of the brush management era.

Factors Influencing
Mechanical Brush Management Methods

In the years from the first efforts at serious mechanical control of brush until about the mid-1970s, several things emerged about woody plant physiology and morphology that were important in the design of practices. One of
the most significant of these was the aggressive resprouting ability following
top removal of several important woody species, including honey mesquite
(*Prosopis glandulosa* var. *glandulosa*) and huisache (*Acacia smallii*), as well as
a host of associated shrub species. Top removal, or even top growth damage,
stimulated buds at the base of stems on subterranean root crowns or on
roots of some species, such as lotebush (*Zizyphus obtusifolia*) and Macartney
rose (*Rosa bracteata*). Therefore, mechanical practices, fire, or even biological control by grazing animals that resulted in top removal provided only
short-term relief from resprouting woody plants. The aggressiveness of this
regrowth was observed by many and documented by Powell et al. (1972)
who showed that huisache cut near ground line on April 1 elongated approximately 4 feet of new growth by October 1 of the same year.

Seedling survival after top growth removal is also significant. Scifres et al.
(1971) reported that 60% of seedlings survived after being cut above the
cotyledonary axil 7 days after emergence and 95% survived after 7 weeks.
Seedlings that were cut 1 month after emergence resprouted within 5 days.
Once a seedling is established, it is virtually impossible to cause mortality
with mechanical equipment that provides only top removal. Although the

seedlings will suffer mortality if cut below the cotyledonary axil, this area of the plant is too close to ground level for effective clipping with equipment on range landscapes.

It became obvious that mechanical brush control practices were often followed by an unwanted spread of pricklypear (*Opuntia* spp.) Pricklypear density increased by a factor of 2 to 3 times on rootplowed, rootplowed and raked, and on chained areas compared to adjacent untreated areas (Dodd 1968). Thousands of acres of South Texas that had moderate to sparse stands of pricklypear before chaining or rootplowing were converted to solid pricklypear patches by these practices (Meadors et al. 1973). Grubbing of mesquite in the Texas Rolling Plains had similar, although less dramatic, results where pricklypear was associated with mesquite and was spread by mechanical grubbing equipment.

By the mid-1970s, the cost of broadcast mechanical practices was high enough to make a single treatment, such as chaining or even rootplowing, only marginally economical in most cases within their effective treatment lives. This brought recognition of the need for a more strategic, long-term approach and planning for low-cost, follow-up practices to stretch benefits of initial high-cost treatments (Scifres et al. 1985). Hundreds of thousands of acres were chained in the 1950s and 1960s with no maintenance treatments. Similarly, areas were rootplowed, or rootplowed, raked, and seeded to introduced grass species with no long-term maintenance of woody plant reinvasion. As cost of initial treatments escalated it became more difficult to show acceptable returns on investment without maintaining the maximum benefits from these treatments for 10 to 20 years.

It also became obvious that there were significant differences in the potential of different ecological sites (range sites) to pay for investments in woody plant management (Allison and Rechenthin 1956). This led to more discriminating locations of treatments on the landscape. The first recognition of site differentials was based on soil depth, inherent fertility, and productivity potential with relation to forage for livestock. Near the end of the period in the late 1960s and early 1970s, wildlife habitat became a consideration in the design of mechanical treatments, with vegetation types and their physical structure and nutritional utility gaining in importance. Shallow ridge sites where species such as guajillo (*Acacia berlandieri*) were present or riparian areas with mesic environments (including large trees, dense shade, and mast) were not usually treated. However, this was still primarily the era of brush strips in South Texas, where long, parallel, alternating strips of brush and cleared areas were installed. Within the time period, it was unusual for travel corridors to be a consideration in the designs and, although strips provided good edge effect, there was often less thought given to saving high-utility areas than to the geometric pattern.

Watershed characteristics and water loss were factors in justifying brush management in the 1950s and 1960s. The series of publications by Smith and Rechenthin (1964) brought attention to the water wasted by undesirable woody plants on Texas rangelands, as did the story of Rocky Creek on the Flat Top Ranch (a dry creek that began to flow after brush control in the watershed). While some ranchers, urban dwellers, and political leaders might have recognized the significant relationship between rangeland vegetation management and water quantity and quality, there was no evidence during the period of enough concern to support action.

Chronology of Development and Application of Mechanical Brush Control Practices

As early as the turn of the last century, land managers recognized that the increasing density of brush, particularly mesquite, would be one of the greatest problems of maintaining rangelands in productive form (Wilkinson 1957). Young et al. (1948) stated that range specialists are confronted with a threefold problem. First, efficient and economical ways must be found to remove the noxious plant forms from infested range areas. Second, once these growths are removed, landowners must be encouraged to utilize the forage value of the range to a maximum capacity and to exercise sufficient care in doing so to avoid reinfestation with noxious plants. Third, techniques of building up run-down ranges and restoring cleared ranges to productivity must be developed. An array of mechanical tools would be used in this effort, evolving from simple manual tools to complex heavy equipment (Fig. 2.1).

Texas ranchers have been grubbing brush from their pastures since the mid-nineteenth century. During the 1890s, approximately 1,000 families

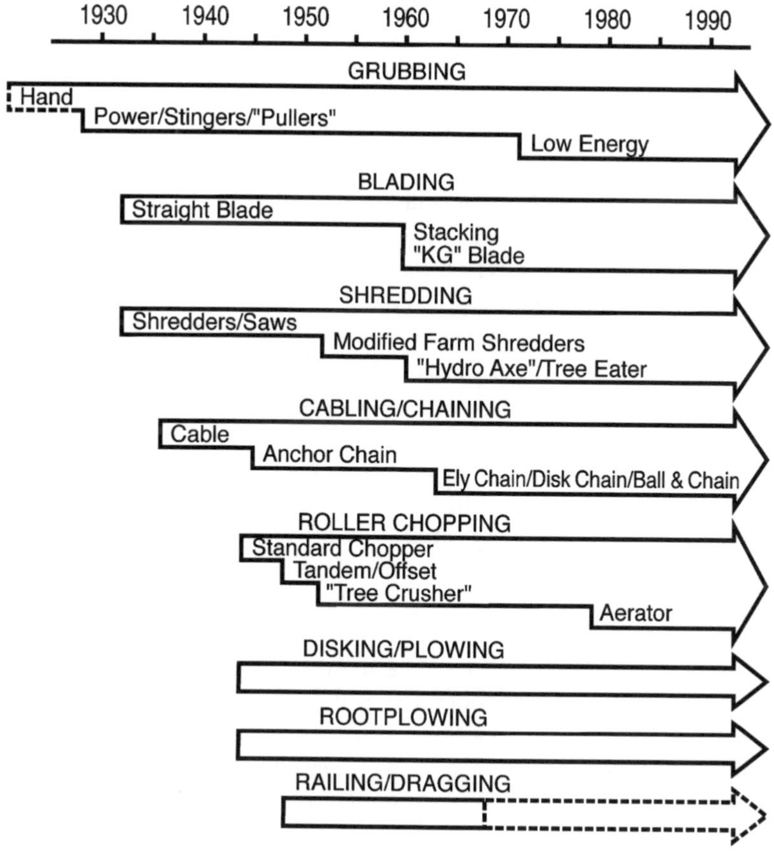

Figure 2.1.
A General Chronology of Mechanical Brush Management.

were employed by King Ranch to dig out mesquite and other brush growth with hand axes and grubbing hoes. One worker could clear less than an acre a week (Wilkinson 1957). There are many other records and accounts that this was a very common practice in the early 1900s. The Jornada Experimental Range in New Mexico hand-grubbed 4,265 acres as late as 1958 (Herbel et al. 1958).

The development of power equipment to grub brush is attributable to both equipment manufacturers and ranchers. In 1937, V. V. Parr attempted to grub mesquite using a pneumatic air hammer equipped with a cutting blade. The idea was abandoned because it was too slow and laborious. In 1938, J. S. Bridwell, a rancher in Northwest Texas, attempted to control mesquite with a bulldozer. Bridwell, working in cooperation with The Texas Agricultural Experiment Station, designed a "stinger" mounted on the blade of the bulldozer (Fisher et al. 1973). Many different forms of mini-rootplows that could be pulled behind farm tractors to grub woody plants were built in blacksmith shops or on ranches. Further improvements by the 1970s resulted in present-day low-energy grubbing equipment.

One of the earliest heavy machines to be used in an effort to control brush growth was the bulldozer, or crawler tractor with its "cat" treads and heavy, scraping blade. While some crawler tractors were in use for brush control before World War II, their availability increased dramatically after the war and made possible the emergence of many conservation contractors looking for brush control and earth moving work. A number of improvements on the bulldozer were made over the years. One such machine was the tree dozer, which was used successfully for mesquite control at the Texas A&M Spur substation and on King Ranch. This machine was an extra-powerful bulldozer with a plow-like attachment and lift (Young et al. 1948). The KG Blade evolved ca. 1960.

Shredding brush with power equipment was initiated in the late 1930s. In 1942, a circular saw mounted on a farm tractor was developed to cut brush close to ground level (Fig. 2.2). It was reported to be difficult to operate and had frequent breakdowns, especially working in dense brush stands. Attempts to develop a large chain saw mounted on a crawler tractor were not successful (Fisher et al. 1973). Experiments at the Beeville, Texas, Experiment Station in the mid-1940s used mobile rotating power saws to cut brush at ground level (Young et al. 1948).

Modified farm shredders were in use by the late 1940s (Fig. 2.3). Commercial roto-beaters were evaluated in 1949. By 1950, corn stalk shredders, custom-built rails, and rotary cutters were being tested for rangeland brush control. This line of evolution developed from agricultural implements for disposal of a crop residue, to rangeland brush beaters, to "tree eaters." It moved toward specialized equipment that was primarily useful for planting site preparation and slash disposal in forestry as typified by such machines as the Hydro-Axe in the 1960s (Young et al. 1983).

Cabling to control heavy brush was first used in the 1930s. Cabling evolved into chaining with a ship anchor chain substituted for the cable. Used first in Hawaii, anchor chains were introduced to the mainland in the late 1950s and tried at several locations in the Southwest and Intermountain

Figure 2.2.
Circular Saw.
Courtesy Harold Wiedemann

Figure 2.3.
Hydroaxe.
Courtesy Wayne T. Hamilton

areas (Young et al. 1983). Anchor chains were commonly used in Texas for mesquite control in the 1950s and 1960s. Smooth anchor chains usually produced better brush control than cables, but often failed to give adequate control and seedbed preparation. Modified chains were developed at Ely, Nevada (called the Ely Chain) and St. George, Utah (called the Dixie-Sager Chain).

King Ranch records indicate the first mechanized pasture improvement involving plowing was initiated on the ranch in 1915. Two Buffalo Pitts Traction Engines (iron-wheeled steam tractors) were equipped with three-blade moldboard plows. It is believed that this was the first time a plow was pulled by tractor equipment for pasture maintenance in a cattle ranching operation (Wilkinson 1957). The steam-powered tractors were superseded about 1918 by more efficient Twin City gasoline tractors that were also used to pull plows.

Plowing operations were greatly improved by the advent of the Caterpillar tractor, and some very effective land clearing was accomplished by using a very heavy disk plow especially designed to be pulled by these crawler tractors. A disk plow was imported from Australia and tested in Idaho in 1947. From this plow, the plow which became known as the brushland plow was developed.

In 1933, William K. Holt undertook studies in cooperation with King Ranch to develop brush control equipment that resulted in the present-day rootplow in 1949. In 1935, King Ranch tested the RD-8 Diesel Caterpillar tractor, attached with a knockdown bar, or ram, and a V-blade to pull stumps after the trees were knocked down. The LeTourneau Manufacturing Company of Peoria, Illinois built this equipment (the tree dozer, a mechanical land clearing device), which was to spread throughout the world. LeTourneau was then requested to build a large steel half-round plow blade to be pulled by the tractor. When completed, this loop was pulled beneath the surface of the ground, slicing a 4-foot swath. A wedge-shaped blade developed from the idea and was eventually produced in a 9-foot model. This was the first practical rootplow.

Rootplowing became very popular for mesquite control in Texas and the Southwest by 1961. The most commonly used rootplow was mounted on a heavy-duty, crawler-type tractor that pulled an 8- to 10-foot, V-shaped blade 10 to 18 inches below the soil surface. Rootplowing had become an effective control treatment for mesquite in Texas, Oklahoma, and the Southwest by the late 1950s and early 1960s (Allison and Rechenthin 1956, Carter 1958).

There was a definite shift in mechanical methods of brush control during the 45-year period (1930–75), from the use of hand grubbing of small acreages to chaining or chopping of extensive acreages to rootplowing and seeding of smaller blocks of rangelands. Ranch managers consistently were the innovators of new, promising brush control practices. They were prominent during the 1930s and 1940s in the use of chaining or chopping, and they led the shift to rootplowing and seeding in the 1950s (Davis and Spicer 1965).

Description of the Mechanical Practices from the Early Days to the Mid-1970s

Hand Grubbing. Grubbing is one of the oldest methods of physically removing individual plants and was originally done by hand with shovels, axes, and grubbing hoes (Fig. 2.4). This method has been the most effective mechanical practice, especially for crown-sprouting plants, if practiced correctly (Scifres 1980). Hand grubbing may be effectively used as a maintenance practice for small brush plants when the number of plants per acre is small. This labor intensive practice may be used to control nonsprouting species and species that sprout from the stem base if they are uprooted below the lowermost bud. Hand grubbing is best accomplished when the soil is moist (Welch 1991).

Mechanical Power Grubbing. Power grubbing implements have been successfully mounted on crawler and wheeled tractors, with tremendous im-

Figure 2.4.
Hand Grubbing.
Courtesy Wayne T. Hamilton

provements in efficiency. The time required to remove woody plants from rangeland with power grubbing depends upon the size of the plants, stand density, type of growth, soil texture, and moisture content. The soil must be moist enough to allow a high percentage of the plants to be grubbed deeply enough to prevent regrowth. Power grubbing is effective on nonsprouting species and species that sprout from the stem base, provided they are uprooted below the lowermost bud, and with scattered plants that are large enough to be seen easily by the equipment operator. Various types of power grubbers have been developed and are used on small crawler and rubber-tired tractors. Pits left in the soil surface where brush plants are removed allow a good chance for establishing desirable grasses if seeds are scattered in the pits in early spring. The soil surface may become extremely rough if high densities of brush are grubbed.

Blading (Bulldozing). A bulldozer or crawler tractor equipped with a heavy-duty pusher blade is used to sever woody stems at or below the soil surface. Since few plants are uprooted, this practice is best adapted for use on large nonsprouting species in scattered stands. If sprouting species are bull-dozed, they can be expected to resprout unless the bud zone is removed (Welch 1991). The bulldozer blade is generally not efficient for clearing large tracts of rangeland solely for the purposes of improving native forage stands. Bulldozers are best adapted for the removal of large trees, especially on relatively small areas that are destined for complete conversion to tame pastures (Scifres 1980). A negative factor of bulldozing is that topsoil may be removed and placed in brush piles. The KG blade is an adaptation of bull-dozing that consists of a deep concave and angled blade. The leading edge of the blade runs almost parallel with the soil surface providing good cutting action on woody plants. Cut brush rides onto the deeply curved blade and is rolled to the lower end and deposited in a windrow parallel to the direction of travel.

Figure 2.5.
Brush Stacker.
Courtesy Wayne T. Hamilton

Raking—Stacking—Root Raking. The brush rake is a front-end rake pushed by a crawler tractor to pile debris left by a previous practice. Brush rakes have open tines that gather debris without major accumulations of soil. They may be used on either disturbed or firm soil surfaces. The stacker is a special modified front-end rake. It is designed to uproot or shear off woody plants at ground level and gathers them with less loss of debris than the brush rake (Fig. 2.5). Modifications include turned-in ends (slightly cupped) and a steel plate across the tines near the soil surface. Additional plates may be added to the bottom tines to support the stacker's weight and hold it in the correct position at the soil surface. Soil disturbance is usually minimal when the equipment is correctly applied. The implement works on a firm soil surface and is especially effective for removal of pricklypear and the top growth of mature, dense Macartney rose. Drag-type root rakes have long tines that travel in the soil profile and remove litter and debris, as well as viable buds left after root-plowing, thus contributing to better total woody plant mortality and seed-bed preparation (Welch et al. 1985).

Cutters and Saws. As described in the historical overview, saws were experimented with briefly during the period as a means of removing the top growth of woody plants. Cutters, or sickle-bar cutters, were also used to mow small woody plants. Both of these implements gave way to shredders and roller choppers and have not been significant equipment for rangeland brush management for many years.

Shredders (Modified Farm-type). Shredding uniformly removes brush top growth but rarely kills woody plants capable of sprouting from roots or stem bases. Drag-type shredders are most efficient on plants with stem basal diameters of less than 2 inches, although heavy-duty, hydraulically operated shredders may remove woody plants with trunk diameters of 4 inches or more. Repeated shredding generally causes the number of stems and size of the basal stems to increase. Fulbright (1987) reported that repeated shredding every 3 years had little effect on density and canopy cover of high-, medium-, and low-value browse plants for white-tailed deer (*Odocoileus virginianus*). However, densities of exceptionally palatable plants were lower on shredded than on nonshredded areas. Brush species diversity was also lower on shredded rangelands (Hamilton et al. 1981). Plants that have been shredded repeatedly are more difficult to control with herbicides and may require more energy to remove by grubbing than plants that have not been shredded. Shredding may increase the plant densities of Macartney rose and pricklypear because fragments of rose canes or pricklypear pads scattered over the soil surface may take root. Spreading of such species is minimized by shredding during hot, dry periods. Although shredding provides only short-term control of most undesirable plants, it may allow sufficient time for grass to grow and provide fine fuel for prescribed burning; may increase browse availability and quality by increasing the number of young, succulent sprouts; and may also improve livestock handling efficiency by increasing accessibility and visibility for the manager.

Hydro-Axe. The Hydro-Axe is a large, self-propelled shredding unit utilizing an articulated, rubber-tired tractor and a front-end shredding unit that is powered by a hydraulic motor. The motor turns a heavy flywheel enclosed in a canopy. Two free-swinging blades are attached to the flywheel with heavy pins. This machine is capable of cutting large brush; however, as brush size increases, the cost of operation per unit of land also increases so that stem diameters of less than 4 inches are most practical.

Cabling. Cabling is similar to chaining but, because of their lighter weight, cables (usually 2.5 to 3 inches in diameter) tend to ride over the tops of small brush and woody debris, leaving many plants intact. Cabling is most effective on upright, nonsprouting species of moderate size, such as Ashe juniper (*Juniperus ashei*), and when the soil moisture content is conducive to uprooting the plants (Welch 1991). Cabling will spread pricklypear when conducted under conditions optimum for woody plant removal. However, cabling during dry periods has been used to control cholla (*Opuntia* spp.). Soil disturbance is slight.

Smooth Anchor Chain. The chaining operation consists of dragging a heavy ship anchor chain, usually 150- to 300-feet long, in a loop behind two large crawler tractors. Swath width, usually 75 to 150 feet, varies with the size of the tractors and the size and thickness of the brush. The tractors should be driven far enough apart to attain the maximum swath width but close enough together to maintain continuous forward motion. This is accomplished by a long loop in the chain that allows it to be pulled from straight ahead, thus reducing pull from the side that is hard on equipment. Anchor chains weighing 80 pounds or more per foot replaced heavy cables for dragging down brush. The heavy chains are more flexible, work closer to the ground, and have less tendency to ride over dense brush than do cables. Chaining is used to knock down and thin moderate to thick stands of brush but chaining alone gives only temporary control. It is most effective on trees

Figure 2.6.
Disk Chain.
Courtesy Wayne T. Hamilton

4 to 18 inches in diameter in a density of no more than 400 plants per acre. Small, "switchy" brush will bend under the chain or break off above the soil surface. Soil moisture must be sufficient for plant crowns and/or lateral roots to be pulled completely out of the soil. However, chaining under moist conditions may dramatically increase the cover of pricklypear. Two-way chaining, covering the area twice in opposite directions, usually gives better control than one-way chaining (Scifres et al. 1976). Chaining can be used on rough, rocky terrain with only moderate soil disturbance.

Disk Chain. Disk chains are anchor chains with disks (often scalloped) welded to every other chain link (Fig. 2.6). The idea for these chains originated in Australia, where a 100-foot length of disk chain was used on lands operated by King Ranch, Inc. of Texas (McKenzie et al. 1984). Disk chains have been used primarily for smoothing rootplowed areas to improve a seedbed, although they also serve to remove severed roots from the soil and reduce brush resprouting potential.

Ely Chain. Ely chains are anchor chains with bars welded on each of the links. This modification to smooth anchor chains was first developed by John K. Chambers of Ely, Nevada. The bars can be flat metal bars approximately 1-inch thick, or they can be sections of railroad rails. Ely chains have been used in the West to uproot big sagebrush (*Artemisia tridentata*) and other shrub species too limber for smooth chains or cables. McKenzie et al. (1984) reported that about 50% of big sagebrush was uprooted by one pass of the Ely chain and an additional 20–30% by a second pass. The bars on the chain links provide added surface area and corners that catch woody plant stems and improve pulling capacity compared to smooth chains. Ely chains are equipped with swivels at each end that allow the chain to rotate (Young et al. 1983). An important additional feature of Ely chains is that they provide much more soil disturbance than smooth chains and greatly enhance seedbeds. Ely chaining can be expected to be slightly more expensive than smooth chaining.

Ball and Chain. A ball and chain system was developed for brush control in steep terrain where it is impossible to operate large tractors in parallel positions. This modification to chaining was probably first used in the mountains of southern California (McKenzie et al. 1984). The ball was made from a surplus antisubmarine net buoy with a 5- or 6-foot diameter. The steel-walled buoy was filled completely with water, sand, or concrete and attached to one end of a chain. The water-filled ball weighing 1.5 to 2.0 tons was used to hold one end of the chain down slope while a tractor dragged the other end along ridge tops. The concrete-filled ball weighed about 5 tons and presented a problem to transport.

Dixie-Sager Chain. This chain was first built in the late 1960s by Forest Service range managers in southwestern Utah. The materials included an anchor chain, railroad rail, and track rollers. The chain was 250-feet long and weighed 20,000 pounds. There were 235 links with 6-inch pieces of railroad rails welded lengthwise on the outfaces of the links to act as digger teeth and fifteen smooth links on each end. In operation, the chain twisted like a giant rototiller on the swivels. The Dixie-Sager chain, like the Ely chain, could provide good soil scarification. It is not known by the authors if the chain was used in Texas.

Roller Choppers. Young et al. (1948) reported brush cutters (roller choppers) in operation on Texas rangelands. The earliest roller choppers were hollow heavy metal drums with blades mounted across the drum surface perpendicular to the direction of pull (Fig. 2.7). E. L. Caldwell and Sons, of Corpus Christi, Texas, is credited with development of the first implement of its type to be tested on rangelands (Pechanec 1950). The Pacific Southwest Forest and Range Experiment Station followed with an implement called the brushland roller, built by T. G. Schmeiser Co. of Fresno, California (Hull 1953). The drums of most roller choppers could be filled with water to increase weight. The cutting power of roller choppers is determined by the weight of the unit, the speed of pull (momentum applied to the blades), and the amount of surface area contact with woody plant stems along the blade. Traditional choppers can be individual or multiple units and are usually pulled with a single crawler tractor. Choppers provide a simple top removal function with less uniformity of cut stems than is associated with shredders. Distinct advantages of roller choppers over shredders are seedbed preparation and fewer breakdowns. Roller choppers leave a ridge and furrow effect on the soil surface that holds water and promotes seed germination and seedling establishment. In early work with roller choppers in South Texas in 1953, Allison and Rechenthin (1956) reported that 22% of the brush was killed by roller chopping, but after chopping the brush resumed vigorous growth.

LeTourneau Tree Crusher. A large, self-propelled variety of roller choppers was manufactured by the LeTourneau company. These machines were large

Figure 2.7.
Roller Chopper.
Courtesy Wayne T. Hamilton

and powerful enough to take down heavy tropical forests in South America. They were also used in hardwood and mixed conifer–hardwood forests in East Texas and parts of the southeastern United States. The design of these machines was unique, using a GMC 8V71 diesel engine to power a generator that, in turn, powered electric motors in each wheel. The three wheels were the chopping units and featured angular blades that tended to cause greater damage to cut material than perpendicular blades.

Rootplows. Like chaining, cabling, and other mechanical practices requiring crawler tractors, the post-World War II era saw a dramatic increase in use of these land treatments as tractors became available (McKenzie et al. 1984). Holt Machinery Company was working with King Ranch in the 1930s on development of equipment capable of removing brush (Young et al. 1983) and rootplowing was being applied on King Ranch and in South Texas by the late 1940s. Holt built the famous double plow for King Ranch and tens of thousands of acres were rootplowed using these machines that featured two D8 tractors mounted side-by-side pulling a double V-shaped blade (Fig. 2.8). This plow was capable of taking on undisturbed stands of mesquite with hardly a "grunt or groan." Another feature of the double plow was the funnel blade on the front that forced everything in the swath width under the tractor and over the blades.

Although the double plow garnered much attention, single D8 tractors were being used at the same time on thousands of acres. Carter (1958) reported that between 1954 and 1958, 250,000 acres in South Texas were rootplowed at a cost of $2,000,000, or an average of $8.00 per acre. Smith and Rechenthin (1964) reported that rootplowing cost between $10 and $20 per acre. Plowed areas were commonly seeded to adapted introduced species, such as blue panicgrass (*Panicum antidotale*) and buffelgrass (*Cenchrus ciliaris*) in South Texas. Rootplows look and perform today very much as they did 50 years ago, although cable controls have given way in part to hydraulics. One innovation of the rootplow was the side bar plow that was apparently pushed by a rubber-tired tractor. The photos available of this plow indicate that it may have been used in light brush stands. Another innovation included a rootplow with an attachment that elevated the plowed soil onto a belt, shook the soil away from the root material, and gathered the roots on a rack that could be raised to dump the debris. There were at least two different versions of this machine demonstrated in South Texas, but they did not become generally accepted equipment. Fins, usually three in number and approximately 2-feet long, were often welded on the top of rootplow blades at about a 30° angle. These fins helped to raise material cut by the blade onto the soil surface and loosen many of the shallow-rooted plants that might otherwise survive (Fisher et al. 1973).

Railing. In the western United States, the practice of railing has been applied primarily for the control of big sagebrush. In Texas, two or more railroad rails dragged in tandem, or clusters of rails have been used for control of pricklypear and other cacti (Scifres 1980). Maximum cactus control was obtained by railing when the soil surface was extremely dry and when hot, dry weather followed the treatment and desiccated the pads. The mode of action of railing is to cut and mash the epidermis of pricklypear cladophylls so that they will dry rapidly and die before resprouting. Railing can also be used to knock down small woody plants, such as big sagebrush, uprooting or breaking off stems. Very large I-beams or H-beams are also used for this purpose and have enough weight to hold an edge of the beam against the soil surface to uproot some woody plants or shear off brittle species.

Disking. Heavy disk plows are used to control small, shallow-rooted brush species such as whitebrush (*Aloysia gratissima*) (Welch et al. 1985). The disks were usually scalloped and depth of cut was highly dependent upon soil

Figure 2.8.
King Ranch Rootplow®.
*Courtesy King Ranch
Archives, King Ranch, Inc.*

conditions, weight of the unit, and size and density of woody plants. In work near Pearsall, Texas, C. E. Fisher (personal communication 1975) reported excellent kills of whitebrush by disking in the fall, seeding to small grains, and then disking again in the early spring. Moderate rates of kill have been obtained on blackbrush acacia (*Acacia rigidula*) and other South Texas species, particularly where soil allows penetration of disks below the bud zone of woody plants. The brushland plow, or stump-jump plow, a heavily constructed disk plow designed to allow pairs of disks to move separately from others and ride over obstacles, has been successfully used on rangeland (Young et al. 1983).

Summary

Mechanical brush management from the early 1900s to 1975 was a time of innovation, development, and experimentation with equipment. While some of this equipment never found general acceptance, the major mechanical practices in use today were developed during this period. It was during this time that powerful crawler tractors came into use with implements that were able to physically modify vast areas of brush in the southwestern United States. Unfortunately, treatments were often applied before the ecological consequences were fully understood. Much needed to be learned about woody plant physiology and morphology, the need for long-term strategic planning, and inclusion of maintenance practices to stretch benefits of high cost initial reclamation treatments. These shortfalls in understanding resulted in the spread of species, such as pricklypear, and rapid loss of initial treatment benefits to aggressive regrowth by many other species that sprouted readily from stem basal buds and root crowns. However, by 1975, land managers had at their disposal an array of mechanical equipment that could effectively provide both woody plant top removal (shredding, roller chopping, etc.) and whole plant removal treatments (grubbing, rootplowing). Moreover, several of these methods provided good seedbed preparation for revegetation.

During the 1950s and 1960s, mechanical practices, primarily broadcast treatments such as chaining, were applied on millions of rangeland acres, primarily as a means to increase forage production for livestock. Shortly before the end of the period in the early 1970s, the increasing value of wildlife resources on private lands began to dictate to land managers the need for careful consideration of habitat in brush management operations (as opposed to earlier eradication and control philosophies). This fostered the use of brush patterns, alternating cleared and brushy areas, in attempts to preserve habitat for important game animal species.

Mechanical practices have the capability to modify landscapes and facilitate revegetation that cannot be accomplished with any other method. For this reason, they will continue to be important as tools available to managers to accomplish specific land management goals. They are especially valuable when used in conjunction with other methods in an integrated, strategic, and ecologically sound planning process.

Literature Cited

Allison, D. V., and C. A. Rechenthin. 1956. Rootplowing proved best method of brush control in South Texas. Journal of Range Management 9:130–33.

Carter, M. G. 1958. Reclaiming Texas brushland range. Journal of Range Management 11:1–5.

Davis, R. B., and R. L. Spicer. 1965. Status of the practice of brush control in the Rio Grande Plain. Texas Parks and Wildlife Department Bulletin 46.

Dodd, J. D. 1968. Mechanical control of pricklypear and other woody plant species on the Rio Grande Plains. Journal of Range Management 21:366–70.

Fisher, C. E., H. T. Wiedemann, C. H. Meadors, and J. H. Brock. 1973. Mechanical control of mesquite. Pages 46–52 *in* C. J. Scifres, R. W. Bovey, C. E. Fisher, G. O. Hoffman, and R. D. Lewis, editors. Mesquite, growth and development, management, economics, control, uses. Texas Agricultural Experiment Station Research Monograph 1.

Fulbright, T. E. 1987. Effects of repeated shredding on a guajillo (*Acacia berlandieri*) community. Texas Journal of Agriculture and Natural Resources 1:32–33.

Hamilton, W. T., L. M. Kitchen, and C. J. Scifres. 1981. Height replacement of selected woody plants following burning or shredding. Texas Agricultural Experiment Station Bulletin 1361.

Herbel, C., F. Ares, and J. Bridges. 1958. Handgrubbing mesquite in the semidesert grassland. Journal of Range Management 11:267–70.

Hull, A. C. 1953. Report of the range seeding committee. U.S. Forest Service. Washington, D.C.

McKenzie, D., F. R. Jensen, T. N. Johnsen, Jr., and J. A. Young. 1984. Chains for mechanical brush control. Rangelands 6:122–27.

Meadors, C. H., C. E. Fisher, R. H. Haas, and G. O. Hoffman. 1973. Combinations of methods and maintenance control of mesquite. Pages 53–59 *in* C. J. Scifres, R. W. Bovey, C. E. Fisher, G. O. Hoffman, and R. D. Lewis, editors. Mesquite, growth and development, management, economics, control, uses. Texas Agricultural Experiment Station Research Monograph 1.

Pechanec, J. F. 1950. Report of the range seeding committee. Pacific Northwest Forest and Range Experiment Station, Portland, Oregon.

Powell, J., T. W. Box, and C. V. Baker. 1972. Growth rate of sprouts after top removal of huisache (*Acacia farnesiana* (L.) Willd.) (*Leguminosae*) in South Texas. The Southwestern Naturalist 17:191–95.

Scifres, C. J. 1980. Brush management: principles and practices for Texas and the Southwest. Texas A&M University Press, College Station.

———, and R. R. Hahn. 1971. Response of honey mesquite seedlings to top removal. Journal of Range Management 24:296–98.

———, W. T. Hamilton, J. R. Conner, J. M. Inglis, G. A. Rasmussen, R. P. Smith, J. W. Stuth, and T. G. Welch. 1985. Integrated brush management systems for South Texas: development and implementation. Texas Agricultural Experiment Station Bulletin B-1493.

———, J. L. Mutz, and G. P. Durham. 1976. Range improvement following chaining of South Texas mixed brush. Journal of Range Management 29:418–21.

Smith, H. N., and C. A. Rechenthin. 1964. Grassland restoration. Part II. Brush control. USDA, Natural Resources Conservation Service, Temple, Texas.

Welch, T. G. 1991. Brush management methods. Texas Agricultural Extension Service Bulletin 5004.

————, R. P. Smith, and G. A. Rasmussen. 1985. Brush management technologies. Pages 15–24 *in* C. J. Scifres, W. T. Hamilton, J. R. Conner, J. M. Inglis, G. A. Rasmussen, R. P. Smith, J. W. Stuth, and T. G. Welch, editors. Integrated brush management systems for South Texas: development and implementation. Texas Agricultural Experiment Station Bulletin 1493.

Wilkinson, L. F. 1957. Defense against brush encroachment. Appendix XI. Pages 709–12 *in* T. Lea, author. The King Ranch. Volume 2. Little, Brown and Company, Boston.

Young, J. A., R. A. Evans, and D. W. McKenzie. 1983. History of brush control on western U.S. rangelands. Pages 17–25 *in* Kirk C. McDaniel, editor. Brush management symposium. Society for Range Management.

Young, V. A., F. R. Anderwald, and W. G. McCully. 1948. Brush problems on Texas ranges. Texas Agricultural Experiment Station Miscellaneous Publication 21.

3　Current State of the Art

Harold Wiedemann

Brush-dominated rangelands occur over vast areas of Texas that were previously dominated by grasses. Coping with excessive tree and shrub cover has been a costly and often futile activity of ranchers for several decades. Historically, brush was viewed only as a nuisance to livestock production, and brush eradication was the prevailing management paradigm of many ranchers throughout the 1950s. Large-scale, broadcast mechanical or chemical methods were applied over entire pastures or ranches. Follow-up, maintenance brush control, and proper grazing management were not utilized; hence, many programs failed.

In the 1960s, it became apparent that brush eradication was neither physically possible nor economically feasible, so brush control became the prevailing philosophy. Management goals continued to include total kill of targeted woody plants. About 1975, the phrase "brush management" became more popular and reflected the notion that some woody plants had value. Wildlife in Texas was becoming more important as an economic entity during this time. Additionally, environmentalists were starting to call for a reduction in herbicide use. During the 1980s, stakeholders began to realize the value of addressing resource management practices simultaneously. This led to the development of integrated brush management (Hamilton 1985).

Range scientists, resource management agencies, and landowners are now recognizing that woody plants have both tangible and intrinsic values. This, and smaller-sized land holdings and various other reasons, has brought about the current paradigm of brush sculpting. Brush sculpting is a concept of sculpting brush-infested rangeland for multiple use, including wildlife habitat, watershed management, recreational enterprises, endangered species, and landscape enhancement, as well as traditional livestock grazing (Wiedemann et al. 1999). These factors have influenced the current mechanical brush control devices in many ways. Each will be discussed.

Selective Thinning

Individual tree treatment is accomplished by grubbing or clipping and is an ideal method to sculpt brush-infested land. Sculpting can involve such

Figure 3.1.
Low-energy grubber.
*Courtesy Cross and
Harold Wiedemann, 1983*

Figure 3.2.
Wheel-loader grubber.

Figure 3.3.
Farm-tractor grubber.

Table 3.1. Mechanical techniques to prevent the regrowth of nine different brush species.*

Species	Technique
Mesquite	Sever taproot below basal crown (below bud zone), 6 to 14 inch depth, depends on size of tree
Redberry juniper	Sever taproot below basal crown, 6 to 12 inch depth, depends on size of tree
Blueberry (Ashe) juniper	Sever trunk above or below ground level, does not sprout from roots or basal crown
Algerita	Remove basal crown and buried stems under entire canopy area, 4 to 6 inches depth
Huisache	Sever taproot below basal crown, 6 to 12 inch depth, depends on size of tree
Twisted acacia	Sprouts from roots, remove as many as possible
Blackbrush	Sever taproot below second lateral, 6 to 12 inches deep, depends on size of tree
Whitebrush	Remove basal crown, depth of 4 to 6 inches
Catclaw	Sever taproot below first lateral and remove all buried stem with adventitious roots

*Based on grubbing studies listed in Table 3.2.

Table 3.2. Efficacy of the low-energy grubber (Fig. 3.1) operating in seven different brush species.*

Species	% Plant kill	Trees/acre	Dollars/acre**
Mesquite	80	20 to 100	3.00 to 12.00
Juniper	98	30 to 175	4.50 to 27.00
Huisache	75	75 to 225	9.50 to 30.00
Algerita	93	15 to 80	5.50 to 16.50
Twisted acacia	0	30 to 250	3.50 to 16.00
Blackbrush	86	20 to 130	6.50 to 19.00
Catclaw	85	50 to 150	8.50 to 20.50

*Adapted from Wiedemann (1997).
**Based on a contractor's cost of $45/hr to operate on a ranch site.

practices as leaving islands of brush with connecting corridors to provide a safe habitat for wildlife and a protected pathway for their movement between sites, while cleared areas provide plants for grazing. Grubbing implies below ground severing, while clipping implies above ground severing. Grubbing equipment will be discussed first.

Mechanical grubbing is the severing of tree roots below ground by a sharp, U-shaped blade mounted on a tractor (Fig. 3.1). Tractors can be crawlers, wheel loaders (Fig. 3.2), or farm-type (Fig. 3.3) depending on the size of trees to be grubbed and type of terrain. Table 3.1 describes the best technique to achieve good plant root kills when grubbing various brush species in Texas.

Low-energy Grubber

Low-energy grubbing is the use of a small tractor on small trees. This can be effective and cost efficient if tree densities are not too high (Wiedemann et al. 1977). These tractors usually have hydraulically assisted blades that enhance the output by tearing roots loose as the blade is rotated. Table 3.2 lists the performance of a 65-hp crawler tractor with a hydraulic-assisted blade (Fig. 3.1) grubbing seven different brush species. Performance curves are shown in Figure 3.4. Grubbing rates vary due to tree size, density, distribution, soil moisture, and type of terrain. Grubbing is best suited to tree infestations of 25 to 250 trees per acre.

Research using hydraulic force to assist in uprooting trees was started in the early 1970s (Wiedemann et al. 1977). Supplementing tree-uprooting forces with hydraulics allowed smaller, less costly tractors to be utilized. The result was the low-energy grubber. Tractor sales and grubber construction averaged more than a million dollars a year for five years in the late 1970s.

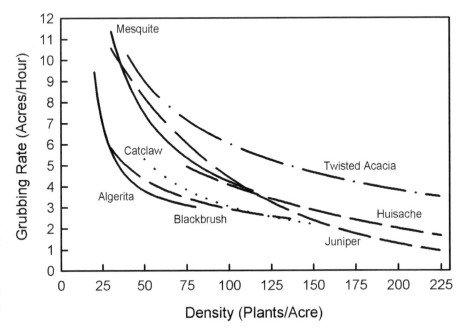

Figure 3.4.
Performance
curves for a
65-hp crawler
tractor grubbing
seven brush
species. A field
efficiency factor of
70 to 85% should
be anticipated.

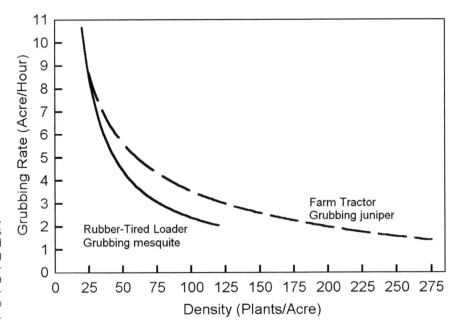

Figure 3.5.
Performance curves
for a wheeled
loader grubbing
mesquite 2- to 6-
feet tall and for a
farm tractor grub-
bing junipers 2- to
4-feet tall.

Figure 3.6.
Track-loader grubber.
Courtesy HOLT-CAT, San Antonio, Texas

The concept of hydraulic assistance has spawned a niche industry in Texas marketing novel grubbers for small tractors.

Loaders

With the advent of foam filling of off-road tires, the use of rubber-tired equipment on thorn-infested rangeland became practical (Wiedemann and Cross 1982). Wheel loaders are especially useful for grubbing (Fig. 3.2) because they provide excellent vision for the operator, can travel on roads between sites, and the bucket can be useful for material handling jobs. Crawler tractors have to be hauled between sites. Performance of a wheeled loader in mesquite (*Prosopis* spp.) regrowth 10 years following rootplowing is shown in Figure 3.5. In a grubbing comparison between an equal size (80 hp) loader (Fig. 3.2) and crawler tractor, the loader had 38% less soil disturbance and 43% less fuel consumption than the crawler. Productivity of the loader was the same as the crawler at 19 trees/acre but 42% less than the crawler at 140 trees/acre density.

Farm tractors with front-end loaders are handy for grubbing juvenile trees (Fig. 3.3) and performance in small junipers (cedars; *Juniperus* spp.) is shown in Figure 3.5. Track-type loaders are also practical for grubbing because the forward location of the cab provides the operator with a good view of the grubbing blade and the small cleats on the track grouser allow minimum soil disturbance (Fig. 3.6).

Three-point-hitch Grubbers

A popular method for grubbing limited acreage of small trees is to use a three-point-hitch grubber on the rear of a farm tractor. Some grubber styles require the tractor to drive over the tree first while others back the tractor to the tree and use the three-point hitch to lift the tree from the soil (Fig. 3.7). Grubbing trees by backing into them averaged 155 mesquites/hour (Mc-

Figure 3.7.
3-point-hitch grubber.

Figure 3.8.
Excavator grubber.
*Courtesy Darrell N. Ueckert,
San Angelo, Texas*

Farland and Ueckert 1982) while grubbing with front-mounted units on a crawler averaged 288 mesquites/hour and 432 small junipers/hour (Wiedemann et al. 1977, Wiedemann and Cross 1981).

Excavator

The most recent addition to the list of grubbers is an excavator. Excavators are track-type, high-capacity backhoes that are front mounted (Fig. 3.8).

With the boom extended, they can work a 50-foot swath, while moving in a straight line. The bucket, equipped with rock-digging teeth and two-prong-clamshell clamp, is very effective in removing junipers from rocky soil and stacking them. A U-shaped grubbing blade can be used in place of the bucket. Observations by scientists estimate 200 to 500 trees per hour can be removed. The air-conditioned cab, joystick controls, and small cleats on the track grousers provide the operator with a smooth operating machine.

Skid-steer Loaders

Brush species, such as Ashe juniper (*Juniperus ashei*), which do not sprout from the roots can be clipped above ground rather than uprooted below ground. Skid-steer loaders accomplish this using hydraulic shears (Fig. 3.9). Because of availability and low cost, they have become popular in sculpting landscapes. When shearing sprouting species (mesquite, redberry juniper [*Juniperus pinchotii*]), some contractors spray the stump with herbicide to reduce regrowth (McGinty and Ueckert 1997).

Selective Clearing

Selective clearing implies that selected areas are cleared of all woody species leaving a mosaic pattern or strips of cleared areas within the brushy land-scape. The cleared areas should be seeded with native or introduced grasses and shrubs that meet multiple use goals. Treatments can involve removing all aboveground growth, severing all roots at a given depth, or removing root systems from the soil. Clearing usually involves a combination of methods. The current machines and their application are discussed in this section.

Chains

A ship anchor chain pulled between two crawler tractors is widely used for tree felling because it can open an area quickly and is low-cost. Chains vary in length from 200 to 400 feet, weigh from 40 to 75 pounds per foot, and are

Figure 3.9.
Skid-steer loader with shears.
Courtesy Darrell N. Ueckert, San Angelo, Texas

Figure 3.10.
Elevated chain.

Figure 3.11.
Disk-chain-diker.
*Courtesy Harold Wiedemann
and Cross, 1994*

pulled in a U-shape. Chaining is used in dense to moderate stands of trees (trunk diameters greater than 3 in.) and is most effective in uprooting when soil moisture is high. It is not effective on shrubs or small trees with limber stems. Effectiveness is short lived because of regrowth and chaining should be used in combination with other treatments for maximum effectiveness. In North Texas, mesquite is chained 2 to 3 years following aerial spraying. In South Texas, dense stands of mixed brush are chained and stacked prior to subsequent treatments (Fisher et al. 1973).

Modified Chains

Modification of an anchor chain is the addition of a device to enhance the performance of the chain for brush manipulation and/or seedbed preparation. Examples are as follows.

Elevated chains. On individual tree tests, an elevated striking height reduced felling force by 67% and 84% compared to ground level striking on Ashe juniper in southern Oklahoma and redberry juniper in North Texas, respectively (Wiedemann and Cross 1996a). Elevated chaining is accomplished by attaching a rotating ball in the center of the chain pulled by two crawler tractors (Fig. 3.10). This one-way chaining method, if followed by prescribed burning, can achieve 98% plant kill in Ashe juniper. Redberry juniper, a sprouting species, is still under study using the chain and burn strategy. A 4-foot-diameter ball worked best in junipers 9- to 18-feet tall while a 6-foot ball did better in trees 18- to 45-feet tall (Wiedemann and Cross 1996b).

Disk-chain-diker. A unique development for limited brush control, but mainly, seedbed preparation on debris-littered land is the disk-chain-diker (Fig. 3.11). It was designed to follow rootplowing, but it can also be used on undisturbed sites when shrubs are less than 8-feet tall. It tills, smoothes, and forms small basins in the soil all in one pass and is energy efficient (Wiedemann and Cross 1994). A disk chain is an anchor chain with disk blades welded to alternate chain links. Disking action occurs when the chain, with swivels attached to each end, rotates as it is pulled diagonally. A flexing roller holds the disk-chain gangs in place. The chain diker, which is attached to the rear of the roller, uses special shaped blades welded to opposing sides of each link of a large anchor chain. As it is pulled over tilled land, the chain rotates and the blades leave a broadcast pattern of diamond-shaped basins 4-inches deep. Pulling requirements depend on the size of each component; a standard size unit requires 515 pounds of force per blade and the usual number is twenty blades. A twenty-blade unit is 35-feet wide and requires a 165- to 200-hp crawler tractor for pulling. A detailed explanation of the unit is provided by Wiedemann (1990).

In seeding studies over a 3-year period, grass densities were increased 92% by the disk chain compared with seedbeds prepared by smooth chaining in clay loam soil. There was no significant difference in grass densities between seedbeds prepared by disk chaining or offset disking, but both were significantly higher than chaining alone (Wiedemann and Cross 2000). Basins prepared by the chain diker increased grass stands from 33% to 2.6 times the density of grass stands on non-diked areas when growing-season rainfall was less than 20 inches (Wiedemann and Cross 2001). There was no advantage from diking when growing-season rainfall was above 20 inches. Since much of western Texas receives less than 20 inches of rainfall, it would be advantageous in many areas to include chain diking as part of seedbed preparation for rangeland seeding. Chain diking reduced runoff by 40% compared with non-diked treatments over a 3-year period on a slope of 0.3% (Wiedemann and Clark 1996).

Rootplows

A rootplow has a heavy-duty, V-shaped, horizontal blade, 10- to 16-feet wide pulled by a large crawler tractor at a depth of 12 to 14 inches (Fig. 3.12). This operation severs roots, preventing regrowth of nearly all brush species

Figure 3.12.
Rootplow®.
*Courtesy HOLT-CAT,
San Antonio, Texas*

except those with shallow root systems such as whitebrush (*Aloysia gratissima*) and pricklypear (*Opuntia* spp.). Chaining or raking following plowing helps to smooth the soil surface and remove sprouting species or stumps. Rootplows have been in use since the 1940s to clear dense stands of mesquite and other hard-to-kill brush species in preparation for seeding grasses or crops (Fisher et al. 1973). Commercial rootplowing averages about 2 acres/hour. Sculpting dense brush-infested areas by selective plowing and seeding with plants favorable for wildlife habitat, grazing animals, and watershed management could enhance the multiple use value of depleted rangeland on fertile soils. The most recent change in rootplows has been the development of regrowth plows.

Regrowth Rootplows

Holt Company of Texas (changed to HOLT CAT in 2002) has started manufacturing a line of regrowth plows (Fig. 3.13) and rakes for areas where brush regrowth is present on land previously cleared with conventional rootplows. They are especially useful in coastal Bermudagrass (*Cynodon dactylon*) pastures in parts of South Texas. Performance is best when tree trunk diameters are 4 inches or less. The plows resemble conventional rootplows but have been downsized to fit Caterpillar D-6 crawlers, rubber-tracked Challengers, or large farm tractors (Holt 1997). These 10-foot-wide units use quick hitches, and are much more energy efficient and cost effective than conventional rootplows.

The regrowth root rake has been designed to operate in concert with the regrowth plow. These 14-foot-wide units remove roots from the soil and pile them along with any aboveground brush debris (Holt 1997). They use the same quick hitch as the regrowth plows.

Renovators/Aerators

Roller chopping of brush has been accomplished by a large, rotating drum with a series of longitudinally mounted blades. A recent advancement in roller choppers is the use of small blades welded to the heavy drums in a staggered, cylindrical pattern; these units are called renovators or aerators (Fig. 3.14)(Lawson 1994). The advantages of the renovators are that the small blades chop debris and form basins in the soil to capture and hold rainfall. In addition, the staggered, cylindrical blade pattern prevents the vibration caused by the longitudinal blade placement on standard roller choppers. Renovators normally use two drums mounted on a frame similar to an offset disk, and are pulled with a crawler tractor or a special-equipped, rubber-tired tractor. The drum diameters vary from 18 to 42 inches and can be filled with water for weight. Renovators are used in moderate to dense shrub-infested rangeland or pastures to remove top growth of shrubs and to improve rainfall retention. Removal of the top growth produces a flush of regrowth. This is desirable for browsing animals when used on palatable

Figure 3.13.
Regrowth plow.
Courtesy HOLT-CAT,
San Antonio, Texas

Figure 3.14.
Renovator/Aerator.

Figure 3.15.
Self-propelled shredder.

brush species such as shin oak (*Quercus havardii*) or guajillo (*Acacia ber-landieri*). When seeding grass in combination with chopping, the basins enhance seedbed preparation. Roller chopping Bigelow shin oak (*Quercus durandii* var. *breviloba*) averaged 5.3 acres/hour using a 15-foot-wide drum filled with water (Wiedemann et al. 1980).

Disks

Disks used on rangeland are the heavy-duty offset style. Blade diameters range from 24 to 36 inches and units are 8 to 12 feet in width. Disks with 36-inch blades are used for brush control on undisturbed soil while units with blade diameters less than 30 inches are used for seedbed preparation following rootplowing. Whitebrush was controlled by disking in the fall (13% mortality) and then re-disking in the spring after the root crowns had sprouted (91% mortality) (Wiedemann and Cross 1980). Oats were seeded following fall disking, and buffelgrass (*Cenchrus ciliaris*) was seeded following spring disking for livestock grazing. Seedbed prepared by disking (24-in. blades) consistently produced better grass stands than did roller chopping or chaining on rootplowed sites at nine locations in the Edwards Plateau and Rolling Plains (Wiedemann et al. 1979). If excessive timber prevents the use of a disk, then a disk-chain-diker can be used.

Shredders

Brush shredders are patterned after pasture and crop shredders but are designed to withstand more strain. Width is normally 7 feet, but selected units are 15-feet wide. Brush shredding is prone to mechanical failures and usually requires extensive modification of the farm tractor that pulls the unit. Modifications include foam filling of the tires or other approaches to prevent flats, and mounting front and belly-pan guards and a rear guard to protect the back of the operator from flying debris. Shredding brush leaves the plant height level and this is aesthetically pleasing. Regrowth, however, is extensive following shredding of all sprouting shrubs. Downtime was 64%

when shredding Bigelow shin oak with a standard 7-foot shredder in the Edwards Plateau (Wiedemann et al. 1980). Shredders are more applicable for pasture weed control than brush control but they can be used on brush over limited acreage.

Self-propelled shredders are constructed for brush mastication, and a Hydro-Axe unit was very effective in removing top growth of Bigelow shin oak at 2.35 acres/hour (Fig. 3.15). However, they are expensive and not readily available.

Summary

Sculpting brush-dominated rangeland for multiple use has resulted in new opportunities for mechanical brush control methods. Manipulating brush infestations for better wildlife habitat, watershed management, and recreation enterprises often lends itself to mechanical manipulation. This, coupled with new advancements in machines and especially the way in which these machines are used, has helped to keep mechanical brush control as a viable option in brush management.

Proceedings of a recent symposium on brush sculpting are available on the web at http://texnat.tamu.edu/symp/sculptor/ and additional mechanical information is available at http://juniper.tamu.edu/sculptor/.

Literature Cited

Cross, B. T., and H. T. Wiedemann. 1983. Low-energy grubbing with special blade to control algerita. Journal of Range Management 36:601–603.

Fisher, C. E., H. T. Wiedemann, C. H. Meadors, and J. H. Brock. 1973. Mechanical control of mesquite. Pages 46–52 *in* Mesquite. Texas Agricultural Experiment Station Research Monograph 1.

Hamilton, W. T. 1985. Initiating IBMS. Pages 9–14 *in* C. J. Scifres, W. T. Hamilton, J. R. Conner, J. M. Inglis, G. A. Rasmussen, R. P. Smith, J. W. Stuth, and T. G. Welch, editors. Integrated brush management systems for South Texas: development and implementation. Texas Agricultural Experiment Station Bulletin 1493.

Holt Company of Texas. 1997. Product literature. P.O. Box 207916, San Antonio, Texas 78220-7916.

Lawson Cattle & Equipment, Inc. 1994. Pasture aerator product literature. 2954 Hilliard Isle Rd., Kissimmee, Florida 34744.

McFarland, M. L., and D. N. Ueckert. 1982. Mesquite control: use of a three-point hitch mounted, hydraulically assisted grubber, PR-3981:48–50. *In:* Texas Agricultural Experiment Station CPR-3968-4014.

McGinty, A., and D. N. Ueckert. 1997. Brush busters: how to beat mesquite. Texas Agricultural Extension Service & Texas Agricultural Experiment Station Leaflet L-5144.

Wiedemann, H. T. 1990. Disk-chain-diker implement selection and construction. Center Technical Report No. 90-1. Chillicothe-Vernon Agricultural Research and Extension Center, Vernon, Texas.

———. 1997. Factors to consider when sculpting brush: mechanical treatment options. Pages 88–95 *in* D. Rollins, D. N. Ueckert, and C. G. Brown, editors. Proceedings brush sculptors symposium. Texas Agricultural Extension Service, San Angelo.

———, J. H. Brock, C. E. Fisher, and B. T. Cross. 1979. Seed metering and placement devices for rangeland seeder. Transactions of the ASAE 22: 972–77.

———, and L. E. Clark. 1996. Chain diking effects on runoff and winter wheat yield. Agronomy Journal 88:541–44.

———, and B. T. Cross. 1980. Evaluation of equipment for control of whitebrush. Texas Agricultural Experiment Station CPR-3665:101–102.

———, and ———. 1981. Low-energy grubbing for control of junipers. Journal of Range Management 34:235–37.

———, and ———. 1982. Performance of front-mounted grubber on rubber tired equipment, PR-3982:50–53. *In* Texas Agricultural Experiment Station CPR-3968-4014.

———, and ———. 1994. Chain diker draft and power requirement. Transactions of the ASAE 37:389–93.

———, and ———. 1996*a*. Draft requirements to fell junipers. Journal of Range Management 49:174–78.

———, and ———. 1996*b*. Draft requirements for tree felling by chaining. Paper No. 965003. ASAE, St. Joseph, Missouri.

———, and ———. 2000. Disk chain effects on seeded grass establishment. Journal of Range Management 53:62–67.

———, and ———. 2001. Chain diker effects on seeded grass establishment following disk chaining. Journal of Range Management 54:138–43.

———, ———, and C. E. Fisher. 1977. Low-energy grubber for controlling brush. Transactions of the ASAE 20:210–14.

———, C. H. Meadors, and C. E. Fisher. 1980. Bigelow shin oak control. Texas Agricultural Experiment Station CPR-3665:28–29.

———, D. Rollins, D. N. Ueckert, and A. McGinty. 1999. Sculpting brush-dominated rangeland for multiple use. Pages 233–34 *in* D. Eldridge and D. Freudenberger, editors. Proceedings 6th International Rangeland Congress, Townsville, Queensland, Australia.

4   The Future of Mechanical Treatments for Brush Management
What is Next?

Rory Burroughs,
Mike Gibbs,
Robert K. Lyons,
and
Colin McGahey

Mechanical methods for brush management have been in use for over 60 years; however, there have not been many new procedures developed within the last 30 years. With the exception of improvements to heavy equipment and basic design modifications to implements, the mode of action remains the same for various mechanical treatments. Practices such as rootplowing, chaining, and disking are time tested and proven methods for treating brush and the use of these and other mechanical applications will certainly continue and perhaps increase in the future.

There are three major reasons why the use of mechanical treatments will continue to be popular. The first relates to the increased value that has been placed on the recreational use of rangelands. While multiple use values are a major consideration, in many areas of the state wildlife has become the single most important income-producing operation on ranches. Mechanical treatments are compatible with this wildlife management emphasis. They allow for precise location of treatments while leaving untreated areas that have a high utility value for wildlife species. Even broadcast practices, such as rootplowing, can be applied along contours or to delineate specific polygons on the landscape that are important for wildlife habitat. Mechanical treatments also avoid problems with damages caused by chemical applications when nontarget areas are in close proximity to target areas, and they are viewed as more environmentally friendly by many landowners.

Mechanical practices can provide soil disturbance and seedbed preparation for wildlife food plants. Because of soil disturbance, most mechanical practices tend to increase the forb components on rangelands. Many forbs are of great value to wildlife species because of their seeds, relatively high protein content, and digestibility. However, other plants that are undesirable, such as common goldenweed (*Isocoma coronopifolia*), may be stimulated by mechanical soil disturbance and require that care be taken in planning the appropriate control technology.

A second reason for continued use of mechanical practices in the future involves a change in the trend of land ownership. A growing number of rural landowners today do not live on the ranch. Most of these owners have income produced from areas other than ranch operations and do not have to make a living from the land. The disposable income generated away from the ranch is often used to improve the ranch, a luxury that was not commonly available to traditional ranch owners. The availability of income to invest in land treatments and the desire to implement fast changes on range landscapes tend to favor mechanical practices among these landowners. Mechanical treatments can provide fast and dramatic changes in vegetation, including woody plant presence, density, and structure.

Increased information and technology are the third reason closely related to future use of mechanical methods of brush management. With a better understanding of ecological principles and the ability to accurately measure and plan brush management projects using Geographic Information Systems (GIS) and Global Positioning Systems (GPS), landowners can effectively utilize a variety of available mechanical options. These technologies (GIS and GPS) facilitate "sculpting" of landscapes to optimize the soils, topography, and vegetation to meet very specific habitat management objectives.

Recreational Uses of Rangelands

People with a wide variety of interests are using rangelands for recreation. These users enjoy activities such as hiking, camping, mountain biking, birding and wildlife viewing, rock or artifact hunting, and game hunting. Optimization of such multiple uses of rangelands requires landowners to consider a variety of vegetation management options. Owners who emphasize game hunting, or a combination of hunting, livestock production, and recreation, rely heavily on mechanical brush management to meet spatial and structural landscape design requirements.

Hunting has many economic impacts on rural areas. It is often the driving force in rural land real estate markets. Leasing rangelands for hunting generates from six to twelve dollars per acre depending on location in the state. Many rural landowners are encouraged to manage for wildlife because of the economic incentives derived from hunting and the major consideration in managing wildlife is creating and maintaining the appropriate habitat.

With this emphasis on wildlife, and thus on habitat, brush management on many ranches is focusing on brush sculpting, or the selective removal of woody vegetation in a design that favors both wildlife and livestock. Mechanical treatments are very compatible with brush sculpting because the high degree of selectivity they offer allows land managers to create optimal wildlife habitat within the available land resources.

It should be mentioned that there are also habitat risks associated with brush management, including mechanical practices. Landowners should be aware of the trade-offs involved in removal of brush species that favor one wildlife species while negatively affecting another. For example, nesting habitat of certain bird species can be damaged by honey mesquite (*Prosopis glandulosa*) removal (Nolte and Fulbright 1996).

Land Ownership Trends and Educational Roles

The future of rural land in Texas largely depends on demographics of the next generation of landowners. The "Texas Land Rush of the Twenty-first Century" is occurring slowly, but surely, as more and more people are acquiring property away from urban areas. The resulting subdivision of traditional ranches and decreasing property size are changing the face of rural landscapes. There is an increasing need for emphasis on proper management of small properties owned by people with little or no experience in land management. Issues such as water quantity and quality are moving to the forefront and proper management of rural ecosystems is needed to ensure overall health of the land. Many of today's new landowners look to mechanical practices to make changes on landscapes that serve their perception of best use. However, they often are not aware of the need for development of long-range plans to minimize habitat damage and optimize desired ecological and environmental results.

Today's rural landowners represent a different group of individuals than existed in the past. Many of the new landowners are absentees and they represent an increasingly large segment of the rural population in Texas. These are landowners who typically do not reside permanently on the rural property they own and who have income derived from sources other than operations on the ranch. Absentee landowners are generally well educated, albeit in subjects unrelated to rangeland or wildlife management issues. However, they are usually interested in proper management and proper ecological balance for their land and they tend to be open to new ideas.

The educational role for new landowners cannot be filled totally by existing state and federal programs, such as the Texas Cooperative Extension and the Natural Resources Conservation Service. In many instances, including the planning and application of brush management practices, the time available for landowners to meet with technical assistance personnel does not match the time that these landowners have away from their principal businesses in the city. This can lead to decisions to apply long-lasting mechanical treatments on the land without proper regard for long-range impacts on desired land uses. Contractors who apply mechanical and other practices to modify rangeland on these properties are being pressed into educational roles in an effort to ensure that habitat is enhanced, rather than diminished, in the process. More effort is needed to prepare special publications, web-based materials, videos, and other media sources to quickly reach new landowners after the land purchase and before critical decisions are made that may have long-term negative impacts on the land and vegetation.

Information and Technology

Aldo Leopold observes that the most outstanding scientific discovery of the 20th century would probably be the complexity of the land (1949). Ecosystem management reflects Leopold's concept of the land's complexity. With growing demands on rangelands from an ever-increasing human population, the complexity of the land organism is being studied more than ever.

Ecosystem management best describes how rangelands should be managed today, and incorporates all aspects of the landscape: climate, soil characteristics, and plant physiology, as well as the requirements of species that occur within the system. Humans are a part of the ecosystem and their decisions that influence ecosystems must be considered in management plans as well. Brush management is an integral component in managing many rangeland ecosystems and mechanical treatments provide land managers with a great degree of flexibility for treating undesirable woody vegetation. The use of brush management, including mechanical methods will continue and should increase in popularity as an option in land management.

On the technological side of Leopold's thought is the growing use of Geographic Information Systems (GIS) and Global Positioning Systems (GPS) in rangeland applications. Complex relationships in ecology are more readily understood with the information provided by GIS and GPS systems. The additions of these technologies to brush management have had a greater impact on mechanical treatments than any other recent development in the field. For contractors, these technologies have made equipment use more efficient, helped to better predict and manage costs, as well as produce a higher quality final product. The use of GPS units on ground and aerial brush management equipment is already at hand. Large equipment manufacturers will be installing GPS systems directly on the equipment for use by the operator. These technological advantages will facilitate the increasing use of mechanical brush management methods as more precise delineations of range landscapes increase in importance for the reasons previously stated.

Delineation of landscape features of significance to habitat and subsequent treatment designs can be done on digitized maps with available GIS software. The longitude and latitude coordinates from these features can be programmed into GPS units on mechanical equipment that allows the operator to identify areas for treatments and areas to be left untreated, and to follow lines, such as contoured strips, that have been preselected on the digital maps. The increased interest in the use of GIS and GPS has fostered development of companies that provide landowners with the newest technologies available. Companies, such as Kiva Consulting, an on-site GIS and GPS ranch mapping company, and Land Enhancement Services, a heavy machinery land improvement company, work together to provide landowners with "packaged" planning and applications capability.

The key component in brush management is both short-term and long-term planning (20 or more years in the future). The brush species that occur on Texas rangelands are tenacious and in order to maintain the best combination of plants to meet management objectives over time, land managers must plan treatments for the long term. They must look beyond the immediate project, and consider the effects on the ecosystem over extended planning horizons. What will a rootplowed field look like 20 years after the initial treatment with no follow-up management? The answer, of course, is that brush will return and probably with fewer, and perhaps less desirable, species (mostly plants like honey mesquite, huisache [*Acacia smallii*], and pricklypear [*Opuntia* spp.]) (Hamilton et al. 1983, Fulbright and Beasom 1987, Ruthven et al. 1993, Nolte et al. 1994).

This same problem of longevity of the initial treatment is even more significant for many other mechanical practices, including chaining, dozing, or roller chopping. Land managers must be able to "see" into the future of initial treatments and plan for the follow-up or maintenance practices necessary to stretch the benefits of initial practices over longer time periods. This long-term extension of initial treatment benefits is absolutely essential for economic viability of brush management. Treatment combinations and synergistic effects between treatments should also be considered.

GIS technology allows managers to create project maps that incorporate several key management components (Figs. 4.1, 4.2). Maps that overlay soil and topographical data, ecological sites, and brush densities enable managers to be more effective in the long term. For example, Plan Map A (Fig. 4.1a) shows the use of GIS to help landowners and managers visualize

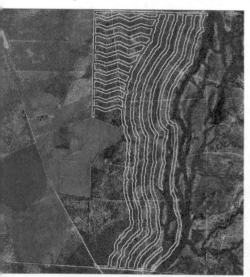

Figure 4.1a. (*left*) Plan Map A. Plan maps created using GIS technologies are transferred to the field using GPS. These maps help the landowners and managers visualize the final product before the equipment reaches the field. Note the second strip is not continuous, as a potential problem was identified during the planning process. The strip intersected the creek, and treatments performed in this area would pose a risk to operators and create accelerated erosion. *Courtesy Land Enhancement Services*

Figure 4.1b. (*above*) GPS allows the contractor to accurately transfer the design from the plan map onto theground. This image is an aerial photograph of the finished product from plan map A. *Courtesy Land Enhancement Services*

Figure 4.1c. Additional images of the final product from plan map A. *Courtesy Land Enhancement Services*

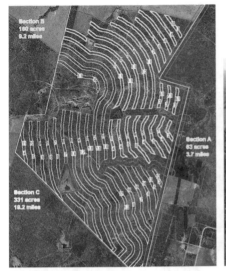

Figure 4.2a. Plan Map B. This brush sculpting plan was developed with cattle production as the primary emphasis. However, the landowner could not ignore the value of improved wildlife habitat. By removing brush in the contoured pattern, areas for grazing were created that were also beneficial for wildlife. Wildlife "honey holes" were identified on the plan map so that they would not be altered. Numbered strips with calculated acreages and distances on the map aided communications between the operators and the landowner. *Courtesy Land Enhancement Services*

Figure 4.2b. This image is an aerial photograph from plan map B. The contoured design of the strips provided screening cover for wildlife. Approximately 200 yards was the maximum distance that could be observed on any given strip. By leaving islands of brush, habitat and patterning were enhanced for wildlife while providing additional shade for livestock. *Courtesy Land Enhancement Services*

Figure 4.2c. An additional aerial image from plan map B showing large mesquites left for wildlife screening cover and shade for livestock. *Courtesy Land Enhancement Services*

the final product before equipment reaches the field. GPS allows the contractor to accurately transfer the design from the plan map (Fig. 4.1a) onto the ground (Figs. 4.1b, 4.1c). In another example, Plan Map B (Fig. 4.2a) shows a brush sculpting plan developed with cattle production as the primary goal. However, the landowner could not ignore the value of improved wildlife habitat. By removing brush in a contoured pattern, areas were created that were beneficial for both cattle grazing and wildlife. Wildlife "honey holes" were identified on the plan map to avoid disturbance. Contoured strips provided wildlife screening cover with a maximum 200-yard visibility on any open area (Fig. 4.2b). Large mesquite trees were left for wildlife cover screen and livestock shade (Fig. 4.2c).

The ability to accurately measure distances and acreages is another benefit of using these technologies, both to landowners and contractors. Information and ideas can be arranged before any treatments are performed.

A major advantage to equipment operators is having existing structures and features highlighted on a map. Water wells, fences, gas lines, and wildlife areas of high utility are identified on the project map and their locations can be transferred to GPS units for use by both equipment operators and land managers.

These technologies, along with education and experience, have helped create the concept of brush sculpting. Historically, treatments were done fence line to fence line or in broad open patterns. Currently, more managers are considering the needs of wildlife and sculpting rangeland to meet their requirements. Narrower, contoured strips, fewer open expanses and more brush sculpting are common today and have prospects for increased use in the future. These very specific spatial decisions for placement of treatments make GIS and GPS technologies essential in the planning process.

What is Next?

Because of the variety of uses for rangelands, education will become an underlying need for new landowners who have new management goals, increased awareness and understanding of ecological processes, and the addition of technologies to aid land managers. Fundamental principles of range management, secondary plant succession, how plants grow and the principles of defoliation, range proper use and grazing management, and principles of brush and weed management are some of the areas that should be addressed. Educated managers and land stewards will continue to include mechanical treatments in their plans for ecosystem health, and, hopefully, their decisions will be based on sound ecosystem management. There will be no new "magical" implement invented any time soon that will effectively treat the variety of brush problems. Existing mechanical techniques, perhaps with modifications, are and will be an integral component of these new management philosophies.

What is taking traditional methods of mechanical treatments into the twenty-first century? The integration of soil characteristics, plant species requirements, climate patterns, wildlife and livestock management objectives, along with our increasing knowledge of these processes, are allowing managers and contractors to make traditional mechanical methods fit the new century and new brush management philosophies.

Literature Cited

Fulbright, T. E., and S. L. Beasom. 1987. Long-term effects of mechanical treatments on white-tailed deer browse. Wildlife Society Bulletin 15: 560–64.

Hamilton, W. T., L. M. Kitchen, and C. J. Scifres. 1983. Height replacement of selected woody plants following burning or shredding. Texas Agricultural Experiment Station Bulletin 1361.

Leopold, A. 1949. A Sand County almanac and sketches here and there. Oxford Unifersity Press, New York.

Nolte, K. R., and T. E. Fulbright. 1996. Nesting ecology of scissor-tailed flycatchers in South Texas. Wilson Bulletin 108:302–16.

———, T. M. Gabor, M. W. Hehman, M. A. Asleson, T. E. Fulbright, and J. C. Rutledge. 1994. Long-term effects of brush management on vegetation diversity in ephemeral drainages. Journal of Range Management 47: 457–59.

Ruthven, D. C., III, T. E. Fulbright, S. L. Beasom, and E. C. Hellgren. 1993. Long-term effects of root plowing on vegetation in the eastern South Texas Plains. Journal of Range Management 46:351–54.

Chemical Brush Management

5 Chemical Weed and Brush Control
Where We Have Been

Rodney W. Bovey

A comprehensive review of the *Journal of Range Management* indicated that during the past 50 years there were many more scientific papers published on chemical woody plant control than any other method. This was true regardless of the time period investigated. Even during the last 10-year period, from 1990 to 2000, more papers were published on plant control using herbicides than papers on plant control using fire, biological, or mechanical means. Economic constraints and governmental restrictions have regulated the use of chemicals to control plants from the 1970s to the present. During the 1970s and 1980s, there were more than fifty-four papers published on chemical brush control in each 10-year period. Even during the 1980s, when prescribed burning gained new popularity, there were still more than twice as many papers published about use of herbicides (55) versus use of fire (26) for vegetation control and management. These papers do not include chemicals used in herbaceous weed control, integrated brush management systems (IBMS), or studies where several methods were compared. It clearly shows the importance of herbicides, or the perceived importance of herbicides, in weed and woody plant control whether used alone or with other methods.

History and Development

Some highly effective chemicals have been developed for weeds and woody plant control and are listed in Appendix 5.1. Limitations on their use are usually economical. Managers must make the right connection between the proper herbicide and the target woody plant or plants, as well as considerations about the herbaceous weed population present. Agricultural herbicides undergo extensive toxicological, environmental, and use benefit tests before they are released for widespread use.

The use of herbicides for woody plant control has sometimes been discovered after their use for control of annual and perennial herbaceous weed control. The history of 2,4,5-T is an exception to this pattern. As early as 1947, Dow AgroSciences researchers found that 2,4,5-T was effective against certain brambles (*Rubus* spp.) and other weeds resistant to 2,4-D (Barrons and Coulter 1947). Similarly, it was reported in 1949 that when the ester of 2,4,5-T was applied to the foliage of honey mesquite (*Prosopis glandulosa* var. *glandulosa*) it was more effective than several formulations of 2,4-D or other chemicals (Young and Fisher 1949).

As early as 1948, Fisher and Young (1948) reported that sodium arsenate, sodium arsenite, ammonium sulfamate, sulfamic acid, ammonium thiocyanate, 2,4-D, and 2,4,5-T were the only chemicals out of several hundred tested that were absorbed by mesquite foliage and translocated in sufficient amounts to kill all dormant buds on the underground stem. Fisher and Young (1948) indicated that kerosene and diesel fuel had been used extensively for mesquite control by application around the base of the plant to completely wet the underground stem. They also mentioned that oils including diesel fuel had been studied as diluents alone and with water with the butyl and isopropyl esters of 2,4-D and 2,4,5-T for mesquite control.

At the same time, control methods were being developed by the Texas Agricultural Experiment Station for cedar (*Juniperus* spp.), pricklypear cactus (*Opuntia* spp.), oaks (*Quercus* spp.), and mixed brush in east-central and South Texas (Darrow and McCully 1959).

Klingman (1961) stated in 1961 that the use of herbicides to control brush and undesirable trees in the United States had expanded rapidly since about 1950. He further stated the use of chemicals has generally proven to be more effective and less costly than most other methods. Although chemicals are still highly effective today and are used in pastures, rangelands, industrial sites, rights-of-way, and forestry, they are no longer inexpensive. The cost of 2,4-D is still reasonable (2,4-D ester at 0.5 lb/A is about $1.75). However, triclopyr and dicamba cost 5 times as much as 2,4-D for the same application rate (Bovey 1996). Is the cost associated with inflation, high production costs, or requirements associated with compliance to government laws and regulations or all of the above? The reasons for the high cost may be difficult to identify. Herbicide use is greatly hampered by cost in the market place, and is limited to the more productive land sites or special situations. It is apparent from Appendix 5.1 that there has been little new herbicide development for grazing land applications since the 1970s.

Accumulated Knowledge

Herbicides. We know a great deal about the chemical properties of herbicides used in weed and brush control. This enables the applicator to select herbicides in relation to the target weeds and brush to achieve maximum efficiency, safety, and economics. Each herbicide has a profile of weeds controlled, behavior in the environment, toxicology, ecological effects, mode of action, and cost of treatment. Responsible and effective herbicide use depends upon user knowledge of available chemistry.

Herbicides commonly used for weed and brush control include foliar applied amitrole, clopyralid, 2,4-D, dicamba, dichlorprop, diquat, fosamine, glyphosate, picloram, triclopyr, and paraquat. Of this group, amitrole, 2,4-D, dichlorprop, diquat, fosamine, glyphosate, and paraquat enter plants mainly through the foliage, while the others have both foliar and root activity. Diesel oil and kerosene enter plants primarily through foliage and stems and are used as herbicide diluents. Diquat and paraquat are contact herbicides applied to foliage only. Tebuthiuron and hexazinone are soil applied usually as a granule or pellet.

Some useful mixtures for weed and brush management include 2,4-D + dichlorprop, 2,4-D + triclopyr, 2,4-D + picloram, 2,4-D + dicamba and picloram + triclopyr, picloram + dicamba, picloram + clopyralid, triclopyr + clopyralid, and others. Herbicide mixtures are used because they may be synergistic and increase herbicide efficacy on target weeds and brush. Mixtures also broaden the spectrum of weeds and brush controlled, reduce total herbicide cost by using a less expensive but effective herbicide in the mixture, or reduce possible forage or soil residues. Herbicide mixtures may also reduce movement problems to ground water or surface runoff water.

Herbicide Application Technology. Formulated herbicides, as discussed, are of little value if methods of application and equipment are not available to treat weed problems in a safe and practical manner. Equipment for applying chemicals must disperse the material in sometimes very small amounts at a uniform rate per acre. Spraying is the most common method of applying herbicides. Sprays are useful since small quantities of herbicides can be diluted to permit even coverage of plant or soil surfaces.

Woody plants and weeds can be killed with herbicides in different ways. Herbicides can be applied by (1) spraying onto foliage, (2) wiping onto stems and foliage, (3) spraying basal bark or stumps, (4) injection into the sapwood of trees by mechanical devices or through frills or notches cut into the tree, and (4) soil application.

Methods of application include broadcast sprays and individual plant treatment. The Brush Busters technology discussed in later chapters is the most recent technology for control of honey mesquite, pricklypear, redberry juniper (*Juniperus pinchotii*), and blueberry juniper (*Juniperus ashei*). Other methods include cut surface and injection treatments with herbicides, including cut stump applications. Soil treatment with woody plant herbicides can be done with pellets or spot treatment to the soil under individual plants.

Sprays can be applied to weeds and brush with hand-carried, ground, or aircraft equipment. Selection of application equipment depends on weed and brush density, species, and area. Rough terrain and tall vegetation may limit the use of ground or hand-carried equipment. Where stands are scattered, individual plants can be treated with foliar sprays, basal stem, cut surface, and injection treatment, or soil application. Special wiping devices are also used to treat individual plants in small or scattered stands. It is essential to calibrate application equipment and use up-to-date equipment in good repair. Calibration charts and procedures are available from the chemical manufacturers, state extension and experiment station personnel, and other sources. Applying herbicides, cleaning equipment, and disposing of containers and waste products must be done in accordance with label instructions and EPA requirements.

Herbicide Residues in the Environment

Amitrole and fosamine are lost rapidly from the soil due to microbial activity and other means. These compounds do not become an environmental problem if they are used according to label specifications (Appendix 5.2). Food crops must be free of any amitrole residue.

Diquat, paraquat, and glyphosate are strongly adsorbed to soil making them virtually biologically unavailable. Diquat and paraquat are destroyed if exposed to sunlight on plant and soil surfaces. Microbial breakdown of these compounds is apparently very slow in decaying plants and soils. Glyphosate is degraded in soil and water by microbial activity. Mobility of these herbicides in most soils will not be a problem because of their strong adsorption to soil. They have low potential for movement in runoff water.

Dicamba, in moist, warm soil has a half-life of <14 days as a result of microbial degradation. Half-life in native grasses and litter is 3 to 4 weeks. Under simulated rainfall conditions, a maximum of 5.5% of dicamba applied to a watershed was removed in runoff water. Dicamba levels found in streams after application to large watersheds were several orders of magnitude below threshold response levels for fish and mammals.

The phenoxy herbicides such as 2,4-D and diclorprop are short lived in the environment and have limited mobility; therefore, movement into groundwater is unlikely. Phenoxys are rapidly decomposed by soil microbes, sunlight, and plant metabolism. Phenoxy herbicides are generally less phytotoxic to broadleaf plants than is picloram. However, preventing spray drift or vapors to susceptible plants such as cotton is essential.

Picloram degrades within 3 to 6 months in Texas soils. Persistence will be longer in cooler climates. The half-life of this herbicide varies widely depending upon rainfall and soil temperature. Picloram tends to leach to lower soil depths, but most remains in the upper meter of soil. Picloram may move in surface runoff water, but its removal from watersheds is usually less than 5% of the total amount applied. Picloram is degraded slowly by soil microorganisms and plant metabolism but is degraded rapidly by sunlight. Picloram is phytotoxic to a wide range of plants, especially broadleaf plants. Therefore, care must be taken to limit its movement.

Clopyralid is chemically similar to picloram but has a shorter half-life in soil than picloram and is subject to degradation by soil microbes. It resists degradation by sunlight. Clopyralid moves in water sources in a manner similar to picloram but is not phytotoxic to as many plant species as picloram.

In Maryland, wheat, corn, and okra could be grown 8 days after application of triclopyr at 3 lb/A to soil. Kidney beans, squash, and potatoes could be grown in less than 3 months after triclopyr application. In Texas, triclopyr persisted for only 3 months after summer application and 6 months after fall application. The mode of breakdown by these compounds in soils is by leaching, photodegradation, and microbial activity. Mobility in runoff water is similar to 2,4-D.

Metsulfuron is moderately persistent in soil with typical half-life of 30 days. Degradation by soil microbes is slow, and nonmicrobal hydrolysis is slow at high pH and relatively rapid at lower pH. Degradation rates increase at high soil temperature and high soil moisture.

Hexazinone is mobile in runoff water and readily leaches in some soils. Spot-gun application to brush species indicated limited movement and transport from treated watersheds in stream discharge. Half-life varied from 1 to 6 months in soil depending upon location.

In semiarid and humid regions, tebuthiuron may persist for long periods. Tebuthiuron is readily adsorbed in soil that has high organic matter or high clay content but may leach in soils that are low in organic matter or have low clay content. Tebuthiuron content, however, in forage plants is typically well below legal residue limits when applied as pellets. Concentrations of tebuthiuron in runoff water decreased rapidly to less than <0.05 ppm after 3 months from a watershed application in Central Texas. Tebuthiuron resists photodecomposition and volatilization, and breakdown by microbial activity is slow.

Bromacil is degraded in soils by microbial activity. Disappearance varies with geographical location. More rapid loss occurs in warmer soils. Bromacil is considered a moderately to highly persistent herbicide especially at rates of 4.5 lb/A and above. It is moderately mobile in the environment.

Imazapyr controls many weeds and woody plants. It is highly persistent in soils and may persist for 2 years. Microbial degradation is the principal means of imazapyr dissipation in soil. Dissipation in shallow ponds is relatively rapid. Imazapyr is not very mobile in soil and contamination from runoff into streams appears unlikely.

Toxicology and Safety

Everyone working with agricultural chemicals wants to know the toxicity of the phytocide to themselves and other organisms (Appendix 5.3). Toxicity to test organisms is given as the LD_{50}, expressed as milligrams (mg) of toxicant per kilogram (kg) of body weight (mg/kg), the dose that kills 50% of the test animals, usually the laboratory rat. For mammalian toxicity it can be expressed as oral acute toxicity and toxicity is determined (short term) at the end of 24 hours (Ware 1989).

The LC_{50} is the median lethal concentration, a concentration that kills 50% of the test organisms, expressed as mg or cubic centimeters (cc), if liquid, per animal. It is also the concentration expressed as parts per million (ppm) or parts per billion (ppb) in the environment (usually water) that kills 50% of the test organisms exposed (Ware 1989).

Chronic toxicity is defined as the toxicity of a material determined beyond 24 hours and usually after several weeks of exposure. The "no effect level" (NOEL) is also desirable information of an herbicide or pesticide to determine if the application is being done at a safe level. Very toxic pesticides have an LD_{50} of 50 to 500 for a single oral dose (mg/kg) and an LD_{50} of 200 to 1000 for a single dermal dose for rabbits (mg/kg) (Klaassen et al. 1986). Paraquat and diquat are the only herbicides listed in Appendix 5.3 that fit the very toxic category. Herbicides that are moderately toxic include 2,4-D, dicamba, dichlorprop, hexazinone, tebuthiuron, and triclopyr. LD_{50} for moderately toxic compounds are from 500 to 5000 mg/kg oral dose for the rat (Klaassen et al. 1986). Amitrole, bromacil, clopyralid, diesel fuel, glyphosate, imazapyr, metsulfuron, and picloram are only sightly toxic at acute oral LD_{50} (rat) of 5000 to 15,000 (mg/kg). Fosamine at 24,000 mg/kg is practically nontoxic (>15,000 mg/kg). If the rabbit dermal category for slightly toxic of 2000 to 20,000 (mg/kg) is considered, dicamba, dichlorprop, hexazinone, and imazapyr can be added to the slightly toxic list.

Herbicide Effects on Crops

An added benefit of woody plant control is usually control of herbaceous weeds associated with the woody plants. The herbicide is sometimes selected to manage both herbaceous and woody vegetation. Because of this, herbaceous crop and desirable vegetation may be extremely sensitive to the chemicals used. Desirable plants adjacent to weed and brush areas may be damaged by volatility (movement by vapors in air) of the herbicide moving to nontarget areas. The amount of fumes or vapors given off by 2,4-D, for example, is related to the vapor pressure of the chemical and high temperature. 2,4-D acid and amine salts have very low volatility and cause little or no volatility hazard, whereas, methyl, ethyl, and isopropyl esters of 2,4-D are very volatile. Low volatile esters of 2,4-D and other hormone-like herbicides are made by using high molecular weight alcohols. In addition, an ether linkage further reduces the volatility.

The relative volatilities of 2,4-D esters have been measured by exposing selected test plants in bags or bell jars to vapors of herbicide for a designated time and air temperature. Leaf epinasty, stem curvature, leaf modification, stem proliferation, and growth inhibition are some manifestations of herbicide effect to demonstrate its presence. Volatility may also be measured by trapping the herbicide and quantifying it by gas chromatography or other chemical analysis. Damage to a number of plants, especially broadleaf plants, has been demonstrated in the laboratory at extremely low rates of 2,4-D and observed in the field. However, in the field, injury to plants (such as crops) by volatile herbicides is sometimes difficult to demonstrate because of the dilution effect and dispersion by air currents. In crop sensitive areas, high volatile esters of 2,4-D are usually prohibited.

Spray drift, or accidental application of herbicides, can cause injury and can be readily demonstrated in agronomic and horticulture crops, especially dicots. Application of 0.01 lb/A of 2,4-D at the seedling stage of cotton delayed maturity and reduced yield. Most other herbicides are not as injurious as 2,4-D on cotton. Soybeans tolerated 2,4-D amine in the early stages of growth but became more sensitive as they matured. Exposure of 0.25 lb/A reduced yields at all stages of growth. Picloram and dicamba were more injurious than 2,4-D to soybeans applied at pre-bloom. At flowering, dicamba at 0.31 lb/A and picloram at 0.008 lb/A reduced soybean yield about 50%. Tomato and root crops were more sensitive to 2,4-D than other vegetable crops tested. Lettuce showed epinasty, necrotic and chlorotic areas within 24 hours after treatment with >50 g/plant. Imazapyr persisted in soil in the greenhouse for over 1 year and forage grasses and herbs were highly sensitive to residual carry over damage. Bean and squash were tolerant of imazapyr residues. Hormone-like herbicides were generally more phytotoxic to dicots and tolerated by monocots at reduced rates that simulate spray drift.

Ecological Effects

Numerous studies show that grass and forb production can be significantly increased by adequate woody plant control with herbicides. Such results have been documented in many different climatic regions with a diverse array of woody plants. Increased grass and forb production was usually measured 2 to 5 years following treatment. Therefore, the treatment benefit may not always be long-term, or we may simply not know the long-term effect of the treatment because most studies have been short-term. Resulting woody plant control on grazing lands increased livestock production and improved wildlife habitat and populations of species that have an affinity for grassland vegetation. Herbicide treatment may reduce forb production during the first growing season but usually forbs recover by the second growing season. Herbicide treatment may not be justified in light, scattered brush stands or stands on poor sites. Herbicides are useful in integrated brush management systems in combination with fire or mechanical methods. For example, low rates of picloram can be used on pricklypear cactus after fire to achieve excellent control in West Texas. Soil-applied herbicides such as tebuthiuron can be used at reduced rates from 0.3 to 0.5 lb/A to thin big sagebrush and increase plant and animal diversity. Spraying strips of brush and leaving alternate untreated areas may significantly increase livestock forage as well as maintaining wildlife habitat and food plants. Forage quality is not adversely affected by herbicide use and is sometimes improved (crude protein). Cattle may prefer forage in herbicide-treated plots.

Woody plants are usually vigorous competitors and tend to regenerate rapidly if disturbed and left untreated. Therefore, follow-up treatments with some control method are desired to maintain both herbaceous vegetation and productivity.

In rangeland, forest, and noncrop lands herbicides may temporarily reduce wildlife numbers not because of toxicity but because of reduced food plants or cover.

Herbicide Efficacy

Chemical management procedures have been developed for several hundred herbaceous weeds and woody plants. These data are provided by manufacturers, state extension and state experiment stations, as well as U.S. Department of Agriculture research and technical bulletins and papers.

Economics

Treatment of weed and woody plant problems on rangeland and forests may be necessary for economic production of livestock, wildlife, or forest products, if weed problems become too severe. Economic production, however, may be confined to the more productive sites with minimal, infrequent, or no expenditure on the nonproductive sites. Land managers must decide on the goals they want to attain and on the cost/benefit ratio that will involve improvements for aesthetics, fire suppression, or other reasons than economic return. Information and computer decision making systems are available on the web for some weed problems. Such resources are also available from some state universities, industries, or the U.S. Department of Agriculture.

Physiology and Mode of Action

Several thousand research papers and bulletins have been written on herbicides, especially the phenoxy herbicides, relative to their mode of action, absorption, translocation, and fate in plants. Such knowledge is essential for determining optimum efficacy at minimal herbicide rates and understanding their behavior in different environments. Such knowledge is also useful in developing new chemicals and enhancing activity of currently used herbicides.

Summary

A comprehensive review of the *Journal of Range Management* indicated that there were far more scientific papers published on chemical woody plant control than any other method during the last 50 years. This was true regardless of the time period investigated, including the most recent 10-year period from 1990 to 2000. Such information clearly shows the importance of herbicide use in weed and brush management. Some highly effective herbicides have been developed, for example, 2,4-D, and dichlorprop in the 1940s for weed and brush management. Most herbicides currently available were developed from the 1950s to the 1970s. Economic constraints and government laws and regulations have hampered herbicide development; therefore, it is extremely important that currently available herbicides be reregistered and retained. There is an enormous body of data and knowledge on herbicide physical properties, chemistry, and behavior in the environment, as well as toxicological effects on many organisms, including humans. Further development in application technology, ecology, physiology, and economics is being pursued.

Literature Cited

Barrons, K. C., and L. L. Coulter. 1947. The specific effect of 2,4,5-trichlorophenoxy acetic acid on members of the genus Rubus and certain other 2,4-D resistant species. North Central Weed Control Conference Research Report 4:255.

Bovey, R. W. 1996. Use of 2,4-D and other phenoxy herbicides on pastureland, rangeland, alfalfa forage, and noxious weeds in the United States. Pages 76–86 *in* O. C. Burnside, editor. Biological and economics assessment of benefits from use of phenoxy herbicides in the United States. USDA, NAIAP Report No. 1, PA-96.

Darrow, R. A., and W. G. McCully. 1959. Brush control and range improvement in the post oak-blackjack oak area of Texas. Texas Agricultural Experiment Station and Texas Agricultural Extension Service, Texas A&M University, Bulletin 942.

Fisher, C. E., and D. W. Young. 1948. Some factors influencing the penetration and mobility of chemicals in the mesquite plant. Proceedings North Central Weed Control Conference 6:197–202.

Klaassen, C. D., M. O. Amdur, and J. Doull, editors. 1986. Casarett and Doull's toxicology. The basic science of poisons. Third edition. Macmillan Publishing Co., New York.

Klingman, G. C. 1961. Weed control: as a science. John Wiley & Sons, Inc., New York.

Ware, G. W. 1989. The pesticide book. Third edition. Thomas Publishing, Fresno, California.

Young, D. W., and C. E. Fisher. 1949. Treatments to the foliage of mesquite (*Prosopis juliflora*). North Central Weed Control Conference Research Report 6:147.

Appendix 5.1. History and development of herbicides used in weed and woody plant management.

Herbicide	Discovered or reported (year)	Country, researcher, or company	First USA use	Basic producer (1998)
Amitrole	1953	Union carbide	1954	CFPI Agro
Bromacil	1961	DuPont	1963	DuPont
Clopyralid	1961	—	1978	Chimac – Agriphar, S.A.
2,4-D	1942	Zimmerman	1944	Several
Dicamba	1958	Hitchcock S.B. Richter, Velsicol Chem. Corp.	—*	Novartis
Dichlorprop	1944	Zimmerman & Hitchcock	1961	BASF AG
Diesel fuel			1930s	Several
Diquat	1955	Dyestuffs Div. ICI, G.B.	1955	Zeneca
Fosamine	1974	DuPont	—*	DuPont
Glyphosate	1971	Monsanto Co.	1974	Several
Hexazinone	1975	DuPont	—*	DuPont
Imazapyr	Late 1970s	Amer. Cyanamid	1981	American Cyanamid
Metsulfuron	1983	DuPont	1986	DuPont
Paraquat	1958	Dyestuffs Div. ICI, G.B.	1959	Several
Picloram	1960	Dow AgroSciences	1963	Dow AgroSciences
Tebuthiuron	1970	Air Supply, Inc.	1974	Dow AgroSciences
Triclopyr	1975	Dow AgroSciences	—*	Chimac – Agriphar, S.A.

*Data were not available for first USA use for dicamba, fosamine, hexazinone, and triclopyr.

Appendix 5.2. Residual activity of herbicides used in weed and woody plant management in soil, plant, and water sources.

Herbicide	Soil	Plants	Water sources	Precautions
Amitrole	Low	Moderate	Low	Prevent residues on food crops
Bromacil	Mod-High	High	Mobile	Prevent soil and water mobility
Clopyralid	Moderate	Moderate	Moderate	Prevent spray drift
2,4-D	Low	Low	Low	Prevent spray drift
Dicamba	Low	Low	Low	Prevent spray drift
Dichlorprop	Low	Low	Low	Prevent spray drift
Diesel oil	Low	Low	Low	Protect skin
Diquat	Very Low	High	Low	Protective gear
Fosamine	Low	Low	Low	Prevent spray drift
Glyphosate	Very Low	High	Low	Prevent spray drift
Hexazinone	Moderate	Moderate	Mobile	Prevent soil and water mobility
Imazapyr	High	Moderate	Low	Prevent spray drift
Metsulfuron	Moderate	Moderate	Low	Prevent soil particle mobility
Paraquat	Very Low	High	Low	Protective gear
Picloram	Mod-High	Moderate	Mobile	Protect from water sources
Tebuthiuron	High	High	Low	Avoid application near large trees
Triclopyr	Moderate	Moderate	Low	Prevent spray drift

All herbicides listed are degraded by soil microbes.
Diquat, metsulfuron, paraquat, and picloram are very slowly degraded by soil microbes.

Appendix 5.3. Mammalian toxicity of herbicides used in weed and woody plant management.

Herbicide	Toxicity rating	Acute oral LD_{50} (rat) (mg/kg)	Dermal LD_{50} (rabbit) (mg/kg)	Inhalation LC_{50} (rat) (g/L-14-h)
Amitrole	Low	>5,000	>2,000	NA[a]
Bromacil	Low	5,200	>5,000	>4.8
Clopyralid	Low	>5,000	>2,000	1.3
2,4-D	Moderate	764	>2,000	1.8
Dicamba	Moderate	1,707	>2,000	>9.6
Dichlorprop	Moderate	800	>4,000	NA
Diesel oil	Low	7,400	>4,100	NA
Diquat	High	230	>400	NA
Fosamine	Very Low	24,4000	>1,638	NA
Glyphosate	Low	>5,000	>5,000	NA
Hexazinone	Moderate	1,690	>6,000	>4.5 (1-h)
Imazapyr	Low	>5,000	>2,000	>1.3
Metsulfuron	Low	>5,000	>2,000	>5.3
Paraquat	High	150	>240	nontoxic
Picloram	Low	>5,000	>2,000	>0.04
Tebuthiuron	Moderate	644	>200	NA
Triclopyr	Moderate	713	>2,000	NA

Source: Farm Chemicals Handbook, 1997. Meister Publishing Co., Willoughy, OH and WSSA Herbicide Handbook, 7th Ed. 1994. Champaign, Illinois.
[a]NA = Not available.

6   A Paradigm Shift

Rob Mitchell,
Steve Whisenant,
and
Ron Sosebee

Controlling unwanted plants with chemicals is not an invention of the twentieth century. For thousands of years, salt has been recognized as an agent to
control plant growth. In Judges 9:45 of the Old Testament, Abimelech de-
feated the city of Shechem and scattered salt on the soil, to prevent his enemies from growing food in this area. More recently, kerosene was applied to
the base of honey mesquite (*Prosopis glandulosa*) to control plants in Texas
and Oklahoma (Young et al. 1983).

Plant control with synthetic herbicides began with the discovery of 2,4-D
[(2,4-dichlorophenoxy)acetic acid] in 1942 (Hammer and Tukey 1944). The
application of 2,4-D on rangeland is still recommended for controlling numerous broadleaf herbaceous weeds. It is used alone or in combination with
other herbicides to control many woody plants (McGinty et al. 2001).

One of the most widely publicized herbicides has been 2,4,5-T [(2,4,5-
trichlorophenoxy)acetic acid]. Carson (1962) referred to herbicides such as
2,4,5-T as "elixirs of death," and ushered in an emotional campaign to free
the world from the bondage of these "biocides." The use of 2,4,5-T and Sil-
vex [2-(2,4,5-trichlorophenoxy)propionic acid] on rangelands became the
standard for controlling honey mesquite for more than three decades, until
their sale was banned in the United States and Canada in 1983 (Vallentine
1989).

The availability of more selective herbicides and application methods for
brush management have remained largely unchanged for 20 years. Although
the development of new chemicals is still important, most recent work has
focused on fine-tuning the delivery of existing herbicides to reduce damage
to nontarget weeds, and to make herbicide application more "user friendly."

While the chemicals, basic treatment methods, and species of concern
have remained somewhat constant in recent years, nearly every other variable influencing brush management decision-making has changed. The average size of ranches has declined, which makes aerial applications less applicable. New landowners, many with nontraditional goals and little land
management experience, are making the brush management decisions. Increasingly, these landowners are not restricted by the economics of produc-

tion agriculture. Public funding of watershed-scale brush management programs is also being used to manage water resources. If successful, these watershed-scale programs will likely be expanded throughout the southwestern United States.

Traditional landowners have responded to this radically altered economic environment by changing their brush management goals and strategies. For example, wildlife habitat concerns and aesthetic interests have changed the brush management goals on many ranches. Interest in non-game animals and endangered species has reduced the use of broadcast herbicide applications in many areas. Public concern about negative herbicide impacts on wildlife continues to grow, even though little information suggests they occur. For example, the broadcast application of clopyralid (3,6-dichloro-2-pyridinecarboxylic acid) had no negative effects on northern bobwhite (*Colinus virginianus*) chick hatchability, growth, or immunocompetence when applied directly to simulated nests (Dabbert et al. 1997). Broad-spectrum, broadcast control methods have become less attractive to wildlife managers than selective methods that allow managers to pick-and-choose brush species and landscape patterns for herbicide treatment. The use of selective herbicides with reduced residual activity is partially replacing, and in other situations being used in addition to, broad-spectrum, persistent chemicals.

In this changing environment, scientists have reexamined previous assumptions about the practicality of individual plant treatments. Several changes began to occur after the basic assumptions about the use of individual plant treatments were reevaluated. These changes led to the development of the Brush Busters program, an integrated marketing effort to disseminate brush management information to the user (McGinty and Ueckert 1995, McGinty and Ueckert 1996, Ueckert and McGinty 1997). The widespread availability of backpack sprayers, all-terrain vehicles (ATV), and 12-volt ATV sprayers simplified treatment techniques and improved labor efficiency. Equipping 15- to 25-gallon ATV sprayers with three hoses and spray wands further increased labor efficiency during individual plant treatments. The use of dye spray markers greatly improved the efficiency with which pastures could be treated, by reducing the number of plants that were treated multiple times or not treated at all. Using ConeJet 5500-X1 nozzles increased the precision application of stem sprays, while reducing the amount of spray used. These new efficiencies and refined techniques have altered our paradigm about the economic feasibility of individual plant treatments. Consequently, individual plant treatments are widely used because they are highly effective and they are an appropriate technology for the goals of many landowners.

Individual Plant versus Broadcast Herbicide Treatments

Treating individual plants with herbicides has become far more common in the last 10 years than any previous time in the history of brush control. Individual plant treatments are attractive because of the relatively small equipment investment, high degree of selectivity, flexible timing of labor requirements, and high mortality of target plants if herbicides are properly applied.

Individual plant treatments allow you to select the species, size, sex (in dioecious species), and even location of brush that is killed or left untreated. However, costs escalate rapidly with individual plant treatments as the density and size of treated brush increase (Ueckert and McGinty 1999a, b, c).

Although broadcast treatments such as aerial spraying are not automatically more expensive on denser, older stands, they may be less effective if herbicide applications are not properly timed. Broadcast herbicide applications may be restricted by nearby susceptible crops or by the presence of desirable brush species that may also be susceptible. It is just as important to understand what species are tolerant of each herbicide as it is to know which species are susceptible to that herbicide. This knowledge provides the foundation for selective broadcast applications. Broadcast applications of less selective herbicides may even be applied in specific patterns (strips, grids, or along topographic boundaries) to provide a lesser degree of selectivity and provide wildlife habitat diversity.

We illustrate a few of the most effective herbicide treatments for honey mesquite, junipers (*Juniperus* spp.), and pricklypear (*Opuntia* spp.). This is not a comprehensive list, but it provides examples of broadcast and individual plant treatments that effectively control some of the most common rangeland brush and weed problems in the southwestern United States.

Mesquite

Mesquite has received more attention than any other brush species on southwestern rangelands. Although numerous broadcast application techniques, aircraft types, herbicides, formulations, and rates have been evaluated in the past, the broadcast treatments of past decades seldom achieved more than 25% root-kill (Dahl and Sosebee 1984). Today, 25% root-kill would be considered a disaster. Dozens of large-scale research plots have consistently produced mesquite root-kill greater than 60%, and often greater than 75% when a mixture of Reclaim® (clopyralid) and Remedy® (triclopyr; [(3,5,6-trichloro-2-pyridinyl)oxy]acetic acid) (0.25+ 0.25 lb. a.e. acre) is used under appropriate conditions (Table 6.1). Studies conducted by scientists with the Texas Agricultural Experiment Station, Texas Agricultural Extension Service, Texas Tech University, Dow AgroSciences, New Mexico State University, the USDA-ARS, and others have consistently produced acceptable mesquite mortality.

Even the most effective herbicide combinations will not be successful if they are applied under improper conditions. The most important consider-

Table 6.1. Mesquite mortality 2 years after aerial application to research plots in Texas and New Mexico.

Treatment	Studies (number)	Average mortality (%)
Reclaim® and Remedy® (0.25 + 0.25 lb. a.e./ac)	18	70
Reclaim® (0.50 lb. a.e./ac)	13	55
Remedy® (0.50 lb. a.e./ac)	11	14
Reclaim® and Tordon® 22K (0.25 + 0.25 lb. a.e./ac)	13	54

Source: Summary provided by Darrell Ueckert.

ation is to apply the spray mixture uniformly to healthy, mature foliage that is at the proper physiological stage and under proper environmental conditions. In most cases, the herbicide used is secondary to the physiological status of the plant and the environmental parameters at the time of herbicide application. Dahl and Sosebee (1984) identified several environmental factors that contribute to the success of aerial herbicide application on mesquite. The most important environmental parameter is soil temperature. Soil temperature must exceed 75 °F at 12–18 inches below the soil surface. Additionally, the mesquite canopy should not contain light green foliage, and the canopy should be reduced by no more than 25% by insects, drought, or hail. During application, wind speed should be between 2 and 10 miles per hour, ambient air temperature should not exceed 90–95 °F, and, if possible, relative humidity should be greater than 50%. Most importantly, one should always read and follow label directions. In addition to the previously mentioned parameters, plants must be physiologically capable of responding to the herbicide once the herbicide is absorbed by the plant. The herbicide must be translocated to the perennating organs and tissues in order to affect root mortality in the target species (see Chapter 8, *this book*).

The best aerial applications put a uniform distribution of spray droplets over the entire leaf surface. Numerous factors contribute to a good deposition of spray droplets, but it usually requires the application of at least 4 gallons of spray mixture per acre (Whisenant et al. 1993). Adding diesel to the spray mixture in a 1:5 diesel:water emulsion is often recommended to improve herbicide absorption into the leaf, thus increasing mortality. However, since broadcast herbicides must enter the plant through the leaf material and be translocated from the leaf to the perennating organs and tissues, it is critical not to get too much diesel in the spray mixture, or it will cause necrosis of the leaf tissue prior to optimum herbicide absorption or translocation. A 1:20 or even 1:40 diesel:water emulsion might be more appropriate if application is to occur when air temperatures are high.

Spraying individual mesquite plants with foliage or stem sprays is very effective when conducted under proper conditions (Table 6.2). The Brush Busters leaf spray recommendation calls for a spray mixture of 0.5% Reclaim® + 0.5% Remedy®. This herbicide combination can be applied in either water or in a diesel:water emulsion. A surfactant should be used with the water mixture (0.25% of spray mixture). Each plant should be sprayed until all the leaves are glistening, but not dripping. It is imperative to spray each stem since translocation across stems does not occur. Adding a dye to the spray mixture improves efficiency by reducing the number of plants that are sprayed multiple times or not sprayed at all, as well as insuring all stems and leaves are sprayed. This spray mixture usually provides 80% or greater root-kill (Table 6.2). Another effective foliar application is a 1% solution of Reclaim® in water sprayed until all the leaves are glistening, but not dripping. Although using a 0.75% solution has provided greater than 80% root-kill on mesquite less than 6 feet tall under research conditions (Mitchell et al. 1998), we recommend a 1% solution for field applications.

The Brush Busters recommendation for stem spraying mesquite is 15% Remedy® + 85% diesel fuel for small (less than 1.5 in. diameter) mesquite

Table 6.2. Mesquite mortality 2 years after treatment using the Brush Busters stem or leaf spray, a leaf spray containing Remedy® and Tordon® 22K at 5 locations (Ueckert et al. 1999, McGinty et al. 2001), and leaf spray containing 0.75% Reclaim® (Mitchell et al. 1998).

Treatment	Herbicide mixture	Average mortality (%)
Stem spray	15% Remedy® + 85% diesel	80
Leaf spray	0.5% Remedy® + 0.5% Reclaim® in water with 5% diesel + emulsifier	80
Leaf spray	0.5% Remedy® + 0.5% Reclaim® + 0.25% surfactant in water	>76
Leaf spray	0.5% Remedy® + 0.5% Tordon® 22K in water with 5% diesel + emulsifier	28
Leaf spray	0.75% Reclaim® in water	>80

with smooth bark. Larger stems with rough bark require a 25% Remedy® mixture in diesel. Using a Conejet 5500-X1 nozzle, spray this mixture lightly, but evenly on the lower 12 inches of each stem. Spray all sides of the stem until wet, but runoff is unnecessary. This method is most effective in hot weather, but works well all year. Stem spraying becomes more difficult and expensive on multiple stemmed plants. Dense grass around the base of mesquite can intercept the spray, reducing efficiency and efficacy, and increasing labor.

Junipers

Several management options are available for juniper species. Mechanical treatments such as dozing, chaining, rootplowing, and hand removal are all viable alternatives. Additionally, fire may be the most effective and least expensive management alternative in many situations, and can cost as little as $3 per acre (Mitchell et al. 2000). The capability to resprout makes redberry juniper (*Juniperus pinchotii*) more difficult to control than nonsprouting juniper species such as Ashe juniper (*J. ashei*) and eastern red cedar (*J. virginiana*). Hand grubbing can be very effective on juniper seedlings. Ueckert and Whisenant (1982) reported 100% mortality for redberry juniper seedlings that were cut at the soil surface or hand grubbed 2 to 6 inches below the soil surface, regardless of treatment date. Although redberry juniper is relatively easy and inexpensive to control as seedlings and juvenile trees, action is not usually taken until trees are "mature" and there is an obvious decrease in herbage production. There are no effective broadcast herbicide treatments for either Ashe or redberry juniper. Thus, herbicide treatments for juniper are limited to individual plant treatments that use foliar sprays, spot applications to the soil, basal applications, or cut-stump treatments to resprouting species.

Foliar sprays are most effective on trees that are less than 3 feet tall (McGinty and Ueckert 1996). Sprays containing 1% Tordon® 22K (picloram; 4-amino-3,5,6-trichloro-2-picolinic acid) in water plus 0.25% surfactant applied to the foliage until the point of runoff resulted in 91% mortality (McGinty and Ueckert 2001). Foliar sprays are most effective in the late spring and summer when plants are actively growing.

Soil spot applications can be very effective even on large trees, but treatment response can be slow. Spot applications of Velpar® L [3-cyclohexyl-6-

Table 6.3. Redberry juniper mortality following cutting 4 in. above the soil surface and/or application of Tordon® 22K in the Texas Rolling Plains (from Tunnell and Mitchell 2001).

Treatment	Mortality (%)
Cut only	7
Basal	
Spray only 1%	60
Spray only 10%	86
Spray only 20%	93
Cut stump	
Cut & spray 1%	77
Cut & spray 10%	100
Cut & spray 20%	100
Soil spot	
4 cc/3 ft of plant height	68

(dimethylamino)-1-methyl-1,3,5-triazine-2,4(lH,3H)-dione] (2 cc/3 ft of plant height) resulted in 93% juniper mortality (McGinty and Ueckert 2001). Treating redberry juniper with Tordon® 22K (4 cc/3 ft of plant height) killed 68% of the trees between 3 and 10 feet tall (Tunnell and Mitchell 2001). Soil spot applications are made with an exact delivery hand-gun and are most effective when applied to the soil under the canopy of smaller trees (<3 ft). The treatment effectiveness is more reliable when applied prior to a significant rainfall event, or when the soil is moist. For larger trees requiring more than one spot, doses should be applied on opposite sides of the plant. Always apply spot treatments on the uphill side of plants growing on slopes. The effectiveness of soil-applied herbicides is reduced by high clay and organic matter contents.

Basal application of Tordon® 22K has effectively controlled redberry juniper trees between 3 and 10 feet tall (Tunnell and Mitchell 2001). Applying a 1% solution of Tordon® 22K in water killed 60% of the trees. Increasing the concentration to 10% Tordon® 22K increased average mortality to 86%. However, increasing the concentration to 20% Tordon® 22K only increased average mortality to 93%. Consequently, a basal application of 10% Tordon® 22K in water optimizes mortality while minimizing treatment cost.

A cut-stump treatment is necessary if mature redberry junipers are to be cut above the soil surface. Cutting 3- to 10-feet tall redberry juniper to a stump height of 4 inches killed only 7% of the trees (Tunnell and Mitchell 2001). Immediately spraying the cut stumps with 1% Tordon® 22K + 99% water resulted in 77% mortality. Increasing the concentration of the spray solution to 10 or 20% applied immediately after cutting resulted in 100% mortality. Additionally, 4% Tordon® 22K + 96% water has resulted in ≥90% mortality (McGinty et al. 2001). Consequently, if the management objectives include removing the trees, then we recommend cutting the trees and immediately treating the stumps with 4 to 10% Tordon® 22K in water. However, the trade-off for increased mortality with cutting and spraying is increased labor costs.

Junipers can be difficult to manage, and management approaches can be labor intensive. Benefits of the individual plant treatments are the specificity in the application, and the ability to sculpt the landscape for livestock or wildlife. Removing junipers with individual plant treatments can rapidly change the complexion of small areas. Individual plant treatments are more difficult to apply to large trees or in areas with high plant densities. However, individual plant treatments might still be the preferred option for managing juniper when large-scale mechanical treatments or fire are not wanted or are not possible (Table 6.3).

Pricklypear

Pricklypear can be controlled with either broadcast or individual plant treatments (Table 6.4). Broadcast applications will be most practical where plant densities exceed 350 to 400 plants per acre, but can be less effective than individual plant sprays (McGinty et al. 2001). Aerial applications of 1 pint to 1 quart Tordon® 22K (0.25 to 0.5 lbs a.i. picloram) per acre can be expected to reduce pricklypear cover by 50 to 85% when applied in 4 gallons of 1:5 diesel:water emulsion. The 1-pint per acre rate is generally restricted to the Texas High Plains. Broadcast applications made with ground equipment should apply the same rate of Tordon® 22K, but requires 20 to 25 gallons of spray mixture (with 0.25–0.50% surfactant) per acre. Broadcast applications are generally recommended in late summer or autumn when total nonstructural carbohydrates (TNC) are increasing in organs supporting perennating buds (Potter et al. 1986).

Pricklypear is an excellent example of the synergism between burning and herbicides. Pricklypear is more susceptible to picloram after fire top-kills most of the established pads and stems (Ueckert et al. 1988, Blair et al. 1993). Burning in early March reduced canopy cover by at least 59% compared to initial measurements (Table 6.4; Blair et al. 1993). A mid- to late May broadcast application of picloram at 0.12 and 0.25 lb a.i. per acre to burned areas reduced pricklypear canopy cover by 98% 3 years after treatment. Although successful pricklypear control has been achieved with as little picloram as 0.12 lb a.i. per acre after burning under research conditions, picloram manufacturers do not recommend the application of less than 0.25 lb a.i. per acre. Consequently, if an area has been burned and over 90% of the pricklypear pads have been scorched, the broadcast application

Table 6.4. Expected pricklypear canopy reduction following burning with or without broadcast herbicide treatments (Blair et al. 1993), and individual plant and aerial broadcast treatments (from McGinty et al. 2001).

Treatment	Herbicide mixture	Expected canopy reduction (%)
Prescribed burning	None	≥59
Prescribed burning	0.12 lb a.i. per acre Tordon® 22K in water + 0.1% emulsifier	≥82
Prescribed burning	0.25 lb a.i. per acre Tordon® 22K in water + 0.1% emulsifier	≥77
Hand spray pads and stems	1% Tordon® 22K in water	>75
Aerial application to undamaged plants	1 pint Tordon® 22K per acre applied in 4 gallons spray (1:5 diesel:water emulsion)	50–75
Aerial application to undamaged plants	1 quart Tordon® 22K per acre applied in 4 gallons spray (1:5 diesel:water emulsion)	80–90

of picloram can be reduced from 0.5 lb a.i. per acre to at least 0.25 lb a.i. per acre. Burning likely increases picloram efficacy by removing the grass canopy, which reduces interception of the herbicide by the litter, and by eliminating old, decadent pricklypear pads, and increasing the physiological activity in pricklypear tissues. It is important to understand that picloram enters pricklypear through the cuticle of the pads and through the roots. Consequently, effective pricklypear control depends on the uniform application of picloram to the pad as well as the incorporation of picloram into the soil water solution.

Spraying individual pricklypear plants with 1% Tordon® 22K (plus 0.25% surfactant in water carrier) can be more effective than broadcast applications (McGinty et al. 2001). Canopy reductions of 75 to 100% are common with the individual plant spray methods. Pricklypear can be sprayed most of the year, with the exception of very cold weather, or during extremely dry conditions. Pads should be sprayed until they are wet, just prior to runoff (Ueckert and McGinty 1997). Pricklypear mortality occurs more rapidly when both sides of the pads and stems are sprayed, and when rainfall is received within a few weeks after sprays are applied.

Conclusion

We are coming full circle in chemical control of brush and weeds. The first large-scale herbicide applications for brush management were individual plant treatments with kerosene. We then progressed into broadcast aerial application using many herbicides with varying degrees of success. We learned volumes of information about the ecophysiology of many species, which has proven to be critical in understanding brush management. Today, changes in land ownership patterns, management goals, and public concern for herbicide use and wildlife habitat have elucidated the need for precision application of herbicides for brush management, challenging the paradigm that bigger is better. Albert Einstein stated, "Not everything that can be counted counts, and not everything that counts can be counted." We have the responsibility and opportunity to identify the things that count on rangelands, and develop treatment options that address the problems at hand.

Literature Cited

Blair, B. K., C. M. Britton, and D. N. Ueckert. 1993. Pricklypear control with fire and herbicides on the Texas Rolling Plains. Texas Journal of Agriculture and Natural Resources 6:87–97.

Carson, R. L. 1962. Silent spring. Houghton Mifflin Co., New York.

Dabbert, C. B., R. B. Mitchell, and D. Oberheu. 1997. Northern bobwhite egg hatchability and chick immunocompetence following a field application of clopyralid. Bulletin of Environmental Contamination and Toxicology 58:801–806.

Dahl, B. E., and R. E. Sosebee. 1984. Timing—the key to herbicidal control of mesquite. Texas Tech University Management Note 2. Texas Tech University Press, Lubbock.

Hammer, C. L., and H. B. Tukey. 1944. Selective herbicidal action of midsummer and fall applications of (2,4-dichlorophenoxy) acetic acid. Botanical Gazette 106:232–33.

McGinty, A., J. F. Cadenhead, W. T. Hamilton, C. W. Hanselka, D. N. Ueckert, and S. G. Whisenant. 2001. Chemical Weed and Brush Control Suggestions for Rangeland. Texas Agricultural Extension Service Bulletin B-1466.

———, and D. N. Ueckert. 1995. Brush Busters—how to beat mesquite. Texas Agricultural Extension Service and Texas Agricultural Experiment Station Publication L-5144.

———, and ———. 1996. Brush Busters—how to master cedar. Texas Agricultural Extension Service and Texas Agricultural Experiment Station Publication L-5160.

———, and ———. 2001. The Brush Busters Success Story. Rangelands 23:3–8.

Mitchell, R., C. Britton, B. Racher, E. Fish, and E. Atkinson. 2000. Prescribed fire costs on juniper-infested rangeland. Rangelands 22:7–10.

———, R. Sosebee, B. McFarland, and R. Mata-Gonzalez. 1998. Mesquite management with summer and fall clopyralid applications. Page 74 *in* Society for Range Management Abstracts.

Potter, R. L., J. L. Petersen, and D. N. Ueckert. 1986. Seasonal trends of total non-structural carbohydrates in Lindheimer pricklypear (*Opuntia lindheimeri*). Weed Science 34:361–65.

Tunnell, S. J., and R. B. Mitchell. 2001. Redberry juniper response to picloram and top removal in the Texas Rolling Plains. Texas Journal of Agriculture and Natural Resources 14:112–16.

Ueckert, D. N., and A. McGinty. 1997. Brush Busters: How to take care of pricklypear and other cacti. Texas Agricultural Extension Service and Texas Agricultural Experiment Station Publication L-5171.

———, and ———. 1999*a*. Brush Busters: how to estimate costs for controlling pricklypear. Texas Agricultural Extension Service and Texas Agricultural Experiment Station Publication L-5290.

———, and ———. 1999*b*. Brush Busters: how to estimate costs for controlling small cedar. Texas Agricultural Extension Service and Texas Agricultural Experiment Station Publication L-5292.

———, and ———. 1999*c*. Brush Busters: how to estimate costs for controlling small mesquite. Texas Agricultural Extension Service and Texas Agricultural Experiment Station Publication L-5291.

———, ———, and U. P. Kreuter. 1999. Brush Busters: marketing *Prosopis* management technology. Volume 2. Pages 580–81 *in* D. Eldredge and D. Freudenberger, editors. VI International Rangeland Congress, Inc., Townsville, Queensland, Australia.

———, J. L. Peterson, R. L. Potter, J. D. Whipple, and M. W. Wagner. 1988. Managing pricklypear with herbicides and fire. Pages 10–15 *in* Texas Agricultural Experiment Station Report 4570.

———, and S. G. Whisenant. 1982. Individual plant treatments for controlling redberry juniper seedlings. Journal of Range Management 35:419–23.

Vallentine, J. F. 1989. Range development and improvements. Third edtion. Academic Press, Inc., San Diego, California.

Whisenant, S. G., L. F. Bouse, R. A. Crane, and R. W. Bovey. 1993. Droplet size and spray volume effects on honey mesquite mortality with clopyralid. Journal of Range Management 46:257–61.

Young, J. A., R. A. Evans, and D. W. McKenzie. 1983. History of brush control on western U.S. rangelands. Pages 17–25 *in* K. C. McDaniel, editor. Proceedings brush management symposium. 17 February 1983, Albuquerque, New Mexico. Society for Range Management.

Future of Rangeland Chemical Weed and Brush Control
A Texas Range Scientist's Viewpoint

76   The next 20 or more years will be interesting in respect to the use of chemicals for the management of rangeland weeds and brush. While some may view the future with pessimism, I do not. In my opinion, herbicides will continue to be a valuable management tool on rangelands for a very long time. I am especially excited about several new, promising technologies, which will give us the ability to literally sculpt brush on rangelands to meet specific goals.

It must be understood that my opinions and views of the future were formed from working a couple of decades as a District-based Extension Range Specialist in a private land state. My vision of the next 20 years is specific for this state, and may not be valid for other regions, particularly public land states or areas of the country with other demographics.

Herbicides

In the mid-1980s, I placed all the herbicides labeled for rangeland on the tailgate of my pickup and took a photograph (Fig. 7.1). Little did I know then, how important that photograph would become. Because now, that simple black and white picture illustrates how little change there has been in the herbicides we use on rangeland over the past 15 or more years. If you look at the photograph, you will notice some trade names have changed. For example, Grazon PC is now Tordon 22K, Grazon ET was changed to Remedy, etc. But if you look closely you will also recognize the active ingredients represented on the pickup tailgate in the mid-1980s are, with few exceptions, the same we have for use today.

It is said, "The best way to predict the future is to look to the past." Based on the past, I predict there will be few, if any, additions to our present arsenal of range herbicides over the next 20 years. Almost certainly there will be no new "magic bullets" that represent a significant new chemistry of herbicides. Rangeland is a small market for most chemical companies, thus they devote little resources toward the development of new products for rangeland. Most of the herbicides we have now were developed for other markets

Figure 7.1.
Herbicides from the 1980s.

first. University range research scientists have worked with very few "numbered" (new) compounds in the past 20 years.

But the future is not necessarily dark. The herbicides we have today are all tested and proven by time. They are known to be effective and safe, and have been through the EPA review process several times. As such, I believe we will keep most of these herbicides over the next 20 years.

As technology advances and the ability to detect ever-smaller quantities of herbicides in the environment improves, we can expect increasingly stringent EPA labeling requirements. I believe most of our present herbicides will hold up well to these higher standards. Unfortunately, the process of re-labeling compounds over the years is a tremendous cost passed on to the end user. If we lose a herbicide in the next two decades, it will most likely be due to the high cost of re-registration rather than the inability to meet new safety and environmental regulations.

One of the greatest future restrictions on rangeland herbicides may be endangered species protection. For example, when Arsenal was recently labeled for control of salt cedar (*Tamarix gallica*) in Texas, a two-mile "no treatment" buffer was established on both sides of the Colorado River in Runnels, Coke, and Mitchell Counties to protect the Texas poppy mallow (*Callirhoe digitata*). There are only a few known colonies of Texas poppy mallow known to exist along this entire stretch of river and they exist on a different soil type as compared to those areas occupied by salt cedar. This spray buffer is extreme to say the least, and prevents control of this invasive, undesirable plant along a large section of the river. It also eliminates any hope of long-term control of salt cedar down river.

Research

For decades, universities have served as the foundation for research on the use of herbicides to control rangeland brush and weeds. Unfortunately, in recent years, research scientists have had only an occasional new herbicide to work with and limited funding opportunities for this type of research. There is no reason to believe this will change. Without new herbicides developed by industry, there will be little motivation or opportunity for research scientists to work in the area of new product development. Instead, I believe their efforts will, by necessity, be focused in the areas described below.

The first is finding new uses for old molecules. A recent example is the herbicide Arsenal. This compound was used for years for broad spectrum plant control in rights-of-way, on areas not planted with crops, etc. Because it was nonelective, it was never labeled for use on Texas rangelands. Fortunately, researchers in New Mexico developed a new use for this old herbicide (Duncan and McDonnell 1998). They found Arsenal can control salt cedar when applied as an aerial broadcast treatment. Because of several unique characteristics in terms of where this plant grows and lack of understory vegetation, herbicide selectivity is not a major limitation. As a result, Arsenal was recently labeled for use on Texas rangelands for salt cedar control.

The second area pertains to herbicide application equipment. On rangeland we are using essentially the same basic spray systems we used 40 years ago. There have been some recent advances and modifications, such as the use of special low volume nozzles for herbicide stem sprays, and using ATVs as spray platforms (Ueckert et al. 1997). Hopefully, over the next 20 years, researchers will develop spray systems that will greatly improve our ability to apply the herbicide directly to the target plant. For example, there is a need to automate individual plant treatments. For many reasons, which will be discussed later, selective spraying will become increasingly important. Unfortunately, selective spraying (individual plant treatment) is labor intensive. With advances in the ability to detect individual plant species based on chlorophyll reflectance and other technologies, the automation of individual plant treatments will be more likely.

With few new herbicides to work with, researchers will hopefully devote time to the development of new adjuvants for herbicide applications. The use of adjuvants when applying liquid rangeland herbicides has not moved much beyond the use of dyes, surfactant, oil-water emulsions, and drift control additives (McGinty et al. 2000). We need better dyes, with colors that are highly visible on lush green vegetation. We need adjuvants that will substantially reduce volitization of herbicides, and we need adjuvants to improve the absorption and translocation of herbicides within the plant.

We know little about the proper timing of herbicide applications on many of our rangeland species. Some plants like mesquite (*Prosopis* spp.) (Wan and Sosebee 1990) and pricklypear (*Opuntia* spp.) (Petersen et al. 1988) have been well researched, but for most of our species, the timing of our herbicide applications is made without even basic knowledge of carbohydrate flow or impact of growth stage on control.

Finally, I believe over the next 20 years researchers will continue to develop new systems for control of major noxious plants. We know the single treatment approach usually increases cost and reduces success. When treatments are integrated (i.e., fire and herbicides for control of pricklypear), the amount of herbicide used and costs are usually reduced, plus initial control and treatment life are improved. These systems usually make our herbicides work more effectively. We have these systems defined in detail for prickly-pear (Eckert et al. 1988), Macartney rose (*Rosa bracteata*) (Scifres 1975), and to a lesser extent mesquite and cedar (*Juniperus* spp.). We need the same for salt cedar, catclaw (*Acacia* spp.), huisache (*Acacia smallii*), and many others.

I did not include genetic engineering in the above list. The manipulation of genes has been used with great success with field crops to develop plants resistant to specific herbicides or insects (i.e., Bt and Roundup ready cotton). This new technology represents a major leap in the effective and efficient use of herbicides. Unfortunately, genetic engineering will have little impact, at least in the next 15 to 20 years, on chemical weed and brush control on rangelands. Plants on rangeland are indigenous. Rangelands are not "planted" as are grain sorghum or cotton. Thus, it is, at the very least, impractical to introduce gene-altered plants into rangeland plant communities. There may be some limited opportunities for genetic engineering with pasture grasses. For example, it may be possible to eliminate the toxicity problems associated with Kleingrass (*Panicum coloratum*). Since the potential economic rewards of genetic engineering are small on rangeland as compared to field crops or vegetables, I doubt the application of this technology to rangelands will receive much attention from industry or research.

Technology Transfer

Over the next 10 to 20 years, I believe we will see a continued trend that shifts University–Land Grant College resources allocated to chemical control of rangeland plants from research to technology transfer. Again, the past is the best view of the future. Now, as compared to 20 years ago, there are fewer Experiment Station Research Scientists actively involved in research directly related to the use of herbicides on rangeland. More and more of the applied research (development of rates, timing, etc.) has shifted to Extension Range Specialists. I would also argue that one of our most serious limitations to the effective use of herbicides on rangelands is not the lack of new technology, but the proper use and adoption of the technology we already have. That is why I believe technology transfer will be so important in the future. In this present era of the "Information Revolution," the possibilities related to technology transfer are beyond imagination. Our ability to inform and educate is improving every day. Through the Internet, landowners/managers can access information and people, anywhere in the world, any time, day or night. EXSEL (Welch et al. 1991), an expert system to provide Texas weed and brush control recommendations, has been available on the Internet for several years. A pilot project has recently been initiated in Texas to evaluate the use of digital imagery, computers, and the web to provide timely and accurate weed and brush control recommendations to landowners and managers. Called Texas Digital Diagnostics, this computer-based system will allow a landowner to send digital images and other pertinent information to experts for plant identification or for individual help with weed and brush control problems. These types of information and service systems will undoubtedly become more available and powerful in the years to come.

Teaching

I have seen one trend over my career as a District-based Extension Specialist that has been troubling. Many university disciplines (botany, wildlife, recreation and parks, etc.) produce graduates who take careers that directly impact the management of rangelands (Environmental Protection Agency, U.S. Fish and Wildlife Service, Texas Department of Agriculture, Texas Parks and Wildlife, etc.). These graduates are well schooled in their specific discipline. Many have or will make decisions that directly affect the use of herbicides on rangelands. Endangered species protection is a good example. Unfortunately, most do not have a single course related to herbicides or range improvements in general, and furthermore, many have developed a negative paradigm toward herbicides and chemical pesticides in general. How can an architect design a practical, safe, useable, and affordable building without understanding the basic construction techniques used to build it? How can an individual make sound, practical decisions concerning habitat management for wildlife on rangeland, or endangered species protection, without at least a basic knowledge of the tools used to manage rangelands?

The End User

In my opinion, the changing demographics of Texas landowners will have a pronounced impact on the use of herbicides on rangelands. Three factors are involved. Texas ranches are becoming smaller and more urbanized, non-traditional owners are more common, and the goals and expectations of the landowners for their ranch do not necessarily include livestock (Hanselka et al. 1990).

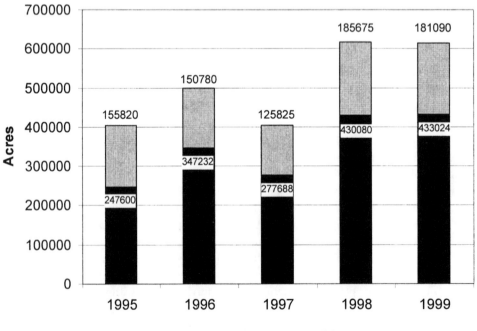

Figure 7.2. Leaf Spray vs. Stem Spray over the Years.

The breakup of larger ranches into 50-, 100-, or 200-acre tracts has been taking place for some time. This trend becomes more pronounced as you move from west to east in the state. Smaller ranch size (I hesitate to call these ranches) and the close proximity of other homes, vineyards, orchards, golf courses, etc. have resulted in the increasing use of individual plant herbicide treatments, and the decreased use of broadcast aerial applications. In many areas of the state, the aerial broadcast application of herbicides is no longer an option. In fact, in these areas it is often impossible to find an aerial applicator.

Individual plant treatments for brush control on rangeland never received much attention from researchers or industry until the latter part of the 1980s. At that time, several different stem spray methods were developed and promoted for woody plant control. By the mid-1990s, the Brush Busters program (McGinty and Ueckert 1995, 1996; Ueckert and McGinty 1997), which simplified treatment options and stressed early treatment with individual plant treatments, was initiated. With the changing demographics of Texas rangeland owners, and the growing importance of wildlife, there is an increasing demand for effective, targeted brush control. The timing could not have been more perfect. The result has been a tremendous increase in the use of individual plant treatments in Texas.

Marketing data provided by Dow AgroSciences has made it possible to document this change over the past 5 years (Fig. 7.2). Although the assumptions used to estimate total acreage treated each year may be subject to argument, the trends are not.

Since 1995, when Brush Busters was first initiated, there has been a pronounced growth in the estimated number of acres of mesquite treated using ground applied, individual plant treatments. From 1995 to 1999 there was an estimated 16% increase in the acreage of mesquite treated with individual plant leaf sprays, a 74% increase in the acres of mesquite stem sprayed, and a 52% overall increase in the acreage of mesquite controlled with individual plant, herbicide treatments. This large growth in the use of stem sprays to control mesquite is not surprising when you consider (1) a single, nonrestricted herbicide is used, (2) that herbicide (Remedy) is relatively inexpensive and available in 1-gallon containers, (3) stem sprays can be used any time of the year, (4) stem sprays have reduced risk of off-target damage, and (5) the only equipment required is a backpack sprayer. The appeal of the stem spray to this growing group of users is obvious. The trend toward greater use of individual plant treatments and the declining use of aerial broadcast will continue for years to come. This has serious implications for agencies, especially those concerned with technology transfer. How do we educate a large and growing number of small acreage landowners, as compared to what historically has been a relatively low number of commercial applicators and larger ranchers?

This brings us to a relatively new user of herbicides on rangeland. In general, this group of individuals has little-to-no background in agriculture. They purchase land for retirement, for a weekend getaway, for the hunting, etc. This growing group of potential users can be characterized by a general lack of knowledge about herbicides and range improvement practices, a high level of concern about the safety and environmental consequences of using herbicides, and they are a stranger to most traditional agricultural educational or technical assistance agencies and groups. They do not participate in Extension tours, field days, or educational meetings. Many work in towns or cities and cannot attend traditional educational programs, and others do not live in the same county as their property. Fortunately, this group as a whole is educated, computer literate, and has a strong commitment to conservation ethics. Programs similar to Brush Busters, that can be disseminated over the Internet, that are simple, jargon free, promote hand treatments, and that are selective and safe, will be increasingly important over the next couple of decades for educating this rapidly growing group of users.

These landowners bring with them new opportunities in terms of rangeland weed and brush control. Their goals and expectations often vary from the traditional. Most do not expect livestock to pay the cost of owning and managing the land. Many care little or nothing about livestock. They own the land simply for the aesthetics, recreational use, or wildlife. In other words, the poor old cow, sheep, and goat do not have to pay the entire cost of range improvement practices. When an owner must generate revenue from rangeland to support living expenses, that owner can only spend money if the rangeland makes money. The low financial rate of return from livestock has been a serious limitation to most range improvement practices in the past. With the new type of landowner, ranch revenue is not always important. The landowner may simply wish to control mesquite for the aesthetic value or for personal hunting, etc. It is similar to adding a porch on a house. The cost does not have to be recouped from energy savings due to shading that side of the house. It is completely acceptable to build a porch just because it looks good. Now we have a growing group of landowners with the luxury of saying, "I would like to control cedar just because it makes my place look better." This is a significant change from the traditional manner in which range improvements were justified. In the future, we will have more and more opportunity to improve rangelands without the financial constraints related to livestock production. The challenge will be to educate this new owner as to what is healthy rangeland and how to properly use tools like herbicides to improve or maintain that health.

The need for water by our cities, agriculture, industry, and recreation over the next 20 years will have a significant impact on brush control in this state. For the first time, in 1999, the Texas legislature funded brush control for an entire watershed. Much of the mesquite and cedar on the North Concho watershed will be removed to provide additional flow to O. C. Fisher Reservoir, which is used by the city of San Angelo. Feasibility studies are currently in progress on eight other watersheds within the state. This trend will continue. During the recent "Texas Community Futures Forum," conducted by the Texas Agricultural Extension Service, over 230 counties identified water as a critical issue over the next 5 years. With the increasing demand for water and the inability of landowners to bear the entire cost of brush control to produce water, there will have to be substantial public funding. Herbicides will by necessity be a major tool used in these watersheds.

GIS/GPS/DOQs

What do GIS (Geographic Information System), GPS (Global Positioning System), and DOQs (Digital Orthophoto Quadrangles) have to do with the future use of herbicides on rangelands? The answer is: "A lot."

We have traveled through three eras in rangeland weed and brush control and are now in the fourth. When herbicides were first developed, it was believed brush could be eradicated. It did not take long to see the fallacy of this paradigm. Shortly thereafter, the word "control" became common in the literature. This was the realization brush could not be eradicated, but it was possible to have some impact on how much brush you have and where it grows. By the mid-1970s, "management" was the word of choice. With the escalating importance of wildlife as a source of ranch revenue, brush became valuable.

As we move into the twenty-first century, we are entering an era best described as "brush sculpting" (Rollins 1997). We now have the tools to plan and implement selective brush control practices, including herbicides, at the landscape level. DOQs provide affordable, high resolution (one meter), color infrared, geo-referenced photography that can be used to plan brush control treatments. GIS can take the areas selected for treatment, no matter what the shape or size, and transfer that information from the photograph to the spray plane. GPS then guides the pilot to the treatment site and then through each pass, telling the pilot when to turn the herbicide on or off. This technology can also be used with heavy equipment, ground spray rigs, etc. The use of GPS, GIS, and DOQs will become more and more commonplace over the next 10 to 20 years, giving us the ability to accurately and effectively plan and implement brush control practices at the landscape level. We will truly be able to sculpt rangelands to meet future needs or goals.

Summary

Through the next couple of decades, herbicides will continue to be a major tool for the management and control of weeds and brush on rangeland. During this time period we cannot expect to have new "silver bullets" added to our herbicide arsenal. Hopefully, we will keep all or most of our present herbicides. Some of the major changes to expect include a growing user group with nontraditional goals and needs that don't necessarily include livestock production. One benefit will be less financial constraints on the use of range improvement methods, such as herbicides. A major challenge will be education of these individuals. As the state becomes more urbanized and ranch size decreases, there will be a continued shift from aerial broadcast applications to individual plant treatments, which will provide new opportunities for commercial applicators, and a rethinking of traditional markets by the chemical industry. I believe we will have large-scale, public funding of brush control on Texas rangelands, with water serving as the catalyst. Although we cannot expect significant technological advancements in the herbicides we use, we will benefit from other technologies such as GIS, GPS, and DOQ photography and improved application technology. With these new tools we will have the ability to sculpt rangelands with a degree of precision never before possible.

Literature Cited

Duncan, K. W., and K. C. McDaniel. 1998. Saltcedar (*Tamarix* spp.) management with imazapyr. Weed Technology 12:337–44.

Hanselka, C. W., A. McGinty, B. S. Rector, R. C. Rowan, and L. D. White. 1990. Grazing and brush management on Texas rangelands—an analysis of management decisions. Texas Agricultural Extension Service Unnumbered Publication.

McGinty, A., J. F. Cadenhead, W. Hamilton, W. C. Hanselka, D. N. Ueckert, and S. G. Whisenant. 2000. Chemical weed and brush control suggestions for rangeland. Texas Agricultural Extension Service Publication No. B-1466.

———, and D. Ueckert. 1995. Brush Busters—how to beat mesquite. Texas Agricultural Extension Service Publication No. L-5144.

———, and ———. 1996. Brush Busters—how to master cedar. Texas Agricultural Extension Service Publication No. L-5160.

Petersen, J. L., D. N. Ueckert, and R. L. Potter. 1988. Herbicidal control of pricklypear cactus in western Texas. Journal of Range Management 41:313–16.

Rollins, D. 1997. Applied landscaping: a primer for brush sculptors. Pages 127–33 *in* D. Rollins, D. N. Ueckert, and C. G. Brown, editors. Proceedings brush sculptors symposium. Texas Agricultural Extension Service, San Angelo.

Scifres, C. J. 1975. Systems for improving Macartney rose infested Coastal Prairie rangeland. Texas Agricultural Experiment Station Publication No. MP-1225.

Ueckert, D., and A. McGinty. 1997. Brush Busters—how to take care of pricklypear and other cacti. Texas Agricultural Extension Service Publication No. L-5171.

———, ———, and D. A. Addison. 1997. Brush Busters: common-sense brush control for rangelands. Down to Earth 52:34–39.

———, J. L. Petersen, R. L. Potter, J. D. Whipple, and M. W. Wagner. 1988. Managing pricklypear with herbicides and fire. Pages 10–15 *in* Texas Agricultural Experiment Station Progress Report 4570.

Wan, C., and R. E. Sosebee. 1990. Relationship of photosynthetic rate and edaphic factors to root carbohydrate trends in honey mesquite. Journal of Range Management 43:171–76.

Welch, T. G., W. T. Hamilton, S. W. Deiss, B. R. Myrick, and B. Lyons. 1991. EXSEL: an expert system for brush and weed control technology. Pages 41–44 *in* Proceedings international conference on decision support systems for resource management. College Station, Texas.

8 Timing
The Key To Successful Brush
And Weed Control With Herbicides

Ronald E. Sosebee

Mesquite (*Prosopis glandulosa*) has been the nemesis of southwestern rangelands for many years, seemingly always. We have been attempting to control
mesquite at least since the 1940s. And yet, we still have the brush problem
with us. It is often said that we are no nearer today than we were 40 or 50
years ago in our understanding of how to control noxious plants, regardless
of the species. However, if one is cognizant of the phenological stage and the
physiological status of the plant as well as the environmental conditions at
the time of applying herbicide, the target species can be effectively controlled. This chapter will primarily address aerial spraying of foliar-applied
herbicides, since satisfactory control is most difficult to achieve. Some attention will also be given to both individual plant treatment (basal and spot-
foliar application of herbicides) and soil application of dry herbicides.

One of the primary tenets of controlling noxious species is recognizing
the time at which herbicides are translocated to the perennating organs (i.e.,
buds) and tissues. Since foliar-applied herbicides can be translocated via the
carbohydrate (total nonstructural carbohydrates; TNCs) stream in the plant,
it is important to know the TNC trends and the energy allocation patterns
within plants (source: sink relationships, Cobb and Kirkwood 2000). Several
years ago, Pitelka (1977) identified energy allocation patterns in three different lupines; an annual, an herb, and a nonsprouting shrub (Table 8.1). It is
interesting to note in plants from all three growth habits the amount of energy that is allocated to the flowering/reproductive process. As is the case,
the flowering process requires a substantial amount of energy, which signifi-

Table 8.1. Energy allocation (%) in *Lupinus* sp.

	L. annus (Annual)	*L. variicolor* (Herb)	*L. arboreous* (Shrub)
Reproductive tissue	61	18	20
Seeds	29	5	6
Stems	—	—	50
Roots	3–4	40	—

Source: Adapted from Pitelka (1977).

cantly affects one's ability to control both herbaceous and woody plants. One can conclude from Pitelka's data that in order to achieve a high degree of chemical control, the plants must be sprayed either before or after the flowering stage, but not during the initial reproductive phase.

Categories of Woody and Herbaceous Weeds

For the sake of simplicity, noxious plants will be categorized and discussed in the following categories: (1) annuals (summer annuals/winter annuals/biennials), (2) hard-to-kill herbaceous perennial weeds, (3) suffrutescent (half) shrubs, (4) cacti, and (5) woody plants (sprouting and nonsprouting). Consideration of long- and short-shoots is very important when planning herbicidal control of woody plant resprouts. Long-shoots in woody plants are primarily vegetative shoots, whereas, short-shoots are primarily reproductive shoots (discussed in more detail later in the chapter).

Annuals

Annuals are relatively easy to control chemically. However, they should be sprayed during the vegetative stage. After the plants become reproductive and bolt (produce a flower stalk), they are very difficult to control. Many annuals, at least in the southern and southwestern United States, germinate and become established during late summer, fall, and early winter if soil water is available. They remain vegetative throughout the winter as rosettes and bolt in the spring when air temperatures become warm. This gives them a head start on the warm-season grasses and creates weed problems, such as common broomweed (*Amphiachyris dracunculoides*). Common broomweed, for example, and other annuals are easily controlled if sprayed anytime before the plant bolts (usually mid- to late spring). After the plant bolts, it is difficult to impossible to control chemically. Cold air temperature at the time of spraying can be important if the plant is not sufficiently physiologically active. Ueckert et al. (1980) found that bitterweed (*Hymenoxys odorata*) was difficult to kill if sprayed when air temperatures were <70 °F.

Perennial Herbaceous Weeds

Many perennial herbaceous weeds such as silverleaf nightshade (*Solanum eleagnifolium*), field bindweed (*Convolvulus arvensis*), blueweed sunflower (*Helianthus ciliaris*), and leafy spurge (*Euphorbia esula*) have the reputation of being difficult to kill. Most of our problems stem from improper timing of herbicide application. Herbicide application typically occurs when the plants are actively growing, which usually coincides with the flowering/reproductive stage. Silverleaf nightshade, for example, has traditionally been sprayed during the reproductive phase when the plant is in the purple flower stage. Top-kill is obtained but root-kill is not. If silverleaf nightshade is sprayed after the plant has advanced to the greenberry stage, the TNC translocation trend is to the roots (Fig. 8.1), the perennating tissue from which new shoots arise during the next spring, and the plants are easily root-killed (Stubblefield 1986). Available soil water (reflected in irrigated and nonirrigated plants) affects the magnitude of the trend of TNC translocation, but not necessarily the direction of the trend.

Personal experience indicates that field bindweed is also relatively easy to control with herbicides if the plants are sprayed during the post-flower stage.

Suffrutescent (Half) Shrubs

As with perennial herbaceous weeds, half shrubs such as broom snakeweed (*Gutierrezia sarothrae*) were traditionally sprayed during late spring or early summer during the active growth stage. With the discovery that translocation of TNC (Fig. 8.2) is to the stem bases and roots (the perennating tissues; Courtney 1984) in the post-flower stage, which occurs during the fall (Sosebee and Dahl 1991), broom snakeweed can be easily controlled. Broom snakeweed is similar to silverleaf nightshade in that soil water influenced by range site (Fig 8.3) affects the magnitude of the TNC trend, but not the direction of the trend.

Environmental conditions are not strong influences in chemically controlling broom snakeweed. Snakeweed is an evergreen plant in the southwestern United States, if soil water is not limiting. Therefore, as long as the plants have adequate leaf area in the autumn to spray, there is enough soil water to support sufficient physiological activity to render the plants responsive to herbicide application. Air temperatures are only important when subfreezing temperatures can freeze the spray solution during application and render the spray equipment nonfunctional.

One could conclude that if broom snakeweed, and similar species, were sprayed in the autumn (October 1 until December 31 in the southwestern

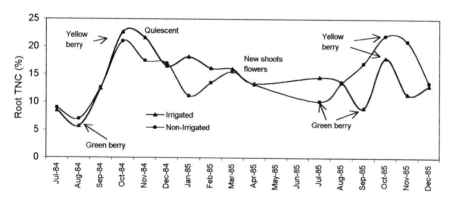

Figure 8.1.
Average total nonstructural carbohydrate (TNC) trends in silverleaf nightshade growing under irrigation and no irrigation.
Courtesy Sosebee and Dahl, 1991

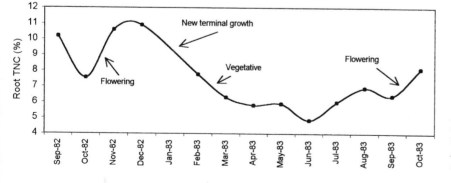

Figure 8.2.
Average total nonstructural carbohydrate (TNC) trends of broom snakeweed.
Adapted from Sosebee and Dahl, 1991

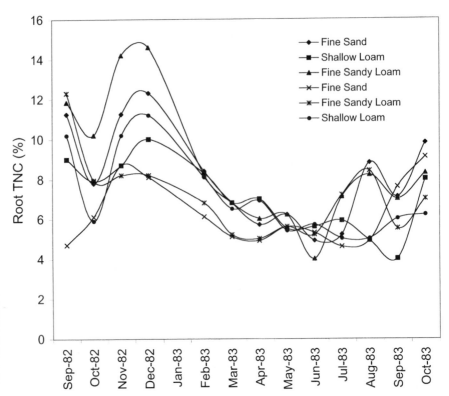

Figure 8.3.
Influence of range
site on total
nonstructural
carbohydrate (TNC)
trends in broom
snakeweed.
*Courtesy Sosebee
and Dahl, 1991*

United States), it could easily be killed. Broom snakeweed is not a root sprouter, but rather new growth is initiated from buds along the basal stems; therefore, if the plant is top-killed, the entire plant is killed.

Cacti

Cacti are different kinds of plants. They are CAM plants (i.e., they are characterized by the crassulacean acid metabolism photosynthetic pathway), which means that their stomata are not open during the daytime, but rather at night. Since cacti have no leaves (or only rudimentary leaves), the stems (pads or joints) are the primary regions of photosynthetic activity. Therefore, herbicides must be absorbed into the stems. Although stomata are closed during the daytime, herbicide entry into the plant is through the stem epidermis rather than through the stomata.

Pricklypear (*Opuntia lindheimeri*) is most effectively controlled when the herbicides are applied post-fruit ("tuna") production (Potter et al. 1986, Peterson et al. 1988), i.e., in the autumn. Translocation of TNCs in cholla (*Opuntia imbricata*) occurs post-fruit production, as in other species (Kunst 1988). Each pricklypear pad and each cholla joint are independent units, and they do not readily translocate photosynthate between pads or joints. Therefore, it is very important to spray every pad and joint when cacti are to be sprayed with herbicides. Any stem (pad or joint) missed will remain alive. As with other species, TNCs are translocated to the roots after fruit production (Fig. 8.4), but the critical point in controlling cacti is herbicide cover-

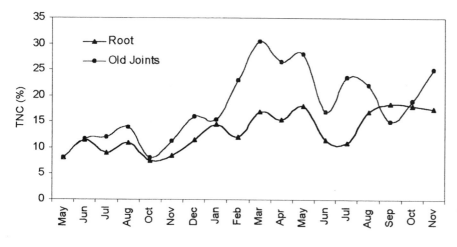

Figure 8.4.
Average total non-structural carbohydrate (TNC) trends of roots and old joints of cholla. Adapted from Kunst, 1988

age of every joint to assure control (Kunst 1988). If cholla were to be aerially sprayed, late summer and autumn would be a more desirable time to spray.

Woody Plants: Nonsprouting Shrubs and Trees

Nonsprouting woody plants are not usually problem species. However, some are problems, such as Ashe juniper (*Juniperus ashei*). If nonsprouting species are susceptible to herbicides, they are relatively easy to control. The primary consideration is that the plants are actively photosynthesizing at the time of herbicide application. Once the herbicide is incorporated into the photosynthate stream and translocated to perennating tissues and storage organs in the shoots, the plant is easily killed.

Although most of the noxious shrubs in the Southwest are sprouting species, one of the most common nonsprouting shrubs in the West is big sagebrush (*Artemisia tridentata*). Big sagebrush is relatively easy to control if two criteria are met: (1) the plant is actively growing (i.e., actively photosynthesizing and "leader" length is expanding), and (2) the soil is wet. Although the literature does not define wet soil, the implication is that there is adequate soil water to promote active growth. Under these conditions, big sagebrush (and other similar nonsprouting species) can easily be controlled.

Sprouting Shrubs and Trees

The main problem in controlling noxious shrubs and trees on Texas and other southwestern rangelands is that most of the problem species resprout after the shoots, or tops, are killed or injured. One of the major nemeses of Southwest rangelands is mesquite. Many attempts have been made over the past 60 years to control mesquite. But, it remains a problem on many Texas rangelands.

Mesquite is relatively easy to control if two criteria are met: (1) soil temperature at 12 to 18 inches must be at least 75 °F, preferably higher, and (2) the plant must be physiologically capable of responding to foliar-applied herbicides, i.e., the TNCs must be translocated to the perennating tissues in the basal bud zone. If these two criteria are met at the time of aerial application, one can expect a high degree of mesquite control. If both of these criteria are not met concurrently at the time of aerial application, less than satisfactory control will be obtained.

Several years ago, Dahl et al. (1971) identified soil temperature as the most important environmental parameter affecting mesquite's ability to respond to foliar application of herbicides (Fig. 8.5). This information was confirmed from 1970 through 1976 when commercial aerial applications of mesquite in Texas and eastern New Mexico were monitored throughout the Rolling Plains, parts of the Trans-Pecos, parts of the Edwards Plateau, and parts of the High Plains. In cooperation with several aerial applicators, approximately one hundred sites were selected per year and twenty-five trees per site per year were individually identified and permanently marked for future reference on warm, cool, and intermediate sites throughout West Texas, the Texas Panhandle, and eastern New Mexico. If the soil temperature was <70 °F at the time of herbicide application, no mesquite were root-killed. Root-kill increased as soil temperature increased up to at least 86 °F. Mesquite root-kills as high as 98% were obtained where the soil temperature was near 86 °F (and the physiological conditions were appropriate).

Soil temperature is important from the standpoint of both photosynthesis and translocation. Synthesis of hormones and plant growth regulators in the roots is strongly influenced by soil temperature. Some of the hormones produced in the roots are essential for photosynthesis in the leaves. If the hormones are neither produced in the root tips nor translocated to the leaves, photosynthesis is significantly reduced or ceased. Likewise, if synthesis of hormones and growth regulators that are required for translocation of photosynthates (i.e., carbohydrates) are adversely affected by cooler soil temperatures at the time of aerial application of herbicides, then TNC translocation (and the herbicide that moves with the carbohydrate stream) to the basal bud zone is reduced or ceased. Consequently, the plant has no opportunity to respond to the herbicide application. Also, photosynthate produced during any day is essentially all translocated from the leaves (and daily temporary sinks) during the night following synthesis. For these reasons, it is imperative that soil temperatures be known the day of spraying and not necessarily what they were either a few days before or a few days after spraying.

Subsequently, we found that the physiological status of mesquite trees at the time of spraying was equally as important as the soil temperature (Sosebee and Dahl 1991). In order to achieve satisfactory mesquite control (when the soil temperature is appropriate), the trees must translocate TNCs to the basal bud zone. TNC translocation to the basal bud zone of mesquite trees essentially occurs during two periods in the annual cycle of the trees: (1) yellow flower to pod formation, 42 to 63 days post-budbreak, and (2) post-pod elongation, 72 to about 85 days post-budbreak (Fig. 8.6).

The flower spike and white flower stages (budbreak until about 42 days post-budbreak), the reproductive stage, and the period of pod elongation require a tremendous amount of energy input; therefore, no TNCs are translocated to the basal bud zone. Hence, it is nearly impossible to root-kill mesquite if the plants are aerially sprayed during these growth stages. These

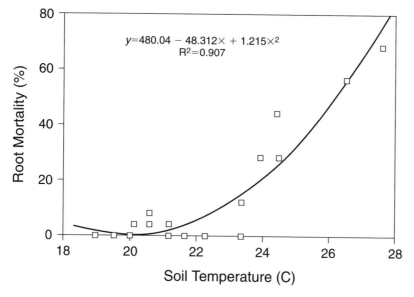

$$y = 480.04 - 48.312x + 1.215x^2$$
$$R^2 = 0.907$$

Figure 8.5.
Influence of soil temperature
(30 cm depth) on mesquite
mortality. Adapted from Dahl
et al., 1971

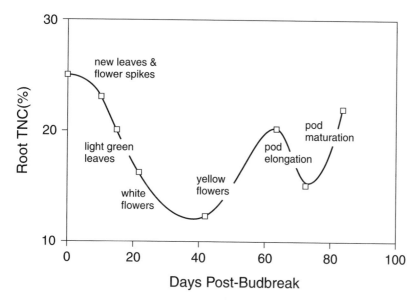

Figure 8.6.
Average nonstructural
carbohydrate (TNC) trends
in mesquite.
Courtesy Sosebee and Dahl,
1991

results are a refinement of the recommendation made many years ago by
Fisher et al. (1959). After the basal bud is "recharged" with TNC (about
midsummer), the carbohydrates presumably are translocated to the sink areas (parenchymatous tissues) around the aerial buds from which new shoots
will arise the next spring and from which the new aerial shoots will derive
the energy for their initial growth.

One could conclude, then, that mesquite is (1) very difficult to control if
sprayed during the first 42 days post-budbreak, regardless of the soil temperature, (2) relatively easy to control 42 to 63 days post-budbreak, if the soil
temperature is 75 °F, or higher (the higher, the better), (3) nearly impossible
to control during pod elongation, 63 to 72 days post-budbreak, regardless of
the soil temperature, and (4) most easily controlled post-pod elongation, 72

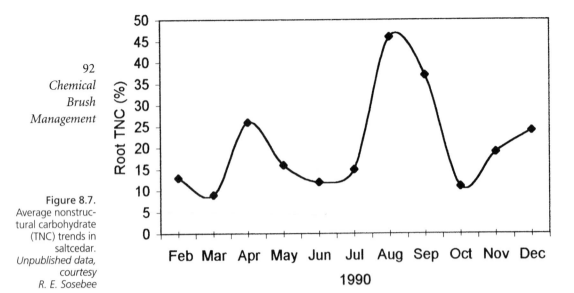

Figure 8.7.
Average nonstruc-
tural carbohydrate
(TNC) trends in
saltcedar.
Unpublished data,
courtesy
R. E. Sosebee

to 85 days post-budbreak, if the soil temperature is 75 °F, or higher. If one lives in an area where susceptible crops prevent spraying during the most desirable times to achieve maximum control of mesquite, then one must accept suppression or minimal root-kill as alternatives to maximum control.

Salt cedar (*Tamarix gallica*) is a major noxious woody plant that grows in riparian areas. It is a phreatophyte that is "choking" many of the river systems in Texas and throughout the western United States. Control of salt cedar has been difficult for at least two reasons: (1) herbicides approved for aquatic systems are very limited, and (2) traditionally, we have sprayed it during the early part of the growing season, which occurs during the flowering/reproductive stage (rendering the plant nonsusceptible to herbicide application). Our data (Sosebee, unpublished data) would suggest that according to the TNC translocation pattern, the optimum time to spray salt cedar is late summer to early fall (Fig. 8.7).

Personal experience indicates that spraying yucca (*Yucca* spp.) "over-the-top" after flowering (about 2 to 3 weeks) will yield successful control.

Individual Plant Treatments (IPT)
Spot-foliar Application of Herbicides

Timing is much less critical for spot-foliar application of herbicides than it is with aerial application. In aerial application, 4 gallons of total volume (or similar amount) is recommended per acre of land (4 gallons/43,560 ft^2 or 0.012 oz/ft^2). Therefore, timing is ultra critical when so little herbicide solution is used in aerial application. In IPT, spot-foliar treatment trees are usually sprayed "to wet." Hence, each tree or shrub receives a larger amount of herbicide solution and the tree's system apparently is "flooded." Mesquite can be effectively controlled by IPT spot-foliar application anytime between mid-May and September 1. For similar reasons, soil temperature is not a critical consideration.

The most important consideration in spraying regrowth or resprouts for which IPT is most commonly used is the physiological age of the resprouts (Fig. 8.8). Are the resprouts long-shoots (vegetative shoots) or short-shoots (reproductive shoots)? Long-shoots are those with long internodes, sometimes called "water sprouts." They are fast growing and remain vegetative. Therefore, most, if not all, of the photosynthate that is produced by the leaves goes to support the structural growth of the resprouts and none goes to the basal bud zone.

In contrast to long-shoots, the short-shoots are those in which the internodes are not, or have not, elongated, but rather have begun to produce flowers, i.e., reproductive shoots. Sometimes these short-shoots are called "spurs" on fruit trees, such as apple. It is from these spurs that apples are produced. If the resprouts have advanced to the short-shoot stage, which has nothing, necessarily, to do with chronological age of the resprouts, then the resprouts are relatively easy to control with IPT because the TNC translocation pattern is to the basal bud zone and not into structural material for the stems.

Basal Application of Herbicides

Conventional basal application of diesel oil or low volume application of diesel oil and herbicide mixture to shrubs or trees such as mesquite is quite effective. Timing of application is not a factor. Basal treatments can be applied anytime during the year. If conventional application of diesel oil (which includes pouring or spraying diesel oil on the soil around the base of the plant) is used, the soil should be dry. Diesel oil does not infiltrate well into wet soil and it is imperative that the diesel oil envelop the basal bud zone if this method is used. If low volume basal application of diesel oil and herbicide is used (which involves spraying only the lower 12 to 14 inches of the stem base), there are no restrictions on the time at which applications can be made.

Soil-applied Herbicides

IPT of soil-applied herbicides such as tebuthiuron, picloram, and hexazinone can be applied almost anytime during the year, depending upon rainfall. The most effective time of application, however, is shortly before anticipated rainfall. It is important that these herbicides be carried into the soil with infiltration of rainfall and incorporated into the soil solution so they

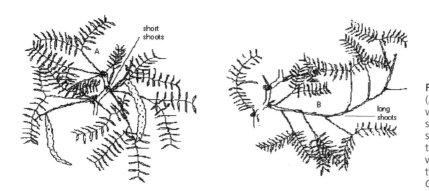

Figure 8.8.
(A) Mesquite stem segment with predominantly short shoots (note almost total absence of internode elongation); (B) mesquite branch with a long shoot showing typical internode elongation. *Courtesy Dahl, 1995*

can be absorbed by the target plant. If picloram is not incorporated into the soil solution within 60 days or so, it tends to photodegrade and its effectiveness is significantly reduced. Tebuthiuron and hexazinone are not as sensitive to UV radiation as is picloram; therefore, their effectiveness can last for several months while residing at the soil surface.

Timing of aerial application of dry herbicides such as tebuthiuron to sand shinnery oak (*Quercus havardii*) is similar to timing considerations for IPT soil-applied herbicides. The dry herbicides should be applied before the anticipated rainfall in order to achieve effectiveness the year of herbicide application. If the herbicide is applied after the rainfall season, the effectiveness will still be realized, but it will be delayed until the next growing season. Our research in the late 1970s indicates, as a precaution, that tebuthiuron applied in the winter and early spring had less deleterious effect on the grass in the plant community. Tebuthiuron applied in May (during early spring growth) significantly reduced grass production, at least during the year of herbicide application. Therefore, dry herbicides should be applied during the dormant season and long enough before grass growth begins, preferably February or earlier, to avoid grass injury.

Summary

Brush and weed control should be easier than we often make it. Although no one has all of the answers for control, we have a wealth of information from which we can draw to develop control measures for noxious species. If we know how a plant grows and the environmental conditions at the time of spraying, we can usually develop a satisfactory control program for that species. One should target the species to be controlled. If more than one species is selected for control, chances are they will not be in the same physiological stage at the same time. The result is that a compromise is made in which satisfactory control is achieved in neither species.

Specific guidelines for control are as follows:

1. Annuals: spray in the vegetative stage,
2. Perennial herbs: spray post-flower,
3. Half-shrubs: spray post-flower,
4. Cacti: spray post-fruit and cover every pad or joint,
5. Woody non-sprouters: spray when the plant is actively photosynthesizing and translocating to the sink areas, and
6. Woody sprouters: spray post-flower or post-fruit and when the environmental conditions are conducive to herbicide translocation to the sink areas.

For effective herbicidal control, plants must be sprayed at a time in which they can be responsive to an herbicide. Therefore, timing of herbicide application depends upon the phenological stage/physiological status of a plant and often the environmental conditions at the time of herbicide application.

Literature Cited

Cobb, A. H., and R. C. Kirkwood. 2000. Challenges for herbicide movement. Pages 1–24 *in* A. H. Cobb and R. C. Kirkwood, editors. Herbicides and their mechanisms of action. CRC Press, L.L.C., Cleveland, Ohio.

Courtney, R. W. 1984. Influence of site characteristics and phenology on carbohydrate trends in broom snakeweed (*Xanthocephalum sarothrae*). Thesis, Texas Tech University, Lubbock.

Dahl, B. E. 1995. Developmental morphology of plants. Pages 22–58 *in* D. J. Bedunah and R. E. Sosebee, editors. Wildland plants: physiological ecology and developmental morphology. Society for Range Management, Denver, Colorado.

———, R. B. Wadley, M. R. George, and J. L. Talbot. 1971. Influence of site on mesquite mortality from 2,4,5-T. Journal of Range Management 24: 210–15.

Fisher, C. E., C. H. Meador, R. Behrens, E. D. Robinson, P. T. Marion, and H. L. Morton. 1959. Control of mesquite on grazing lands. Texas Agricultural Experiment Station Bulletin 835.

Kunst, C. R. G. 1988. Carbohydrate trends in *Opuntia imbricata* (Haw.) D.C. (Cholla). Thesis, Texas Tech University, Lubbock.

Petersen, J. L., D. N. Ueckert, and R. L. Potter. 1988. Herbicidal control of pricklypear cactus in western Texas. Journal of Range Management 41:313–16.

Pitelka, L. F. 1977. Energy allocation in annual and perennial lupines (*Lupinus:* Leguminosae). Ecology 58:1055–65.

Potter, R. L., J. L. Petersen, and D. N. Ueckert. 1986. Seasonal trends of total nonstructural carbohydrates in Lindheimer pricklypear (*Opuntia lindheimeri*). Weed Science 34:361–65.

Sosebee, R. E., and B. E. Dahl. 1991. Timing of herbicide application for effective weed control: a plant's ability to respond. Pages 115–26 *in* L. F. James, J. O. Evans, M. H. Ralphs, and R. D. Childs, editors. Noxious Range Weeds. Westview Press, Boulder, Colorado.

Stubblefield, R. E. 1986. Influence of phenology on carbohydrate trends and herbicide translocation in silverleaf nightshade (*Solanum eleagnifolium* Cav.). Thesis, Texas Tech University, Lubbock.

Ueckert, D. N., C. J. Scifres, S. G. Whisenant, and J. L. Mutz. 1980. Control of bitterweed with herbicides. Journal of Range Management 33:4654–69.

Biological Brush Management

9   A Historical Perspective
Darrell N. Ueckert

Biological control is defined as the deliberate use of natural enemies—such
as parasites, predators, and pathogens—to suppress the growth or reduce
the population of their host plant. Classical biological control involves the
carefully regulated importation, conservation, or augmentation of highly selective natural enemies—insects, mites, nematodes, or plant pathogens—of
plant species that cause major ecological and economic problems over wide
geographical areas. All phases of classical biological control programs are
handled by highly trained professionals in federal or state agencies. With selection of the appropriate livestock species and careful attention to timing,
intensity, and duration of grazing, individual landowners can use vertebrates
—goats, sheep, or cattle—to reduce the abundance of some low-value or
noxious woody and herbaceous plants on rangeland within the confines of
their property boundaries. This is possible because food preferences differ
among the animal species and because relative palatability varies among
plant species and seasonally. This paper presents an overview of classical biological control and the use of vertebrates for biological control of noxious
or low-value weeds and woody plants on rangeland and gives the highlights
of biological control projects in Texas.

Advantages of Biological Control

The advantages of classical biological control programs over other methods
of weed control include (1) reasonably permanent management of the
target plant, (2) no harmful side effects, (3) attack is limited to a specific target weed or a very small group of closely related species, (4) agents are self-
perpetuating, often density dependent and self disseminating, (5) costs are
nonrecurring, (6) risks are known and evaluated before a biological control
agent is introduced, (7) high benefit:cost ratios for successful programs, and
(8) once biological control is established, no further inputs are needed
(Wapshere et al. 1989). The obvious advantage realized by ranchers who can
use goats, sheep, or cattle for biological control of brush and weeds is that the
animals produce income and are important ranch enterprises. From the
ecological and environmental perspective, biological control is an ideal so-

lution to weed and brush problems, but like all methods of control, it has certain advantages, certain limitations, and specific applications. Biological control, by itself, has rarely been a total solution to any rangeland weed and brush problem. It should be considered only as one component in an integrated weed or brush management system.

Constraints to Classical Biological Control

Classical biological control is generally not applicable for controlling brush or weeds that (1) are highly valued under certain circumstances, (2) are closely related to valuable crop, ornamental, or endangered plant species, (3) require immediate control, (4) need to be totally eliminated from an area or which can be tolerated only at very low densities, (5) are geographically localized or have low economic impact, or (6) occur on cropland under intense cultivation, frequent crop rotation, or heavy pesticide treatment (Goeden 1977). Classical biological control is ideally suited for controlling perennial plant species, which are major pests, growing in relatively stable or undisturbed habitats, such as rangelands (DeLoach 1980). Some annual and biennial plants can also be controlled biologically.

Early Examples of Biological Control

The first recorded example of the biological control of a weed was the intentional introduction of a cochineal insect, *Dactylopius ceylonicus,* which was actually thought to be *D. coccus,* a species cultured as a source of carmine dye, to northern India from Brazil in 1795 (Goeden 1988). The cochineal did not develop well on the intended cultivated pricklypear species (*Opuntia ficus-indica*) but rapidly transferred to, and controlled a weedy pricklypear species, *O. vulgaris,* which had been introduced into India from South America. After the value of this cochineal insect for control of *O. vulgaris* was recognized, it was intentionally introduced into southern India from 1836 to 1838. The insect completely controlled *O. vulgaris* in India. The cochineal was introduced into Sri Lanka (Ceylon) prior to 1865 and successfully controlled *O. vulgaris* throughout that country.

The next use of biological control of weeds occurred in the early 1900s. Twenty-three species of insects, collected on lantana (*Lantana camara*) in Mexico, were shipped to Hawaii and released on lantana. Eight of the species established (Perkins and Swezey 1924). Thereafter, research on biological control of weeds has expanded, with eighty-seven weed species presently having one or more natural enemies intentionally used for their control in the United States and Canada. Over 180 weed species have been targeted in biological control programs worldwide (Julien 1992).

The Principles of Natural Control

Classical biological control is based upon the fact that populations of all living organisms fluctuate over time due to the combined action of the biotic (living) and abiotic (nonliving) components of the environment. This natural phenomenon is referred to as "natural control." Most of the major herbaceous, woody, and succulent weed species on rangeland in Texas and the western U.S. have natural enemies that are intrinsically capable of greatly reducing the population densities of their hosts. These natural enemies do not greatly reduce the populations of their host plants because they are in turn limited by their own parasites and predators or other environmental factors (Wilson 1964). The literature on the impacts of native insects on specific plants and on the composition of plant communities and succession has been reviewed by Huffaker (1957, 1959, 1964), Scifres (1980), and Watts et al. (1989).

The overall goal in classical biological control of weeds and brush on rangeland is to reduce the population and influence of the target species below an ecologically or economically acceptable level, i.e., to improve the ecological system so that the target species do not overwhelm plant communities or cause damage to livestock. Eradication of the target plant is never the goal of biological control, because total elimination of the host plant, i.e., the target species, would result in the total die-off of the natural enemies. These principles should also be abided by when ranchers use goats, sheep, or cattle for natural control of noxious or low-value range plants to minimize the risk of damaging the desirable grasses, forbs, and woody plants. Excellent reviews of the science of biological control have been written by Huffaker (1957, 1959, 1964), Goeden (1977), Scifres (1980), and Quimby et al. (1991).

Biological Control Agents

Insects, mites, nematodes, plant pathogens, and herbivores have been used as biotic agents for weed control. The application and use of competitive plants or plants that excrete secondary plant compounds which reduce the ability of other plants to germinate, establish, and grow (allelopathy) is not part of traditional biological control. Similarly, the application of phytotoxic compounds extracted or derived from plants and microorganisms is not part of traditional biological control, although these approaches are sometimes considered within the broad topic of biological control.

Insects have received the most attention as biocontrol agents for weeds because of (1) the great complexity of the insect world (about 1 million different species), (2) the high degree of host specificity exhibited by some insects, (3) the diverse niches that insects occupy (different species may attack all structures of a plant), and (4) the fact that insects control their hosts in a stable manner, i.e., the availability of the food supply determines the population density of the insect population. The use of plant diseases and herbivores for biological control will be addressed in the last two sections of this chapter.

Biological Control Candidates

Most classical biological control projects have targeted plant species that have been accidentally or intentionally introduced into new areas free from their natural enemies. These alien species are often innocuous in their native habitats because they host a complex of phytophagous (plant feeding) or phytopathogenic (plant disease) organisms that contribute to their natural control. However, they quickly become aggressive and widespread in the new habitat where the indigenous insects and pathogens do not attack the introduced plants. However, native plant species may also be viable candidates for biological control, as noted by the following examples. Substantial control of a native species of pricklypear (*Opuntia littoralis*) and *O. littoralis* X *O. oricola* hybrids, which closely resembled *O. littoralis,* and partial control of *O. oricola* and hybrids which closely resembled this species, was achieved on rangelands on Santa Cruz Island off the coast of southern California by the successful introduction of a cochineal insect (*Dactylopius opuntiae*) from Mexico via Australia and Hawaii (Goeden et al. 1967). The insects were introduced in 1951, had dispersed throughout the island by 1961, and had controlled the pricklypear by 1966. It should be pointed out that the eradication of thousands of wild sheep and hogs to reduce grazing pressure, and the subsequent implementation of proper stocking with cattle occurred simultaneously with the biological control program. This management effort reintroduced another biotic factor, competition from herbaceous plants, which also contributed to the decline of pricklypear on the island. A second example is the native manuka weed (*Leptospermum scoparium*), which was controlled in New Zealand in the 1940s by the accidental introduction of a mealybug (*Eriococcus orariensis*) from Australia (Hoy 1961). The third example is Bermuda cedar (*Juniperus bermudiana*), which was greatly reduced in Bermuda by the accidental introduction of two scale insects (Wilson 1964). Unfortunate examples of control of beneficial native plants from the accidental introduction of insects and pathogens include (1) control of American chestnut (*Castanea americana*) by the introduced fungus *Endothia parasitica,* and (2) control of the American elm (*Ulmus americana*) by the introduced European elm bark beetle (*Scolytus multistriatus*) and a parasitic fungus (*Ceratostomella ulmi*) that it carries.

Procedures for Classical Biological Control Programs

Classical biological control of weeds involves the importation, conservation, or augmentation of natural enemies. The U.S. Department of Agriculture's (USDA) Agricultural Research Service and other agencies and organizations follow a complex procedure for locating, screening, releasing, and monitoring biocontrol agents of weeds (Rees et al. 1996). Every effort is taken to ensure that a particular weed species is an appropriate candidate for a biological control program, that introduced organisms are limited in host range, do not threaten endangered and native plants, and that introduced agents are not parasitized or diseased. Petitions are written during three phases of the investigations. The first petition requests permission to work on a specific plant and its agents, and must show that the target weed is a suitable candidate for a biological control program. The second petition requests permission to introduce biological control agents into quarantine for host-specificity testing. After all host-range testing is completed, a third petition containing the test results is written as an Environmental Assessment, or risk assessment. These petitions are sent to, and must be approved by Plant Protection and Quarantine (PPQ), a branch of the USDA Animal and Plant Health Inspection Service (APHIS). A group of professionals called the "Technical Advisory Group on the Introduction of Biological Control Agents of Weeds" (TAG) advises APHIS-PPQ on the accuracy and completeness of the host-specificity testing and ensures that the concerns of the

Endangered Species Act and the Native and Endangered Plant Act are addressed. Those who want to release biological control agents in their states and/or to move biological control agents across state lines must complete and submit a form PPQ-526 "Application and Permit to Move Live Plant Pests or Noxious Weeds." This form must be sent through the Department of Agriculture in the state in which the release will be made. If approved there, it is forwarded to USDA-APHIS-PPQ, Biological Assessment and Taxonomic Support. When this is signed by PPQ, a copy will be returned to the applicant as an approval record (Rees et al. 1996).

Selecting Appropriate Weed Species for Biological Control

The first step in a biocontrol program is to pick an appropriate weed or brush candidate. Introduced species are usually the best candidates, but species we refer to as natives should not be ruled out because some of our major native brush species in Texas were actually introduced onto this continent several hundred to several million years ago. For example, mesquite (*Prosopis glandulosa*) was probably introduced into North America from South America several million years ago; creosotebush (*Larrea tridentata*) was introduced from South America 11,000 to 14,000 years ago; and whitebrush (*Aloysia gratissima*) was probably introduced later by early Spanish explorers (DeLoach 1980).

Since biocontrol projects are long-term, expensive, and must be reviewed and approved by APHIS-PPQ, extensive data are needed to justify a new project and the target weed or brush species. DeLoach (1980) developed a scoring system to rank the major weed and brush species of Texas for biological control based on damage caused, beneficial and ecological values, and success potential (Table 9.1). The top candidates, according to his ranking, were perennial broomweed (*Gutierrezia* spp.), whitebrush, tarbush (*Flourensia cernua*), and bitterweed (*Hymenoxys odorata*). DeLoach felt that creosotebush, mesquite, and salt cedar (*Tamarix* spp.) would also be excellent candidates if the conflicts of interest between beneficial and harmful values could be resolved. African rue (*Peganum harmala*), locoweed (*Astragalus* spp.), threadleaf groundsel (*Senecio longilobus*), huisache (*Acacia farnesiana*), retama (*Parkinsonia aculeata*), and pricklypear cactus (*Opuntia* spp.) ranked lower because of greater conflicts of interest or because natural enemies are not yet known. Junipers (*Juniperus* spp.), scrub oaks (*Quercus* spp.), and Macartney rose (*Rosa bracteata*) were judged as unsuitable candidates for biological control because of their great beneficial or ecological values or because they were too closely related to plants of great value (DeLoach 1980).

Conflicts of Interest: Varying Views of the Values of Candidate Plants

Conflicts of interest relative to the status of a plant as a "weed" are a major consideration and constraint to the widespread use of biological control, especially by the introduction of alien insects or other biological control agents. The urgency of controlling pricklypear in Australia in the 1920s was unchallengeable because of its aggressiveness and widespread threat to the

Table 9.1. Ranking of weeds on rangelands of Texas and the southwestern United States relative to suitability for biological control.

Rank	Species	Damage caused[a]	Direct beneficial values[b]	Ecological value[c]	Success potential[d]
1[e]	Broomweed	71 (US)	0	4	7
2	Whitebrush	7 (TX)	3	2	2
3	Tarbush	7 (TX)	1	2	8
4	Bitterweed	7 (US)	0	3	10
5	Baccharis	3 (TX)	1	2	4
6	Creosotebush	30 (US&MX)	9	6	6
7	Mesquite	94 (US)	13	8	5,9
8	Saltcedar	1 (TX)	6	6	1
9	African rue	0.7 (TX)	0	0	12
10	Loco	11 (US)	1	6	11
11	Senecio	11 (?)	0	6	15
12	Huisache	3 (TX)	8	6	13
13	Retama	3 (TX)	5	2	14
14	Cactus	26 (US)	14	8	3
15	Juniper	22 (TX)	8	10−P	16
16	Scrub oaks	36 (TX)	20+	P	18
17	Macartney rose	0.3 (TX)	1	P	17

Source: Adapted from DeLoach (1980).

[a]Acres infested (millions) times a soil productivity factor.

[b]A summation of values as ornamental plants or for honey production, human food, supplementary grazing, fuel or fiber, industrial chemicals or drugs.

[c]Based upon the number of native species in genus or genus complex, whether the weed or a near relative is a dominant species in nature, the plant's value to wildlife, and whether closely related species are useful for food, fiber, fuel, or as ornamentals.

[d]Based upon whether effective natural enemies are known to exist, if these will attack our weed species, if homologs to these natural enemies are present in the U.S., and the degree of host specificity needed.

[e]On a scale of 1 to 17, with 1 being the most suitable and 17 being the least suitable.

country's economy. However, in many other countries, including the United States and Mexico, pricklypear is highly valued in some localities as livestock fodder, human food, a source of water for livestock, and for wildlife food and cover. The importation of the South American pricklypear moth, *Cactoblastis cactorum,* which successfully controlled pricklypear in Australia, into the United States has long been denied, even though pricklypear is widely regarded as a major weed problem on millions of acres of rangeland in Texas (Huffaker 1959).

Cedar or juniper is a major problem on Texas rangelands. However, several closely related species are highly valued as ornamentals; eastern red cedar (*J. virginiana*) is valuable for lumber; Ashe juniper (*J. ashei*) is valuable for fence posts and aromatic oils; and over forty species of wildlife feed on junipers (DeLoach 1980). DeLoach (1985) has thoroughly reviewed the conflicts of interest over the beneficial and undesirable aspects of mesquite in the United States.

Salt cedar is another interesting example of the conflict of interest problem. While salt cedar is widely regarded as a major user of water and cause of deterioration of native riparian habitats in the western United States, it is used for nesting in a few areas by the southwestern population of willow flycatcher (*Empidonax traillii extimus*), an endangered bird species. U.S. Fish

& Wildlife Service personnel at Albuquerque, New Mexico have held up the release of leaf beetles, which have been introduced for biological control of salt cedar, because they felt the beetles might control salt cedar too quickly, i.e., before the native willows, which are the flycatcher's normal nesting sites, are able to recover and grow sufficiently to supply nesting sites for the birds (Jack DeLoach, personal communication).

Steps Followed in Biological Control Projects

After a weed species has been approved for a biological control project, the steps to be followed, in chronological order, are (1) foreign exploration, (2) biological studies and "host-specificity testing" of promising biocontrol agents to assure their level of host specificity within their country of origin, (3) quarantine and additional host-specificity testing of the subject organisms after they are imported to the new country, (4) culture, release, and colonization of the organisms in the new country, and (5) evaluation of the results of their release (Huffaker 1957).

Foreign Exploration. Surveys of the natural enemies of a weed in the country where it is a problem are normally conducted prior to or simultaneously with foreign exploration to determine if insects are already present that attack the plant's flowers, seeds, leaves, stems, roots, etc. Foreign exploration for potential biocontrol agents should be done near the site of origin of the weed species or its genus and in areas with climate similar to that where the weed occurs in the country where it is a problem. The site of origin of the genus is usually the region with the most genetic diversity within a species, usually with the greatest number of species, and where forms with the lowest number of chromosomes are found (DeLoach 1978). The search may be broadened to areas where very close relatives of the target weed species occur if the target species itself does not occur in other countries.

Usually many natural enemies of a weed will be found during foreign surveys. Since it requires approximately one scientist year to conduct the studies necessary to demonstrate that any one natural enemy is safe to introduce as a biological control agent, it is prudent to be able to recognize agents that have the greatest possibility of being effective, both to reduce the cost and the failure rate. Harris (1973) and Goeden (1983) proposed scoring systems for the selection of effective insects as biological control agents. The scoring systems were based on the following attributes or characteristics of the insect: host specificity; the types of direct and indirect damage inflicted; phenology of attack; number of generations per year; number of progeny per generation; extrinsic mortality factors; feeding behavior (solitary vs. gregarious); compatibility with other control agents; adaptation of the insect to the range of habitats infested by the weed; prior effectiveness of the insect in biological control projects; and size (body weight) of the insect.

Host-specificity Testing. Host-specificity testing is done initially in the country of origin of the potential biological control agent, and subsequently while the organism is in quarantine within the country where it will be utilized.

Host-specificity testing is done to assure that the organism will not feed upon, and cannot complete its life cycle on beneficial plants. The introduction of foreign biotic suppressants has met with great success in the past, and careful testing has prevented the introduction of organisms that might damage beneficial cultivated and native plants (Huffaker 1957, DeLoach 1978).

Quarantine. The containers used to ship biocontrol organisms are of sturdy, tight construction and covered with fine-mesh cloth sewn at all seams to safeguard against escape in the event the packages become damaged during transit. Upon arrival in the new country, the containers are opened only in approved quarantine rooms. The quarantine phase of a biological control project serves not only to prevent the premature, accidental release of the potential biocontrol agent(s), but also for screening out and destroying other phytophagous insects and any parasites, predators, or diseases of the agent(s) (Huffaker 1957). Host-specificity testing is done during the quarantine phase.

Culture and Colonization. Other critical steps in biological control include the culture and colonization of the agents. With most natural enemies being introduced for biological control, it is very desirable or essential to mass-culture the organisms and release them in great numbers. The culturing of a biocontrol organism requires that large numbers of the host plant must be maintained under conditions that are favorable for growth of the plants and the organism(s). Also, if the organism(s) have been imported from the opposite hemisphere, then its life cycle must be synchronized with the phenological conditions of the local environment at the sites where it will be released. The cultures of biocontrol agents should be released at carefully selected times, relative to the day (A.M. vs. P.M.) and season, and to sites that are not all ecologically similar. A majority of the release sites should possess attributes believed to conform to the requirements of the agent(s) (Huffaker 1957).

Evaluation. A final and critical step in biological control is the evaluation of results (Huffaker 1957). This involves taking "before and after" photographs from permanently marked photo points to pictorially record the impact of the biocontrol agents on the target species. It is also critically important to keep a permanent record of the population densities of the target weed and the biocontrol agents using appropriate quantitative, ecological sampling procedures and adequate sampling. The responses of associated vegetation at the release sites and other sites eventually colonized by the biocontrol agents should be monitored by similar sampling procedures. The biocontrol agents should be eliminated from small "check" plots, using an appropriate insecticidal check-method, to scientifically document the effects of the released insects on the weed populations. Such information can be invaluable in explaining why control worked in some areas and not in others. Evaluation studies should examine the impact of the program on plant succession, soil conservation, and impacts on the watershed and wildlife habitat values of the land. Huffaker and Kennett's (1959) 10-year study of vegetation changes associated with the biological control of Klamathweed (*Hypericum perforatum*) is an excellent example of how biological control projects should be quantitatively evaluated.

Successful Biological Weed Control Projects

Biological control of weeds has had a history of considerable success. De-Bach (1974) stated that of forty-one projects attempted in the world in the last 80 years, eight were rated as completely successful (no further controls needed), nine gave substantial control, fourteen partial control, and 75% had achieved a "measurable degree" of success. Biological control agents have been released against thirty-eight weed species in the continental United States and Canada since 1945, resulting in substantial to complete control for about one-third of these species (see Chapter 10, *this book*).

The most notable classical example of success with biological weed control is credited to the Australians (Dodd 1936, 1940). About six species of pricklypear were imported into Australia in the late 1800s as ornamentals. There were no native pricklypear present on the Australian continent, thus the introduced species did not encounter any predators, parasites, or diseases. These species, especially *Opuntia stricta,* spread prolifically, infesting about 60 million acres by 1925. About 30 million acres were so densely infested that they were rendered useless for agriculture. It was estimated in 1925 that the pricklypear infestation was increasing at the rate of about 1 million acres annually. Beginning in 1921, Australian entomologists searched the United States, Mexico, and Argentina for insects to import for pricklypear control. About fifty species of cactus arthropods were studied and twelve species were introduced and established in Australia. During 1921–25, several species were reared in large numbers and released in the field, including the Pyralidae moth-borer, *Olycella junctolineella,* the Coreid bug, *Chelinidea tabulata,* the cochineal insect, *Dactylopius tomentosa,* and the Acarid mite, *Tetranychus desertorum.* These agents were well established throughout the pricklypear-infested region and were gradually beginning to have an effect on the pricklypear. During 1925, about 2,750 eggs of the cactus moth, *Cactoblastis cactorum,* were brought into Australia from Argentina. These were increased in the insectary and over 2 million eggs were released in the field in 1926 at nineteen locations. During 1928–30, approximately 3 billion of these insects were distributed throughout the pricklypear area. Feeding by *C. cactorum* caused a major collapse and destruction of the Australian pricklypear infestation during 1930–32. A regrowth of the damaged pricklypear and the appearance of new pricklypear seedlings caused a great deal of anxiety during 1931–33, but during the next 2 years the *C. cactorum* populations increased and controlled the regrowth and seedlings. This control is still in effect today, with pricklypear remaining only as isolated plants.

The classical success story in the United States involved Klamathweed, also known as St. Johnswort. This forb was accidentally introduced into the eastern United States from Europe in the early 1800s and was first reported in northern California in about 1900. By the 1940s, Klamathweed had infested about 5 million acres of rangeland in California and the Pacific Northwest. Klamathweed seriously competes with native grasses, and it causes photosensitization in white-face cattle. In 1944, entomologists with the University of California and USDA introduced two species of leaf beetles, *Chrysolina quadrigemina* and *C. hyperica,* into California from Australia. The Australians had earlier introduced these insects into their country from France for biological control of Klamathweed. After host-specificity testing, the insects were released in 1945 and 1946. Within a few years, these insects reduced Klamathweed to 1% of its former abundance. The benefit of this biological weed control program to California alone was estimated at $51 million in 1964 (Holloway and Huffaker 1951, Huffaker and Kennett 1959, Holloway 1964).

Biological Control Projects on Weeds and Brush in Texas

The review of biological control projects in the United States and Canada by Watson (1993) listed about two dozen plant species that occur on rangelands or pastures in Texas that have been the subject of biological control investigations. Among those listed, the only species that are major weeds on Texas rangelands were broom snakeweed (*Gutierrezia [Xanthocephalum] sarothrae*) and threadleaf snakeweed (*G. microcephala*). Following is a historical account of some of the more important projects. The current status of these projects will be discussed in Chapter 10 (*this book*).

Broom Snakeweed and Threadleaf Snakeweed

The native insects associated with the snakeweeds in Texas and eastern New Mexico were surveyed prior to the foreign exploration (Foster et al. 1981). Cordo and DeLoach (1992) conducted foreign exploration for natural enemies of snakeweeds in Argentina. They found a weevil (*Heilipodus ventralis*) that feeds on the roots and crowns of the snakeweeds and have introduced and released this weevil on snakeweeds in Texas. The current status of this biological control project will be discussed in Chapter 10 (*this book*).

Field Bindweed

A mite (*Aceria malherbae*) (Eriophyidae) from Greece that causes leaf deformation and galling of the stems and leaves of field bindweed (*Convolvulus arvensis*) has been introduced and subsequently released and established in Texas (Boldt and Sobhian 1993). Methods to redistribute the bindweed gall mite and to document its impact are now being studied (Michels 1999). A moth that defoliates field bindweed (*Tyta luctuosa*) (Noctuidae) has also been introduced into Texas, but attempts to establish it in the state failed because of interference by the red imported fire ant (J. A. Jackman, Biological Control of the Weeds website, bc4weeds@tamu.edu). Field bindweed occurs on rangelands, but is primarily a problem in cultivated land.

Puncturevine (Goathead)

Two weevils that feed in the seed pods (*Microlarinus lareynii*) and stems (*M. lypriformis*) of puncturevine (also called goathead) (*Tribulus terrestris*), an exotic weed from the Old World, were introduced into the United States from Italy in 1961 and subsequently released in Howard and Potter Counties, Texas in 1962 (Maddox 1976). The weevils became established in Howard County, but not in Potter County. Over the next 4 years, the seed weevils and puncturevine plants infested with them were widely distributed to many counties (Daniels and Wiese 1967). By the fall of 1966, the seed weevil had spread over the Texas Rolling Plains and southern High Plains. Sampling in fourteen counties during 1965 revealed 44 to 92% infestation of puncturevine burs with the seed weevils. Sampling in ten counties during 1966 indicated 40 to 95% bur infestation. By the mid-1970s, the puncturevine seed weevil had apparently reached an ecological balance with its host, with both the insect and the weed existing at low levels (Rummel and Arnold 1992). However, puncturevine populations began increasing rapidly during the mid-1980s, probably due to a die-off of the seed weevils resulting from extremely cold temperatures during December 1983 and January 1984. A survey in nine counties in 1991 showed that only 4 to 50% of the puncturevine burs were attacked. About 28,000 of the seed weevils were purchased from a California insectary and released in the Texas High Plains. A subsequent survey in 1992 indicated that the weevils has increased above 1991 levels in a few counties, but did not conclusively show that the release had generally been effective (Rummel and Arnold 1992). Eventual elimination of puncturevine by this insect is unlikely because each of the five sections of a puncturevine bur have three seeds, and some healthy seeds usually remain in burs attacked by the weevil (Daniels and Wiese 1967).

Silverleaf Nightshade

Researchers in Texas have found that a native nematode (*Ditylenchus [Nothanguina] phyllobia*), which causes the formation of galls on the leaves and stems of silverleaf nightshade (*Solanum elaeagnifolium*), could significantly reduce the vigor and abundance of this plant. However, methods to mass rear this nematode and to commercialize its use have not been developed (Orr et al. 1975). The nematode attacks silverleaf nightshade throughout much of Texas, but little is known about its mechanisms of dispersal (C. J. DeLoach, personal communication). Silverleaf nightshade is native to Texas.

Mesquite

Surveys have been conducted to assess the insects that attack mesquite (*Prosopis* spp.) in several states and countries (Ward et al. 1977, Cordo and DeLoach 1987) and an assessment of the conflicts of interest relative to mesquite as a candidate for biological control has been completed (DeLoach 1985). However, mesquite has never been cleared as a viable candidate for biological control; consequently, no alien insects have ever been introduced into Texas for the purpose of mesquite control. Biological control programs against mesquite were initiated in 1985 in South Africa (Zimmermann 1991, Moran et al. 1993) and in 1994 in Australia (van Klinken and Campbell 2001). The mesquite seed-feeding insects, *Algarobius prosopis, A. bottimeri*, and *Neltumius arizonensis* were the only insects released in South Africa because mesquite was considered to have some beneficial values there. The two species of *Algarobius* were also released and established in Queensland and Western Australia (Donnelly et al. 1997), but their impact was not expected to be significant because herbivores consume most mesquite pods before these insects have the opportunity to damage the seeds (Moran et al. 1993, Coetzer and Hoffmann 1997). The Australians also tested four insects which attacked mesquite foliage and its reproductive structures prior to their consumption by vertebrate herbivores, including a coreid bug (*Mozena obtusa*), a stem-girdling cerambycid (*Oncideres rhodosticta*), a sap-feeding psyllid (*Prosopidopsylla flava*), and a leaf-tying gelechiid moth (defoliator) (*Evippe* sp.). The latter two species from Argentina were host specific to mesquite, and they were released in four of the Australian territories. *Evippe* sp. has established at most release sites and is causing heavy (50–100%), prolonged defoliation of some mesquite infestations (van Klinken and Campbell 2001).

Salt Cedar

A project on biological control of salt cedar, which is a major pest along rivers and streams and around lakes and ponds in Texas, was initiated in 1987 by Dr. Jack DeLoach. Salt cedar was introduced into the United States from Eurasia in the 1800s as an ornamental. A leaf beetle (*Diorhabda elongata*) (Chrysomelidae) that defoliates salt cedar has been introduced into Texas from western China and eastern Kazakhstan (see Chapter 10, *this book*). The beetles reproductive biology and damage to salt cedar are currently being studied in field cages. It has been approved for release, pending the results from these investigations. A manna scale (*Trabutina mannipara*) (Pseudococcidae) found in Israel that feeds on the plant sap of salt cedar and which may inject toxic saliva into the plant may also have potential for biological control of this plant (DeLoach 1996). The host range and biology of the manna scale have been studied in quarantine at Temple, Texas, and the release of this insect has been approved by TAG.

Musk Thistle

Musk thistle (*Carduus nutans*) was introduced from Eurasia in about 1853 and was first reported in Texas in about 1940 (Cory 1940). It has become a problem weed in rangelands, pastures, cropland, and highway rights-of-way in several areas of the Texas Hill Country and also occurs locally in the panhandle and in Central and North Texas. Weevils (*Rhinocyllus conicus*) (Curculionidae) that attack the seed heads of musk thistle (Boldt and DeLoach 1985) were released near Kerrville in 1987. Their establishment was confirmed in 1992, but they had only dispersed about 1.5 miles from the release site. This weevil has been highly successful in controlling musk thistle after an establishment period of 5 to 6 years (Jackman et al. 1992, Boldt and Jackman 1993). Other insects that have been released for biological control of musk thistle in Texas include the musk thistle rosette weevil (*Trichosirocalus horridus*) (Curculionidae), the musk thistle flower fly (*Cheilosia corydon*), and the musk thistle leaf beetle (*Psylliodes chalcomera*) (Chrysomelidae). No establishment of these insects has been documented (J. A. Jackson, Biological Control of the Weeds Website: bc4weeds.tamu.edu).

Russian Thistle (Tumbleweed)

A stem boring moth (*Coleophora parthenica*) was released in South and West
Texas for biological control of Russian thistle (*Salsola iberica*), an exotic
weed from Asia. These insects established, but they had little effect on the
Russian thistle (Goeden and Ricker 1979, Muller et al. 1990).

Plant Diseases for Biological Control

Plant diseases have recently been used to a limited extent in a "bioherbicide"
or "biological herbicide" approach for weed control. This approach involves
the application of inoculum of a weed pathogen in a manner analogous to
chemical herbicide applications (Templeton 1982). Worldwide bioherbicide
research was reviewed by Charudattan (1991). The bioherbicide approach
uses an inundative strategy and is based on the fundamental principles of
epidemiology. In this approach, an abundant supply of virulent inoculum is
universally dispersed onto a susceptible weed population, with careful attention to timing to take advantage of favorable environmental conditions
and the most susceptible stage of the weed's life cycle. Some progress has
been made in formulating the inoculum to avoid unfavorable environmental conditions and to facilitate application. Bioherbicides have been com-
mercially developed from fungi for control of strangler vine (*Morrenia odorata*) in Florida citrus groves (DeVine®, a liquid formulation of *Phytophtora
palmivora*); northern jointvetch (*Aeschynomene virginica*) in rice and soybeans in Arkansas, Louisiana, and Mississippi (Collego®, a dry powder
formulation of *Colletotrichum gloeosporioides* f.sp. *aeschynomene*); round-
leaved mallow (*Malva pusilla*) in flax and lentils in Canada (BioMal®, a
dry formulation of *Colletotrichum gloeosporioides* f.sp. *malvae*); and dodder
(*Cuscuta* spp.) in soybeans in China (LUBAO 2, *Colletotrichum gloeosporioides* f.sp.*cuscutae*) (Watson 1993).

No biological herbicides have been developed for control of weeds or
woody plants on rangelands. However, recent work has shown that a rhizobacteria (*Pseudomonas* spp.) may have potential for suppressing downy
brome or cheatgrass (*Bromus tectorum*), a major invasive weed of rangelands
in the Intermountain region of the western United States (Kennedy et al.
1991). Researchers in Oklahoma found that common persimmon (*Diospyros virginiana*) on rangelands could be controlled very effectively by inocu-
lating cut stumps or wounds made to the stems with a spore suspension of
the persimmon wilt organism, *Cephalosporium diospyri,* or by shooting the
trees with shotgun pellets impregnated with the conidia (spores) of this organism (Crandall and Baker 1950, Wilson 1965, Griffith 1970). Seedlings of
Texas persimmon (*D. texana*) in Oklahoma were found susceptible to this
wilt, but mature Texas persimmon were not susceptible to this wilt organism in studies done in the 1980s in Texas (D. N. Ueckert, unpublished data).
A bracket fungus, *Ganoderma zonatum,* has been reported to kill honey mesquite in the Rolling Plains of Texas. Attempts to inoculate mesquite growing
on rangeland with this fungus by a variety of methods during the 1950s
failed, but mesquite seedlings growing in sterilized soil suffered 100% mortality when inoculated with the fungus (Fisher and Meadors 1952, Fisher

et al. 1953, Behrens et al. 1954, Norton and Behrens 1955). Mature mesquite in the field was not successfully inoculated with *G. zonatum* during the 1980s (D. N. Ueckert and R. Tabor, unpublished data).

Biological Control of Weeds and Brush with Vertebrates

Continuous, heavy grazing by a single species of domestic livestock exerts stress on the animal species' preferred food plants, shifts the competitive advantage to the plants not preferred, and over time allows the less palatable plants to increase in abundance and dominate the plant community. However, livestock can also be used to suppress or control undesirable plants. Control of weeds and brush with vertebrates, such as sheep and goats, has been used for many years, but it is considerably different from classical biological control because the densities and behavior of the animals are under the arbitrary control of people, i.e., they are not allowed to react, as populations, to changes in the abundance of the weeds (Huffaker 1964). Some species of weeds and woody plants can be controlled by modifying the intensity of grazing (stocking rate), timing of grazing, and/or the kind and class of livestock. A distinctive advantage of using domestic livestock for weed control, as opposed to insects or pathogens, is that they have market value and can be a profitable ranch enterprise while controlling undesirable weeds and woody plants (Magee 1957). The ecological advantages of grazing with more than one species of herbivore have been reviewed by Walker (1994).

Changing the species composition of a plant community with livestock is possible because food preferences differ among the animal species and because relative palatability varies among plant species and seasonally. Changing the composition of a plant community in a desirable direction with livestock may necessitate switching from a single-species to a multispecies livestock grazing system or to a nontraditional livestock species. The successful use of livestock for weed and brush control demands strict attention to management because timing and intensity of use or defoliation are critical. The target species must be repeatedly and severely defoliated, but the sheep, goats, or cattle must be removed prior to severe defoliation of the desirable forage species and/or the pasture must be rested during critical times to allow the desirable forages to completely recover. The literature on the effectiveness of cattle, sheep, and goats in controlling weeds was recently reviewed by Gillen and Scifres (1991), Quimby et al. (1991), and Popay and Field (1996).

Goats

The annual diet of goats can vary greatly depending upon the availability of different foods, but, on average, consists of about 30% grass, 10% forbs, and 60% shrubs (Van Dyne et al. 1980). Goats are well adapted for feeding on woody plants because their mobile upper lip and prehensile tongue allow them to select leaves and twig tips, even on thorny plants, and because of their ability to climb and graze in the canopies of woody plants by standing on their hind legs. Effective control of several woody species, including several species of oaks (*Quercus* spp.), sumac (*Rhus* spp.), greenbriar (*Smilax* spp.), hawthorn (*Crataegus* spp.), beautyberry (*Callicarpa americana*), yaupon (*Ilex vomitoria*), sweetgum (*Liquidambar styraciflua*), retama (*Parkinsonia aculeata*), honeysuckle (*Lonicera* spp.), sassafras (*Sassafras albidum*), guajillo (*Acacia berlandieri*), blackbrush (*Acacia rigidula*), trumpet-creeper (*Campsis radicans*), hackberry (*Celtis* spp.), mesquite, and juniper has been accomplished by the use of goats (Darrow and McCully 1959, Rechenthin et al. 1964, Merrill and Taylor 1976).

Many ranchers in Texas have historically used goats to maintain their liveoak (*Quercus virginiana*) savannas, i.e., to kill liveoak root sprouts and prevent the formation of thicketized liveoak mottes. Upon discontinuing goat grazing, many have observed a very rapid establishment of blueberry juniper (*J. ashei*) seedlings—indicating the secondary benefit of goats for juniper control not previously realized. Grazing rangeland heavily infested with seedlings and saplings of redberry juniper (*J. pinchotii*) with Spanish goats for short periods during midwinter at a stocking density of 290 to 580 goat days/acre, for 2 consecutive years in the northern Edwards Plateau killed 30 to 34% of the young junipers (Ueckert 1997). The current status of research on using goats and prescribed fire for juniper control is discussed in Chapter 12 (*this book*).

Mature algerita (agarito) (*Mahonia trifoliolata*) is relatively unpalatable to goats because of its sharp leaf spines, but the tender basal regrowth that appears following top-removal methods, such as fire or blading, is a preferred goat food. Algerita infestations in west-central Texas can be suppressed and managed by the integrated use of fire and goating.

Yearlong stocking rates of goats commonly used to control sprouts are usually one goat to 2 or 3 acres. However, short-term grazing at higher stocking densities such as five to eight goats per acre for a 30-day period is more effective. A high degree of defoliation for about 3 consecutive years is usually necessary to achieve a high level of brush control. Subsequent light stocking with goats grazed in combination with cattle or sheep may provide maintenance control.

Grazing by goats is usually most effective if used immediately following other brush treatments—such as mechanical or chemical methods or fire—which reduce the height and foliage volume of the target species, stimulate basal sprouting of palatable regrowth, and initiate a depletion of carbohydrate reserves stored in the plants' roots and basal crowns. Two-way chaining in 1969 followed by stocking at 45 animal units (85% Spanish goats) per section for 5 years in a two-pasture rotational grazing system at the Sonora Research Station reduced the canopy of a mixture of liveoak, shinoak (*Q. mohriana*), mesquite, juniper, sacahuista (*Nolina texana*), and pricklypear by 83% (Merrill and Taylor 1976). Spanish goats are more effective than Angora goats as biological control agents for woody plants. A potential problem with using goats for woody plant control is that their preferred food plants are often those preferred by deer (Severson and Debano 1991, Nelle 2001). Reduced forage diversity and nutritional stress in deer herds can result if goat grazing and deer populations are not carefully managed.

Sheep

Sheep diets can also be highly variable, but, on average, they consist of about 50% grass, 30% forbs, and 20% shrubs (Van Dyne et al. 1980). Under proper management, sheep can be very valuable in natural resource management (Shelton 1994). Sheep grazing can be a very desirable and effective weed control method, especially where other control methods are limited by environmental and economic constraints (Olson and Lacey 1994). Sheep are used extensively to suppress weeds on cropland being fallowed in Victoria, Australia (Armor 1987). Judicious timing and control of the intensity of grazing with sheep can be used to control certain weeds. For example, annual broomweeds (*Amphiachyris* spp., *Gutierrezia texana,* and *Xanthocephalum gymnospermoides*) can be controlled or suppressed if sheep are grazed at a high stocking rate on infested pastures in late winter and early spring while these annual weeds are in the rosette stage. Sheep avoid annual broomweed infestations after the plants have bolted.

Sheep can be useful for managing some plant species that are very toxic to cattle. Larkspurs (*Delphinium* spp.) are highly toxic to cattle, but sheep are more resistant to the secondary compounds in this plant. Under some conditions, sheep utilize large amounts of larkspur and it can be a source of nutrients. Intensive management of sheep by bedding or holding them on larkspur infestations has resulted in heavy, nonselective grazing of the weeds in the U.S. Intermountain West (Ralphs et al. 1991, Ralphs and Olsen 1992). Sheep can be used to graze larkspur-infested pastures before cattle are allowed access.

Leafy spurge (*Euphorbia esula*), a major alien weed in the Intermountain region and north-central United States, is avoided by cattle because of its latex content, but it is readily eaten by sheep and goats (Fay 1991). Infestations of this weed can be controlled by grazing with sheep and goats, but grazing must be started early in the growing season and mature stands must be mowed before being grazed (Landgraf et al. 1984, Lym and Kirby 1987). The seeds of leafy spurge are passed through the digestive tract of both sheep and goats, but sheep were more effective than goats in reducing the germinability and viability of the seeds (Lacey et al. 1992). Animals that have been grazing on leafy spurge should be confined for 5 days to allow all the seeds to pass from their digestive tract before being moved to leafy spurge-free pastures. Walker et al. (1992) suggested that previous training could make sheep more effective for controlling leafy spurge. Lambs with previous experience of eating leafy spurge had a higher relative preference for leafy spurge, spent more time grazing it, and were considered more effective as biological control agents.

Frischknecht and Harris (1973) reported that grazing with sheep in late autumn would effectively control big sagebrush (*Artemisia tridentata*), if the practice was initiated early during its invasion of improved pastures. Effective control was maintained on sites where the density of sagebrush plants was about 1.5 plants per 100 ft^2. The greatest effect of sheep grazing on sagebrush was the reduction in size of existing plants, rather than direct plant mortality. However, heavy feeding by sheep greatly reduced the capacity of sagebrush to produce flower stalks and seeds. Sheep had little effect on big sagebrush on sites where there were more than thirteen plants per 100 ft^2. This indicates that a high ratio of sheep to sagebrush was essential to achieve a significant level of suppression.

Cattle

On average, the yearlong diet of cattle consists of about 70% grass, 15% forbs, and 15% browse (Van Dyne et al. 1980). Cattle consume significant amounts of forbs when they are available, in certain growth stages, and especially during periods of stress or drought. They also consume a wide variety of browse plants, including winged elm (*Ulmus alata*), oaks, Macartney rose, mesquite, and hackberry, but they normally only eat the leaves and twig tips. Hackberry seedlings and saplings that are accessible are often kept hedged and maintained in a shrub growth form by cattle grazing. Small soapweed (*Yucca glauca*) has been controlled by grazing with mature cattle during winter in the sandhills of Nebraska (Vallentine 1971). Cattle utilized over 50% of the growth of sprouts of salt cedar during summer in an Arizona study (Gary 1960).

Seedlings and saplings of willow baccharis (*Baccharis salicina*) are eaten by cattle, hence mature willow baccharis plants are usually rare in pastures with a history of cattle grazing (Mutz et al. 1979). This woody weed often invades grasslands that have been mechanically disturbed or severely overgrazed, then completely protected from cattle grazing for a period of time. Mature willow baccharis is only slightly used by cattle.

There is at least one example of using cattle to manage a weed that is toxic to sheep. Pastures infested with woolly paperflower (*Psilostrophe tagetina*) in the Trans-Pecos region of Texas are often grazed with cattle before sheep are allowed to graze to reduce sheep intoxication on this toxic plant (W. A. McGinty, personal communication).

Literature Cited

Armor, R. L. 1987. Non-chemical weed control in Victorian dryland crops—the dream and the reality. Proceedings Australian Weeds Conference 8: 24–26.

Behrens, R., C. E. Fisher, and C. H. Meadors, Jr. 1954. Biological control of mesquite. Annual Report. Mesquite control studies. Weed Investigations Section, Field Crops Research Branch, USDA and Texas Agricultural Experiment Station. Substation No. 7, Spur.

Boldt, P. E., and C. J. DeLoach. 1985. Evaluating *Rhinocyllus conicus* Froel. (Coleoptera: Curculionidae), an introduced weevil for the biological control of *Carduus* and *Silybum* thistles. Bulletin Entomological Society America 26:355–58.

———, and J. A. Jackman. 1993. Establishment of *Rhinocyllus conicus* Froelich on *Carduus macrocaphalus* in Texas. Southwestern Entomologist 18:173–81.

———, and R. Sobhian. 1993. Release and establishment of *Aceria malherbae* (Acari: Eriophyidae) for control of field bindweed in Texas. Environmental Entomology 22:234–37.

Charudattan, R. 1991. The mycoherbicide approach with plant pathogens. Pages 24–57 *in* D. O. TeBeest, editor. Microbial control of weeds. Chapman & Hall, New York.

Coetzer, W., and J. H. Hoffmann. 1997. Establishment of *Neltumius arizonensis* (Coleoptera: Bruchidae) on mesquite (*Prosopis* species: Mimosaceae) in South Africa. Biological Control 10: 187–92.

Cordo, H. A., and C. J. DeLoach. 1987. Insects that attack mesquite (*Prosopis* spp.) in Argentina and Paraguay: their possible use for biological control in the United States. USDA Agricultural Research Service ARS-62.

———, and ———. 1992. Occurrence of snakeweeds (*Gutierrezia:* Compositae) and their natural enemies in Argentina: implications for biological control in the United States. Biological Control 2:143–58.

Cory, V. L. 1940. Six thistles recently introduced into Texas. Madrona 5:200–201.

Crandall, B. C., and W. L. Baker. 1950. The wilt disease of American persimmon caused by *Cephalosporium diospyri.* Phytopathology 40:307–25.

Daniels, N. E., and A. F. Wiese. 1967. Survival and spread of the puncturevine seed weevil in Texas. Texas Agricultural Experiment Station Miscellaneous Publication MP-827.

Darrow, R. A., and W. G. McCully. 1959. Brush control and range improvement in the post oak-blackjack oak area of Texas. Texas Agricultural Experiment Station and Texas Agricultural Extension Service Bulletin 942.

DeBach, P. 1974. Biological control by natural enemies. Cambridge University Press, London.

DeLoach, C. J. 1978. Considerations in introducing foreign biotic agents to control native weeds of rangelands. Pages 39–50 *in* T. E. Freeman, editor. Proceedings IV International Symposium on Biological Control of Weeds. Aug.30–Sept.2, 1976. Institute of Food and Agricultural Sciences, University of Florida, Gainesville.

———. 1980. Prognosis for biological control of weeds of southwestern U.S. rangelands. Pages 175–99 *in* Proceedings V International Symposium on Biological Control of Weeds. Brisbane, Australia, 1980.

———. 1985. Conflicts of interest over beneficial and undesirable aspects of mesquite (*Prosopis* spp.) in the United States as related to biological control. Pages 301–40 *in* E. S. Delfosse, editor. Proceedings VI International Symposium Biological Control of Weeds. August 19–25, 1984. Vancouver, Canada.

Dodd, A. P. 1936. The control and eradication of prickly-pear in Australia. Bulletin of Entomological Research 27:503–17.

———. 1940. The biological campaign against prickly pear. Commonwealth Prickly Pear Board, Brisbane, Australia.

Donnelly, G., J. Dodd, and S. Addison. 1997. Biological control of mesquite with insects. Pages 10–11 *in* Annual Report on Weed and Pest Animal Research, Queensland Department of Natural Resources, Technical Highlights 1996–97.

Fay, P. K. 1991. Controlling leafy spurge with grazing animals. Pages 193–99 *in* L. F. James, J. O. Evans, M. H. Ralphs, and R. D. Child, editors. Noxious range weeds. Westview Press, Boulder, Colorado.

Fisher, C. E., and C. H. Meadors, Jr. 1952. Biological control of mesquite. Annual Report. Mesquite control studies. Texas Agricultural Experiment Station Substation No. 7, Spur.

———, ———, and R. Behrens. 1953. Biological control of mesquite. Annual Report. Mesquite control studies. Texas Agricultural Experiment Station Substation No. 7, Spur, and the Section of Weeds Investigations, Field Crops Research Branch, USDA, Unpublished Report.

Foster, D. E., D. N. Ueckert, and C. J. DeLoach. 1981. Insects associated with broom snakeweed (*Xanthocephalum sarothrae*) and threadleaf snakeweed (*Xanthocephalum microcephala*) in West Texas and eastern New Mexico. Journal of Range Management 34:446–54.

Frischknecht, N. C., and L. E. Harris. 1973. Sheep can control sagebrush on seeded range if _ _ _. Utah Science. March 1973. Utah State University, Logan.

Gary, H. L. 1960. Utilization of five-stamen tamarisk by cattle. Rocky Mountain Forest and Range Experiment Station Research Note 51.

Gillen, R. L., and C. J. Scifres. 1991. Selective grazing as a weed control method. Pages 369–76 *in* D. Pimentel, editor. CRC handbook of pest management in agriculture. Second edition. Volume 2. CRC Press, Inc., Boca Raton, Florida.

Goeden, R. D. 1977. Biological control of weeds. Pages 43–47 *in* B. Truelove, editor. Research methods in weed science. Southern Weed Science Society, Auburn Printing, Inc., Auburn, Alabama.

———. 1983. Critique and revision of Harris' scoring system for selection of insect agents in biological control of weeds. Protection Ecology 5:287–301.

———. 1988. A capsule history of biological control of weeds. Biocontrol News & Information 9:55–61.

———, C. A. Fleschner, and D. W. Ricker. 1967. Biological control of prickly pear cacti on Santa Cruz Island, California. California Agricultural Experiment Station. Hilgardia 38:579–606.

———, and D. W. Ricker. 1979. Field analysis of *Coleophora parthenica* (Lep.: Coleophoridae) as an imported natural enemy of Russian thistle, *Salsola iberica,* in the Coachella valley of southern California. Environmental Entomology 8:1099–1101.

Griffith, C. A. 1970. The use of persimmon wilt (*Cephalosporium diospyri*) for control of common persimmon (*Diospyros virginiana*). Proceedings Southern Weed Science Society 1970:254–57.

Harris, P. 1973. The selection of effective agents for the biological control of weeds. Canadian Entomologist 105:1495–1503.

Holloway, J. K. 1964. Projects in biological control of weeds. Pages 650–70 *in* P. DeBach, editor. Biological control of insect pests and weeds. Reinhold Publishing Corporation, New York.

———, and C. B. Huffaker. 1951. The role of *Chrysolina gemellata* in the biological control of Klamath weed. Journal of Economic Entomology 44:244–47.

Hoy, J. M. 1961. *Eriococcus orariensis* Hoy and other Coccoidea associated with *Leptospermum* Forst. species in New Zealand. New Zealand Department of Scientific Industries Research Bulletin No. 141.

Huffaker, C. B. 1957. Fundamentals of biological control of weeds. University of California, Berkeley. Hilgardia 27:101–57.

———. 1959. Biological control of weeds with insects. Annual Review of Entomology 4:251–76.

———. 1964. Fundamentals of biological weed control. Pages 631–49 *in* P. DeBach, editor. Biological control of insect pests and weeds. Reinhold Publishing Corporation, New York.

———, and C. E. Kennett. 1959. A ten-year study of vegetational changes associated with biological control of Klamath weed. Journal of Range Management 12:69–82.

Jackman, J. A., P. Boldt, J. W. Stewart, and T. W. Fuchs. 1992. Biological control of musk thistle in Texas. *In* Biological Pest Control. Texas Agricultural Extension Service Leaflet L-5067.

Julien, M. H., editor. 1992. Biological control of weeds: a world catalogue of agents and their target weeds. Third edition. CAB International, Wallington, Australia, in association with Australian Centre of International Agricultural Research (ACIAR), Canberra.

Kennedy, A. C., L. F. Elliott, F. L. Young, and C. L. Douglas. 1991. Rhizobacteria suppressive to the weed downy brome. Soil Science Society of America Journal 55:722–27.

Lacey, J. R., R. Wallander, and K. Olson-Rutz. 1992. Recovery, germinability, and viability of leafy spurge (*Euphorbia esula*) seeds ingested by sheep and goats. Weed Technology 6:599–602.

Landgraf, B. K., P. K. Fay, and K. M. Havstad. 1984. Utilization of leafy spurge (*Euphorbia esula*) by sheep. Weed Science 32:348–52.

Lym, R. G., and D. R. Kirby. 1987. Cattle foraging behavior in leafy spurge (*Euphorbia esula*)-infested rangeland. Weed Technology 1:314–18.

Maddox, D. M. 1976. History of weevils on puncturevine in and near the United States. Weed Science 24:414–19.

Magee, A. C. 1957. Goats pay for clearing Grand Prairie rangeland. Texas Agricultural Experiment Station Miscellaneous Publication 206.

Merrill, L. B., and C. A. Taylor. 1976. Take note of the versatile goat. Rangeman's Journal 3:74–76.

Michels, J. 1999. Gall mite shows promise against field bindweed. Texas Biological Control News. Texas Agricultural Extension Service.

Moran, V. C., J. H. Hoffmann, and H. G. Zimmermann. 1993. Objectives, constraints, and tactics in the biological control of mesquite weeds (*Prosopis*) in South Africa. Biological Control 3:80–83.

Muller, H., G. S. Nuessly, and R. D. Goeden. 1990. Natural enemies and host-plant asynchrony contributing to the failure of the introduced moth, *Coleophora parthenica* Meyrick (Lepidoptera: Coleophoridae), to control Russian thistle. Agriculture, Ecosystems and Environment 32:133–42.

Mutz, J. L., C. J. Scifres, W. C. Mohr, and D. L. Drawe. 1979. Control of willow baccharis and spiny aster with pelleted herbicides. Texas Agricultural Experiment Station Bulletin B-1194.

Nelle, S. A. 2001. Ecological implications of using goats for control of juniper in Texas. Pages 352–355 *in* E. D. McArthur and D. J. Fairbanks, compilers. Shrubland ecosystem genetics and biodiversity: proceedings; June 13–15, 2000; Provo, Utah. Proceedings RMRS-P-21. Ogden, UT: U.S. Department of Agriculture, Forest Service, Rocky Mountain Research Station.

Norton, D. C., and R. Behrens. 1955. *Ganoderma zonatum* associated with dying mesquite. Annual Report. Mesquite control studies. Field Crops Research Branch, USDA and Texas Agricultural Experiment Station Substation No. 7, Spur.

Olson, B. E., and J. R. Lacey. 1994. Sheep: a method for controlling rangeland weeds. Sheep Research Journal Special Issue 1994:105–12.

Orr, C. C., J. R. Abernathy, and E. B. Hudspeth. 1975. *Nothanguina phyllobia,* a nematode parasite of silverleaf nightshade. Plant Disease Reporter 59:416–18.

Perkins, R. C. L., and O. H. Swezey. 1924. The introduction into Hawaii of insects that attack lantana. Hawaiian Sugar Planters' Association Experiment Station Entomological Services Bulletin 16.

Popay, I., and R. Field. 1996. Grazing animals as weed control agents. Weed Technology 10:217–31.

Quimby, P. C., Jr., W. L. Bruckart, C. J. DeLoach, L. Knutson, and M. H. Ralphs. 1991. Biological control of rangeland weeds. Pages 84–102 *in* L. F. James, J. O. Evans, M. H. Ralphs, and R. D. Child, editors. Noxious range weeds. Westview Press, Boulder, Colorado.

Ralphs, M. H., J. E. Bowns, and G. D. Manners. 1991. Utilization of larkspur by sheep. Journal of Range Management 44:619–22.

———, and J. D. Olsen. 1992. Prior grazing by sheep reduces waxy larkspur consumption by cattle. Journal of Range Management 45:136–39.

Rechenthin, C. A., H. M. Bell, R. J. Pederson, and D. B. Polk. 1964. Grassland restoration. Part II. Brush control. USDA Soil Conservation Service, Temple, Texas.

Rees, N. E., P. C. Quimby, Jr., G. L. Piper, E. M. Combs, C. E. Turner, N. R. Spencer, and L. V. Knutson. 1996. Biological control of weeds in the West. Western Society of Weed Science, in cooperation with USDA Agricultural Research Service, Montana Department of Agriculture, and Montana State University, Bozeman.

Rummel, D. R., and M. D. Arnold. 1992. Status of the puncturevine seed weevil in the Texas southern high plains. Southwestern Entomologist 17:347–49.

Scifres, C. J. 1980. Biological brush management. Pages 245–61 *in* C. J. Scifres. Brush management: principles and practices for Texas and the Southwest. Texas A&M University Press, College Station.

Severson, K. E., and L. F. Debano. 1991. Influence of Spanish goats on vegetation and soils in Arizona chaparral. Journal of Range Management 44:111–17.

Shelton, M., editor. 1994. The role of sheep grazing in natural resource management. Sheep Research Journal Special Issue 1994.

Templeton, G. E. 1982. Biological herbicides: discovery, development, deployment. Weed Science 30:430–33.

Ueckert, D. N. 1997. Juniper control and management. Pages 23–34 *in* Proceedings 1997 juniper symposium. Texas Agricultural Experiment Station, San Angelo, Technical Report 97-1.

Vallentine, J. F. 1971. Range development and improvements. Brigham Young University Press, Provo, Utah.

Van Dyne, G. M., N. R. Brockington, Z. Sxocs, J. Duek, and C. A. Ribic. 1980. Large herbivore sub-systems. Pages 269–537 *in* A. I. Breymeyer and G. M. Van Dyne, editors. Grasslands, systems analysis and man. Cambridge University Press, Cambridge.

van Klinken, R. D., and S. D. Campbell. 2001. The biology of Australian weeds 37. *Prosopis* L. species. Plant Protection Quarterly 16:2–20.

Walker, J. W. 1994. Multispecies grazing: the ecological advantage. Sheep Research Journal Special Issue 1994:52–64.

———, K. G. Hemenway, P. G. Hatfield, and H. A. Glimp. 1992. Training lambs to be weed eaters: studies with leafy spurge. Journal of Range Management 45:245–49.

Wapshere, A. J., E. S. Delfosse, and J. M. Cullen. 1989. Recent developments in biological control of weeds. Crop Protection 8:227–50.

Ward, C. R., C. W. O'Brien, L. B. O'Brien, D. E. Foster, and E. W. Huddleston. 1977. Annotated checklist of new world insects associated with *Prosopis* (mesquite). USDA Agricultural Research Service Technical Bulletin 1557.

Watson, A. K., editor. 1993. Biological control of weeds handbook. Monograph Series No. 7. Weed Science Society of America, Champaign, Illinois.

Watts, J. G., G. B. Hewitt, E. W. Huddleston, H. G. Kinzer, R. J. Lavigne, and D. N. Ueckert. 1989. Rangeland entomology. Second edition. Society for Range Management, Denver, Colorado.

Wilson, C. L. 1965. Considerations of the use of persimmon wilt as a silvicide for weed persimmons. Plant Disease Report 49:780–91.

Wilson, F. 1964. The biological control of weeds. Annual Review of Entomology 9:225–44.

Zimmermann, H. G. 1991. Biological control of mesquite, *Prosopis* spp. (Fabaceae), in South Africa. Agriculture, Ecosystems and Environment 37:175–86.

10   Current State Of The Art

C. Jack DeLoach
and
Phil A. Lewis

A veritable flood of exotic plants have been introduced intentionally or accidentally into North America since the arrival of European explorers and
settlers. Many of these plants have increased enormously in their new environment, mainly because the controlling natural enemies (insects and plant
pathogens) in the Old World were not brought with them and the native
North American insects and pathogens do not attack them, or else cause
little damage. For years, these exotic invaders have seriously threatened agricultural and natural ecosystems, as well as many rare or endangered indigenous plants and animals. Public awareness now has culminated in passage of
Presidential Executive Order 13112: Invasive Species of February 3, 1999,
which seeks to control the spread of nonnative species of plants and animals
that are in the United States. Many of these exotic, invasive species are weeds
that are difficult and expensive to control by conventional chemical and
mechanical means; these controls also damage many nontarget plants in
rangelands and natural areas, pollute soil and groundwater, and increase soil
erosion.

Biological control, primarily by the introduction of the natural enemies
of the weed from its homeland, but also sometimes by augmenting or conserving the natural enemies already here, has been used successfully to
control introduced, and sometimes indigenous, weeds since the mid-1800s.
This method is highly host specific to the target weed, does not damage the
ecosystem, and provides permanent, low-cost control. Darrell Ueckert has
described this methodology and usage in Chapter 9 (*this book*). In the continental United States and Canada, biological control agents have been released against thirty-eight weed species since 1945. Substantial to complete
control has been obtained for about one-third of these and research is continuing on others.

In this chapter, we address the current state of research on major terrestrial weeds in the southwestern United States, and some of the issues that
affect this field of research. Recent reviews of biological control of North
American weeds have been written by DeLoach (1981, 1989, 1991, 1995, and
1997), Kelleher and Hulme (1984), DeLoach et al. (1986), Buckingham

(1994), Nechols et al. (1995), Rees et al. (1996), and Julien and Griffiths (1999). Many aspects of the control of these weeds have been covered in the proceedings of the ten international symposia on biological control of weeds, now held every 4 years. Because of space constraints, many original references are not cited and the reader is referred to review papers on some of the weeds.

Selection of Weeds for Biological Control

The desirability of biological control for an invasive or native weed species may be determined by an analysis of its harmful and beneficial values (both economic and ecological), and of its potential for successful biological control (mostly the potential for finding and developing insects or plant pathogens that can control it) (DeLoach 1981, Peschken and McClay 1995). Harmful values include competition with beneficial plants in agricultural or natural ecosystems, use of water, salinization of soil, desertification, toxicity to livestock or wildlife, degradation of wildlife habitat, toxicity or allergenicity to humans, etc. Beneficial values include use of the weed by wildlife or livestock, or as a part of natural plant communities (in the case of native weeds), soil stabilization and control of water and wind erosion, use as ornamentals, for honey production, production of fiber, chemicals or medicines, etc.

Most of the major weeds of southwestern rangelands are native woody species, whereas most from the northwestern United States and Canada are introduced herbaceous species (Platt 1959). Many of the native southwestern weeds are from genera that also have species native in similar climatic zones of southern South America. Some of these genera with a disjunct distribution of species originated in North America (snakeweeds and loco, the latter also native throughout northern Eurasia) and some genera originated in South America (mesquite, creosotebush, whitebrush, baccharis). All of these species have some insects or plant pathogens in South America that do not occur in North America, which appear sufficiently host specific to introduce here. In general, more host-specific insects occur in the continent where the weed genus originated, since more time for evolution occurred there, than in the continent to which the weed later spread.

Our attempt to control native weeds by introducing foreign natural enemies is the first attempt in North America and the first attempt in a continental area anywhere (three previous projects were all on islands discussed by Darrell Ueckert in Chapter 9, *this book*) (DeLoach 1995). Although these native species were not recognized as damaging by the early explorers and settlers of the region, they increased enormously under later management practices. Many are now permanently established at high densities except where effective control methods are periodically applied. Many exotic weeds have invaded the Southwest—most of them also in other western areas—especially from Europe, Asia, and South America. Some of these have relatives in the same genus native in North America but most have only more distant relatives (different genus or even different family). These taxonomic relationships are important if introduced natural enemies are to be used for control. Natural enemies that will not damage closely related native plants are much more difficult to find, and sometimes may not exist.

Status of Control of Various Exotic Weeds

For many years, the introduction of foreign insects and occasionally of plant pathogens has been the most commonly used and most successful method for biological control of weeds. This was discussed by Darrell Ueckert in Chapter 9 (*this book*). Unfortunately, only a few of the major weeds of southwestern rangelands are introduced (Platt 1959). We have developed controls for two of them, salt cedar and field bindweed. Controls have been developed in California and Montana for four others that we have applied in our region, discussed below. We have new programs for research on three others: African rue, Russian olive, and camelthorn.

Puncturevine (Tribulus terrestris) *(Zygophyllaceae).* Puncturevine is a prostrate, spreading plant of arid areas, introduced from the Old World. It has sharp spines on the fruits that are very painful to the feet of children and pets. The spines can even puncture bicycle tires. The plants can reach 3 to 4 yards across in favorable areas. It has invaded large areas from Texas to California to Florida. Two weevil species were introduced from Italy in 1961, *Microlarinus lareynii* that feeds in the seeds and *M. lypriformis* that feeds in the stems. The two species together have provided 80% control in California and complete control in Hawaii but insufficient control in some other areas (Andres and Goeden 1995). Complete control was obtained in much of Texas but the weeds reestablished after the beetles apparently died during the severe freeze of 1983. However, reintroduction of the beetles appears to have resulted in successful control again.

Musk Thistle Complex (Carduus nutans, C. thoermeri, C. macrocephalus) *(Compositae).* Biological control of musk thistle has been one of the most successful projects in the United States. The seed-head weevil, *Rhinocyllus conicus,* was introduced into Canada from Europe in 1968 and into the United States in 1969. It attacks, to some degree, nine species of thistles but gives best control of musk thistle (*C. nutans*), resulting in 80 to 99% reduction in stands in Montana (Rees 1977), Missouri (Ben Puttler, University of Missouri, Columbia, personal communication), Virginia (Kok and Surles 1975) and other states. A rosette weevil (*Trichosirocalus horridus*) was released in 1974 and provides some control in Kansas, Missouri, and Virginia. Two other European insects have been released in the United States, a syrphid fly (*Cheilosia corydon*) in Maryland in 1989 and a flea beetle (*Psylliodes chalcomera*) near Kerrville, Texas in 1977, but establishment is not confirmed (see review by Andres and Rees 1995 and Rees et al. 1996). In Central Texas and much of New Mexico, musk thistle recently has become a serious pest. *R. conicus* is giving substantial control here, with nearly all seed heads infested, and stands greatly reduced. A small amount of damage to native, nontarget *Cirsium* thistles (predicted in the original host-range testing) in

Nebraska has caused great furor among some in the environmentalist community and concern among biological control workers (McEvoy and Coombs 2000).

Russian Thistle (Salsola australis) *(Chenopodiaceae).* Two species of this genus of desert plants have been introduced from Asia, and now infest 102 million acres in the western United States (Platt 1959). In Texas and New Mexico, Russian thistle occurs mostly on disturbed soil along highways and in abandoned cultivated fields (see review by DeLoach et al. 1986). Two species of coleophorid moths were introduced into California in the 1970s from Pakistan, *Coleophora parthenica* whose larvae bore in the pith of the stems and *C. klimeschiella* whose larvae feed on the foliage. Although both became widely established and sometimes abundant, they caused very little damage to the plant (Pemberton 1980).

We released *C. parthenica* near Rio Grande City, Texas in 1997; it has spread widely and the larvae are often abundant in the stems but the plants are not noticeably damaged and we have not observed any reduction in stands. We also released *C. klimeschilla* near Saragosa in western Texas but it did not become established, probably because the landowner burned the site soon after release. At the time this research was underway in the 1970s, searching for natural enemies near the center of the plant's distribution in central USSR was not possible. However, limited explorations have been conducted recently in Turkmenistan and China where numerous insects probably occur. With more effort, the possibility of finding safe, effective control agents appears to be good.

Leafy Spurge (Euphorbia esula) *(Euphorbiaceae).* This is a deep-rooted, perennial herb native throughout Eurasia that is difficult to control by conventional methods. It forms dense stands over large areas, seriously competes with forage plants, and is poisonous to livestock. It has invaded much of southern Canada and the northern third of the United States. It is especially serious in Montana, Wyoming, and the Dakotas. Leafy spurge has spread southward to New Mexico where it is now invading northern areas and the Sacramento Mountain area. Since 1966, thirteen species of Eurasian insects have been tested and released into Canada and the United States. Nine of these species have become established, and others are under study. The most effective to date are several species of *Aphthona* fleabeetles, whose larvae feed on the roots and the adults on the foliage. Each species has its own microclimate and soil preference, and dispersal is slow at first, reducing spurge cover from 90% to 2% over 2.5 acres after 4 years, but dispersal later becomes more rapid. Control is now spectacular in several areas of several miles in diameter, with little spurge remaining. These areas have been replaced with a good stand of forage grasses (see review by Pemberton 1995 and Rees et al. 1996). Three of the *Aphthona* beetles recently have been released in New Mexico by Dave Thompson at New Mexico State University, Las Cruces. Two of these, *Aphthona nigriscutis* and *A. lacertosa*, are giving good control.

Field Bindweed (Convolvulus arvensis) *(Convolvulaceae).* This exotic weed from Eurasia has become a serious pest in cultivated crops, pastures, and natural areas over most of the United States and Canada, with the most seriously affected areas from Central Texas through the Great Plains and northern Rockies. High host specificity of control agents is required because of the danger of attack on several native *Calystegia* species in the Pacific states and on sweet potato. Research progress was reviewed by Rosenthal (1995).

Explorations in southern Europe and Turkey by Rosenthal and Buckingham (1982) and others revealed several promising control insects. Quarantine testing by Rosenthal at Albany, California and Temple, Texas resulted in an APHIS permit to release the defoliating moth, *Tyta luctuosa,* and an eriophyiid mite, *Aceria malherbae,* in the central United States but not on the Pacific Coast. We released *T. luctuosa* near Temple, Texas and in Oklahoma, Arkansas, Missouri, Kansas, Iowa, Maryland, and New Jersey but establishment has never been confirmed. Research is continuing by Jim Nechols at Kansas State University.

The mite, *A. malherbae,* was released near Amarillo, Texas in 1989 by Paul Boldt and Tom Robbins (USDA-ARS, Temple, Texas), but it spread little. At another site 35 miles away, the plots were accidentally mowed in 1998 and the mite spread 600 yards along the mowed road in 2 weeks. Since then, approximately 160 new sites have been established in northern Texas, and another 150 in sites in New Mexico, southwestern Kansas, Oklahoma, and southeastern Colorado. The mite has established and overwintered in these areas and is spreading rapidly (with mowing). Within a year after establishment, the mites reduce field bindweed biomass by 75%. They overwinter on the roots, weaken the plants, and the next year prevent flowering and seed production and reduce the plants to small rosettes that do not twine on crop plants and cause little damage. After a few years, complete control may be achieved (Jerry Michaels, Texas A&M University, Amarillo, personal communication).

Salt Cedar (primarily Tamarix ramosissima *) (Tamaricaceae).* Salt cedar is a deciduous, facultatively phreatophytic, shrub to small tree, from central Asia that has heavily invaded western riparian areas and lakeshores since the 1920s. It is adapted to areas of saline soil and shallow groundwater, is fire tolerant, and is resistant to attack by North American insects. It has displaced native plant communities with nearly monotypic thickets and has seriously degraded wildlife habitats. Dense stands lower water tables, increase salinity levels, and promote intense wildfires. It interacts synergistically with practically all human-produced ecological changes (dams, groundwater pumping, livestock grazing, conventional weed controls, etc.) to increase its own competitive advantage. Salt cedar dries up water sources for wildlife in desert areas. It exacerbates wildfires that kill wildlife and burn nests of breeding birds, and it modifies stream channels, backwaters, and water quality to the detriment of fish and other aquatic animals. Salt cedar provides reduced quality and diversity of insects, its fruits and seeds are too small, and its foliage is unpalatable as food for most wildlife and bird species (reviewed by DeLoach 1989, DeLoach et al. 1996).

Nevertheless, in areas where salt cedar has replaced the native wildlife habitat, some wildlife species do utilize salt cedar as cover, nesting substrate, and to feed on the pollinating adult insects that come to its flowers. In recent years, the endangered southwestern subspecies of the willow flycatcher (*Empidonax traillii extimus*) has begun nesting in salt cedar, and in several areas of Arizona it nests entirely in salt cedar. This has produced great concern among flycatcher biologists and endangered species experts over the fate of the flycatcher if salt cedar is controlled (reviewed by DeLoach et al. 2000).

Tamarix is a genus of fifty-four species of mostly small trees that evolved in temperate, semiarid, saline areas of central Asia; no species are native in the Western Hemisphere. The primary weedy species in the United States, *Tamarix ramosissima* is native from eastern Turkey and across central Asia to north-central China (Baum 1978). Ten species of *Tamarix* have been introduced into the United States as ornamentals or for erosion control. *T. ramosissima* occurs from northern Mexico to Montana and from the central Great Plains to the Pacific. Another species, *T. parviflora*, is becoming weedy in California. One species, the large, evergreen, cold-intolerant athel (*T. aphylla*) is a low quality but often used shade tree in the desert Southwest; it is not a target for control. The other species are weakly naturalized in areas of the western, southwestern, and southeastern United States (Crins 1989). The Tamaricaceae and the Frankeniaceae form a two-family group, usually placed in the small order Tamaricales, that are not closely related to other plant families. Six species of *Frankenia* are native shrubs of occasional abundance and low ecological value in the United States and northern Mexico, four of these in the United States. In North America, these and athel are the only plants of concern for nontarget attack by introduced biological control agents. Of the many species of insects in Asia that are associated with *Tamarix*, only very few also are associated with *Frankenia*.

We began research on salt cedar in 1987 and submitted a comprehensive review of its harmful and beneficial values and of its possibility for successful control as a petition to the Technical Advisory Group for Biological Control Agents of Weeds (TAG) in June 1989 asking their advice on beginning a project on biological control, which they subsequently recommended. We then began overseas exploration and testing of natural enemies. More than 300 insect species are known from *Tamarix* in Asia, very few of which attack other genera of plants (Kovalev 1995). Our cooperators in Montpellier, France; Tel Aviv, Israel; Ashghabat, Turkmenistan; Almaty, Kazakhstan; and Urumqi and Beijing, China currently are testing some twenty insect species as candidates for introduction into the United States. We have begun testing ten of these in quarantine at Temple, Texas. We have completed testing three species, a leaf beetle, *Diorhabda elongata* from China and Kazakhstan; a mealybug, *Trabutina mannipara* from Israel; and a foliage-feeding weevil, *Coniatus tamarisci* from France (DeLoach et al. 1996).

Host-range studies of *D. elongata* show that it is safe to release into nature in North America. A review of the literature and museum records by Asian and European scientists revealed that *D. elongata* is known only from several species of the genus *Tamarix*. Formal host-range testing in quarantine at Temple, Texas from 1992 to 2001 revealed that *D. elongata* fed and completed their development only on *Tamarix* (50 to 80% from egg to adult) but that 8 to 13% completed development from egg to adult on *Frankenia*. However, tests in 10×10 ft outdoor cages at Temple demonstrated that the adults are only slightly attracted to and lay only a few eggs on *Frankenia jamesii* (ca. 2% as many as on *Tamarix*) and were not attracted to and laid no eggs on the other two species of *Frankenia* tested, including the endangered *F. johnstonii* from South Texas. These tests provide definitive data indicating that *D. elongata* is highly unlikely to damage *Frankenia* or any other plant species if released into nature (DeLoach et al. 2003, Lewis et al. 2003).

We received TAG recommendation for field release and were prepared to release both *D. elongata* and *T. mannipara* into the field during the summer of 1994. However, after the southwestern willow flycatcher was placed on the Federal Endangered Species list in March 1994, a Biological Assessment and clearance by the USDI Fish and Wildlife Service (FWS) was required. This was prepared at Temple and submitted to Region 2, FWS, Albuquerque, New Mexico on October 17, 1997. However, concern by flycatcher biologists of Region 2, and a philosophical opposition to biological control in general, prevented a decision to release the insects. At a meeting with FWS personnel of Region 1 and Region 6 at Reno, Nevada in June 1998, it was agreed that we should submit a proposal to conduct research releases in field cages during 1 year, to be followed by 2 years of research after release from the cages at these sites. FWS would then review the results after the 3 years and issue a Biological Opinion regarding further releases and dispersal of the insects. This Research Proposal was submitted to FWS on August 28, 1998. A Letter of Concurrence was signed by Fish and Wildlife Service on June 3, 1999 approving releases at ten sites in Texas, Colorado, Wyoming, Utah, Nevada, and California, but eliminating the proposed sites in New Mexico. An Environmental Assessment was prepared by APHIS, and a Finding of No Significant Impact was signed by APHIS on July 7, 1999. Permits for release into field cages at the various sites were issued by APHIS during July 1999. The beetles were released into the cages at eight of the sites during August 1999, at one more site in August 2000, and at the tenth site during 2001. The beetles overwintered at five sites during the winter of 1999 to 2000. At all five sites they increased greatly in numbers and completely defoliated salt cedar in the cages during the summer of 2000, such that new cages had to be established, and some beetles transferred there, to prevent them from starving. Releases from the eight original field cages into nature were made during May 2001. Release of *T. mannipara* is pending development of cages that would prevent its escape into the field. A positive response from TAG on the release of *C. tamarisci* was received in May 2001; National Environmental Policy Act (NEPA) and the Endangered Species Act (ESA) clearances now must be obtained.

Status of Control of Various Native Weeds

Native plants usually become weedy pests because of environmental changes produced by the European settlers and due to interactions with natural events. The increase in abundance of some native plants has been enormous. Snakeweeds, broomweeds, mesquite, pricklypear cactus, junipers, and some others probably are 100 to 1,000 times more abundant today than before 1800. The major causes probably are abusive overgrazing by livestock in the early years (although management in most areas has greatly improved in recent years), spread of seeds by livestock, suppression of grassland fires, droughts, and increasing atmospheric CO_2 levels which favor growth of woody plants over warm-season grasses (see review by DeLoach 1995). Unfortunately, good management alone does not improve weed-dominated rangelands, as demonstrated in long-term studies—some active control measure is required first. Conventional herbicidal and mechanical controls are expensive and short lived (8–12 years) and ranchers rarely recover the cost of control before maintenance control treatments are needed. Also, many of the conventional control treatments are broad-spectrum and damage many nontarget plants. Biological control could offer permanent, low-cost, environmentally friendly control. The ecological principles are the same as for the more familiar and frequently used biological control of introduced weeds, as discussed in the previous section.

However, several factors interact to make biological control of native weeds more difficult than for introduced weeds. Native weeds often have numerous species of mammals, birds, and insects (including endangered species) that depend on them in varying degrees for food and shelter. They often have many close plant relatives (especially if the genus of the weed also is native) that should not be damaged by the control agents. In addition, the weed species itself usually is not native in other continents and so control agents must come from another species of the weed genus. Such control agents may not establish on the weed species itself or may not cause much damage. These factors combine to make the discovery of both highly host-specific and highly effective control agents very difficult. Nevertheless, the need for control of major native weeds of rangelands and natural areas is so desperate, the inadequacies and damage caused by broad-spectrum conventional controls so great, and the concepts of biological control so appealing that its use should be investigated (DeLoach 1995). Following is a discussion of the evaluation of and research done on several native weeds by ARS at Temple, Texas from 1974 to 1994.

Snakeweeds (Gutierrezia sarothrae *and* G. microcephala) *(Compositae).* The genus *Gutierrezia* originated in southwestern North America where sixteen species are native (Lane 1985). Twelve species also later evolved in South America, mostly in Argentina and Chile (Solbrig 1966). These were rather uncommon plants before the beginning of large-scale ranching in the Southwest; however, snakeweeds are now probably the most damaging weeds of rangelands and some Native American tribal lands in New Mexico (Huddleston and Pieper 1990), in much of western Texas (McGinty and Welch 1987), and in Arizona. They infest 142 million acres from central Mexico to Montana and from the central Great Plains to California. In some areas they are toxic to cattle, causing abortions, and they have little to no beneficial values. They, together with the also hugely abundant and damaging but nontoxic annual broomweeds (*Gutierrezia* spp. and *Amphiachyris* spp.), seriously compete with forage grasses and are unpalatable to livestock.

Some 338 species of insects attack snakeweeds in the Southwest (Foster et al. 1981, Richman and Thompson 1999), some of which sporadically cause great damage. Cordo and DeLoach (1992) listed seventy-nine species of phytophagous insects, a mite, and a pathogen from snakeweeds in Argentina. Several of these appear to be reasonable candidates for introduction into the United States, including five species of root borers, two flower and seed feeders, a leaf beetle, and two stem-galling insects. We extensively tested two of the stem borers in Argentina and in quarantine at Temple, Texas: the large root-boring weevil *Heilipodus ventralis* (Cordo et al. 1999, DeLoach and Cuda 1999) and the root-boring moth *Carmenta haematica* (Cordo et al. 1995a,b). Both cause heavy damage in Argentina that, combined with drought, kills many plants, and both appear sufficiently host specific to release. From 1988 to 1994, we released several thousand eggs, young larvae or adults of *H. ventralis,* by a variety of methods during spring, summer, or fall at sixteen locations in central and western Texas and in eastern and central New Mexico. However, we never detected reproduction or establishment in the field although rarely young larvae grew for awhile before dying. A thorough follow-up survey of all sites in September 1999 again failed to reveal any adults or larvae. We never successfully reared *C. haematica* to adults in quarantine at Temple; therefore, we never requested a release permit for it.

The reasons for this lack of establishment of *H. ventralis* are not clear. Climate could have been adverse in some (but probably not all) areas when releases were made. We believe the most likely cause was that the insects were not adapted to the North American snakeweed species (which are all different from the South American species). Females readily laid eggs in the stems in the laboratory but the larvae were unable to develop in them, probably either because of nutritional inadequacies or because of a lack of the plant chemicals that stimulate feeding. However, we did rear some adults from eggs on potted U.S. snakeweed plants in the quarantine tests, though survival to large larvae or adults was only 6 to 28% (DeLoach and Cuda 1999).

Some of the other promising insects from Argentina still might be successful if further research were done. Daniel Gandolfo, of the USDA-ARS Biological Control Laboratory at Hurlingham, Argentina conducted research on two flower-feeding insects, which might also attack annual broomweeds. This research was not followed to conclusion because of possible conflicts and damage to the large number of closely related and non-harmful native plant species in North America.

Honey Mesquite (Prosopis glandulosa) *and Velvet Mesquite* (P. velutina) (*Leguminosae*). The genus *Prosopis,* with forty-four presently recognized species, underwent its greatest speciation in southern South America (Argentina, Paraguay, and Chile) where thirty-one species occur (Burkart 1976). The genus dispersed to North America 36 to 25 million years ago (Smeins 1983). Today, nine species occur in Mexico, with four of these also in the United States. Under natural, pre-European-settlement conditions, mesquites grew mostly along the floodplains of streams, and in association with many other brush species in savannahs of South Texas (Johnson 1963). During the past 100 years, they have spread rapidly into upland areas for the reasons discussed above and now occupy some 44 million acres of grazing lands in the United States (Platt 1959). Only velvet mesquite in Arizona and Sonora and honey mesquite in other southwestern states and Mexico cause great damage to the grazing livestock industry. In large areas of northwestern Texas, nearly unbroken stands of mesquite, sometimes more than 50 miles in diameter now occupy the former continuous grasslands (personal observation).

In arid, sandy areas mesquites reduce herbage yields by 85% in dense stands (Kennedy 1970, Dahl et al. 1978) and contribute to sand dune formation and desertification (Wright 1982), especially on overgrazed rangeland in the absence of fires. Management of livestock in mesquite-infested areas is difficult because the stock cannot be found or removed from mesquite thickets. In Texas, mesquite reduced potential livestock productivity of a 130-county area by $143 million/year (Osborn and Witkowski 1974) and caused a total decrease in economic activity statewide of $200 to 500 million annually.

Mesquite also has considerable beneficial value for food, cover, and breeding sites for several species of birds and mammals. It may have beneficial value by acting as a nursery plant for shrub species that are important as browse, mast, and nesting cover for many wildlife species (Franco-Pizana et al. 1995, 1996). Livestock feed on the mature beans and in Mexico they are collected, ground, and used for livestock feed (see review by DeLoach 1985). The seeds are eaten by jackrabbits (*Lepus californicus*) and mesquite foliage constitutes 2–56% (average ca. 20%) of the diet of small mammals in various studies but these animals also significantly damaged forage grasses when abundant (reviewed by DeLoach 1985). White-tailed deer (*Odocoileus virginianus*), mule deer (*Odocoileus hemionus*), and antelope (*Antilocapra americana*) ate little of the foliage (1–9%; average approximately 6% of the diet) but ate more of the beans (12–43% of the diet) during midsummer. Mesquite is an important food for Gambel's quail (*Lophortyx gambelii*) (10–25% of the diet) but other birds eat little or none (Martin et al. 1951). Mesquite is host to many species of insects, which sometimes reach large populations. These are fed on by several species of insectivorous birds and mammals, but this is little documented. However, more recent reports indicate high usage of mesquite by some bird species for nesting at some locations, such as by the scissor-tailed flycatcher (*Muscivora forfic*) at one location in South Texas (Nolte and Fulbright 1996), but this bird nests in a wide variety of trees in other areas. Screwbean mesquite (*P. pubescens*) has great value for wildlife in riparian areas. Mesquite also has a great value as an ornamental shade tree (DeLoach unpublished data), for soil nitrogen fixation (Johnson and Mayeux 1990), and a lesser value for barbecue wood, crafts, honey production, etc.

Ward et al. (1977) reported 657 species of phytophagous insects from mesquite in the United States and Mexico. Cordo and DeLoach (1987) reported that 393 species of insects and a mite attacked mesquites in southern South America, 199 of which were new records collected by them. They estimated that seventy-seven species appeared to have potential for biological control, with thirty-eight species considered rather promising; of these, thirteen attacked seeds, two buds, twelve foliage, and eleven limbs or trunks. A few of these have been introduced into South Africa and Australia for biological control, where they are causing substantial damage to introduced mesquites (van Klinken and Heard 1998; Impson et al. 1999; R. D. van Klinken, T. H. Heard, and R. Zonnerveld 2000. CSIRO Entomology, Indooroopilly, Brisbane, Queensland, Australia, unpublished report).

The most promising method of biological control of mesquite in the southwestern United States probably would be to introduce pod and seed-feeding insects from Argentina. If these were effective, the potential of mesquite to re-infest areas controlled by other methods would be reduced, and little harm would be inflicted to its beneficial values. Seed-feeding bruchid beetles introduced into South Africa from the United States have reduced seed production there by up to 49% in unfenced areas and to 92% in areas fenced to exclude livestock (Impson et al. 1999); a defoliating moth introduced into Australia from Argentina is beginning to provide control there (van Klinken and Heard 2000). Although mesquite is very damaging to the ranching industry and its enormous invasion of previous grasslands has drastically changed the natural ecosystem, we also recognize the numerous ecological, aesthetic, and economic benefits of mesquite. Also, public opinion in the United States is increasingly opposed to biological control of any native plant, especially of a dominant species such as mesquite. Even though the large number of promising control insects in Argentina and Paraguay indicate that mesquite likely could be substantially controlled (Cordo and De-Loach 1987), at present we do not believe that information reviewed by DeLoach (1985) is sufficient to resolve the conflicts of interest in favor of classical biological control. No mesquite insects have been introduced into North America and no plans have been made to do so.

Creosotebush (Larrea tridentata) *(Zygophyllaceae).* The genus *Larrea* originated in semiarid areas of western Argentina where four species occur. The ancestor of our only species dispersed to southwestern North America, probably through seeds carried by migrating birds. Pollen records from packrat middens indicate that it arrived approximately 14,000 years ago, then rapidly spread across the Chihuahuan, Sonoran, and Mojave deserts. Creosotebush is in the same family (*Zygophyllaceae*) with puncturevine, caltrops, and African rue, many of which are poisonous weeds, but some of which are native plants that should not be harmed by introduced control agents (reviewed by Mabry et al. 1977, Campos-Lopez et al. 1979, DeLoach 1979).

The area infested by cresotebush has increased greatly in recent years, especially during periods of drought. It occupies approximately 47 million acres in the drier deserts of the southwestern United States and northern Mexico (Platt 1959). Earlier observations reported it mostly on the steeper slopes but it now occupies lowlands also. Plants often grow uniformly spaced a few yards apart. Its lateral roots remove soil moisture between the plants which then, especially with overgrazing, eliminates most forage plants, leaving bare soil. Creosotebush has potential for production of fungicides, antioxidants, and other chemicals (though pilot development in Mexico was not economical), and for soil stabilization in arid areas severely overgrazed (Campos-Lopez et al. 1979).

Paul Boldt and Tom Robbins (unpublished data, USDA-ARS, Temple, Texas) found 106 species of phytophagous insects on creosotebush in the southwestern United States and northern Mexico. About 110 insect species are known to feed and develop on *Larrea* in Argentina (Cordo and DeLoach 1993). Several of these appear to be promising biocontrol agents, including scale insects and some walkingstick-like insects in the genus *Astroma*. The latter were tested by Daniel Gandolfo at the USDA-ARS laboratory in Hurlingham, Argentina and by Paul Boldt at Temple, Texas (unpublished data). However, the conflicts of interest between the harmful and beneficial values of creosotebush have not been resolved and so approval of the project or for release of the insects was not requested from the USDA/APHIS Technical Advisory Group on Biological Control of Weeds (TAG).

Willow Baccharis (Baccharis neglecta) *(Compositae).* Willow baccharis is a weed of only modest importance in Central to South Texas. It often infests abandoned cultivated fields converted to grazing and may form light to dense stands (see review by Boldt 1989). Some twenty-four species are native in the Southwest, some extending to the Atlantic. It has little beneficial values. The insects attacking several species have been surveyed by Boldt and Robbins (1987), who reported ca. 50 and by Palmer (1987) who reported 100 species of foliage and sap-sucking insects on willow baccharis.

The site of origin of the genus is South America, where more than 400 species are native, with a center of distribution in Brazil but with several species extending into northern Argentina. Surveys for natural enemies were conducted in Brazil and the United States in the 1970s and 1980s by Australian scientists, who then introduced several insects into Australia, some of which are giving partial control of the exotic and invasive *Baccharis halimifolia* (McFadyen 1985). This research indicated that control in Texas possibly could be obtained quickly and easily by using the insects already developed in Australia. Therefore, we tested two of these insects at Temple, a leaf beetle *Stolas fuscata* from Argentina, and a cerambycid stem borer *Megacyllene mellyi* from Brazil. Both were specific to the genus *Baccharis* but attacked seepwillow (*B. salicifolia*) in quarantine to a greater extent than it attacked willow baccharis; since seepwillow is not a pest and has value for wildlife, these insects were not released. We also introduced a gall midge, *Rhopalomyia californica* from *B. pilularis* in California but it did not establish. Given the large number of insects on *Baccharis* in South America, biocontrol of willow baccharis in Texas would appear to have a good chance of success but would require a large effort in exploration and testing to find a control agent sufficiently host specific and effective.

Whitebrush (Aloysia gratissima) *(Verbenaceae).* Whitebrush is a rather minor weed of importance mostly in rangelands in central and western Texas, southern New Mexico, and northern Mexico. It forms thickets that reduce forage production and interfere with livestock movement but extensive, dense stands are not common. The genus originated in southern South

America where about twenty-one species are recognized, mostly from northern Argentina and southern Brazil to Peru. Seven species occur in Mexico, two of these also in the United States. *A. grattisima* is native in both North and South America. In the United States, whitebrush is of little benefit to wildlife and has little economic benefit except that it produces an excellent table honey. Whitebrush can be controlled with chemical herbicides (Scifres et al. 1979) or by disking (Bozzo et al. 1992). Few insects develop on it in the United States (reviewed by Cordo and DeLoach 1995). We found eighty-two insect species and four plant pathogens on whitebrush in Argentina, Paraguay, and southern Brazil during 6 years of surveying, in addition to the thirty-six species previously reported. A stem-boring buprestid beetle, a large crown-boring cerambycid beetle, a scale insect, a bark-feeding moth larva, a twig-girdling cerambycid and a rust fungus appeared to have possible value as biological control agents (Cordo and DeLoach 1995). None of these natural enemies have been tested as control agents and we have no plans for introducing them into the United States.

Bitterweed (Hymenoxys odorata) *and Pingue* (H. richardsonii) *(Compositae).* The winter annual bitterweed is a serious pest in the Edwards Plateau of Texas and in northern Mexico and the perennial pingue is a pest in New Mexico, Arizona, and Colorado. Both are poisonous to sheep. During the drought of the 1930s more than half of many flocks died in Texas and great losses occurred again during the drought of the 1950s. The genus *Hymenoxys* originated in southwestern North America where twenty-four species are native but four different annual species are native in southern South America (Sanderson 1975). *Hymenoxys* has little to no economic or wildlife benefit. Paul Boldt and Tom Robbins (unpublished data) reported thirty-one species of mostly polyphagous insects on *H. odorata* in western Texas. In Argentina, we found a few insect species that could have potential for biological control; most notable were an unidentified fly whose larvae feed in the petioles and two species of moths whose larvae feed in the crown and roots.

Tarbush (Flourensia cernua) *(Compositae).* Tarbush often grows in similar areas with creosotebush, but usually in the lower areas with more moisture and heavier soils. The genus contains thirty-one species of desert shrubs restricted to the Western Hemisphere, thirteen species in southwestern North America, and eighteen in South America (mostly in Argentina and Peru) (Dillon 1976). Richerson and Boldt (1995) found eighty-eight species of phytophagous insects on tarbush in the southwestern United States and northern Mexico, but none caused much damage. In rather limited exploration in the low mountains from central to northern Argentina, H. A. Cordo and C. J. DeLoach found rather numerous lepidopterous and large cerambycid larvae boring in the crowns and stems as well as weevils that feed on the foliage.

Cactus: Pricklypear, Cholla, and Tasajillo (Opuntia *spp.*) *(Cactaceae).* The genus *Opuntia*, with 187 species, is native only in the Western Hemisphere.

In subgenus *Opuntia* (pricklypear), forty-eight species are native in the United States, twenty-three in South America, and thirty-one in Brazil and on islands (Benson 1982). Several species are rare, threatened, or endangered. Some species of pricklypear have increased greatly in density on rangelands in recent years through the spread of seed by livestock and wildlife, brush control by chaining, and other mechanical methods that spread the detached pads, and other factors.

Pricklypear causes great damage to the livestock industry in the southwestern United States and northern Mexico. These cacti infest 77 million acres in the United States (Platt 1959), with half of this in Texas. Pricklypear spines and glochids cause great damage to the mouth, tongue, throat, and stomach of livestock, especially of cattle and sheep (Migaki et al. 1969, Merrill et al. 1980, Ueckert 1993) and even in wildlife (elk; *Cervus canadensis*) (R. N. Ueckert and J. Reagor, personal communication), and the hard seeds cause rumen impaction. Affected animals often are unable to eat, lose weight, and sometimes die. Dense stands of pricklypear reduce forage production available for livestock (Bement 1968, Price et al. 1985), and interfere with handling and movement of livestock (Dameron and Smith 1939).

Pricklypear has considerable beneficial value for wildlife; forty-four species utilize it and it is a major part of the diets of the javelina (*Dicotyles tajacu*), antelope ground squirrels (*Ammospermophilus interpres*), and white-throated wood rats (*Neotoma mexicana*) (Martin et al. 1951). Pricklypears are cultivated in Mexico and conserved in Texas for emergency drought feed for cattle (González 1971), the fruits and young pads are used as human food, and they are widely planted as ornamentals (Bailey and Bailey 1976).

Large numbers of insects have evolved with these plants, most of which are host specific to *Opuntia* or at least to the Cactaceae, because of its very different physiology and ecology. Several of these have been introduced as biological control agents from the United States, Mexico, and Argentina for control of various pricklypear species that have been introduced into other areas of the world; these projects have produced substantial to complete control in India, Sri Lanka, Australia (Dodd 1940), Hawaii, South Africa (Moran and Zimmermann 1991), and on several oceanic islands (Julien and Griffiths 1999) as discussed by Darrell Ueckert in Chapter 9 (*this book*). Since these projects have been highly successful, and pricklypear is very damaging in the southwestern United States, livestock producers often inquire about biological control of cacti in the United States.

Biological control of pricklypear in Australia and South Africa is perfectly acceptable because these countries have no native species. However, both environmental and economic considerations would make pricklypear biological control in the United States extremely risky, although a reduction in density of the overabundant species would be beneficial to agriculture and not harmful to the environment. Numerous insects in South America could be useful for control, and some, especially the famous Argentine moth, *Cactoblastis cactorum,* could be highly effective. However, because of the many closely related *Opuntia* species in southwestern North America, these insects would almost certainly attack nontarget species here, probably including some endangered species, and could do great damage to them. An extremely highly host-specific natural enemy would be required to control the pest species and not damage the nontarget species. This does not seem possible because the North American pest species of *Opuntia* are all different from the South American species; the natural enemies in South America then would occur on different species and by definition would not be species specific. Attack by introduced natural enemies on nontarget species in other plant families would be highly unlikely and has not occurred. Biological control by augmenting the effectiveness of some of the few known native plant pathogens could be safe and effective in the United States, but augmentation of native insects is probably too expensive.

Discussion

From the point of view of biological control, we may divide weeds into two major categories: introduced and exotic. Both types may become highly invasive, though from different causes, and cause great damage in rangelands and sometimes also in natural areas. Here, we review research on biological control of eight native and six introduced weeds of southwestern rangelands, where control has been or is being attempted or considered by the approach of introducing natural enemies (insects, or potentially also plant pathogens) from ecologically isolated regions (other continents). In the Southwest, most of the major weeds are native, woody plants, whereas in the northern areas of the West, most major weeds are exotic, invasive herbaceous plants (Platt 1959). As pointed out by Darrell Ueckert (see Chapter 9, *this book*), biological control of exotic weeds by introducing host-specific natural enemies that provide control in their homeland (the "classical" approach) has been widely used and often highly successful worldwide and in North America and Hawaii for more than 100 years now (Julien and Griffiths 1999). In over 350 releases of exotics worldwide for weed biocontrol, only eight cases are known where the insect has caused some minor damage to a nonhost/nontarget plant. None of these occurrences resulted in any economic or serious environmental harm, and the majority of these were predicted during host-range testing. This topic will be discussed further in Chapter 11 (*this book*).

Research by our team at Temple, Texas since 1974 to control native weeds by introducing natural enemies (which we call the "neoclassical" approach) from other continents is the first attempt worldwide for biological control of native weeds in a continental area. Two earlier projects were highly successful against native pricklypear cacti on two small islands, St. Kitts in the Caribbean (Bennett 1971) and Santa Cruz off the coast of California (Goeden and Ricker 1981). Native and exotic plants become invasive and dominate ecosystems (become weedy) for different reasons: exotics primarily because they were introduced without the natural enemies that suppressed their population increase in their homeland; and natives primarily because of human or management influences in the local ecosystem (DeLoach 1995). Of course, both exotic and native plants are influenced by human modifications, such as overgrazing, suppression of fires, and lowered water tables. Also, the dramatic 33% increase in atmospheric CO_2 during the past 150 years gives woody and herbaceous plants (C_3 metabolic carbon pathway) a strong competitive advantage over warm-season grasses (C_4 plants) (Polley et al. 1992).

The philosophy and methodology of biological control also is different for exotic and native weeds. Natural enemies of exotic weeds normally are collected from the weed species itself in its homeland; therefore, they are sure to attack the weed and highly specific natural enemies often can be found that attack only the weed species. Natural enemies of native weeds normally must be selected from a different plant species but of the same weed genus, because the weed species itself usually is not native in two different continents, though the genus may be native in both regions. These natural enemies are not restricted to only the weed species, but may (or may not) also attack other closely related plant species. If such nontarget attack does not occur or is minimal, and if the nontarget plants do not have great ecological or economic value, then the use of such natural enemies may be acceptable in order to control a weed highly damaging both to agriculture and the ecosystem that has no other acceptable and efficient method of control.

Our review indicates that several native southwestern rangeland weeds have potential for biological control, although we have not yet been successful with any of them. These weed genera have disjunct distributions, with native species in both North and South America, and with damaging natural enemies in South America that do not occur in North America. However, both logic and our experience indicate that controlling native weeds is more difficult than controlling exotics. The native weeds whose genus evolved in North America are likely to have many close relatives, requiring highly host-specific natural enemies. The exotic natural enemies coming from a different plant species may not damage the target weed, and beneficial values of native weeds, especially for wildlife, are likely to be greater than for exotic weeds, which arguably are never essential for native wildlife.

On the other hand, efforts to control exotic weeds seem destined to be highly successful. Several exotic weeds for which biological controls have been developed in other areas of the United States have, or are now, invading the Southwest, such as puncturevine, musk thistle, leafy spurge, yellow starthistle, and others. In these cases, researchers of our team at Temple and at New Mexico State University and Texas A&M University have introduced natural enemies from California or Montana that are rapidly providing control. The original research on these and other weeds was done by USDA-ARS scientists either at Temple or at Albany, California or by Canadian entomologists and their overseas cooperators. The recent explosive dispersal and effectiveness of the field bindweed mite illustrates the sometimes serendipitous nature of biological control research. The extremely complex ecological interactions between salt cedar, native plant communities, and the abiotic environment at the lower trophic level, and between salt cedar and native wildlife communities (including endangered species) at the higher trophic level, illustrate the degree of insight, revision of theory, and interaction between different schools of thought and between different organizations and agencies necessary to resolve conflicts of interest and to develop an effective control program.

We actually introduced and released an Argentine insect to control snakeweeds, but it did not establish in the field. We plan no further research on biocontrol of native weeds. In a way, this is regrettable because some possibilities for success exist. In the future, changes in our national goals or our increasing human population needs may dictate some population suppression of some out-of-control native plants. If so, our research will provide guidelines for implementing this.

Literature Cited

Andres, L. A., and R. D. Goeden. 1995. Puncturevine. Pages 318–21 *in* J. R. Nechols, L. A. Andres, J. W. Beardsley, R. D. Goeden, and C. G. Jackson, editors. Biological control in the western United States. Accomplishments and benefits of Regional Research Project W-84, 1964–1989. University of California, Division of Agriculture and Natural Resources Publication 3361.

———, and N. E. Rees. 1995. Musk thistle *Carduus nutans* L. Asteraceae. Pages 248–51 *in* J. R. Nechols, L. A. Andres, J. W. Beardsley, R. D. Goeden, and C. G. Jackson, editors. Biological control in the western United States. Accomplishments and benefits of Regional Research Project W-84, 1964–1989. University of California, Division of Agriculture and Natural Resources Publication 3361.

Bailey, L. H., and E. Z. Bailey. 1976. Hortus third: a concise dictionary of plants cultivated in the United States and Canada. MacMillan Publishing Co., Inc., New York.

Baum, B. R. 1978. The genus *Tamarix*. Israel Academy of Sciences and Humanities, Jerusalem.

Bement, R. E. 1968. Plains pricklypear: relation to grazing intensity and blue grama yield on central great plains. Journal of Range Management 21:83–86.

Bennett, F. D. 1971. Some recent successes in the field of biological control in the West Indies. Anales el Congresso Latinoamericano de Entomologia 14:369–73.

Benson, L. 1982. The cacti of the United States and Canada. Stanford University Press, California.

Boldt, P. E. 1989. *Baccharis* (Asteraceae), a review of its taxonomy, phytochemistry, ecology, economic status, natural enemies and the potential for its biological control in the United States. USDA Agricultural Research Service MP 1674.

———, and T. O. Robbins. 1987. Phytophagous and pollinating insect fauna of *Baccharis neglecta* (Compositae) in Texas. Environmental Entomology 16:887–95.

Bozzo, J. A., S. L. Beasom, and T. E. Fulbright. 1992. Vegetation responses to 2 brush management practices in South Texas. Journal of Range Management 45:170–75.

Buckingham, G. R. 1994. Biological control of aquatic weeds. Pages 413–80 *in* D. Rosen, F. D. Bennett, and J. L. Capinera, editors. Pest management in the subtropics: biological control—a Florida perspective. Intercept, Ltd., Andover, Hampshire, U.K.

Burkart, A. 1976. A monograph of the genus *Prosopis* (Leguminosae subfamily Mimosoideae). Journal of the Arnold Arboretum 57:217–525.

Campos-Lopez, E., T. J. Mabry, and S. F. Tavison, editors. 1979. Serie el Desierto. Volume 2. Larrea. Centro de Investigación en Química Aplicada, Saltillo, Coahuila, Mexico.

Cordo, H. A., and C. J. DeLoach. 1987. Insects that attack mesquite (*Prosopis* spp.)

in Argentina and Paraguay: their possible use for biological control in the United States. USDA Agricultural Research Service ARS-62.

———, and ———. 1992. Occurrence of snakeweeds (*Gutierrezia:* Compositae) and their natural enemies in Argentina: implications for biological control in the United States. Biological Control 2:143–58.

———, and ———. 1993. Phytophagous insects that attack *Larrea* spp. (Zygophyllaceae) in Argentina and their potential for biocontrol of creosotebush (*L. tridentata*) in North America. Biological Control 3:6–16.

———, and ———. 1995. Natural enemies of the rangeland weed whitebrush (*Aloysia gratissima:* Verbenaceae) in South America: potential for biological control in the United States. Biological Control 5:218–30.

———, ———, and R. Ferrer. 1995*a.* Host range of the Argentine root borer *Carmenta haematica* (Ureta) (Lepidoptera: Sesiidae), a potential biocontrol agent for snakeweeds (*Gutierrezia* spp.) in the United States. Biological Control 5:1–10.

———, ———, ———, and J. Briano. 1995*b.* Bionomics of *Carmenta haematica* (Ureta) (Lepidoptera: Sesiidae) which attacks snakeweeds (*Gutierrezia* spp.) in Argentina. Biological Control 5:11–24.

———, ———, and D. H. Habeck. 1999. Biology of *Heilipodus ventralis* (Coleoptera: Curculionidae), an Argentine weevil for biological control of snakeweeds (*Gutierrezia* spp.) in the United States. Biological Control 15:210–27.

Crins, W. L. 1989. The Tamaricaceae in the southeastern United States. Journal of the Arnold Arboretum 70:403–25.

Dahl, B. E., R. E. Sosebee, J. P. Goen, and C. S. Brumley. 1978. Will mesquite control with 2,4,5-T enhance grass production? Journal of Range Management 31:129–31.

Dameron, W. H., and H. P. Smith. 1939. Pricklypear eradication and control. Texas Agricultural Experiment Station Bulletin 575.

DeLoach, C. J. 1979. Possibilities for biological control of *Larrea.* Pages 127–37 *in* E. Campos-Lopez, T. J. Mabry, and S. F. Tavison, editors. Serie el Desierto. Volume 2. Larrea. Centro de Investigación en Química Aplicada, Saltillo, Coahuila, Mexico.

———. 1981. Prognosis for biological control of weeds of southwestern U.S. rangelands. Proceedings of the International Symposium on Biological Control of Weeds 5:175–99.

———. 1985. Conflicts of interest over beneficial and undesirable aspects of mesquite (*Prosopis* spp.) in the United States as related to biological control. Proceedings of the International Symposium on Biological Control of Weeds 6:301–40.

———. 1989. Prospects for biological control of saltcedar (*Tamarix* spp.) in riparian habitats of the southwestern United States. Proceedings of the International Symposium on Biological Control of Weeds 7:307–14.

———. 1991. Past successes and current prospects in biological control of weeds in the United States and Canada. Natural Areas Journal 11:129–42.

———. 1995. Progress and problems in introductory biological control of native weeds in the U.S. Proceedings of the International Symposium on Biological Control of Weeds 8:111–12.

———. 1997. Biological control of weeds in the United States and Canada. Pages 172–205 *in* J. O. Luken and J. W. Thieret, editors. Assessment and management of plant invasions. Springer-Verlag, New York.

———, P. E. Boldt, H. A. Cordo, H. B. Johnson, and J. P. Cuda. 1986. Weeds common to Mexican and U.S. rangelands: proposals for biological control and ecological studies. Pages 49–68 *in* D. R. Patton, C. E. Gonzales V., A. L. Medina, L. A. Segura T., and R. H. Hamre, technical coordinators. Management and utilization of arid land plants: symposium proceedings. U.S. Forest Service General Technical Report RM-135.

———, R. I. Carruthers, J. E. Lovich, T. L. Dudley, and S. D. Smith. 2000. Ecological interactions in the biological control of saltcedar (*Tamarix* spp.) in the United States: toward a new understanding. Proceedings of the International Symposium on Biological Control of Weeds 10:819–73.

———, and J. P. Cuda. 1999. Host specificity of the Argentine root-boring weevil, *Heilipodus ventralis* (Coleoptera: Curculionidae), a potential biocontrol agent for snakeweeds (*Gutierrezia:* Asteraceae) in western North American rangelands—U.S. Quarantine Tests. Biological Control 15:185–209.

———, D. Gerling, L. Fornasari, R. Sobhian, S. Myartseva, I. D. Mityaev, Q. G. Lu, J. L. Tracy, R. Wang, J. F. Wang, A. Kirk, R. W. Pemberton, V. Chikatunov, R. V. Jashenko, J. E. Johnson, H. Zheng, S. L. Jiang, M. T. Liu, A. P. Liu, and J. Cisneroz. 1996. Biological control programme against saltcedar (*Tamarix* spp.) in the United States of America: progress and problems. Proceedings of the International Symposium on Biological Control of Weeds 9:53–60.

———, P. A. Lewis, J. C. Herr, R. I. Carruthers, J. L. Tracy, and J. Johnson. 2003. Host specificity of the leaf beetle, *Diorhabda elongata deserticola* (Coleoptera: Chrysomelidae) from Asia, a biological control agent for saltcedars (*Tamarix:* Tamaricaceae) in the Western United States. Biological Control 27:117–47.

Dillon, M. 1976. Systematic study of the genus *Flourensia* (Asteraceae-Heliantheae). Thesis, University of Texas, Austin.

Dodd, A. P. 1940. The biological campaign against prickly-pear. Commonwealth Prickly Pear Board, Brisbane, Queensland.

Foster, D. E., D. N. Ueckert, and C. J. DeLoach. 1981. Insects associated with broom snakeweed (*Xanthocephalum sarothrae*) and threadleaf snakeweed (*Xanthocephalum microcephala*) in West Texas and eastern New Mexico. Journal of Range Management 34:446–54.

Franco-Pizana, J. G., T. E. Fulbright, and D. T. Gardiner. 1995. Spatial relationships between shrubs and *Prosopis glandulosa* canopies. Journal of Vegetation Science 6:73–78.

———, ———, ———, and A. R. Tipton. 1996. Shrub emergence and seedling growth in microenvironments created by *Prosopis glandulosa.* Journal of Vegetation Science 7:257–60.

Goeden, R. D., and D. W. Ricker. 1981. Santa Cruz Island—revisited. Sequential photography records the causation, rates of progress, and lasting benefits of successful biological weed control. Proceedings of the International Symposium on Biological Control of Weeds 5:355–65.

González, M. H. 1971. Manipulating shrub-grass plant communities in arid zones for increased animal production. Pages 429–34 *in* C. M. McKell, J. P. Blaisdell, and J. R. Goodin, editors. Wildland shrubs—their biology and utilization. U.S. Forest Service General Technical Report INT-1.

Huddleston, E. W., and R. D. Pieper. 1990. Snakeweed: problems and perspectives. Symposium proceedings. New Mexico State University, Agricultural Experiment Station Bulletin 751.

Impson, F. A. C., V. C. Moran, and J. H. Hoffmann. 1999. A review of the effectiveness of seed-feeding bruchid beetles in the biological control of mesquite, *Prosopis* species (Fabaceae), in South Africa. Pages 81–88 *in* T. Olckers and

M. P. Hill, editors. Biological control of weeds in South Africa (1990–1998). African Entomology Memoir No. 1, Entomological Society of Southern Africa, Johannesburg.

Johnson, H. B., and H. S. Mayeux, Jr. 1990. *Prosopis glandulosa* and the nitrogen balance of rangelands: extent and occurrence of nodulation. Oecologia 84:176–85.

Johnson, M. C. 1963. Past and present grasslands of southern Texas and northeastern Mexico. Ecology 44:456–66.

Julien, M. H., and M. W. Griffiths, editors. 1999. Biological control of weeds: a world catalogue of agents and their target weeds. Fourth edition. CABI Publishing, Wallingford, United Kingdom.

Kelleher, J. S., and M. A. Hulme, editors. 1984. Biological control programmes against insects and weeds in Canada 1969–1980. Commonwealth Agriculture Bureaux, Farnham Royal, Slough, England.

Kennedy, R. P. 1970. Texas brush problems and rangeland productivity: an economic evaluation of the Rolling Plains Resource Area. Dissertation, Texas A&M University, College Station.

Kok, L. T., and W. W. Surles. 1975. Successful biocontrol of musk thistle by an introduced weevil, *Rhinocyllus conicus.* Environmental Entomology 4:1025–27.

Kovalev, O. V. 1995. Coevolution of the tamarisks (Tamaricaceae) and pest arthropods (Insecta; Arachnida: Acarina) with special reference to biological control prospects. Proceedings of Zoological Institute, Russian Academy of Sciences, St. Petersburg, Russia. Volume 29. Pensoft Publishers, Moscow, Russia.

Lane, M. A. 1985. Taxonomy of *Gutierrezia* (Compositae: Astereae) in North America. Systematic Botany 10:7–28.

Lewis, P. A., C. J. DeLoach, J. C. Herr, T. L. Dudley, and R. I. Carruthers. 2003. Assessment of risk to native *Frankenia* shrubs from the Asian leaf beetle, *Diorhabda elongata deserticola* (Coleoptera: Chrysomelidae), introduced for biological control of saltcedars (*Tamarix* spp.) in the western United States. Biological Control 27:148–166.

Mabry, T. J., J. H. Hunziker, and D. R. DiFeo, Jr. 1977. Creosote bush: biology, and chemistry of *Larrea* in New World deserts. US/IBP Synthesis Series 1–6. Dowden, Hutchinson and Ross, Stroundsburg, Pennsylvania.

Martin, A. C., H. S. Zim, and A. L. Nelson. 1951. American wildlife & plants: a guide to wildlife food habits. Dover Publications, Inc., New York.

McEvoy, P. B., and E. M. Coombs. 2000. Why things bite back: unintended consequences of biological weed control. Pages 167–94 *in* P. A. Follett and J. J. Duan, editors. Nontarget effects of biological control. Kluwer Academic, Boston, Mass.

McFadyen, P. I. 1985. Introduction of the gall fly *Rhopalomyia californica* from the U.S.A. into Australia for the control of the weed *Baccharis halimifolia.* Proceedings of the International Symposium on Biological Control of Weeds 6:779–87.

McGinty, A., and T. G. Welch. 1987. Perennial broomweed and Texas ranching. Rangelands 9:246–49.

Merrill, L. B., C. A. Taylor, Jr., R. Dusek, and C. W. Livingston. 1980. Sheep losses from range with heavy pricklypear infestation. Page 91 *in* D. N. Ueckert and J. E. Huston, editors. Rangeland resources research. Texas Agricultural Experiment Station Consolidated Progress Report 3665.

Migaki, G., L. E. Hinson, G. D. Imes, Jr., and F. M. Garner. 1969. Cactus spines in tongues of slaughtered cattle. Journal of the American Veterinary Medical Association 155:1489–92.

Moran, V. C., and H. G. Zimmermann. 1991. Biological control of cactus weeds of minor importance in South Africa. Agriculture, Ecosystems and Environment 37:37–55.

Nechols, J. R., L. A. Andres, J .W. Beardsley, R. D. Goeden, C. G. Jackson, editors. 1995. Biological control in the western United States. Accomplishments and benefits of Regional Research Project W-84, 1964–1989. University of California, Division of Agriculture and Natural Resources Publication 3361.

Nolte, K. R., and T. E. Fulbright. 1996. Nesting ecology of scissor-tailed flycatchers in South Texas. Wilson Bulletin 108:302–16.

Osborne, J. E., and G. V. Witkowski. 1974. Economic impact of brush encroachment in Texas. Southern Journal of Agricultural Economics 6:95–100.

Palmer, W. A. 1987. The phytophagous insect fauna associated with *Baccharis halimifolia* L. and *B. neglecta* Britt. in Texas, Louisiana, and Northern Mexico. Proceedings of the Entomological Society of Washington 89:185–99.

Pemberton, R. W. 1980. The impact of the feeding of *Coleophora parthenica* Meyrick (Lep. Coleophoridae) on the tissues, physiology, and reproduction of its host *Salsola australis* R.B. (Chenopodiaceae). Dissertation, University of California, Berkeley.

———. 1995. Leafy spurge. Pages 289–95 *in* J. R. Nechols, L. A. Andres, J. W. Beardsley, R. D. Goeden, and C. G. Jackson, editors. Biological control in the western United States. Accomplishments and benefits of Regional Research Project W-84, 1964–1989. University of California, Division of Agriculture and Natural Resources Publication 3361.

Peschken, D. P., and A. S. McClay. 1995. Picking the target: a revision of McClay's scoring system to determine the suitability of a weed for classical biological control. Proceedings of the International Symposium on Biological Control of Weeds 8:137–43.

Platt, K. B. 1959. Plant control—some possibilities and limitations. II. Vital statistics of range management. Journal of Range Management 12:194–200.

Polley, H. W., H. B. Johnson, and H. S. Mayeux. 1992. Carbon dioxide and water fluxes of C_3 annuals and C_4 perennials at subambient CO_2 concentrations. Functional Ecology 6:693–703.

Price, D. L., R. K. Heitschmidt, S. A. Dowhower, and J. R. Frasure. 1985. Rangeland vegetation response following control of brownspine pricklypear (*Opuntia phaeacantha*) with herbicides. Weed Science 33:640–43.

Rees, N. E. 1977. Impact of *Rhinocyllus conicus* on thistles in southwestern Montana. Environmental Entomology 6:839–42.

———, P. C. Quimby, Jr., G. L. Piper, E. M. Coombs, C. E. Turner, N. R. Spencer, and L. V. Knutson, editors. 1996. Biological control of weeds in the West. Western Society of Weed Science, Bozeman, Montana.

Richerson, J. V., and P. E. Boldt. 1995. Phytophagous insect fauna of *Flourensia cernua* (Asteraceae: Heliantheae) in Trans-Pecos Texas and Arizona. Environmental Entomology 24:588–94.

Richman, D. B., and D. C. Thompson. 1999. Insect associations with woody snakeweeds in New Mexico, Texas and Arizona. Pages 11–27 *in* J. C. Barlow and D. J. Miller, editors. Papers from the 4th Symposium on Resources of the Chihuahuan Desert Region, United States and Mexico. El Paso, Texas, September 30–October 1, 1993. Chihuahuan Desert Research Institute, Ft. Davis, Texas.

Rosenthal, S. S. 1995. Field bindweed. Pages 286–88 *in* J. R. Nechols, L. A. Andres, J. W. Beardsley, R. D. Goeden, and C. G. Jackson, editors. Biological control in the western United States. Accomplishments and benefits of Regional Research Project W-84, 1964–1989. University of California, Division of Agriculture and Natural Resources Publication 3361.

———, and G. R. Buckingham. 1982. Natural enemies of *Convolvulus arvensis* in western Mediterranean Europe. Hilgardia 50:1–19.

Sanderson, S. C. 1975. A systematic study of North American and South American disjunct species in *Hymenoxys* (Asteraceae). Dissertation, University of Texas, Austin.

Scifres, C. J., J. L. Mutz, and W. T. Hamilton. 1979. Control of mixed brush with tebuthiuron. Journal of Range Management 32:155–58.

Smeins, F. E. 1983. Origin of the brush problem—a geological and ecological perspective of contemporary distributions. Pages 5–16 *in* K. C. McDaniel, editor. Proceedings brush management symposium. Society for Range Management, Albuquerque, New Mexico.

Solbrig, O. T. 1966. The South American species of *Gutierrezia*. Contributions Gray Herbarium 197:3–42.

Ueckert, D. N. 1993. Managing pearmouth in sheep. Ranch Magazine June:26.

van Klinken, R. D., and T. H. Heard. 2000. Estimating the fundamental host range of *Evippe* sp. #1 (Gelechiidae), a potential biocontrol agent for *Prosopis* species (Leguminosae). Biocontrol Science and Technology 10:331–42.

Ward, C. R., C. W. O'Brien, L. B. O'Brien, D. E. Foster, and E. W. Huddleston. 1977. Annotated checklist of New World insects associated with *Prosopis* (mesquite). USDA, Agricultural Research Service Technical Bulletin. 1557:115.

Wright, R. A. 1982. Aspects of desertification in *Prosopis* dunelands of southern New Mexico, U.S.A. Journal of Arid Environments 5:277–84.

11   The Future of Biological Management of Weeds on Rangelands
An Entomologist's Viewpoint

David C. Thompson
and
Kevin T. Gardner

The flood of exotic plants being introduced into North America may be 143 slowing due to increased education and legislation providing resources to monitor and reduce the intentional and accidental introduction of unwanted plants. However, we can expect a massive increase in invasive weed problems on rangelands as the plants introduced over the past 100 years become naturalized and begin to spread (McFadyen 1998). New exotic weeds will continue to be introduced into the United States and ultimately into southwestern rangelands. Some exotic weed problems will be unique to southwestern rangelands and others will simply spread from severely infested sites in northern and western states. In the northern half of the western United States, exotic weeds cause considerable economic damage while native weeds are generally considered to be more important than exotic weeds on most southwestern rangelands (DeLoach 1995).

Weed management on southwestern rangelands during the last couple of decades has relied primarily on the use of herbicides. Although herbicides are the best choice for many weed management programs, there are increasingly more limitations placed on their use (Lym 1998). Many of the exotic weeds that we are faced with managing today are difficult to control with conventional herbicides. Some are tolerant of repeated herbicide applications, many occur in areas where the use of chemicals is unsafe or unwelcome, and others, by today's standards, may not warrant the economic expense involved in controlling them with herbicides. Integrating biological control into the future management of many rangeland weeds will become a necessity for land managers who desire more stable, long-term, self-sustaining control.

Biological control of rangeland weeds is dependent on numerous uncertain factors, including management goals for individual properties, economics, and politics. Most of these are very dynamic and will play important roles in future weed management decisions. Recognizing this fact, the future of weed management, especially using biological control agents, is as unpredictable as the factors that govern it.

The future of biological control on rangelands will continue to emphasize the introduction of the natural enemies of weeds from their country of origin, but there will be more research on augmenting or conserving the natural enemies already in place than in the past. Biological control has experienced many successes that completely eliminated the need for other management alternatives (Julien and Griffiths 1999; see Chapter 9, *this book*). However, the majority of weed biological control programs have established insects and pathogens that negatively influence the fitness and, thus, the competitive abilities of target plants without completely controlling the weed. These many successes are often overlooked, although the agents may have played a very important role in the integrated management of the weed.

In this paper, we discuss the future of biological control as a management tool for terrestrial weeds in the southwestern United States, and some of the issues that affect this field of research.

Weed Management

When considering a weed management program, it is important to understand that no single control option will likely provide a cure-all for any given weed problem over its entire range. A variety of weed management options may be necessary where landowner goals vary. For instance, herbicides are very area specific. Herbicides allow a manager to manage a weed on a target area without influencing the neighbor's property. Conversely, biological control agents do not respect property boundaries and if released on one property will eventually spread to neighboring properties where the target weed is present. The value of a plant, whether positive or negative, often varies between neighboring properties and must be considered when a weed management plan is prescribed. The impact of a weed on the rangeland it occupies, whether economic, ecological, or aesthetic is difficult to assess, especially when more than one land manager is involved.

Weed management decisions are influenced, and often dictated, by ranch economics. Rangelands typically produce small economic yields per unit area compared to other land uses and when coupled with budget constraints, such as increased operational costs and lower market prices, weed management with what once was a profitable method may now be cost prohibitive. Such is the case with herbicidal control of many of our native weed species. Currently, the cost of herbicide treatment exceeds the revenue generated by the treatment on many rangelands (Bangsund et al. 1996). Future weed management strategies obviously will need to benefit the land manager in order to be employed. An advantage of biological control is that the associated costs are reduced the more it is applied, unlike chemical or mechanical control whose costs continue to rise with each application (DeLoach et al. 1986).

Regulations and directives regarding biological control have become more stringent in the recent past. New government administrations undoubtedly will have a bearing on the future of biological control. Continued funding for research and foreign exploration for exotic agents is imperative for the continuation of classical biological control programs. New support for basic ecological research exploring the interactions of target weeds, native plants, exotic and native biological control agents, and the local environment will be essential for the success of future projects.

Native versus Exotic Weeds

In this paper we consider native weeds to be weeds that have either evolved in North America or have been introduced in the recent past (300 years) and have naturalized in North America. Among the weeds we consider as natives are mesquite (*Prosopis* spp.), creosotebush (*Larrea tridentata*), snakeweed (*Gutierrezia* spp.), locoweed (*Astragalus* spp. and *Oxytropis* spp.), and many cacti (*Opuntia* spp.). Some of those considered exotics are leafy spurge (*Euphorbia esula*), salt cedar or tamarix (*Tamarix* spp.), musk thistle (*Carduus nutans*), and the knapweeds (*Centaurea* spp. and *Acroptilon repens*). It is important to distinguish between these groups because we feel the future of biological control will differ between native and exotic weeds.

Biological Control of Exotic Weeds

Classical biological control will continue to be the main avenue for biological control of exotic weeds. Insects and pathogens will continue to be collected from plants in the country where the exotic weed originated, carefully studied to insure host specificity and damage potential, and finally released onto target weed populations in the country it has invaded. There have been numerous successful biological control programs throughout the world (McFadyen 1998; see Chapter 9, *this book*). St. Johnswort (*Hypericum perforatum*), skeleton weed (*Chondrilla juncea*), tansy ragwort *(Senecio jacobaea)*, and musk thistle have either been completely or substantially controlled in a significant portion of their former range in the United States. The most recent success story is the biological control of leafy spurge.

Leafy spurge is one of the most important exotic weeds in the western United States and it continues to expand its range. Biological control work on leafy spurge began in the 1960s by Canadian, European, and U.S. scientists and was significantly expanded in the 1970s and 1980s (Harris 1984, Pemberton 1986). Fifteen different insect species have been tested, approved, and released for biological control of leafy spurge in the United States. Two flea beetles, *Aphthona nigriscutis* and *A. lacertosa,* have provided substantial control. Obviously, this program has taken over 20 years to have moderate success. Future programs will also take several years due to the time involved in foreign exploration, host-specificity testing, and testing of other ecological influences. On the bright side, once an agent is approved, released, and established in one state, it is rarely difficult to move the agent to other states provided that screening and host plant analysis were adequate. Many southwestern states, such as Texas and New Mexico, are at the edge of an exotic weed expansion. Leafy spurge has recently expanded into New Mexico and we have been able to take advantage of the work done on leafy spurge in the northern states. There are many successful insectaries in Montana, Wyoming, and the Dakotas, from which millions of the flea beetles have been collected and redistributed. We have transported and released hundreds of thousands of *A. nigriscutis* and *A. lacertosa* into small leafy spurge infestations in New Mexico over the past 3 years and have obtained good control in a very short time.

The development of a new classical biological control program for a given weed takes 10 to 20 scientist years (Harris 1979). In many cases potential biological control agents are rejected for one or more of a number of reasons. We, as a biological control community, continue to stress the importance of understanding the effects a biological control agent will have on its target weed as well as nontarget plants and the ecosystem as a whole.

Several other factors will also help make future biological control programs for exotic weeds successful. One is the recognition of the importance of monitoring, early detection, and rapid response to a new exotic weed infestation. One of the main reasons management of leafy spurge has been so difficult in the Great Plains is that it was established for over 100 years before it was recognized as a problem. Obviously, new small infestations are more easily managed than extensive, well-established infestations. We also have to educate land managers and the general public that biological control will not eradicate an exotic weed and that the goal of biological control should be to reduce the weed to an acceptable level. The integrated use of several methods of weed control is undoubtedly the surest approach to achieve sustainable, long-term solutions to weed problems. Biological control should become a part of any weed management plan and should be used in conjunction with chemical and mechanical control methods and fire, where these are appropriate. This is the current trend, and more emphasis and research on integrated weed management systems will be seen in the future.

Nontarget Issues in Classical Biological Control

In recent years, the use of foreign insects and plant pathogens to control insect and weed pests has been questioned and severely criticized by some. Much of this criticism is based on a fear of all invading, exotic species and on the disastrous effects produced on native flora and fauna by some of them. Indeed, several disasters have resulted from the intentional introduction of agronomic and ornamental plants (kudzu, salt cedar), or wildlife (nutria) by various specialists, or for biological control by nonbiological control specialists (mongoose, cane toad). Also, many parasitoids and predators have been introduced for control of insect pests (with many highly successful programs), but without prior host-range testing or much consideration for attack on nontarget insect species.

In contrast, biological control of weeds programs have always placed great importance in host specificity to avoid the dangers of nontarget attack on economically important agronomic crops. The early (pre-1940s) workers were excellent naturalists and observed host ranges in the field in the native areas. Later, strict protocols were developed for host-range testing, host plant lists for testing, and a wide variety of formal tests to be used were standardized. After a century of weed biological control work throughout the world there are only eight examples of damage to nontarget plants, the majority of these having been predicted by the original prerelease testing (McFadyen 1998). The decision to release was made with the knowledge that such nontarget attack would cause much less damage than the great damage caused by the invading weeds. In no case has a nontarget impact resulted in serious economic or environmental impact (Kluge 2000).

Much of the recent controversy centered on a paper by Louda et al. (1997), who reported the musk thistle control insect (*Rhinocyllus conicus*) damaging the seed heads of the native Platte thistle (*Cirsium canescens*) in Nebraska. They also speculated that the beetles could someday reach the endangered pitcher's thistle (*C. pitcheri*) in Michigan and threaten it. The authors contended that biological control practitioners had no quantitative data to document the damage caused by musk thistle prior to releasing control agents; therefore, they could not make claims of successful control. Although preliminary data would have been preferable, the enormous reduction in musk thistle and the return of valuable forage plants were obvious in before and after photographs. Consequently, statistics do not seem necessary. In the future, biological control scientists should place more emphasis on quantitative plant ecology studies to document the impacts of noxious weed infestations and the impacts of released biological control agents.

Another implication, that the released biological control insects changed their host range after release (Louda et al. 1997), also is without support. The beetle's attack on new plants does not signify a change in host range, but rather that they never before had encountered that native plant but always had the capacity to attack it. Other researchers have shown *R. conicus* to attack other nontarget *Cirsium* thistles, as predicted in the original host range tests. However, Turner et al. (1987) and Herr (2000) found that although *R. conius* attacked eleven *Cirsium* species in California, significant damage occurred on only one, and no stand reduction was observed on it. This is not to say that host shifts are impossible, but the risk appears to be very small. The criticism that weed control agents are released without proper testing or due consideration is completely without foundation. Both the protocols and the review process are very thorough, and to date, after the release of more than 350 control agents on numerous weed species in fifty-three countries, no unpredicted environmental or economic damage has ever occurred (McFadyen 1998). The probability of significant problems from releases of biological control agents in the future, therefore, seems very low.

Nevertheless, criticism of the processes of biological control has been beneficial to the discipline. It has forced even more care into the process and more careful review before releases are made. Criticisms have forced agencies making and wanting releases to conduct proper monitoring of the impact of the control agents on the target weeds, native vegetation, and if appropriate, on wildlife populations. The more extreme criticisms have unduly alarmed the public, governmental agencies, and environmental interest groups to the point of opposing all biological control projects. In fact, at the 1999 annual meeting of the Regional Project W-185: Biological Control in Pest Management Systems of Plants held in Albuquerque, New Mexico, Nancy Kaufman, Director of Region 2 of the U. S. Fish and Wildlife Service (USFWS), stated that she was philosophically opposed to the introduction of exotic insects for the biological control of weeds. When an administrator in a position as powerful as a USFWS regional director globally dismisses biological control, the future of the discipline becomes subject to political whims rather than science. Considering the very strict controls over testing and review in the present protocols, the very small risks of introducing exotic biological control agents are far outweighed by the enormous damage caused by many exotic, invasive weeds, which have no other acceptable method of control.

Biological Control of Native Weeds

The current, and most likely the future, philosophy and attitude of most scientists associated with biological control, does not support introducing nonnative agents against native plants due to the conflicts of interest between economic and ecological values (see Chapter 10, *this book*). Although native weed species such as mesquite, creosotebush, snakeweed, etc. cause considerable economic loss to the livestock industry in the Southwest, their ecological value, as well as their ornamental value in some cases, are sufficient to discourage the introduction of exotic biological control agents because of the unknown risks to ecological processes and impacts to nontarget organisms. However, many of the most economically costly native weeds are known to have many native phytophagous insects associated with them. Some of these have the potential to suppress—if not eliminate—small, localized populations of their hosts. The conservation and augmentation of these natural enemies in an Integrated Pest Management (IPM) control program may provide an economical management option in the future.

The role herbivorous insects play in restricting the distribution and abundance of native weeds is rarely studied, because the detection of their impacts on plant populations in natural communities can be difficult and complex even for those strongly dependent on a particular plant species. Insects have been shown to limit the distribution and even cause local extinctions of native plants; therefore, future research in this area is warranted. Biological control of native weeds, in the future, almost certainly will be limited to augmentation and conservation of native insects. Augmentation involves the mass rearing and release of insects already present in the ecosystem into weed populations. Because of the low economic value of many southwestern rangelands, augmentation will have limited potential over large acreages (DeLoach 1978, Cuda 1988); however, small isolated native weed infestations could possibly be managed by augmentation of natural enemies. Augmentation could be used to establish a native insect population in an area devoid of them or to build populations up to damaging levels. Conservation includes managing ecosystems to increase the population of the biological control agent (Bernays 1985, Hull and Beers 1985, Newman et al. 1998). Conservation of native weed biological control agents is done through appropriate applications of other management methods or directly by managing for the control agent itself. Many insects that contribute to suppressing native weeds can be conserved through appropriate timing and application of insecticides, herbicides, mechanical control methods, prescribed fire, and livestock grazing management.

Chemical control of snakeweed is often short-lived, and not profitable to land managers. Reinfestation of treated rangeland by snakeweed is most likely due to the cyclic nature of the plant and is related to weather patterns

(Torell et al. 1989). Longevity of herbicide treatments of snakeweed is largely dependent on the amount of precipitation and the season in which it is received. Many landowners are reluctant to utilize chemical control because of the unpredictability of snakeweed reinfestation. An integrated approach using management techniques to conserve native biological control agents to suppress reinvading plants following an herbicide treatment should increase the treatment life of the herbicide application.

The grasshopper, *Hesperotettix viridis,* and the root-boring beetle, *Crossidius pulchelus,* are capable of causing significant mortality to snakeweed populations, especially when their densities are high (Richman and Huddleston 1981, Thompson et al. 1995). Broadcast herbicide treatments across entire landscapes remove these native insects' host plants and may be responsible for low population densities of snakeweed-feeding insects and small, localized populations. Herbicide treatment life may be extended by leaving strips of snakeweed untreated as refugia for its insect enemies (Turcotte 1993). By forcing these insects into the remaining strips, their feeding damage intensifies and more suppression of the weed is realized. More importantly, as new seedlings germinate in the treated area, the insects will move into the treated areas and provide extended control by eliminating some of the seedlings and suppressing others.

The treatment life of prescribed fire used for snakeweed management is also unpredictable. However, due to the discontinuity of fine fuel, fires usually leave unburned portions of the treated area as refugia for snakeweed-feeding insects. The time the burn is conducted can also be important to survival of these beneficial insects. Prescribed burns conducted in the early spring, prior to *H. viridis* egg hatch, may increase the number of the grasshoppers feeding on remaining snakeweed plants and not influence the overall population dynamics of the grasshopper (D. C. Thompson, unpublished data). Burning later in the season, after egg hatch, negatively influences the grasshopper population through direct mortality of the relatively immobile grasshoppers. Incidentally, burns conducted in the early spring (prior to egg hatch) or late fall (after eggs have been laid) may result in greater snakeweed control (McDaniel et al. 2000), than burns conducted in June and July when they cause the most damage to the grasshopper populations (McDaniel et al. 1997).

Problems encountered with proper time, rate, and cost of application, and a large soil seed reserve have also limited the use of herbicides for control of woolly locoweed (*Astragalus mollissimus*) (Ralphs and Cronin 1987, Child and Frasier 1992). McDaniel (1999) reported that woolly locoweed rarely persists in a given area more than a few years because of feeding damage inflicted by larvae of the four-lined locoweed weevil (*Cleonidius trivittatus*). Substantial locoweed mortality results from feeding by more than two weevil larvae per plant (Pomerinke et al. 1995). Therefore, conservation of the four-lined locoweed weevil in northeastern New Mexico is vitally important to the management of wooly locoweed.

Insecticide treatments for grasshopper control on rangeland can also influence beneficial insect populations. However, many treatment programs can be accomplished without deleterious effects on the beneficial insects. If insecticide treatments are applied before below-ground feeding insects, such as *C. trivittatus* larvae and *C. pulchelus* larvae, emerge from the ground as adults there appears to be no effect on the population. Many treatment programs, such as grasshopper control, occur before these beneficial insects emerge from below ground. However, grasshopper control programs will be detrimental to the snakeweed-feeding grasshopper, *H. viridis,* since its life cycle coincides with that of many pest grasshopper species. In the case of grasshopper control, species composition of the grasshopper population must be evaluated prior to treatment. Typically, spray programs have been triggered by grasshopper density alone, without regard to the grasshopper species present. It is common on snakeweed-infested rangelands for *H. viridis* to comprise the majority of the grasshopper population. Spraying with insecticides for rangeland pests is sometimes necessary, but in all cases the effect that the program will have on nontarget insects should be considered.

Many other native weeds, including mesquite, creosotebush, and cactus, have a considerable number of insects and diseases associated with them that undoubtedly exert some level of suppression. The biological control of any of these weeds may be possible in the future as our knowledge of these native insects increases and as technology to enhance their effects on their hosts is developed.

Conclusion

Understanding the influence of biotic factors on the population ecology of weed populations is vital for the development and success of effective integrated weed management strategies. The whole discipline of biological control of weeds depends on the efficiency of biotic factors to suppress or destroy weed populations. The keys to success of future efforts in the biological control of rangeland weeds are to identify the weak links in a weed's life cycle and then discover ways to exploit these weaknesses. The difficulty in importing new biological control agents will force biological control practitioners in the future to select the agents to release more judiciously —requiring increased testing before and after the agents are released.

Literature Cited

Bangsund, D. A., J. A. Leitch, and F. L. Leistritz. 1996. Economics of herbicide control of leafy spurge (*Euphorbia esula* L.). Journal of Agricultural and Resource Economics 21:381–95.

Bernays, E. A. 1985. Arthropods for weed control in IPM systems. Pages 373–91 *in* M. A. Hoy and D. C. Herzog, editors. Biological control in agricultural IPM systems. Academic Press, New York.

Child, R. D., and G. W. Frasier. 1992. ARS range research. Rangelands 14:17–27.

Cuda, J. P. 1988. Viewpoint: comments on the proposed use of native insects for biological control of snakeweeds. Rangelands 10:262–64.

DeLoach, C. J. 1978. Considerations in introducing foreign biotic agents to control native weeds of rangelands. Proceedings of the International Symposium on Biological Control of Weeds 4:39–50.

———. 1995. Progress and problems in introductory biological control of native weeds in the United States. Proceedings of the International Symposium on Biological Control of Weeds 8:111–22.

————, P. E. Boldt, H. A. Cordo, H. B. Johnson, and J. P. Cuda. 1986. Weeds common to Mexican and U.S. rangelands: proposals for biological control and ecological studies. Pages 49–68 *in* D. R. Patton, C. E. Gonzales, A. L. Medina, L. A. Segura, and R. H. Hamre, technical coordinators. Management and utilization of arid land plants: symposium proceedings. U.S. Forest Service, General Technical Report RM-135.

Harris, P. 1979. Cost of biological control of weeds by insects in Canada. Weed Science 27:242–50.

————. 1984. *Euphorbia esula-virgata* complex, leafy spurge, and *E. cyparassias* L., cypress spurge. (Euphorbiaceae). Pages 159–69 *in* J. S. Kelleher and M. A. Hulme, editors. Biological control programmes against insects and weeds in Canada 1969–1980. Commonwealth Agricultural Bureaux Farnham Royal, Slough, England.

Herr, J. C. 2000. Non-target impact of *Rhinocyllus conicus* (Coleoptera: Curculionidae) on rare native California *Cirsium* spp. thistles. Proceedings of the International Symposium on Biological Control of Weeds 10:513.

Hull, L. A., and E. H. Beers. 1985. Ecological selectivity: modifying chemical control practices to preserve natural enemies. Pages 103–22 *in* M. A. Hoy and D. C. Herzog, editors. Biological control in agricultural IPM systems. Academic Press, New York.

Julien, M. H., and M. W. Griffiths. 1999. Biological control of weeds: a world catalogue of agents and their target weeds. Fourth edition. CABI Publishing, Wallingford, United Kingdom.

Kluge, R. L. 2000. The future of biological control of weeds with insects: no more 'paranoia', no more 'honeymoon'. Proceedings of the International Symposium on Biological Control of Weeds 10:459–67.

Louda, S. M., D. Kendall, J. Connor, and D. Simberloff. 1997. Ecological effects of an insect introduced for the biological control of weeds. Science 277:1088–90.

Lym, R. G. 1998. Biology and integrated management of leafy spurge, *Euphorbia esula,* on North Dakota rangeland. Weed Technology 12:367–73.

McDaniel, K. C. 1999. How long does locoweed control last? Pages 62–63 *in* T. M. Sterling and D. C. Thompson, editors. Locoweed Research Updates and Highlights. New Mexico State University Agricultural Experiment Station Bulletin 730.

————, D. B. Carroll, and C. R. Hart. 2000. Broom snakeweed establishment following fire and herbicide treatments. Journal of Range Management 53:239–45.

————, C. R. Hart, and D. B. Carroll. 1997. Broom snakeweed control with fire on New Mexico blue grama rangeland. Journal of Range Management 50:652–59.

McFadyen, R. E. C. 1998. Biological control of weeds. Annual Review of Entomology 43:369–93.

Newman, R. M., D. C. Thompson, and D. B. Richman. 1998. Conservation strategies for the biological control of weeds. Pages 371–96 *in* P. Barbosa, editor. Conservation biological control. Academic Press, San Diego, California.

Pemberton, R. W. 1986. Native plant considerations in the biological control of leafy spurge. Proceedings of the International Symposium on Biological Control of Weeds 6:365–90.

Pomerinke, M. A., D. C. Thompson, and D. L. Clason. 1995. Bionomics of *Cleonidius trivittatus* (Coleoptera: Curculionidae): native biological control of purple locoweed (Rosales: Fabaceae). Environmental Entomology 24:1696–1702.

Ralphs, M. H., and E. H. Cronin. 1987. Locoweed seed in soil: density, longevity, germination, and viability. Weed Science 35:792–95.

Richman, D. B., and E. W. Huddleston. 1981. Root feeding by the beetle, *Crossidius pulchelus* LeConte and other insects on broom snakeweed (*Gutierrezia* spp.) in eastern and central New Mexico. Environmental Entomology 10:53–57.

Thompson, D. C., K. C. McDaniel, L. A. Torell, and D. B. Richman. 1995. Damage potential of *Hesperotettix viridis* (Orthoptera: Acrididae) on a rangeland weed, *Gutierrezia sarothrae.* Environmental Entomology 24:1315–21.

Torell, L. A, K. Williams, and K. C. McDaniel. 1989. Probability of snakeweed die-off and invasion on rangeland. Pages 71–84 *in* E. W. Huddleston and R. D. Pieper, editors. Snakeweed: problems and perspectives. New Mexico State University, Agricultural Experiment Station Bulletin 751.

Turcotte, R. M. 1993. Integrated control of broom snakeweed by strip management at two selected locations in New Mexico. Thesis, New Mexico State University, Las Cruces.

Turner, C. E., R. W. Pemberton, and S. S. Rosenthal. 1987. Host utilization of native *Cirsium* thistles (Asteraceae) by the introduced weevil *Rhinocyllus conicus* (Coleoptera: Curculionidae) in California. Environmental Entomology 16: 111–15.

12 Biological Management of Noxious Brush
A Range Scientist's Viewpoint

Charles A. Taylor, Jr.

Most species of rangeland vegetation that are considered noxious weeds and brush either limit or interfere with land management objectives. These plants may be toxic to livestock, excessive users of water, unpalatable to livestock and wildlife, or they may interfere with forage utilization and livestock handling, reduce habitat values for wildlife, or compete with desirable forage species for sunlight, nutrients, and water. A plant species may be considered noxious at one location but desirable at another because of different goals and objectives of the land manager.

Resource managers often apply one or more weed/brush management methods to achieve their goals and objectives. The four general methods for managing noxious plant species include (1) chemical, (2) cultural or mechanical, (3) fire, and (4) biological methods. The training, experience, and management skill required to implement different noxious plant management strategies vary considerably. For example, mechanical control requires basic expertise for handling heavy equipment, but high inputs of energy and capital. Chemical control requires more expertise than mechanical methods and can also be expensive. Burning has the lowest level of cultural inputs, is much less expensive than mechanical or chemical methods, but requires higher levels of expertise and a commitment to long-term management planning. Biological management of noxious plants may be the least expensive of all treatments but probably requires the greatest level of experience, expertise, management, and understanding of how animals interact with plants. Obviously, the objectives, goals, resources, and experience of the manager will determine the treatment or combination of treatments to be used. Biological methods will be discussed from a range scientist's viewpoint in this paper.

Rangeland Vegetation

Rangeland vegetation is a composite of a diverse group of plant species, usually with broad genetic variability within each species. This diversity is an asset to both the stability of the plant communities and the herbivore as it selects its diet. The diversity in plant species adds stability to the nutrient intake of herbivores by allowing them to shift their diets from species to species as seasons or growing conditions change and as the degree of utilization increases.

The native plants on rangelands have evolved under the pressure of natural selection. Those which are best adapted to survive and reproduce under existing ecological conditions occupy the range sites. Because of this environmental selection, most native range plants have low production potential compared to the production potential of improved pasture forages. The low potential productivity of many rangelands precludes the profitable application of expensive inputs to maintain forage production at levels near site potential—thus, the justification for biological vegetation management. Changing rangeland dominated by noxious plants to rangeland dominated by preferred plants is a major part of the work of rangeland managers and scientists. Managers have employed an array of mechanical implements, herbicides, and fire to reduce noxious plants and increase desirable ones. Cattle, sheep, and goats also have been used to fight the invaders and reestablish the desirables but unfortunately, we have made little progress in molding livestock into powerful range improvement tools. The primary approach used by range managers to increase the consumption of noxious plants has been to increase grazing pressure, and thus force animals to consume the target plants. Unfortunately, this strategy has the potential to damage the desirable plants as well.

Diet Selection

"Relative to its impact on plant community structure, diet selection is by far the most important aspect of foraging behavior," stated Walker (1995:352). Before domestic livestock can be used to manage noxious plants, the animals must choose to consume the target species at a damaging level. Foraging behavioral studies of domestic livestock on rangeland were conducted over 70 years ago (Cory 1927, Fraps and Cory 1940) on the Texas A&M University Research Station at Sonora. This research was followed by studies that evaluated the effectiveness of different grazing management strategies using cattle, sheep, goats, and deer. Different mixtures of livestock species were tested, and an optimal mix of herbivore species, each with a unique preference pattern. This resulted in a more complete utilization of the available vegetative complex than could be obtained using single-species grazing. With this optimal mix, ranch productivity was optimized (Merrill and Young 1954, Taylor 1985). These studies also showed that losses of livestock to poisonous plants were reduced by grazing a mixture of animals compared to single-species grazing (Merrill and Schuster 1978, Taylor and Ralphs 1992).

Esophageally cannulated cattle, sheep, goats, and deer have been used since the 1950s to quantify the relationships between available vegetation, animal preference, and diet quality (Cook and Harris 1950, Heady 1964, Kothmann 1968, Malechek and Leinweber 1972, McCollum 1972, Bryant et al. 1979, Taylor et al. 1980). These studies provided valuable insight into qualitative and quantitative mechanisms of foraging behavior. However, the classical definition of habitat quality as a function of biomass and composition of the vegetative community failed to consider the importance of distribution and seasonal characteristics of plants in determining animal foraging behavior (Senft et al. 1987, Johnson et al. 1992).

The emerging science of landscape ecology is providing tools to bridge the gap between fine-scale species studies (i.e., foraging habits of individual herbivores) and broad-scale system studies. Landscape ecology theory provides a systematic framework for exploring animal response to heterogeneous resource distribution at a variety of spatial and seasonal scales (Forman and Gordon 1986). For example, vegetation resources can be abundant but spatially, seasonally, and nutritionally heterogeneous (Schoener 1987). Preliminary evidence suggests that, for ruminant herbivores, landscape heterogeneity and patterns of resource distribution may be at least as important as absolute biomass for determining foraging response (Murden 1993).

Various modeling and geostatistical methods are currently being used to test predictions regarding herbivore foraging response in relation to patterns of vegetation distribution, landscape heterogeneity, and biomass. However, even while modeling approaches are being developed and validated (McFarland and Kothmann 1992, Teague 1996), there is a current need for some practical guidelines for biological management of vegetation for now and into the near future.

How Does Brush Defend Itself against Herbivory?

To understand how noxious brush and weeds can be biologically managed (i.e., consumed by herbivores) it is essential to understand that all plant species have chemical and/or physical characteristics that can determine their forage value. Some plants contain chemical compounds, called "phytochemicals," that have a wide range of effects on herbivores, depending on environmental factors and management practices. Most browse plants do not produce sufficient quantities of phytochemicals to provide complete protection against herbivory; however, phytochemicals occur in varying concentrations in different species of plants and within different parts of the same plant. In addition, the concentrations may vary seasonally and among various growth stages.

Two examples of phytochemicals are tannins and terpenoids, which are uncommonly high in oak (*Quercus* spp.) and juniper (*Juniperus* spp.) species, respectively. Both of these classes of chemicals reduce the digestibility and palatability of forage and, if consumed in sufficient quantities, can have negative physiological effects on the herbivore. The significance of phytochemicals in relation to biological control of noxious plants is that they present significant chemical barriers to herbivory and are present in most woody plants.

How Do Herbivores Cope with Plant Chemicals?

Even though most woody plants have phytochemicals for plant defense, most herbivores have coevolved with these plants for thousands of years and have developed unique methods for dealing with them. Animals cope with plant defense chemicals by two strategies: foraging behavior and physiological adaptation. Herbivores may learn to avoid or minimize the use of plants containing chemical defenses. They may learn to avoid the plant because of an undesired or unfamiliar taste (novel food) and become tentative in their foraging effort. Or, they may develop a conditioned flavor aversion for certain plants when their consumption is followed by negative gastrointestinal consequences (i.e., nausea or malaise). Conditioned flavor aversion learning has been demonstrated in many herbivores including insects (Bernays and Lee 1988), monogastric mammals (Garcia 1989), and ruminant mammals (Provenza 1995).

The physiological adaptation strategy herbivores use to cope with plant defense chemicals is very complex and may involve many different mechanisms. These include chemical and microbiological detoxification in the gastrointestinal tract; detoxifying enzymes in the liver; and similar enzymes in other tissues. One mechanism is the inactivation of the plant defense chemical by a chemical reaction during the digestive process. For example, tannins found in liveoak (*Quercus virginiana*) have a strong affinity for proteins produced in the saliva of deer. As deer consume liveoak, the tannins are complexed quickly with the saliva protein during the chewing process thereby rendering the compound inconsequential. This is an example of a "first line of defense" against these compounds.

Some phytochemicals can be sequestered in the ingesta, thus preventing their absorption from the gastrointestinal tract and thereby providing detoxification. For example, activated charcoal has been used to bind phytochemicals and prevent their absorption (Hayden and Comstock 1975, Poage et al. 2000). Other chemical compounds and products used to lessen the impact of phytochemicals and enhance intake of plants containing them include polyethylene glycol and monensin. Polyethylene glycol (PEG) is an inert substance which may bind up and "inactivate" plant toxins (i.e., there is the potential for PEG to bind with terpenoids). Theoretically, the PEG-terpenoid complex is too large for absorption and resilient to breakdown in the rumen, and must be, therefore excreted. Monensin has the potential of improving the nutritional plane of the animal and thereby influencing its capacity to detoxify phytochemicals.

Rumen microflora also can be manipulated to detoxify phytochemicals. For example, *Leucaena leucocephala* is a tropical leguminous shrub used for cattle, sheep, and goat forage that contains a phytochemical, mimosine, which is a potent goitrogen and can cause hypothyroidism (Hegarty et al. 1979). Control of mimosine toxicity has been achieved by dosing animals with rumen fluid containing specific bacteria, which are capable of degrading the toxin (Pratchett et al. 1991).

It is beyond the scope of this paper to review the extensive literature on the metabolism of plant phytochemicals; however, some generalizations can be made concerning their overall fate. They are absorbed in the lipid-soluble form and are excreted as water-soluble metabolites. Therefore, metabolism of plant defense chemicals involves enzymatic reactions to convert fat-soluble substances to water-soluble compounds. These metabolic processes, known as biotransformations, may either increase or decrease the toxicity of the ingested phytochemical (Cheek and Shull 1985). This process profoundly affects management of brush by biological methods. For example, goats have a greater tolerance for terpenoids, the class of phyto-chemicals found in juniper, than do other domestic livestock species (Straka 1993). This kind of knowledge is critical for the development of biological management strategies for noxious brush.

Use the Proper Species of Livestock

If a species of livestock exists that will consume the undesirable plant, then manipulating the kinds of livestock may be an easy solution to the problem. For example, an alien plant species in North America, leafy spurge (*Euphorbia esula*), has been managed effectively since the 1930s with sheep and goats (Sedivec et al. 1995). However, many ranchers with leafy spurge-infested rangelands are reluctant to use sheep and goats because adequate labor and management skills for these species are not available (Sell et al. 2000). More than 70% of the ranchers surveyed in western North Dakota felt they did not have the right equipment for sheep, and more than 40% indicated they did not have nor desire to learn the skills necessary to utilize sheep effectively (Sell et al. 2000).

Producer Associations and Cooperatives

Because of the reluctance of ranchers in North Dakota to use sheep for leafy spurge control, research and extension personnel from North Dakota State University conducted a feasibility study for a sheep cooperative for the purpose of managing leafy spurge (Sell et al. 2000). Under the cooperative, facilities, labor, equipment, and management for a 5,000-ewe flock would be pooled to enhance the economic as well as biological aspects of using sheep as a biological management tool. The authors concluded that the financial analysis of the cooperative concept did not guarantee a financial success; however, they did provide an indication of the potential that such a cooperative might have.

Cooperatives are a common activity among rancher and farmer groups, but cooperatives with the purpose of managing noxious plants is a new concept. This kind of activity could potentially increase in the future because it creates a critical mass of people with the same goals and objectives. Examples of two successful cooperatives are the Santa Barbara County Range Improvement Association in California and the Edwards Plateau Prescribed Burning Association in Texas. By pooling equipment, labor, information, training, managerial skills, etc., and providing public relations activities, associations or cooperatives could provide a much more effective means to acquire and manage a particular herbivore species than could an individual.

Biological Management of Juniper: An Example

Juniper is possibly the largest ecological and economical problem encountered by land managers in the Edwards Plateau. Juniper infestations are especially troublesome because of the geographic range and ecological impacts of these plants. Livestock production, water yield and quality, and wildlife habitats are negatively affected, and the costs of conventional control methods are prohibitively high. Juniper, once a minor component of the rangeland flora, has increased because of fire suppression, reduction in goat numbers and distribution, and possibly increases in atmospheric carbon dioxide levels. Junipers now occupy many soil types and plant communities in central and western Texas. Carrying capacity for livestock can be reduced as much as 85% in the transition from grassland to closed-canopy juniper (Dye et al. 1995, Ueckert 1997), and the carrying capacity for most wildlife decreases also (Rollins and Armstrong 1997). Much of this reduction in productivity is the result of the use or interception of precipitation by juniper trees and their litter. The lack of recharge of aquifers, resulting in cessation of seeps and springs, can result as juniper invades a site (Hester et al. 1997).

Juniper can be managed by mechanical and chemical methods, but currently these are not economically viable options for many landowners. Fire may be the most cost-effective method of managing juniper. But, safe and effective use of fire requires high levels of grazing management as well as technical training and experience in prescribed burning. Also, the fear of fire escape and liability due to fire damage and smoke is of great concern, especially as the state becomes more urbanized.

One alternative for addressing the juniper dilemma could be the proper use of goats. Normally, goats will prefer other browse species over juniper because they are more palatable and produce less aversive phytochemicals. However, a promising area of research is measuring how terpenoid production affects juniper palatability. Research at the Texas A&M University Research Station at Sonora has revealed that terpenoid concentrations in young juniper growth are lower than that for old juniper growth and that goats prefer juniper seedlings and regrowth over mature growth (Taylor et al. 2000). Goats will return regularly to utilize the same juniper trees, harvesting the young regrowth. When the tips are browsed off, regrowth sprouts from lateral and basal buds. When these observations were tested in a lab, physiological age of the leaf material was found to have influenced the amount and kind of terpenoids present.

There appears to be a threshold at which juniper leaves become significantly less palatable as the juniper foliage ages and terpenoid concentration increases. This has important management implications. If juniper can be maintained below this threshold with control methods such as fire, consumption of its foliage by goats can be increased. The integrated, sequential use of fire and goats is beneficial because fire keeps juniper foliage within reach of goats; helps maintain a higher goat:juniper ratio, which is critical for effective goating; and results in a preponderance of young juniper foliage with a low concentration of the terpenoids, which are most aversive to goats.

Another potential approach to juniper management is to increase the tolerance of goats to terpenoids. Terpenoids are known to influence forage selection by imposing high detoxification costs; i.e., increases the nutrient demands of the animal in order to neutralize terpenoids (Freeland and Janzen 1974). Because of this additional demand for nutrients, adequate nutrition is important to meet the requirements for detoxification.

A protein supplement, rather than energy, appears to be more beneficial to goats consuming juniper. Goats fed either cottonseed meal or alfalfa as a supplement consumed 40% more juniper than did goats fed a corn supplement. Goats in the control group (no supplement) consumed 30% more juniper than the corn-supplemented goats in feeding trials on the Sonora Research Station (C. A. Taylor, Jr., unpublished data).

Even though juniper intake can be increased by feeding a protein supplement, average intake of juniper by goats remains relatively low (0.8 lb/hd/ day maximum intake for an 80 lb goat). If an average 3-foot-tall juniper tree has 10 pounds of consumable foliage and an 80-pound goat consumes 0.8 lb/hd/day, then it would take the goat over 12 days to consume all of the foliage on the juniper plant. At an infestation of 200 to 300 trees per acre, it would take a very large flock of goats to have a major impact on a stand of juniper. Early treatment of juniper (i.e., seedling stage or soon after new growth is initiated following top-killing treatments) is critical for effective biological control.

Because juniper is one of a few evergreen species on most rangelands, it is consumed in larger amounts during the winter when most other vegetation is dormant and low in quality. Grazing with high goat stocking rates during winter could focus goat utilization on juniper. Such a management strategy could be achieved by dispersing goats across many pastures during spring, summer, and fall but concentrating all goats each winter in a target pasture.

Another possibility is to ship goats to other states during the growing season and then winter them on juniper-infested pastures in Texas. This is currently being practiced by some managers who are summer grazing goats in Missouri, Kansas, and Nebraska and then shipping them back to Texas during the dormant winter period. Under this scenario, goats are being used to manage problem plants in northern states in summer. They are shipped back to Texas because of the severe winters in the more northerly states and can be managed to reduce juniper seedling recruitment in Texas during winter.

The geographic range of goats throughout Texas has decreased significantly from earlier years. Goats are well adapted to most areas of the state, but the reintroduction of goats back into many areas infested with juniper will be difficult because of predators, lack of goat-proof fences, management skills of the landowners, and reluctance of people to reintroduce a livestock species that is perceived as competing with wildlife.

Goats + Fire = The Ultimate Weapon

The invasion and increase of juniper in areas previously dominated by grasses, forbs, and desirable browse have been problems since the Edwards Plateau was fire-proofed by excessive grazing by domestic livestock. This is, in part, due to the terpenoids in juniper, which reduce its palatability. However, terpenoids can be highly flammable (Owens et al. 1998). Ashe juniper (*Juniperus ashei*) is a fire-intolerant plant species and can be killed easily with fire. Redberry juniper (*Juniperus pinchotii*) can be top-killed but is a basal-sprouter and can survive a high burn frequency. The initial response of redberry juniper after fire is to regrow shoots from dormant basal buds rather than invest in terpenoid production. After fire and as new growth emerges, there is a period of leaf cell differentiation and maturation before terpenoid synthesis is initiated. Therefore, the use of prescribed fire as an initial treatment followed with grazing by goats can be a cost-effective management tool to suppress redberry juniper. Goats should be moved into a burned pasture as soon as the juniper begins to grow new foliage that will be low in terpenoids and susceptible to damage by goats. Scheduling burns for the summer or fall works well for this strategy because the immature juniper regrowth will be available during the winter time when most other desirable plants are dormant or totally absent due to the fire. Also, the growth rate of juniper will be slower in the winter than during spring or summer.

Animal Selection, Biotechnology, and Molecular Genetics: Super Juniper-eating Goats

"If we want to change the grazing habits of the animals we must work directly on the genetics of the animal," stated Walker (1995:356). Many of the differences in diet preference between individuals within a herbivore species can be explained by inherited physiological, neurological, or morphological characteristics and can serve as a basis for genetic selection (Launchbaugh et al. 1999). Therefore, animals within a population or flock that can be identified as selecting greater than average amounts of a particular plant species can be selectively bred to create successive generations with exceptional preferences. This is an example of genetic manipulation using traditional animal breeding techniques. It may also be possible to insert a specific gene into a breed of livestock that produces an enzyme required to break down a specific plant phytochemical. For example, wild Ibex goats (*Capra ibex*) may have the ability to detoxify more plant phytochemicals than domesticated goats. If the genes responsible for the detoxification process in the wild goats were identified and inserted into domesticated goats, these genetically modified goats could consume larger quantities of target plants and still retain the gentle nature of domestic goats.

An effort is being made at the Texas A&M University Research Station at Sonora to select and breed goats based on their ability to consume juniper. Preliminary results from the research indicate that percent juniper in goat diets has a heritability of 28%. This indication of genetic control over dietary preferences, coupled with the rapid advances in biotechnology and molecular genetics, holds the promise for developing goats that will target juniper, thus improving one of the tools we have to manage vegetation.

These new emerging technologies will increase the ability to select animals for specific dietary preferences. In addition, fecal analysis with near infrared reflectance spectroscopy (Walker et al. 1998) and laser-induced fluorescence (Anderson et al. 1996) are two technologies that make it possible to screen animals quickly for diet characteristics.

Conclusion

The knowledge that livestock can be managed and/or selectively bred to increase their use of noxious plants and that the consumption of some noxious plants by herbivores can be increased by low-cost treatments such as fire provides many opportunities for managers. Advances in understanding how animals cope with plant defense chemicals and in biotechnology and molecular genetics, provide much promise in developing "designer" livestock for management of problem plant species. The integrated use of these technologies, with conventional management practices, where applicable, along with the formation of associations and cooperatives, to facilitate and promote biological management of noxious plants, represent the future of biological vegetation management.

Literature Cited

Anderson, D. M., P. Nachman, R. E. Estell, T. Ruekgauer, K. M. Havstad, E. L. Fredrickson, and L. W. Murray. 1996. The potential of laser-induced fluorescence (LIF) spectra of sheep feces to determine diet botanical composition. Small Ruminant Research 21:1–10.

Bernays, E. A., and J. C. Lee. 1988. Food aversion learning in the polyphagous grasshopper *Schistocerca americana*. Physiological Entomology 13:131–37.

Bryant, F. C., M. M. Kothmann, and L. B. Merrill. 1979. Diets of sheep, angora goats, Spanish goats, and white-tailed deer under excellent range condition. Journal of Range Management 32:412–17.

Cheek, P. R., and L. R. Shull. 1985. Natural toxicants in feeds and poisonous plants. AVI Publishing Company, Inc., Westport, Connecticut.

Cook, C. W., and L. E. Harris. 1950. The nutritive content of the grazing sheep's diet on summer and winter ranges of Utah. Utah Agricultural Experiment Station Bulletin 342.

Cory, V. L. 1927. Activities of livestock on the range. Texas Agricultural Experiment Station Bulletin 367.

Dye, K. L., II, D. N. Ueckert, and S. G. Whisenant. 1995. Redberry juniper—herbaceous understory interactions. Journal of Range Management 48:100–107.

Forman, R. T. T., and M. Gordon. 1986. Landscape ecology. John Wiley & Sons, New York.

Fraps, G. S., and V. L. Cory. 1940. Composition and utilization of range vegetation of Sutton and Edwards Counties. Texas Agricultural Experiment Station Bulletin 586.

Freeland, W. J., and D. H. Janzen. 1974. Strategies in herbivory by mammals: the role of plant secondary compounds. American Naturalist 108:269–89.

Garcia, J. 1989. Food for Tolman: cognition and cathexis in concert. Pages 45–85 *in* T. Archer and L. Nilsson, editors. Aversion, avoidance and anxiety. Erlbaum, Hillsdale, New Jersey.

Hayden, J. W., and E. G. Comstock. 1975. Use of activated charcoal in acute poisoning. Clinical Toxicology 8:515–33.

Heady, H. F. 1964. Palatability of herbage and animal preference. Journal of Range Management 17:76–82.

Hegarty, M. P., C. P. Lee, G. S. Christie, R. D. Court, and K. P. Haydock. 1979. The goitrogen 3-hydroxy-4(IH)-pyridone, a ruminal metabolite from *Leucaena leucocephala*: effects in mice and rats. Australian Journal of Biological Sciences 32: 27–40.

Hester, J. W., T. L. Thurow, and C. A. Taylor, Jr. 1997. Hydrologic characteristics of vegetation types as affected by prescribed burning. Journal of Range Management 50:199–204.

Johnson, A. R., J. A. Wiens, B. T. Milne, and T. O. Crist. 1992. Animal movements and population dynamics in heterogeneous landscapes. Landscape Ecology 7:63–75.

Kothmann, M. M. 1968. The botanical composition and nutrient content of the diet of sheep grazing on poor condition pasture compared to good condition pasture. Dissertation, Texas A&M University, College Station.

Launchbaugh, K. L., J. W. Walker, and C. A. Taylor, Jr. 1999. Foraging behavior: experience or inheritance? Pages 28–35 *in* K. Launchbaugh, K. Sanders, and J. Mosley, editors. Proceedings grazing behavior of livestock and wildlife. University of Idaho Station Bulletin 70.

Malechek, J. C., and C. L. Leinweber. 1972. Forage selectivity by goats on lightly and heavily grazed range. Journal of Range Management 24:105–108.

McCollum, J. M. 1972. The botanical composition of the diet of white-tailed deer. Thesis, Texas A&M University, College Station.

McFarland, A. M. S., and M. M. Kothmann. 1992. Evaluating diet selection by sheep. Texas Agricultural Experiment Station Progress Report 4935.

Merrill, L. B., and J. L. Schuster. 1978. Grazing management practices affect livestock losses from poisonous plants. Journal of Range Management 31:351–54.

———, and V. A. Young. 1954. Results of grazing single classes of livestock in combination with several classes when stocking rates are constant. Texas Agricultural Experiment Station Progress Report 1726.

Murden, S. B. 1993. Assessing competitive interactions among white-tailed deer and angora goats. Thesis, Texas A&M University, College Station.

Owens, M. K., C. D. Lin, C. A. Taylor, Jr., and S. G. Whisenant. 1998. Seasonal patterns of plant flammability and monoterpenoid content in *Juniperus ashei*. Journal of Chemical Ecology 24:2115–29.

Poage, G. W., III, C. B. Scott, M. G. Bisson, and F. S. Hartmann. 2000. Activated charcoal attenuates bitterweed toxicosis in sheep. Journal of Range Management 53:73–78.

Pratchett, D., R. J. Jones, and F. X. Syrch. 1991. Use of DHP-degrading rumen bacteria to overcome toxicity in cattle grazing irrigated *Leucaena* pasture. Tropical Grasslands 25:268–74.

Provenza, F. D. 1995. Postingestive feedback as an elementary determinant of food preference and intake in ruminants. Journal of Range Management 48:2–17.

Rollins, D., and B. Armstrong. 1997. Cedar through the eyes of wildlife. Pages 23–31 *in* C. A. Taylor, Jr., editor. Proceedings 1997 Juniper Symposium. Texas Agricultural Experiment Station, San Angelo, Technical Report 97-1.

Schoener, T. W. 1987. A brief history of optimal foraging theory. Pages 5–30 *in* A. C. Kamil, J. R. Krebs, and H. R. Pulliam, editors. Foraging behavior. Plenum Press, New York.

Sedivec, K., T. Hanson, and C. Heiser. 1995. Controlling leafy spurge using goats and sheep. North Dakota State University Extension Service Publication R-1093.

Sell, R. S., D. J. Nudell, D. A. Bangsund, F. L. Leistritz, and T. Faller. 2000. Feasibility of a sheep cooperative for grazing leafy spurge. North Dakota Agricultural Experiment Station Report 435, Fargo.

Senft, R. L., M. B. Coughenour, D. W. Bailey, L. R. Rittenhouse, O. E. Sala, and D. M. Swift. 1987. Large herbivore foraging and ecological hierarchies. Bioscience 37:789–99.

Straka, E. J. 1993. Preferences for redberry and blueberry juniper exhibited by cattle, sheep, and goats. Thesis, Texas A&M University, College Station.

Taylor, C. A., Jr. 1985. Multispecies grazing research overview (Texas). Pages 14–19 *in* F. H. Baker and R. K. Jones, editors. Proceedings of a conference on multispecies grazing. Winrock International Institute, Morrilton, Arkansas.

———, N. E. Garza, Jr., and T. D. Brooks. 2000. Germination and subsequent diet selection of *Juniperus ashei* and *Juniperus pinchotii* seedlings by Angora goats. Pages 74–80 *in* Sheep and goat, wool and mohair research report. Texas Agricultural Experiment Station Consolidated Progress Report (2000).

———, M. M. Kothmann, L. B. Merrill, and D. Elledge. 1980. Diet selection by cattle under high-intensity low-frequency, short duration, and Merrill grazing systems. Journal of Range Management 33:428–34.

———, and M. H. Ralphs. 1992. Reducing livestock losses from poisonous plants through grazing management. Journal of Range Management 45:9–12.

Teague, W. R. 1996. A research framework to achieve sustainable use of rangeland. Agriculture, Ecosystems and Environment 57:91–102.

Ueckert, D. N. 1997. Juniper control and management. Pages 23–34 *in* C. A. Taylor, Jr., editor. Proceedings 1997 Juniper Symposium. Texas Agricultural Experiment Station, San Angelo, Technical Report 97-1.

Walker, J. W. 1995. Viewpoint: grazing management and research now and in the next millennium. Journal of Range Management 48:350–57.

———, D. H. Clark, and S. D. McCoy. 1998. Fecal NIRS for predicting percent leafy spurge in diets. Journal of Range Management 51:450–55.

Prescribed Fire

13 Fire Ecology
and the Progression of Prescribed Burning
for Brush Management

C. J. Scifres

Systematic studies of grassland burning in the 1920s and 1930s initiated a science base and provided information on burning as a range management tool. By the early 1960s and 1970s, organized research on burning of rangelands gave rise to the idea of prescribed burning—the methodical application of burning to achieve specified natural resource management and ecological goals. Research from the mid-1960s through the mid-1980s emphasized creating a richer database and building practical experiences that greatly refined the practice of developing fire plans to meet prescribed objectives of range resource managers. During this same period, prescribed burning was being integrated into brush management systems giving rise to increasingly sophisticated predictive economic models and a greater understanding of fire and wildlife management. Technical papers on prescribed burning are still frequently published (using the *Journal of Range Management* as an indicator) but, in the last decade, have tended to emphasize descriptive outcomes of burning applications to different geographic regions.

As I thought about my assignment to address the question, "Where have we been?" in regard to application of fire science and technology for range improvement, a truism became increasingly apparent; that is, the driving forces for advancement of science, regardless of field or discipline, reside with the personalities engaged in developing the underlying theory and its application. Perhaps this has been especially true with range management because it is so much an art as well as a science. This has been particularly true for brush management and prescribed burning. I did not approach my assignment on a global basis, but chose to emphasize the evolution of burning of U.S. rangelands with an eye toward southwestern shrublands where I have most of my experience. And finally, I could not resist thinking about where we might be headed and to make some general observations in that regard.

Where have we been? Certainly, we are immediately reminded that fire has always been with us—humans evolved with fire—but only recently (in evolutionary terms) have we developed the capacity to act as master rather than as servant to fire. There is evidence that humans were burning vegetation for premeditated purposes more than a quarter of a million years ago.

We have, for ages, taken the utilitarian values of vegetation burning for granted and tended to dwell on the negative aspects of fire. When growing up in south-central Oklahoma, I recall many times working to stop grass fires. I never recall anyone in the area intentionally starting one (i.e., practicing management burns). Interestingly, though, it was common practice for the city dwellers to burn their yards in late winter or early spring to remove the duff in preparation for the growing season.

My first exposure to a management application of burning came in Oklahoma during a tour with scientists from several states during the early 1960s. I was a graduate student at Oklahoma State University and my experience up to that point had mostly been with wildfires in south-central Oklahoma. Pat McIlvain, a USDA-ARS range scientist, demonstrated responses of sand shinnery oak (*Quercus havardii*) dominated rangeland to controlled burning. The discussions on the tour stop that morning were unforgettable. No participant was even close to neutral on the subject, although some expressed their views more quietly than did others. Clearly, most of the people present were against burning, especially on such unstable soils in such a dry climate. It later occurred to me that although ranges had been burned for centuries and that the art of burning long had been practiced, the science of prescribed burning was in its infancy. Wayne Hamilton and I tried to capture the thought, "Burning is among the oldest of land management practices, yet fire ecology is relatively young as a science. The agent has remained the same, but the context of its application and the potential for its use have changed dramatically, especially during the past two decades." (Scifres and Hamilton 1993: Preface, page xv).

The Early Science Base

Foresters led the way in conducting scientific research on evaluation of vegetation burning. The publication of the *Proceedings of the Tall Timbers Fire Ecology Conference* was a mainstay source of information. Still, burning of grasslands and the ecological outcomes were discussed in early plant ecology and range management texts. Such texts noted that removing dead vegetation and providing more favorable growing conditions is the main objective in burning grasslands. Early growth may even increase, as shown by Hensel (1923) in respect to the Kansas Prairies (Stoddart and Smith 1934). Work in the 1920s and 1930s included effect of fires upon soils, including hydrology and on forage production, but placed greatest emphasis on shrublands for woody plant control such as "eradicating undesirable plants" (Stoddart and Smith 1955). Later, as range managers began to truly embrace burning as a science and fire as a management tool (or perhaps, first, as a tool that could be managed), fire applications were studied more in arid and semiarid climates. Among the leaders at mid-century was a professor at Kansas State University, Kling Anderson, who began to systematically study the factors influencing fire behavior and grassland/animal responses primarily on little bluestem (*Schizachyrium scoparium*) ranges in the Flint Hills of Kansas. His work was preceded by considerable research which provided a base from which to refine and improve burning as a management tool (Aldous 1934). Burning had become common practice on range that was leased for conditioning steers brought from the south and west for the Midwest markets. I visited Anderson's research sites as a part of a range management class field trip in 1966 and was greatly impressed with the management results and the growing body of knowledge about rangeland burning.

By the early 1960s and 1970s, the knowledge base had expanded significantly. Burning was being applied for various other range improvement objectives, although shrub control was the overriding expected benefit. Vallentine (1971) listed eighteen purposes in addition to shrub control. By the mid-1970s, the idea of "prescribed burning" was a prominent part of range management texts (Heady 1975) leading to Wright and Bailey's (1982) book, *Fire Ecology,* becoming the benchmark work.

Research on Range Burning

In an effort to review trends in research on fire and rangelands, I used the indexes of the *Journal of Range Management* for the past 30 years (1970–99 inclusive) to simply count the number of papers on the topics: (1) wildfire, (2) prescribed burning (prescribed fire), (3) fire, and (4) burning. Understanding that this is a superficial measure in that it does not include work in the broader literature nor does it consider advancing sophistication of research, it does indicate the relative interest by range researchers in burning and rangelands. I arbitrarily evaluated article numbers for sequential 5-year periods (i.e., 1970–74, 1974–79 . . . 1995–99) and then sought the 5-year period with the highest article number.

During the 30-year period, 165 burning-related articles appeared in the *Journal of Range Management,* an average of about 5.5 per year as follows: 1970–74 = 4/yr; 1975–79 = 4.2/yr; 1980–84 = 8.6/yr; 1985–89 = 5/yr; 1990–94 = 6.4/yr; and, 1995–99 = 4.8/yr. At least one article was published every year during the period (only one article was found for each year in 1975 and 1981). Interestingly, the rate of appearance during the arbitrary 5-year increments was fairly uniform (four or five articles per year) except during the periods, 1980–84 and 1990–94. The highest 5-year period was 1982–86 when 48–50 articles appeared (depending on how one counts brief reviews and theses). This translated to ten per year or nearly one-third of the total for the 30-year period being published during that 5-year time span. I then counted the number of authors on the papers without regard to repetition of a particular name or numbers of authors per paper and found that Texas range scientists appeared with the following frequency: 1982 = 30%; 1983 = 42%; 1984 = 38%; 1985 = 29%; and 1986 = 42% of the contributing scientists. Without comparing previous or subsequent periods, one might deduce instinctively that this pattern was related to a resurgence of interest in range burning in Texas in the late 1960s and early 1970s, which I believe to be true.

It would be most interesting to analyze the objectives of the research and the subject content of the papers as an index of any changing approach(es) to range burning. My sense is that research on burning is highly cyclic. We have gone through alternating periods of publishing descriptive articles (outcomes of range burning) to results of highly controlled experiments regarding fire behavior back to descriptive studies. But, again, that observation is instinctive and not couched in careful study. I would also offer the peripheral observation that we continue to need both kinds of research and that the present "quiet" time will pass into another period of active analytical work.

Advancing Burning Applications on Shrublands

After a period of reduced activity in brush control research, range livestock producers in Texas created an organization called the "Brush Control and Range Improvement Association" in the mid-1960s. In addition to state and ARS scientists already headquartered at College Station, both Texas A&M University and Texas Tech University responded to the call for more research by adding research capacity. Henry Wright came to Texas Tech to develop fire technology for brush control with initial emphasis on honey mesquite (*Prosopis glandulosa var. glandulosa*) and redberry juniper (*Juniperus pinchotii*). Wright and his students can be credited with developing solid, broad-based research information that contributed to their development of "prescriptions" for burning range to achieve stated improvement goals. Most of the initial research by the Texas Agricultural Experiment Station (TAES) emphasized herbicide technologies. However, TAES scientist J. L. Dodd already had been working on burning in South Texas for a number of years. Whereas Wright and his colleagues initially emphasized identifying critical variables which influenced fire behavior and responses of individual species, Dodd and his students emphasized responses over time at the plant community level. Both of these researchers were involved in early work on wildlife responses to range burning. By the mid-1970s, Darrell Ueckert had developed an extremely active research program incorporating burning in the Edwards Plateau region. A number of other persons dabbled with prescribed burning during that same time but did not sustain programs. So, for a period of nearly 10 years, research on burning was being actively conducted on grazing lands in North, West, South, and Central Texas.

Most of the work, regardless of geographic province, was conducted with the stalwart support of landowners and their management staffs. The research programs in South Texas, for example, would not have been possible without the unflagging support of P. H. ("Pat") Welder, Ed Harte, Will Harte, B. K. Johnson, Richard Gates, Albert Durham, Sr., Chester Keifer, and many, many others. Much of the definitive work was conducted on the Rob and Bessie Welder Wildlife Foundation Refuge in Sinton, in cooperation with D. Lynn Drawe. These individuals were partners in the truest sense and were responsible for much of the creative thinking that led to more effective applications of prescribed burning for resource improvement, especially in the systems context. Others could easily be named by researchers who worked in the Edwards Plateau and in North Texas and I assume full responsibilities for any oversights.

The Critical Database

By the mid-1970s, considerable information had been accumulated about fire behavior and vegetation responses on shrublands. Some of the more critically important ones are listed below.

Fuel Influences. Data were amassed that not only established that certain kinds of fires were related to certain kinds of fuels but that prediction of fire behavior could be based on fuel characteristics. Data included fuel-water content, volatility, size, arrangement, and other physical and chemical characteristics.

Weather Influences. Weather influences could now be categorized temporally (as preburn, during the burn, and postburn) relative to their influence on fire behavior and expected outcomes of burning the vegetation.

Species Susceptibility to Burning. Much of the work in the 1960s and early 1970s emphasized the response of woody plants to burning because of the influence of brush control on range management decisions.

Impacts of Burning on Soils. Early work was revisited with modern equipment and measuring techniques. Conclusions were drawn regarding range hydrology, soil nutrients, water contents, temperature changes, and other parameters that corrected earlier misconceptions in some cases and greatly added to the body of knowledge concerning environmental responses to burning different vegetation types.

Fire Behavior. During this heyday of systematic fire research, more knowledge was gained about fire behavior on rangelands than was accumulated in all the previous time. This information greatly enhanced managers' abilities to plan and execute burns in a safe manner to achieve very specific objectives.

Standards for Developing Sound Fire Plans and Burning Techniques and Strategies. The information collected during work on the previous five areas was integrated and evaluated systematically on a scientific basis to allow the development of true prescriptions for burning.

Burning and Livestock Management. As information was gathered on response of the environment and the subsequent impacts on forage production and quality, scientists were able to develop "grazing management prescriptions" as an integral part of the burning and overall resource management plans.

Burning and Wildlife. As range burning began to be accepted as a legitimate management tool, wildlife biologists and managers developed increasing interests in the impacts on wildlife populations. During this same period, it became increasingly evident that game management had become a critical economic consideration by ranch managers. Data were collected relative to burning schedules and patterns for optimal enhancement of game populations in harmony with livestock management.

Systems Approach. As the information above was accrued, it became increasingly obvious that the range resource, to be sustained economically and ecologically, must be managed as a system. Equally obvious was the pivotal role of woody plants, both positive and negative, in implementing optimal management of the systems.

The Systems Concept and Role of Burning in Woody Plant Management

Approaches to dealing with unwanted woody plants evolved from the desire for brush eradication to brush control and finally to brush management because three things became clear. First, brush populations were not to be eradicated (and probably should not be) because of technological and economic constraints inherent to rangeland management. Further, brush control was usually less than rewarding given economic, ecological, and management outcomes on the long term. And most important, brush management was more compatible with multiple use goals for rangeland (Scifres 1980). As various treatments were combined to increase efficacy and economic performance, progressively more emphasis was placed on the positive interaction of brush management and other range management procedures and processes. Essentially, brush management had to be put into the context of setting goals and applying all management expertise, technology, and heuristics as an interacting set of activities toward meeting those established goals. Early leadership in researching the economic context for burning was led by Robert Whitson and Richard Connor.

One of the first attempts to create a system was on pastures in the relatively resilient Texas Coastal Prairie, which had been invaded by the introduced vine, Macartney rose (*Rosa bracteata*). The idea of developing integrated brush management systems (later referred to as IBMS) was spawned, but the total system concept had only begun to evolve. Early IBMS was really an orchestrated set of treatments rather than a comprehensive system, but the concept refined quickly as information was gathered. As more was learned the work became more refined and systems were developed for a number of "brush types" in South Texas (Scifres et al. 1985). As important as the underlying technologies in systems was the over-arching philosophy of optimizing economic, management, and ecological outcomes.

A number of niches were immediately found for prescribed burning as the systems concept began to take shape. In many cases, prescribed burning determines the success of the system. Burning removed, at least partially, dead woody top growth left from chemical applications with rate of removal depending on the brush species, weather, and fuel conditions. Herbicide applications killed some woody plants, reducing the woody canopy and thinning the stands which, in turn, released and increased herbaceous species for use as grazing or as fine fuel. Burning created a more uniform forage stand by removing rank top growth of grasses and promoted a flush of forbs and browse with values for both livestock and wildlife. It suppressed woody regrowth, albeit a temporary suppression (which also improved the availability and accessibility of high-quality browse). All of these positive responses accrued through time were above and beyond those when brush was treated with herbicide or mechanical methods alone. And, most important, prescribed burning increased the length of effective range improvement on treated areas; in fact, it offered indefinite perpetuation in some cases.

Management Lessons

As the idea of brush management systems evolved, much of the technology previously available was refined and new and emerging technologies were incorporated. The major lessons learned during the period, 1970–90, are described below.

Building the Economic Context. Techniques for conducting *pro forma* economic situation analyses were developed. Production responses projected agreement from conversion of forage production to stocking rate. Measures of forage production contributed to the ability to project long-term performance. Simple models were developed to forecast forage production through time following initial treatment. This was accomplished using the existing database and adding information from controlled experiments. Then the forage production curves were completed to determine carrying capacity. This was accomplished by incorporating long-held heuristic data and by including controlled statistical measurements under actual grazing conditions. This allowed contrasting projected economic outcomes of alternative treatment sequences and management time lines.

Building the Ecological Context. A clearer understanding of the chronology of brush invasion and establishment was gained, especially by research in South Texas (Archer et al. 1988). The role of fire prior to settlement, the influence of change in burning frequencies, and patterns in the changing nature of grasslands to shrublands became more clearly understood. And, knowing these in light of a deeper understanding of fire behavior, the capability to predict responses to burning increased. The research on brush ecology continues under the leadership of S. A. Archer and his associates.

Building the Management Context. Clarification of the potential role of wildlife and the economic interaction of wildlife and livestock and brush was critical to designing the systems. Burning tends to add value for wildlife when applied following broadcast herbicide application and other treatments.

The single-most important lesson learned from the work on Integrated Brush Management Systems was that effective research in the systems context absolutely requires the orchestrated participation of scientists from an array of disciplines. The work in Texas required the research by wildlife biologists (early work was done by Sam Beasom, Jack Inglis, and Ben Koerth), range scientists (including nutritionists and grazing managers like Jerry Stuth and range scientists like Jim Mutz and Wayne Hamilton), animal scientists (Gary Williams worked with the team on projects near Alice, Texas) and economists (Richard Conner and Bob Whitson were mentioned earlier)—all carefully harmonized toward achieving a common goal. Relative participation would ebb and flow as demanded by the specific research project. The research stimulated work by plant ecologists (Archer et al. 1988), soil scientists (Larry Wilding), entomologists (Pete Teel), and involvement of a number of other disciplines.

The Future

The *Journal of Range Management* recently published a series of feature articles on achievements in range management. In Owensby's article (Owensby 2000:14), he discussed achievements in eight areas of range research. One, although disappointingly brief, was implementation of prescribed burning, "Timing, frequency and fire intensity have been the primary areas of research and fire prescriptions can attain many and varied range management objectives." I would not disagree with that midwestern perspective, understated as it is. We have learned how to effectively and predictably use fire in an extremely diverse and ecologically complex physiographic region. As mentioned earlier, it seems from my peripheral view, however, that research on fire-based management systems is cyclic and has waned in recent years. There may be good reasons for this (if it indeed has happened) but given the increasing amount of information being collected on shrub ecology and changing land use patterns, especially in Texas, it would seem that burning in the systems context would be even more important than before.

Literature Cited

Aldous, A. E. Effect of burning on Kansas bluestem pastures. 1934. Kansas Agricultural Experiment Station Technical Bulletin 38 (cited in Stoddard and Smith 1943).

Archer, S. R., C. J. Scifres, and C. R. Bassham. 1988. Autogenic succession in a subtropical savanna: conversion of grassland to thorn woodland. Ecological Monographs 58:111–27.

Heady, H. F. 1975. Rangeland management. McGraw-Hill Book Co., New York.

Hensel, R. L. 1923. Effect of burning on vegetation in Kansas pastures. Journal of Agricultural Research 23:631–43.

Owensby, C. E. 2000. Achievements in management and utilization by privately-owned rangelands. Journal of Range Management 53:12–16.

Scifres, C. J. 1980. Brush management: principles and practices for Southwest Texas. Texas A&M University Press, College Station.

———, and W. T. Hamilton. 1993. Prescribed burning for brushland management: the South Texas example. Texas A&M University Press, College Station.

———, ———, J. R. Conner, J. W. Stuth, J. M. Inglis, T. G. Welch, G. A. Rasmussen, and R. P. Smith. 1985. Integrated brush management systems for South Texas: development and implementation. Texas Agricultural Experiment Station Bulletin 1493.

Stoddart, L. A., and A. D. Smith. 1943. Range management. McGraw-Hill Book Co., New York.

———, and ———. 1955. Range management. Second edition. McGraw-Hill Book Co., New York.

Vallentine, J. F. 1971. Range development and improvements. Brigham Young University Press, Provo, Utah.

Wright, H. A., and A. W. Bailey. 1982. Fire ecology: United States and Canada. John Wiley and Sons, Inc., New York.

14 Prescribed Burning
Current Policies,
Regulations, and Information Sources

D. Lynn Drawe
and
Allen Rasmussen

As we enter the twenty-first century, interest is increasing in the use of pre-   175
scribed fire to manipulate natural ecosystems in the United States. Federal,
state, and private agencies have come to recognize prescribed fire as a tool
that can be used to economically manipulate vegetation and reduce fire hazards to life and property. However, there is not a general acceptance on how
to incorporate fire into an integrated approach, particularly at the landscape
scale. In many cases the reluctance to use fire is from a lack of knowledge or
critical mass of experienced people. Because of the increasing use of, and/or
the desire to use, prescribed fire, many laws and regulations have come to
pass in recent times. Some of these will facilitate the adoption of prescribed
burning, while others may inhibit the use of fire. This chapter will relate
enough of the current laws concerning prescribed fire and current uses of
prescribed fire to give the reader a general concept of the "state of the art."

Federal Agencies and Regulations

The Clean Air Act has conditioned many of the state and federal regulations
relating to the use of prescribed burning in the United States. Although the
1990 Clean Air Act is a federal law covering the entire country, the states do
much of the work to carry out the act. Under this law, the Environmental
Protection Agency (EPA) sets limits on how much of a pollutant can be in
the air, insuring uniform nationwide health and environmental protections.
Individual states may have stronger pollution controls, but may not have
weaker controls than those set for the whole country. States are required to
develop implementation plans outlining how they will carry out the Clean
Air Act. The EPA must approve each plan, and if not acceptable, EPA can
take over enforcement of the Clean Air Act for that state (http://www.epa
.gov.html). Most states have developed emissions and particulate matter
standards that affect prescribed burning. Standards and regulations are set
for particular kinds of natural fuels. One of the requirements of a prescribed
burn plan is smoke management. If smoke will cause an area to exceed the
limits of an "ozone action" day, prescribed burning is prohibited.

The National Wildfire Coordinating Group (NWCG) is made up of the

USDA Forest Service; four Department of Interior agencies: Bureau of Land Management (BLM), National Park Service (NPS), Bureau of Indian Affairs (BIA), and Fish and Wildlife Service (FWS); and state forestry agencies through the National Association of State Foresters (NASF) (http://www.nwcg.gov). The purpose of NWCG is to coordinate programs of the participating wildfire management agencies to avoid wasteful duplication and to provide a means of constructively working together. The goal of NWCG is to provide more effective execution of each agency's fire management program. The group provides a formalized system to agree on standards of training, equipment, qualifications, and other operational functions. NWCG operates through "working teams," a concept that has provided a means for exchange of knowledge about all dimensions of fire management.

The National Interagency Fire Center (NIFC) in Boise, Idaho is the nation's support center for wildland firefighting (http://www.nifc.gov). Seven federal and state agencies call NIFC home and work together to coordinate and support wildland fire and disaster situations. These agencies include the Bureau of Indian Affairs, Bureau of Land Management, Forest Service, Fish and Wildlife Service, National Association of State Foresters, National Weather Service, and Office of Aircraft Services. When the national fire situation becomes severe, the MAC group is activated. This group consists of the directors of each of the wildland firefighting agencies at NIFC. The MAC group helps set priorities for equipment, supplies, and personnel. All federal agencies at NIFC, as well as the National Association of State Foresters, are members of the National Wildfire Coordinating Group created in 1976 by the Secretaries of Interior and Agriculture to facilitate the development of common practices, standards, and training in the wildfire community.

The disastrous fires in our western states over the past few years have awakened and educated the general public and our elected officials to the fallacies of total fire suppression on our public forests and grasslands. These natural disasters have begun to affect the pocketbook of the people who own property in the rural/urban interface. Public opinion has caused elected officials to recognize this natural factor for its benefits rather than for its detriments. Therefore, because of urging from President George W. Bush and many other elected officials, a National Fire Plan has been prepared and adopted.

The U.S. Department of Agriculture (USDA) and U.S. Department of Interior (USDI) are currently in the second year of National Fire Plan implementation (http://www.fireplan.gov). Significant headway was made in 2001 to meet both the intent and specific direction from the U.S. Congress in the 2001 Interior and Related Agencies Appropriations Act. The National Fire Plan recognizes the importance of providing outreach, education, and support for local communities who must play a primary role in reducing fire hazards in and near their communities; hence, the management of private lands in the wildland/urban interface has become a key factor in the fire-risk equation. A top priority for reducing risk is to reduce fuels in forests and rangelands adjacent to and within communities. Particular emphasis is placed on projects where fuel treatments can also be accomplished on adjoining state, private, or other nonfederal land to extend greater protection across the landscape. The National Fire Plan sees prescribed fire on private lands in the wildland/urban interface as an acceptable hazard fuel reduction option.

The USDI, FWS Partners for Fish and Wildlife Program recognizes prescribed burning as an important and acceptable habitat enhancement technique for removing exotic species and to restore natural disturbance regimes necessary for some wildlife species' survival (http://fire.r9.fws.gov/fm/policy/factsheets/privatelands.htm). The prescribed burning assistance offered through FWS may take the form of informal prescribed fire planning and operations advice, or it may consist of designing and funding a prescribed fire project under a voluntary cooperative agreement with the landowner. If the prescribed fire is for fuel hazard reduction in the wildland/urban interface, Wildland Fire Management funds may be used to pay salaries for fire management personnel. If a site is near a USFWS office, USFWS machinery, equipment, and supplies may be used to complete a restoration project. National wildlife refuges may also enter into prescribed fire agreements directly with private landowners on land adjacent to or within the refuge when burning those lands is beneficial to the refuge and the prescribed fire activities are identified in an approved refuge fire management plan.

The USDI, BLM recognizes the value of using fire to manage public lands (www.nv.blm.usdi.gov). Prescribed burns are planned under specified conditions intended to improve the health of the natural landscape and reduce hazardous build-up of vegetation. Prior to a prescribed burn, BLM involves the public in a land-use planning process to determine fire-related goals and prescriptions. A BLM prescription identifies specific conditions under which a burn will be conducted, including humidity ranges, vegetation moisture levels, wind speed and direction, temperatures, atmospheric conditions, smoke dispersal, and designated boundaries. Naturally ignited fires may be managed to achieve natural resource benefits if appropriate management plans and prescriptions exist for the area. BLM uses fire to fight fire in areas where overgrown vegetation has accumulated unnaturally where fire has been kept out, thus providing fuel for unprecedented, raging fires that may be destructive of both public and private property. BLM managers prevent these costly situations through the use of prescribed burns. BLM encourages homeowners in the wildland/urban interface to construct their homes of fire-resistant material and to maintain a defensible, cleared space from the surrounding wildland with enough space for fire-fighting vehicles and equipment to get in and out quickly. All of the public land agencies would like to use prescribed fire more, but they are often stopped by public appeals that delay or eliminate the use of prescribed fire, particularly at the landscape scales needed. These appeals often result from the lack of trust of what the prescribed burn is to accomplish or philosophical differences on how lands should be managed.

USDA, Natural Resources Conservation Service (NRCS) personnel in Texas are under specific guidelines concerning prescribed burning. They may recommend, plan, and participate in prescribed burns in Texas on all land uses except annually tilled cropland under NRCS Code 338, October 2001 (www.tx.nrcs.usda.gov). Prescribed burning may be recommended by NRCS personnel to control undesirable vegetation, to prepare sites for harvesting, planting, or seeding, to control plant disease, to improve wildlife habitat, to improve plant quantity or quality, to remove slash and debris, to enhance seed and seedling production, to facilitate distribution of grazing and browsing animals, and to restore and maintain ecological sites. Specific prescribed burning guidelines for weather conditions, fire guards, volatile fuels, specific timing, notifications, air quality considerations, employee training, proper clothing and equipment, and a written plan are detailed in the code. Currently, NRCS personnel may write plans and participate in prescribed burns on private land in Texas if they have had the three-day prescribed burning course offered by NRCS, its equivalent offered by universities, or the five-day course for Texas Certified Prescribed Burn Managers. NRCS also has a three-burn experience requirement for employees who write plans and participate in prescribed burns.

State Regulations and Policies
The Texas Prescribed Burning Act

The Texas Prescribed Burning Act, which became law in September 1999, is administered through the Texas Department of Agriculture (TDA). The law guarantees the right of all landowners in the state to burn on their own property, sets up a prescribed burn manager certification system, sets up a Prescribed Burning Board (PBB), and sets up an Advisory Committee (www.state.tx.us/tda/pesticide/burnboard/pes_pbbmain.htm). PBB membership consists of representatives of seven state agencies (TDA, Texas Natural Resources Conservation Commission, Texas State Soil and Water Conservation Board, Texas Parks and Wildlife Department, Texas Agricultural Extension Service, Texas Agricultural Experiment Station, and Texas Forest Service) and five private landowners. The Texas law contains a liability insurance clause that protects the landowner from lawsuits up to the limit of the certified prescribed burn manager's coverage, i.e., one million dollars. No other state puts this kind of protection between the landowner and the possibility of damage claims or lawsuits. Because of difficulties in obtaining liability insurance, additional legislation was necessary to limit claims to two million dollars per insured per year. Information concerning insurance providers is available from TDA.

Certification and training in Texas have been set up by the PBB on a regional basis. The PBB has divided the state into five training regions (South Texas Plains and Coastal Prairie, Edwards Plateau and Trans-Pecos, East Texas Pineywoods, High and Rolling Plains, and Post Oak Savannah and Cross Timbers) with similar vegetation and burning techniques. Within each of these regions a contact agency has been selected to coordinate training and certification for the region. Each region has a certified burn manager training coordinator. These contact agencies and coordinators are responsible to TDA for coordination of training, issuance of certificates, and record keeping. TDA maintains certification records and coordinates statewide training and recertification activities. Prescribed burn managers are initially certified to practice in the region where they received training. They may later decide to become certified in another or several other regions. If so, then they must attend only the single-day specialized course for each new region. Recertification is a continuing process sanctioned by the PBB.

Other States

Recent court rulings in the Southeast have increased the potential liability associated with prescribed burning, having defined prescribed burning as "inherently dangerous." The rulings have stated that hiring a contractor does not relieve landowners of liability for an incident that may occur as a result of prescribed burning on their property. Many states have recently passed "prescribed burning acts" both to allow and to regulate the use of fire within the state. Most of these laws release landowners or prescribed burn managers from liability if the rules of prescribed burning are followed and if negligence is not involved.

In Florida, burning regulations are at least 70 years old; however, in 1990 the Florida Legislature passed the Florida Prescribed Burning Act which provided a definition of prescribed fire, defined standards for prescribed burning, and reduced liability for burners who are properly certified by and abide by the new laws and previously existing regulations (http://edis.ifas.ufl.edu/BODY_FR055). The 1990 Florida act combined and revised all previous statutes related to prescribed burning and fire control. The more important changes include (1) increased attention to fuel reduction in the interface and other wildland areas, (2) increased public education about fire and prescribed burning, (3) much greater liability protection for certified burners, and (4) expanded burn permit conditions.

Mississippi became the second state to pass legislation to address prescribed burning. The 1992 session of its state legislature adopted the Mississippi Prescribed Burning Act establishing prescribed burning as a landowner property right, and authorizing prescribed burning for ecological, silvicultural, and wildlife purposes (http://cfr.msstate.edu/ContinuingEd/frstry.html). An important provision of the Mississippi legislation lowers liability for the certified burn manager and/or the landowner who utilizes a certified burn manager. The act provides that when a prescribed burn is properly planned, documented, and applied by a certified burn manager, no property owners or their agents may be held liable for damage or injury caused by fire or resulting smoke unless negligence is proven. Burn managers are certified in Mississippi through the successful completion of (1) a fire behavior self-study prerequisite, (2) the completion of a formal week-long course for burn managers (or an equivalent course approved by the Mississippi Forestry Commission), and (3) the Mississippi Forestry Commission certification exam. Individuals who are not certified burn managers are not prohibited from prescribed burning, but do not qualify for the added liability protection afforded by certification. Differing from the Texas program, the Mississippi legislation does not require liability insurance.

The primary purpose of the 1996 Alabama Prescribed Burning Act is to reduce the liability associated with prescribed burning if the burner chooses to become certified and follows the requirements of the law (http://www.forestry.state.al.us/pres_burn_cert.htm). The Alabama Legislature found prescribed burning is a landowner property right and a land management tool benefiting the safety of the public, the environment, the natural resources, and the economy of the state. For protection under this act, the following requirements must be met: (1) the burn must be accomplished only when at least one prescribed burn manager is supervising the burn or burns that are being conducted, (2) a written prescription that meets certain requirements is prepared and witnessed or notarized prior to conducting the burn, (3) a burning permit is obtained from the Alabama Forestry Commission, and (4) the burn is conducted pursuant to state laws and rules applicable to prescribed burning.

In 1999, the North Carolina Legislature passed a bill designed to encourage the use of prescribed fire in the state (http://www.ncforestry.org/prescribed_burning_.htm). The bill limits the liability of private landowners who use fire as a part of their forest management program. Under this legislation, local government may not declare smoke from prescribed fire as a public nuisance, and landowner liability for any damage caused by smoke from a prescribed fire is limited provided the burn is conducted by a certified burner and the burn is done in accordance with a prescribed burning plan. Landowners may burn up to 50 acres of their own land provided the burning is done in accordance with a burning plan prepared and approved by a certified burner.

In Oklahoma, the statutes of the Oklahoma Forestry Code as amended by the legislature in 2001 address prescribed burning (www.oda.state.ok.us/main/srvs/agfor). The law states that it is lawful for an owner of croplands, rangelands, or forestlands to set the lands on fire for the purposes of (1) managing and manipulating plant species present—whether grass, weeds, brush, or trees, and (2) destroying detrimental or unwanted plants, plant parts, shrubs, or trees on croplands, rangelands, or forestlands. The law does not exempt or release a person from civil liability for damages or injury incurred as a result of the burn or for criminal liability. The statutes define lawful burning, unlawful burning, and set fines for unlawful burning. The law outlines the procedure for lawfully burning land that describes firelines, personnel, and equipment requirements. It includes a notification requirement to be placed in writing on a form provided by the State Department of Agriculture, and to be filed with the local rural fire department and the Oklahoma Forestry Division 60 days prior to conducting the burn. Oklahoma does not list a certification or a training requirement.

In New Jersey, the State Department of Environmental Protection may issue a permit authorizing prescribed burning with a plan approved by and under the control of the Bureau of Forest Fire Management (www.state.nj.us/dep/aqm_prescribed_burning). The permit may be conditioned upon meteorological factors and any other requirements that the Bureau of Forest Fire Management deems necessary, and is revocable at the discretion of the department. The permit may be issued for a single event or for a period of days, and no prescribed burning shall commence until a permit is issued and current. Any person seeking a permit for prescribed burning must file with the Bureau of Forest Fire Management a permit application on a form provided by the department. The permit application contains information pertinent to the burn, such as name of the burner, location of the burn, and a detailed plan describing the reasons for the burn and how the burn will be carried out.

The 2001 California Prescribed Burning Act permits, regulates, and coordinates the use of prescribed burning and hazard reduction burning while minimizing smoke impacts in the state (http://216.239.51.100.www .valleyair.org.html). California's law is oriented heavily toward smoke management. There is no requirement for people who burn on their own property to be certified nor to have liability insurance; however, other restrictions apply. A person who conducts a prescribed burn in California is required to take an Air Pollution Code approved smoke management class. A smoke management plan must be filed with the fire control district for review and approval. A smoke management plan must include (1) a legal description of the area to be burned, including maps, (2) a description of the type and amounts of fuels to be burned, and (3) the identity and mailing address of the person responsible for the burn. The California law has increasing requirements for areas less than 10 acres, greater than 10 acres, greater than 100 acres, and greater than 250 acres. If a fire is ignited naturally, a "go/no-go" decision must be made if the fire is to be allowed to burn. The decision is made primarily based on smoke management. In California, smoke management guidelines for agricultural and prescribed burning are outlined in a separate law which describes burning permits and divides the state into air pollution control districts.

In Utah, the State Division of Forestry, Fire and State Lands is responsible for approving prescribed burn plans on private and state lands. In the past, agricultural lands were exempt from the smoke management requirements, but with the adoption of the new national fire management plan agricultural burns will have to adhere to smoke management regulations. Currently, these regulations require environmental conditions for the prescribed burn that result in a specified minimum mixing height (http://www.nr.utah.gov/ SLF.htm). While these are very flexible regulations they do little to encourage or protect those who use fire.

Burning Coalitions and Associations

The Texas Prescribed Burning Coalition (TPBC) was organized in April 1998 to influence positive legislation concerning prescribed burning in the state, to foster and support training in the art and science of prescribed burning in Texas, and to disperse accurate information to the public on the subject of prescribed burning. The goal was to "get ahead of the curve" on burning legislation in Texas because it had become obvious to those who organized the effort that urbanization, a general fear of fire, and lack of information on the proper use and positive benefits of fire might soon preclude the use of this valuable tool. We were aware that recent court rulings in the Southeast had increased the potential liability associated with prescribed burning. These rulings defined prescribed burning as "inherently dangerous," and stated that hiring a contractor to conduct the burn does not relieve landowners of the liability for an incident which may occur as a result of a prescribed burn on their property. The TPBC Legislative committee went to work immediately because the 1999 Texas legislature met fast on the heels of the organizational effort. As a result of the coalition's efforts, legislation was introduced in the Texas Legislature, passed both chambers, was signed by Governor Bush, and became law in September 1999.

The Edwards Plateau Prescribed Burning Association, Inc. was established in 1997 to offer training in the use of prescribed fire, increase participation on prescribed burns, pool equipment, and foster a better understanding and appreciation of the value of prescribed fire (Taylor 2001). Currently, there are over ninety landowner members representing approximately 500,000 acres of rangeland across six counties in the organization. The association has conducted more than forty prescribed burns since its inception. Members of the organization are able to get exemptions to burn during burn bans imposed by county commissioners' courts. Support has come in from other organizations such as local fire departments, local soil and water conservation districts, the Texas Forest Service, the Texas Cooperative Extension, and the USDA, NRCS.

Recently, meetings have been held in the Texas Hill Country by landowners to determine if another prescribed burning association might be needed. Landowners from Bandera, Kendall, Kerr, and Medina counties were present, and the association appears to be on its way to formal organization.

Prescribed Fire Training

Universities. Prescribed fire courses at universities were examined to give an idea of the numbers of courses and kinds of training available at various selected schools across the nation. Although not a complete listing, Table 14.1 gives a representative view of the training currently available at these universities. In the western states, most of the fire-related courses are found in natural resources and forestry departments. At the universities in the South and Midwest, most of the fire courses are taught in the range departments.

State Agencies. The Texas Forest Service (TFS), probably typical of most state forest agencies, offers rigorous training for all its employees. TFS training courses are outlined at the TFS web site located at http://txforestservice .tamu.edu. The following courses would be required for TFS "Burn Boss, Type 2," which would be approximately the equivalent of Texas' Certified Prescribed Burn Manager (Bobby Young, Associate Director, TFS, personal communication, Feb. 2000): (1) I-100, Introduction to ICS, (2) S-190, Introduction to Fire Behavior, (3) S-130, Firefighter Training, (4) S-290, Intermediate Fire Behavior, (5) S-234, Ignition Operations, (6) Introduction to Wildland Fire, and (7) Prescribed Fire Boss. These courses are offered through TFS Wildland Fire Academies and are presented several times each year.

National Training Program. The NRCS National Training program has implemented an in-service prescribed burning training program to build the critical mass needed to help local landowners understand how to use fire. The program was first implemented in 1985 at one location. Because of the variability of fuel types, weather conditions, and plant communities involved the program was expanded. It now includes two different classes. The first is to familiarize NRCS employees with fire and the role fire can play in land management and the second is oriented to teach them to write prescribed burn plans. Both of these courses are now taught at requested locations around the country. These are often done in conjunction with other state and federal agencies.

Public Acceptance and the Urban Interface

On private land, prescribed fire comes with risks and rewards under any circumstances, but burning in the urban/wildland interface often brings far greater risks to homes, businesses, and other property adjacent to the burn, and sometimes even to the career of the prescribed burn manager. In spite of the dangers, managers and owners of interface lands often need to use prescribed fire to manage fuel levels, improve wildlife habitat and grazing productivity, and otherwise manage plant and animal communities. Burn-

Table 14.1. Prescribed fire and fire management courses offered at selected universities across the United States.

University	Department	Course #	Course Title (credit hrs)
Auburn	Forestry	Fory 4440	Forest Fire Management (3)
Colorado State	Natural Resources	F224	Wildland Fire Measurements (1)
Iowa State	Forestry	390	Forest Fire Protection and Management (3)
Montana State—Bozeman	Animal Range and Natural Resources	354	Fire Ecology and Management (3)
Oklahoma State	Range Science	RLEM 5760	Special Topics (Wildland Fires) (3)
Oregon State	Forest Resources (Cross listed)	FOR 446, CRN 17452 FW 446, CRN 17623, RNG 446, or CRN 17624	Wildland Fire Ecology (3)
Penn State	Forestry	221	Forest Fire Technology (1)
		320	Forest Fire Management (2)
S. Dakota State	Range Science	421–521	Grassland Fire Ecology (3)
		421A–521A	Grassland Fire Ecology Lab (0)
		621	Grassland Fire Ecology (3)
		621A	Grassland Ecology Lab (0)
Stephen F. Austin State	Forestry	337	Introduction to Fire Management (3)
		438	Fire Use in Land Management (3)
Texas Tech	Range	4304	Fire Ecology and Management (3)
		5304	Fire Behavior and Ecology (3)
Texas A&M	Rangeland Ecology and Management	616	Fire and Natural Resource Management (3)
University of Idaho	Forestry	426	Wildland Fire Management and Ecology (3)
		427	Prescribed Burning Lab (2)
		526	Fire Ecology (3)
University of California, Davis	Environmental Resources	141	Role of Fire in Natural Ecosystems (4)
University of Nevada, Reno	Environmental and Resource Sciences	495, 695	Fire Ecology and Management (3)
Utah State	Forest, Range, and Wildlife Sciences	2210 & 2220	Basic Wildfire Suppression (2)
		4520 & 4530	Wildland Fire Planning and Management (2)
		6050	Rangeland Fire Ecology and Fire Prescription Development (3)
Washington State	Natural Resource Sciences	430	Introduction to Wildland Fire (3)
		437	Wildland Fire Management Lab (1)
		537	Wildland Fire Management Lab (1)

ing in the interface zone requires extra careful planning to safeguard people, property, and resources that may be in harm's way. The local public must be informed of prescribed burn plans. This may be accomplished by articles in local newspapers, fliers, and public meetings. Not only must the public be "brought into the loop," but just as importantly the local fire department must be informed, and if possible, included in the burn. In a very aggressive approach, Florida's Division of Forestry has developed a program called "Fire in Florida's Ecosystems" in which school teachers receive free training courses to help them teach fourth- through eighth-grade children about the natural role of fire (http://www.safnet.org/archive/602_howtowinpub supp.htm).

On public lands, federal agencies are currently following the National Fire Plan, which attempts to bring fire back to natural ecosystems managed by the various agencies. The goal is to restore ecological health and productivity to forests and grasslands through the expanded use of fire as a management tool. Those in federal management-level positions must place priority on public participation as a key step in planning and implementing a growing prescribed fire program on all public lands. In recent years since the spectacular 1988 fire season, the public has become more aware of the role of fire. However, much education is left to be done. The public must come to understand the role of fire in natural ecosystems, and this can only be accomplished through an intensive and continuous education program carried out by all federal land management agencies (Weldon 2002). Fifty years of "Smokey Bear" attitude must be counteracted. The public has the perception that fires burn wood fiber and waste a valuable resource. Ranchers have the attitude that fires burn up valuable forage. Hunters, sightseers, and recreationalists have the attitude that all fire creates scorched earth, which is bad for all natural areas. Smoke management is a major concern that must be addressed by the burn manager. The federal agencies are reacting through public education using all available media, including interacting actively with the public using field trips, demonstrations, and agency fliers made available locally to the public. Risks of burning must be made clear. Managers must listen to the public's concerns and respond rationally. Finally, assessments of the success or failure of public education campaigns must be made, and this knowledge used to correct future campaigns.

Web Sites for Prescribed Burning Information

There is no shortage of fire information available at various places in the Internet. One reference found over a million sites (Higgason 1997). Some of the major web sites are listed below in Table 14.2.

Conclusion

The state of the art of prescribed burning is scientifically sound as far as burning technology and "know how" are concerned, although many facts remain to be learned about the complexities of the application of fire and the responses of ecosystems to each individual set of circumstances. Scifres (2000) is correct in his assumption that the current interest in fire has and will result in much scientific investigation into the subject. Although it is not

Table 14.2. Web sites with information on prescribed burning.

Web Site/Agency Name	Internet Address
Forest Service	http://www.fs.fed.us/land/#fire
FEMA (Federal Emergency Management Agency)	http://www.fema.gov
Firenet	http://www.csu.edu.au/firenet/
NAPI (National Arson Prevention Initiative)	http://166.112.200.140/napi/napi.htm
AFPA (National Fire Protection Association)	http://www.nfpa.org
NICC (National Interagency Coordination Center)	http://www.nifc.gov/sitreprt.html
NIFC (National Interagency Fire Center)	http://www.nifc.gov
USDI Bureau of Land Management	http://www.blm.gov
NOAA (National Oceanic and Atmospheric Administration)	http://www.noaa.gov
USDI Fish and Wildlife Service Fire Management	http://fwspceaa.nifc.r9.fws.gov/olson/firemanagement.html
USFA (U.S. Fire Administration)	http://www.usfa.fema.gov
Wildland Fire Assessment System Maps	http://www.fs.fed.us/land/wfas/welcome.html
Hines Index	http://www.fs.fed.us/land/wfas/hines.gif
Keetch-Byram Drought Index	http://www.fs.fed.us/land/wfas/kdbi.gif
Observed Fire Danger	http://www.fs.fed.us/land/wfas/fd_class.gif
WRCC (Western Regional Climate Center)	http://www.wrcc.sage.dri.edu
Wildland-urban interface	http://www.firewise.org
WESTAR (Western States Air Resources)	http://westar.org
NISE (National Institute for Science Education)	http://whyfiles.news.wisc.edu/018forest_fire/index.html
NPS (USDI National Park Service)	http://www.nps.gov
PLT (Project Learning Tree)	http://eelink.umich.edu/plt.html
Boulder Mountain Fire Authority Training	http://www.bouldermountainfire.org/training/index.html

feasible in this chapter to address all the various burning laws and regulations throughout the United States, a few of the more salient are presented. In the end, the use of fire in our modern society will be determined by the will of the majority and the rule of law rather than by scientific knowledge and the ability of people to safely apply this tool.

Literature Cited

Alabama Forestry Commission. No date. Alabama Prescribed Burn Certification Program. http://www.forestry.state.al.us/publication/CERTIFICATON_PROGRAM.pdf.

———. 2002. Prescribed Burn Certification. http://www.forestry.state.al.us/pres_burn_cert.htm.

Drawe, D. L. 2001. Prescribed Burning Board. The Texas Certified Prescribed Burn Manager Program. www.state.tx.us.tda/pesticide/burnboard/pes_pbbmain.htm.

Higgason, N. R. 1997. Fire information for everyone, any time. Fire Management Notes 57:32–33.

Long, A. J. 2002. Prescribed Burning Regulations in Florida. University of Florida, Cooperative Extension Service, Institute of Food and Agricultural Sciences (UF/IFas). http://aris.sfrc.ufl.edu/faculty/web_pages.

National Fire Plan. 2002. Implementation in FY 2002-Overview. http://www.nv.blm.gov/carson/Fire/2_fuels_using%20fire,htm.

———. 2002. Using fire to manage public lands. http://www.nv.blm.gov/carson/Fire/2_fuels_using%20fire,htm.

National Interagency Fire Center. 2002. Mission and history of the National Interagency Fire Center. http://www.nifc.gov/nifcmiss.html.

National Wildfire Coordinating Group. 2002. NWCG Home Page. NWCG Organization. http://www.nwcg.gov.

Natural Resources Conservation Service. 2001. Prescribed burning. www.tx.nrcs.usda.gov/eng/ Texas.state.

New Jersey State Department of Environmental Protection. 2002. Control and prohibition of open burning. Title 7, Chapter 27, Subchapter2. Prescribed burning. http://www.state.nj.us/dep/aqm /Sub.

Oklahoma Department of Agriculture Forestry Services. 2002. Notification requirements and considerations for safe and lawful prescribed burning in Oklahoma. www.oda.state.ok.us/main /srvs/agform / burnlaw.pdf.

Scifres, C. J. 2000. Where we have been: fire ecology and the profession of prescribed burning for brush management. Pages 139–46 *in* Proceedings rangeland weed and brush management: the next millennium workshop and symposium. October 19–21, 2000, San Angelo, Texas.

Taylor, C. A. 2001. Organizing ranchers for prescribed burning: The Edwards Plateau Prescribed Burning Association, Inc. Texas Agricultural Experiment Station TR 01-2.

U.S. Environmental Protection Agency. 1990. The role of the federal government and the role of the states. http://www.epa.gov/oar/oaqps/pegcaa02.html.

U.S. Fish & Wildlife Service. 2002. Prescribed burning on private lands. http://fire.r9.fws.gov/fm /policy/factsheets/privatelands.htm.

Valleyair. 2001. Rule 4106 Prescribed Burning and Hazard Reduction Burning. www.valleyair.org/ Workshops/postings/8-15-02.

Weldon, L. A. 2002. Dealing with public concerns in restoring fire to the forest. U.S. Forest Service General Technical Report INT-GTR 341. http://www.fs.fed.us/rm /pubs/int_gtr341/gtr341_6.html.

Wilent, S. 2002. How to...win public support for prescribed burning in interface zones. http://www.safnet.org/archive/602_howtowinpubsupp.htm.

15   Effective Application
of Prescribed Burning

B. Keith Blair,
Jeffrey C. Sparks,
and
Joe Franklin

Prescribed burning remains one of the most feasible ways to manipulate vegetation for rangeland management and restoration of natural communities
and is, therefore, an important tool for land managers. However, the actual
application of this tool still leaves many managers with more questions than
answers concerning the best approach to safe and effective use of the practice. How, in a "real world" situation, do you install a prescribed burn? What
are the variables that you need to know and interpret correctly before you
burn? How do you actually determine that the necessary preburn parameters are met? What specific guidelines are helpful? More variables are now
being used in prescriptions, and smoke management is becoming an increasingly critical issue. Prescribed burning in Texas is no longer confined to
the winter months, and is now often used during summer and fall months.
Land managers will often come to the conclusion (and rightfully so) that
there are many interacting factors that contribute to a complex state-of-the-
art system and impact their decision for use of prescribed burning. This
chapter deals with examples of the preburn variables that must be quantified
and interpreted correctly and how such measurements can be made. It also
discusses ways that land managers can find the assistance needed for developing prescribed burning programs for their resources and provides key literature references.

Texas law clearly provides that landowners can burn on their own land in
accordance with the rules for outdoor burning from the Texas Commission
on Environmental Quality. However, the information contained in this
chapter is not intended to prepare people to do a prescribed burn, but rather
to illustrate the important variables involved and how they are measured. If
you have not been trained so that you fully understand the variables that
influence fire behavior and how to measure and interpret them, get assistance. If you do not have actual experience from hands-on participation in
prescribed burns planned and conducted by competent professionals, get
assistance. Because you started a fire and burned an area of your land without a negative incident does not constitute adequate training for planning
and managing prescribed fire. Every burn is different and must be ap-

proached with a good understanding of the interacting influences of the many fuel and environmental variables on fire behavior.

Where Can You Get Assistance?

There are competent contractors available in the state who can help landowners by planning and installing prescribed burns. More will be said about these certified prescribed burn managers and the increasing role they will play in implementing the use of fire in our natural resources. In the past, the Texas Forest Service and Texas Parks and Wildlife have been very helpful to landowners in the conduct of burns and other state and federal agencies have provided assistance as they could. However, most of these agencies have re-examined their roles in prescribed fire on private lands. Prescribed burning associations are becoming a more practical way for many landowners to obtain needed assistance.

Prescribed Burning Associations

It is difficult for state and federal agencies to meet the prescribed burning needs throughout Texas. This is due largely to reductions in staff; program driven initiatives; and an increase in the number of private landowners, both the total number and those who are interested in the use of prescribed fire on their land. It has become very apparent that other avenues are needed to meet the demand for prescribed burning.

Increasing recognition is being given to the benefits for landowners who become part of a prescribed burning association. Several burning associations have been established and more are in the early stages of development. The members are primarily local landowners and are assisted by local, federal, and state agencies. An excellent example of an effective prescribed burning association is the Edwards Plateau Prescribed Burning Association (EPPBA). The EPPBA was established in 1997 and covers six counties with over 100 landowner members. Meetings have been held at other locations in the Texas Hill Country to determine if landowners wanted to form an association similar to the EPPBA. Landowners from the northern Edwards Plateau and the Hill Country have shown interest in forming an association.

Associations are an excellent way to establish a base of crew members, equipment, and experience that are needed for prescribed burns. It is our opinion that burning associations will be the leading avenue by which prescribed burning will be increased on private lands in Texas.

Prescribed Burn Managers

The Texas law that deals with burning provides for the certification of prescribed burn managers. These prescribed burn managers will go through both a rigorous classroom and hands-on training program prior to certification and will carry a minimum of $1,000,000 per occurrence of liability insurance. The burn manager is also required to meet the experience standards set by the Prescribed Burn Board of Texas. It is anticipated that some of these people will be available as contractors to plan and conduct burns on private lands. They will provide an excellent means for land managers to have confidence that burn programs are safely and effectively applied, as well as relief from liability up to the limit of the required insurance coverage.

Using and Refining General Prescribed Burning Prescriptions

The general prescriptions for burning Texas rangelands developed by Texas Tech University (Wright and Bailey 1982) through years of prescribed fire research are still widely accepted and used today. The 60:40 rule serves as an excellent base for safely and effectively conducting prescribed burns. This prescription for blackline burning is as follows: (1) Temperature: 40–60 °F; (2) Relative Humidity: 40–60 %; and (3) Wind Speed: 0–8 mph.

Blacklines refer to an area burned to remove enough combustible material prior to ignition of the main burn (generally the headfire) so that the headfire will not carry through this previously burned area. Blacklines are particularly important in volatile fuel beds, such as those containing juniper (*Juniperus* spp.). When the above conditions are not present during the burning of blacklines, other variables should be monitored to reduce the risk of fire escape. These variables may include herbaceous fuel moisture, juniper leaf moisture, and fine fuel load.

Herbaceous (Fine) Fuel Moisture

One-hour dead fuel (typically grass) moisture is a primary controlling factor of fire behavior on the fire front (Andrews 1986). One-hour live fuel moisture depends on physiological changes in the living plant (Andrews 1986), and influences ignition and spread patterns depending on the distribution, quantity, and moisture content of live vegetation. Herbaceous Fuel Moisture (HFM) is the combination of both live and dead or cured 1-hour fuels.

HFM is obtained by clipping all herbaceous vegetation or fine fuels (fuels <0.25 in. diameter), weighing the sample immediately in the field, and then drying. Weights can be obtained by using a 200- or 300-gram spring scale with 2-gram reading intervals (Fig. 15.1). Samples can be dried in ovens that are manufactured specifically for the purpose and usually require about 72 hours at 140 °F in order to remove all moisture without damage to the sample material. Microwave ovens present an alternative method and will be discussed in more detail later. The fuel moisture percentage is obtained by the following formula: [(Wet Weight − Dry Weight)/Dry weight] × 100. In this case the HFM will be expressed on a dry weight basis. Care should be used when interpreting fuel moisture contents in prescriptions to know if the moisture percentage is expressed on a dry weight or a wet weight basis, even though the dry weight basis is standard. For example, given a wet weight of 100 grams and a dry weight of 75 grams, the fuel moisture on a dry weight basis [(100 − 75)/75] × 100 = 33%. Given the same wet weight of 100 grams and dry weight of 75 grams, the fuel moisture on a wet weight basis [(100 − 75)/100] × 100 = 25%. The difference in the two representations of moisture in the same fuel material can be significant in determining the appropriate prescription.

Figure 15.1.
Stripping of leaves.
Courtesy Keith Blair

Preliminary research indicates a HFM above 60% is needed in order to control fire behavior while blacklining. HFM above this level appears to reduce rate of spread and fireline intensity, while also minimizing spotting (the movement of firebrands, usually down wind, to cause ignition of fuel outside of the target area). The target HFM of 60% applies well to fine fuel loads <1,500 lb/acre, while as the fine fuel load increases, an increase in HFM will also be necessary. Overall, it is still necessary for ⅓ of the fine fuel complex to be cured in order for the fire to carry. However, the control of fire behavior is likely correlated to live fuel moisture (LFM) percentage and fine fuel load. When LFM is above 100%, torching of brush is very uncommon. Therefore, few firebrands are produced and spotting is minimal. When fine fuel loads are light (<1,000 lb/ac), compactness of these fuels is very low, thus creating poor reception for firebrands to land and produce ignition. Texas Tech University has several ongoing research projects examining fire behavior of summer burns under differing environmental conditions and their effects on the vegetation. Preliminary results indicate that 10-hr (0.25 to 1.0 inch diameter dead fuels) fuel moisture may play an important role in firebrand dynamics.

Juniper Leaf Moisture

The objective of prescribed burns in many areas of the Rolling Plains and Edwards Plateau Regions of Texas is often to control redberry juniper (*Juniperus pinchotii*) and/or Ashe juniper (*Juniperus ashei*). Both species fall into the category of high volatile fuels and are, therefore, given priority as an example because of the associated high level of risk. However, results are frequently variable. Holding other variables constant, this is likely due to the juniper leaf moisture (JLM). JLM can vary seasonally (Bunting et al. 1983) and higher JLM values require more fine fuel and/or more intense conditions to provide adequate juniper control. Texas Tech University and Texas Parks and Wildlife have monitored JLM prior to prescribed burns since 1988. For winter burns and fine fuel loads less than 2,000 lb/acre, a JLM less than 75% is often necessary to obtain adequate control of redberry juniper ranging from 4 to 8 feet in height. As JLM increases, good results can still be obtained if fine fuel load also increases. However, once JLM is above 95% it is doubtful that any winter burn would provide adequate control.

In areas such as the western Edwards Plateau it is often difficult to obtain fine fuel loads of 2,000 lb/acre; therefore, more intense fires are necessary to achieve adequate control of juniper. Juniper less than 4 feet tall are easily controlled with moderate intensity fires. However, taller juniper often requires a more intense fire as well as JLM of less than 90%. Once again, fine fuel load will determine the threshold of JLM necessary to achieve good control. Fine fuel load can be estimated by clipping and bagging all fine fuel material in a .25 m² plot, weighing in the field, and drying. The weight in grams of the dry material times 40 and multiplied by .891 gives an estimate of the pounds per acre of dry fine fuel (lb/ac).

Sampling Juniper Leaf Moisture

Samples are obtained by stripping leaves from the ends of stems (Figs. 15.2, 15.3). Samples should be collected from waist to chest high from all sides of the plant and from similarly sized plants within a given range site. Samples should be collected equally from old and new leaves when both are present.

Leaves should be placed in a pre-weighed paper bag. An adequate sample will weigh from 60 to 100 grams. On the bag, the date, time, bag weight, and green weight of the sample are recorded. The green weight is recorded in the field immediately after collecting the sample. Again, a 200- or 300-gram spring scale (Fig. 15.1), reading at 2-gram intervals, can be purchased through various catalogs, such as Ben Meadows Company and Forestry Supplies.

To obtain the JLM reading, the sample must be dried. The quickest method is to use a microwave (Fig. 15.4). The sample is dried on high at 30-second intervals. The bag should be weighed after each 30-second interval.

Figure 15.2.
Stripped leaves.
Courtesy Keith Blair

Figure 15.3.
Bag weighed in the
field with scales.
Courtesy Keith Blair

Figure 15.4.
Microwave with bag.
Courtesy Keith Blair

The sample is dried until it stops losing weight. The sample must be allowed to cool between each interval, especially toward the end of the drying sequence. If the sample feels very hot, then it must be allowed to cool before initiating another drying interval. If the sample begins to combust (smoke, smoldering, or fire present), then the sample is ruined and should be immediately extinguished. It is not recommended to use a microwave located in-side a dwelling or other facilities where individuals may be sensitive to the odor produced by drying juniper.

Once drying is completed, the JLM can be calculated. The bag weight must be subtracted from both the green and dry weight. The formula for obtaining JLM is as follows:

$$\frac{\text{Wet weight} - \text{Dry Weight}}{\text{Dry weight}} \times 100 = \%\text{JLM}$$

Examples:

$$\frac{100g - 50g}{50g} \times 100 = 100\% \text{ JLM}$$

$$\frac{105g - 62g}{62g} \times 100 = 69\% \text{ JLM}$$

Samples should be collected throughout the year to provide information for future reference relating to prescribed burning, drought conditions, and wildfire potential. Other information that is helpful and should be recorded includes average height of plants, ecological site, soil, soil moisture, and latest rainfall.

Following are some general winter burn guidelines based on JLM developed for 4 to 8 ft juniper:

<60%   Drought and/or summer conditions with high fire intensity and possible extreme fire behavior.

60–75%   Relatively dry conditions with high fire intensity, often used for headfires (fires set to burn with the wind; aggressive, wind-driven fires). Adequate fine fuel (>1,200 lb/acre) still needed for successful headfire.

76–85%   Moderate conditions with moderate fire intensity in juniper; often used for burning blacklines. Adequate fine fuel (>2,000 lb/acre) needed for successful headfire.

>85%   Relatively moist conditions with moderate to low fire intensity in juniper; often will experience poor top-kill of juniper. Adequate fine fuel (>3,000 lb/acre) may produce successful headfire.

Summer Prescriptions

Little research has been conducted on the development of summer burn prescriptions in western Texas. However, through several years of applying summer burns, blackline and headfire prescriptions for the eastern Edwards Plateau are proposed in Tables 15.1 and 15.2, respectively. In some cases, winter burns of the same year can be used as the blackline. This would depend on the amount of fine dead fuel that is present at the time of the summer burn. In most years, there would not be enough fuel accumulated following the winter burn to carry a fire. At this time, a minimum blackline width of 1,000 feet or greater is recommended to stop a summer headfire. It is also recommended that the headfire be burned in strips to keep fire behavior in check. Strip fires, or strip headfires, are ignited in the unburned

Table 15.1. Ignition, burning, and control for blacklines in summer.

	Planned or proposed	Actual
Scheduling		
Approximate date(s)	June–September	_____
Time of day	9 a.m. to 1 hr pre-sunset or at night	_____
Acceptable prescription range		
Temperature (broad range)	80°F–100°F	_____
Relative humidity	30–60%	_____
Wind direction	as needed	_____
Wind speed (MPH–eye level)	0–8 mph	_____
Cloud cover (> or <50%)	<50%	_____
Environmental conditions*		
Fine dead fuel moisture	6–12%	_____
10-hr fuel moisture	>8%	_____
Juniper leaf moisture	>80%	_____
Herbaceous fuel moisture	>60%	_____

*Also likely dependent on fine fuel load and live fuel moisture.

Table 15.2. Ignition, burning, and control for headfires in summer.

	Planned or proposed	Actual
Scheduling		
Approximate date(s)	June–September	_____
Time of day	9 a.m. to 1 hr pre-sunset	_____
Acceptable prescription range		
Temperature (broad range)	85°F–100°F	_____
Relative humidity	20–40%	_____
Wind direction	as needed	_____
Wind speed (MPH–eye level)	5–15 mph	_____
Cloud cover (> or <50%)	<50%	_____
Environmental conditions*		
Fine dead fuel moisture	3–8%	_____
Juniper leaf moisture	65–85%	_____
Herbaceous fuel moisture	<50%	_____

*Also likely dependent on fine fuel load.

fuel bed to simultaneously produce a headfire and a backfire. They are normally ignited moving across the area perpendicular to the wind direction and are used to reduce the distance from the headfire to the blackline. This reduces the area of the headfire that needs to be patrolled at a given time and contributes to overall safety of the burn.

Smoke Management

Smoke management is an extremely important element of prescribed fire applications and thus factors affecting the dispersion of smoke should be included in prescribed fire prescriptions. The first step in proper smoke management is to determine the area that will be affected by smoke and identify all smoke sensitive areas (for example: residents, livestock, cities, hospitals, etc.) within this area. When determining the area affected by smoke, use a 30° angle from the burn unit and allow 5 miles for grass fires or backfires (fires that move into the wind, normally set from firebreaks) and 10 miles for headfires or burns greater than 1,000 acres.

Land managers can greatly reduce the impact of smoke if they restrict burning to days when (1) mixing height (maximum height that rapid vertical mixing occurs) is greater than 1,700 feet, (2) transport winds (average wind speed and direction of all winds within the layer bounded by the surface and the mixing height) are 9 mph or greater, (3) background visibility is at least 5 miles, and (4) steps are taken to prevent stumps and snags from burning for long periods of times. Weather information relating to smoke management is given in most "Fire Weather Forecasts" (Fig. 15.5). Prescribed fires initiated that comply with these conditions should not cause a smoke problem.

Season of Burn

Until recently, land managers have primarily confined prescribed burning to the dormant season to meet management objectives of brush reduction, forage production, fuel reduction, and wildlife management. Managers concentrated the use of prescribed fire to the dormant season because fire prescriptions were widely published and understood, burning conditions were

Fire Weather Forecast

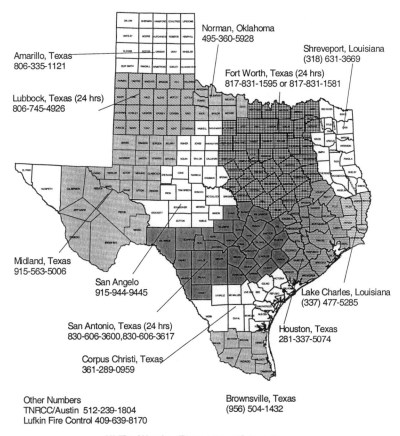

Amarillo, Texas
806-335-1121

Norman, Oklahoma
495-360-5928

Shreveport, Louisiana
(318) 631-3669

Fort Worth, Texas (24 hrs)
817-831-1595 or 817-831-1581

Lubbock, Texas (24 hrs)
806-745-4926

Midland, Texas
915-563-5006

San Angelo
915-944-9445

Lake Charles, Louisiana
(337) 477-5285

San Antonio, Texas (24 hrs)
830-606-3600,830-606-3617

Houston, Texas
281-337-5074

Corpus Christi, Texas
361-289-0959

Other Numbers
TNRCC/Austin 512-239-1804
Lufkin Fire Control 409-639-8170

Brownsville, Texas
(956) 504-1432

All Fire Weather Forecasts on Internet
http://www.boi.noaa.gov/firewx.htm

Figure 15.5.
National Weather Service Fire Weather Forecast.
Courtesy the National Weather Service

predictable and produced good smoke dispersion properties, and managers were experienced with fire behavior under these normally cool and docile, dormant-season burning conditions (Wright and Bailey 1982, Wade and Lunsford 1989, Robbins and Myers 1992). However, recent research indicates that dormant-season fires alone may be ineffective at maintaining communities of endemic species and reducing invasive brush, because they do not mimic natural ecosystem processes (Boerner et al. 1988).

Recent research of historical data indicates that lightning-ignited fires occurred primarily from late spring (May) to late summer (September) (Komarek 1964, Reap 1994). Reap (1994) shows lightning frequencies to be highest in June, July, and August, and lowest in December, January, and February. Fire frequency, fire intensity, and season of burning are major factors in determining the effects of fire on vegetation structure and composition (Lewis and Harshbarger 1976, Platt et al. 1988, Waldrop et al. 1992, Glitzenstein et al. 1995, Masters et al. 1995, Sparks and Masters 1996, and Sparks et al. 1998). Therefore, contemporary prescribed fire regimes that concentrate prescribed fire to the dormant season (November to March) differ from historical fire regimes and may be reshaping communities that evolved under the influence of fire in a different season (Sparks and Masters 1996). These factors taken together have influenced renewed interest in the use of summer burning and, because of the increased intensity and risk associated with such fires, have intensified the need for understanding the influence of variables on fire behavior.

Fire Behavior and Fire Season

Season of fire is often confounded by environmental variables such as weather conditions, fuel type, topography, soils, grazing pressure, and fire frequency (Ohmann and Grigal 1981, Sousa 1984, Wade 1986, Masters et al. 1993, Masters and Engle 1994). These factors affect fire behavior, which directly influences aboveground portions of woody plants (Van Wagner 1973, Rothermel and Deeming 1980, Alexander 1982, Wright and Bailey 1982, Wade 1986, Sparks 1996, Sparks et al. 1999). For example, fireline intensity affects survival of small diameter shrubs and trees (Wade and Johansen 1986, Sparks et al. 1999) and herbaceous composition (Bidwell et al. 1990). The amount of live or green fuel also affects fire behavior, and may reduce fireline intensity (Bragg 1982). Fireline intensity may have an overriding effect on seasonality depending on burning conditions (Glitzenstein et al. 1995, Sparks et al. 1999). These factors vary among specific locations within a region and managers should consider variations for each community type they manage. Recent developments in computer software, such as BEHAVE or BEHAVE PLUS, actually allow resource managers to enter environmental variables to predict fire behavior prior to ignition.

Understanding and Working With County Burn Bans

In Texas, the authority for County Commissioners to issue a burn ban is given by HB2650, 1999. This authority allows them to issue a burn ban for all or parts of a county. The burn ban is normally based on the Keetch-Byram Drought Index (KBDI) described by Keetch and Byram (1968) and calculated by the Texas Forest Service. However, more recently, the Texas Forest Service now uses a combination of variables and indices to facilitate decisions regarding burn bans. An important note here is that the KBDI is a drought index and not necessarily a fire behavior index. Also the KBDI can be highly variable across a county. When the KBDI is high, the potential for fuels to burn in an extreme manner is probable. However, even when the KBDI is high, it is possible to conduct safe prescribed burns when appropriate firebreaks are used and with appropriate dispensation from county officials.

Prescribed burns are based on a written prescription and during periods of high KBDI they will often have preestablished firebreaks. For juniper burns, these firebreaks should be at least 1,000 feet wide for summer burns and 500 feet wide for winter burns. Firebreaks can be blacklines that are burned under a specific prescription to help control the fire or they can be produced by other techniques. For example, some often conduct winter burns adjacent to pastures that will be burned in the summer. Under normal conditions, these pastures will not produce enough fine fuel to carry a fire for at least 1 year. The targeted pasture can then be burned with a wind that would run the fire into the previously burned pasture. Another example would be to use a technique called "grazing out." Although the authors do not personally recommend this technique, it is accomplished by placing large numbers of livestock in adjacent pastures to essentially remove all the fine fuel. An important note here is to make sure that juniper canopy cover is not dense enough to support a crown fire. Further research is needed to determine the thresholds of juniper canopy cover in combination with juniper leaf moisture necessary to stop a fire when fine fuel load is minimal.

Some counties do allow for prescribed burns during a burn ban. Some criteria for this type of exemption may include membership in a prescribed burning association or having a burn plan on file with the county or local conservation agency. HB2650 allows a county to issue a burn ban for all or parts of a county. These "parts" should be well defined to reduce confusion. Some counties use precincts, while others simply split up the county by using major highways. These "parts" can also be areas that are burned under a prescribed burn plan. Lastly, a certified burn manager will be exempt from county burns bans (HB3315) providing they follow the guidelines set by the Texas Prescribed Burn Board.

If county burn bans continue without any leniency toward prescribed burning, then fuel loads will continue to increase and wildfires will become larger and more frequent. This will not only impact the occurrence of wildfires, but will also have negative impacts on wildlife habitat. The general public may eventually conclude that all fire is bad.

Literature Cited

Alexander, M. E. 1982. Calculating and interpreting forest fire intensities. Canadian Journal of Botany 60:349–57.

Andrews, P. L. 1986. BEHAVE: fire behavior prediction and fuel modeling system—BURN subsystem, part 1. U.S. Forest Service General Technical Report INT-194.

Bidwell, T. G. , D. M. Engle, and P. L. Claypool. 1990. Effects of spring headfires and backfires on tallgrass prairie. Journal of Range Management 43:209– 12.

Boerner, R. E. J., T. R. Lord, and J. C. Peterson. 1988. Prescribed burning in the oak-pine forest of the New Jersey Pine Barrens: effects on growth and nutrient dynamics of two *Quercus* species. American Midland Naturalist 120:108–19.

Bragg, T. B. 1982. Seasonal variations in fuel and fuel consumption by fires in a bluestem prairie. Ecology 63:7–11.

Bunting, S. C., H. A. Wright and W. H. Wallace. 1983. Seasonal variation in the ignition time of redberry juniper in West Texas. Journal of Range Management 36:169–71.

Glitzenstein, J. S., W. J. Platt, and D. R. Streng. 1995. Effects of fire regime and habitat on tree dynamics in North Florida longleaf pine savannas. Ecological Monographs 65:441–76.

Keetch, J. J., and G. M. Byram. 1968. A drought index for forest fire control. U.S. Forest Service Research Paper SE-38.

Komarek, E. V. 1964. The natural history of lightning. Proceedings of the Tall Timbers Fire Ecology Conference 3:139–83.

Kulhavy, B. Hooper, and R. Costa, editors. Red-cockaded woodpecker: species recovery, ecology and management. Center for Applied Studies, Stephen F. Austin University, Nacogdoches, Texas.

Lewis, C. E., and T. J. Harshbarger. 1976. Shrub and herbaceous vegetation after 20 years of prescribed burning in South Carolina Coastal Plain. Journal of Range Management 29:13–18.

Masters, R. E., and D. M. Engle. 1994. BEHAVE—Evaluated for prescribed fire planning in mountainous oak-shortleaf pine habitats. Wildlife Society Bulletin 22:184–91.

———, R. L. Lochmiller, and D. M. Engle. 1993. Effects of timber harvest and periodic fire on white-tailed deer forage production. Wildlife Society Bulletin 21:401–11.

———, J. E. Skeen, and J. Whitehead. 1995. Preliminary fire history of McCurtain County Wilderness Area and implications for red-cockaded woodpecker management. Pages 290–302 *in* D. Kulhavy, B. Hooper, and R. Costa, editors. Red-cockaded woodpecker: species recovery, ecology and management. Center for Applied Studies, Stephen F. Austin University, Nacogdoches, Texas.

Ohmann, L. F., and D. F. Grigal. 1981. Contrasting vegetation responses following two forest fires in northeastern Minnesota. American Midland Naturalist 106:54–64.

Platt, W. J., G. W. Evans, and M. M. Davis. 1988. Effects of fire season on flowering forbs and shrubs in longleaf pine forests. Oecologia 76:353–63.

Reap, R. M. 1994. Climatology of lightning frequency. Southern Region Technical Attachment 94-63, November 15. National Weather Service, NOAA, Fort Worth, Texas.

Robbins, L. E., and R. L. Myers. 1992. Seasonal effects of prescribed burning in Florida: a review. Miscellaneous Publication Number 8. Tall Timbers Research Station, Tallahassee, Florida.

Rothermel, R. C., and J. E. Deeming. 1980. Measuring and interpreting fire behavior for correlation with fire effects. U.S. Forest Service General Technical Report INT-93.

Sousa, W. P. 1984. The role of disturbance in natural communities. Annual Review of Ecology and Systematics 15:353–91.

Sparks, J. C. 1996. Effects of growing-season and dormant-season prescribed fire on vegetation in red-cockaded woodpecker clusters. Thesis, Oklahoma State University, Stillwater.

———, and R. E. Masters. 1996. Fire seasonality effects on vegetation in mixed-, tall-, and southeastern pine-grassland communities: a review. Transactions of the North American Wildlife and Natural Resources Conference 61:230–39.

———, ———, D. M. Engle, M. E. Payton, and G. A. Bukenhofer. 1998. Effects of growing-season and dormant-season prescribed fire on herbaceous vegetation in restored pine-grassland communities. International Journal of Vegetation Science 9:133–42.

———, ———, ———, ———, and ———. 1999. Effects of growing-season and dormant-season fire on midstory and understory woody species in restored pine-grassland communities. Wildlife Society Bulletin 27:124–33.

Van Wagner, C. E. 1973. Height of crown scorch in forest fires. Canadian Journal of Forest Research 3:373–78.

Wade, D. D. 1986. Linking fire behavior to its effects on living plant tissue. Pages 112–16 in Proceedings Society of American Foresters National Convention, October 5–8, 1986. Birmingham, Alabama.

———, and R. W. Johansen. 1986. Effects of fire on southern pine: observations and recommendations. U.S. Forest Service General Technical Report SE-41.

———, and J. D. Lunsford. 1989. A guide for prescribed fire in southern forests. U.S. Forest Service Technical Publication R8-TP 11.

Waldrop, T. A., D. L. White, and S. M. Jones. 1992. Fire regimes for pine-grassland communities in the southeastern United States. Forest Ecology and Management 47:195–210.

Wright, H. A., and A. W. Bailey. 1982. Fire ecology: United States and southern Canada. John Wiley & Sons, New York.

R. James Ansley
and
Charles A. Taylor

16   What's Next
The Future of Fire
as a Tool for Managing Brush

200   As economics of profitable ranching become more challenging, one of the hardest decisions to make is how to deal with excessive woody vegetation. Because of its relatively low cost and environmental friendliness, fire is viewed as an extremely viable tool for reducing excess brush. However, serious problems can occur, as we witnessed with the unfortunate prescribed burn that became a destructive wildfire near Los Alamos, New Mexico in 2000. But what does the future hold? In this chapter, we will review some ideas relating to the future of fire as a management tool. Because the future is as much about interacting with people as it is about managing a natural resource, we have divided the chapter into two major sections, an "ecology and management" section, and a "political" section.

Ecological and Management Aspects

Some trends that we see occurring in the future with respect to ecology and management of fire include (1) a more efficient execution of prescribed fires, (2) a greater ability to manipulate fire behavior and effects, (3) increased use of fire within integrated treatment plans, (4) increased use of summer fires, (5) a greater realization of the limitations of fire, and (6) an increased use of fire to manage seeds and seedlings.

More Efficient Execution of Prescribed Fires

As information continues to become easier to access, there will be a greater ability on the part of the resource manager to physically execute a prescribed fire. The manager will have easier access to current weather forecasts, will have better and less expensive instruments to measure weather in the field, and can access imagery of weather patterns via satellite on a laptop computer. The manager will have better access to geo-referenced aerial images when planning a burn. A manager will also have access through the internet for better communication with all people involved in the fire, including neighbors, fire departments, agencies, and weather forecasters. For the onsite crew, better and less expensive radios and perhaps even Global Positioning System (GPS) locators will increase coordination of all crew members. This will result in increased safety for the crew and an increased ability to report spot fires that breach containment, etc.

More and more managers will have access to fire behavior models and, with laptop computers in the field, will be able to predict not only conditions which are safe to burn, but also fire effects on vegetation and soils. Interfacing a fire behavior model on a laptop with a portable weather station would allow a manager to instantaneously track the conditions required to produce a specific fire effect. It may be that such a window of opportunity would exist for only 2 or 3 hours in a day.

Greater Ability to Manipulate Fire Effects

With greater access to information about fire behavior and fire effects on vegetation, the manager will have more options for customizing a fire treatment plan. This may involve planning for different intensities to achieve different management goals. For example, burning under different air temperatures and relative humidities can produce different effects on mesquite (Britton and Wright 1971, Ansley et al. 1998).

There will be an increased use of more specific fire prescriptions. Such prescriptions will go beyond the traditional definition of prescription, which has primarily been used to differentiate an intentional fire from an act of nature, and will move toward achieving more specific effects than were expected in the past. Goals may be different for different pastures within the same ranch. For example, in one pasture the goal may be to top-kill 90% of the mesquite with a summer fire and shift the plant community to 50% cool-season grasses, while in an adjacent pasture, the goal may be to use a lower intensity fire to top-kill only 30% of mesquite and maintain a dominant warm-season grass community. In another example, a low-intensity fire may be desired for mesquite savanna development (Ansley and Jacoby 1998). As we gain more biological information, we will be better able to manipulate individual components of a ranch to different end results with fire.

Increased Use of Fire Within Integrated Treatment Plans

Often, dense stands of brush require mechanical or chemical treatment before prescribed fire is effective. This is because the development of such stands almost completely eliminates herbaceous production, which provides the fine fuels necessary to carry a fire. We believe that the use of prescribed fire in combination with other treatments is an area that will receive increased activity. While this has been discussed within academia for many years (Scifres et al. 1985), there are very few active examples of the planned use of an integrated treatment approach. Thus, this is an area that will receive increased research attention, but also will be applied in a more planned manner by more and more producers. The potential of fire to extend the life of herbicides needs to be explored both from a biological and economic standpoint (Scifres and Hamilton 1993). Herbicide/fire combinations for developing savanna or other management goals are also needed.

Key questions as to how such a program should be implemented remain unanswered. For example, how can fire be used in an integrated system to optimize wildlife habitat? Do I spray first, then burn, or burn first, then spray the brush left after the fire? At what point after an herbicide treatment is it most cost-effective to burn? Often, economic reality will dictate the sequence of treatments.

Increased Use of Summer Fires

There has been a great deal of interest during recent years in the use of summer fires for reducing brush. There is no question that summer fires are more effective than cool-season fires at top-killing mesquite. Some studies in Arizona suggest that velvet mesquite (*Prosopis velutina*) are killed by summer fires (Humphrey 1949, Blydenstein 1957), but increased mortality from summer fires has not been found with honey mesquite (*Prosopis glandulosa* var. *glandulosa*) in Texas (Stanley 1997, Ansley and Jacoby 1998, D. N. Ueckert, unpublished data). Summer fires are also more effective on cactus (*Opuntia* spp.) and juniper (*Juniperus* spp.) species (C. A. Taylor, D. N. Ueckert, unpublished data). Not only are summer fires more effective at reducing brush, some managers feel that summer fires allow one to burn without having an extended preburn grazing deferral. This certainly makes sense in areas dominated by cool-season annual grasses which provide adequate fuel for fire but have no forage value during the summer.

We anticipate that use of summer fires will increase. For example, an informal survey of members of the Edwards Plateau Prescribed Burning Association revealed that summer fire was preferred over cool-season fire by a ratio of 10:1. However, those using summer fire should proceed with caution. Wright and Bailey (1982) suggest that certain warm-season species, such as sideoats grama (*Bouteloua curtipendula* var. *curtipendula*), may be harmed by summer fires. Soil erosion may be increased, while water infiltration rates and soil nutrients may be decreased with intense summer fires (Hester et al. 1997). The question remains, if most natural fires occurred during summer months by lightning strikes, etc., then how were some warm-season perennial mid-grasses, such as sideoats grama, able to persist? It may be the combined effect of fire followed by grazing that actually harms grasses. Research from the Texas Agricultural Experiment Station at Sonora indicates that summer fire enhances warm-season perennial mid-grasses, but their recovery may take longer than grasses that are burned during the cool season. Summer burned pastures should be deferred until the vegetation recovers completely (i.e., one to three growing seasons of complete rest may be required).

Greater Realization of the Limitations of Fire

Our best estimate of the cost of burning medium-sized pastures (approximately 300 to 1,200 acres) in the Texas Rolling Plains and Edwards Plateau, using all the recommended safety procedures (preburned blacklines, dozed perimeter line, etc.), is about $2.50/acre (Ansley et al. 1999a). This compares to the cost of a root-killing herbicide treatment for mesquite of $22–25/acre. There is a perception among many that fire is a somewhat magical tool that can do what more expensive treatments will do at a tenth of the cost. Even though fire is considerably cheaper than other brush treatments, it has very clear limitations, both in ability to properly execute a burn and in its biological effect. These limitations and dealing with them by preplanned actions can be described in the following case study.

A Texas Rolling Plains Case Study

There are many limitations toward executing prescribed fires due to management or climatic constraints. Recent research on the Waggoner Ranch Kite Camp south of Vernon, Texas, offers a good example of such limitations in the use of fire. On the Kite Camp, a 35,000-acre area dominated by honey mesquite and a mixture of cool- and warm-season mid-grasses (no juniper species), we began a project in 1995 to determine if fire could be used within the constraints of a livestock production system. Mesquite were initially at about 10–30% cover. It was not economically feasible to spray herbicide first and use fire as a maintenance tool later. Several rotational grazing systems were established as experimental treatments to determine how many paddocks were needed within this soil type and precipitation zone to make fire work (Teague et al. 1997). There were eight separate systems and thirty-four paddocks total with each paddock about 400 to 1,200 acres. Our goal was to burn thirty-two (the two others were unburned controls) paddocks within a 5-year span (six to eight paddocks per year) and then apply a second burn on each paddock over the next 5 years. All burns were designed to be winter or early spring burns (January–March).

Our results give a good example of the promise and the limitations of fire. On one hand, we burned fourteen paddocks and over 11,000 acres from 1996 to 2000. We were able to burn even though 3 of the 5 years (1996, 1998, 1999) were extreme drought years. On the other hand, we fell far short of our stated goal (Ansley et al. 1999*b*). Moreover, half of the fourteen burns we completed produced less than 50% mesquite top-kill. On the positive side, these fires did create openings in the brush to facilitate a second burn, reduced some of the cactus, and restored some grass vigor.

Overcoming Limitations with Preplanned Actions

There were several factors involved that allowed us to burn in the midst of drought when others could not burn under such conditions. We used pre-burned blacklines (Wright and Bailey 1982). This enabled us to react quickly to the narrow windows of opportunity the weather gave us because, once the blacklines were burned, we could burn the main unit within about 2 or 3 hours at some later date. For example, in 1998, because of bad weather, we had less than 5 days between February 1 and April 1 which were determined to be adequate for burning. We were able to burn three separate paddocks, all more than a mile from each other, on a single day because the blacklines were preburned.

Other factors that allowed us to burn were rotational grazing and a slight reduction in stocking rate from 30 acres/cow to about 36 acres/cow. Rotational grazing enabled us to defer selected paddocks within each system for burning. Finally, our burn units were of a reasonable size (400–1,200 acres). The larger the burn unit, the greater are the limitations of how and when one can burn.

Recognizing Biological or Ecological Limitations of Fire

There are many biological or ecological limitations of fire. Many still view fire as the solution to all ecological problems because it is a natural part of the ecosystem (as opposed to herbicides, for example). However, many studies have shown that for every benefit fire has on some wildlife species, it hurts others or their habitat (Greenlee 1997). Fire can also have extreme and deleterious effects on soils and herbaceous vegetation (Sharrow and Wright 1977, Hobbs et al. 1991, Hester et al. 1997).

Fire also has real limitations as to its effect on brush. Fire will not kill many sprouting species, such as honey mesquite or redberry juniper (*Juniperus pinchotii*), even after numerous repeated fires or summer fires (Ansley and Jacoby 1998). In the case of mesquite, a top-killing fire can turn a plant with a tree-like growth form into a multi-stemmed bush which is probably more competitive with grasses and impairs visibility to a greater degree. Thus, managers of the future need to seriously consider what they will be getting if their goal is a top-killing fire on mesquite. They will most certainly need to be within a management system which allows them to apply fire every 7–10 years, and perhaps more often in different areas of the state (Teague et al. 1997). The same holds true for redberry juniper with the exceptions that (1) regrowth is not as fast as mesquite, and (2) the initial growth form of a mature juniper is no better than what a regrowth juniper will become. In other words, one does not potentially lose the tree as one would in top-killing large mesquite.

In Oklahoma and areas of Texas such as the Edwards Plateau, the juniper species are susceptible to fire and fire has real potential for restoring areas invaded by junipers to grasslands (McNeill 2000). A key element will be implementing management strategies so that fire can be used before juniper gets too big and, through competition, removes all the herbaceous fuel for carrying a fire. Unfortunately, juniper invasions have reduced herbaceous fine fuel loads in much of these areas. Thus, other treatments such as mechanical chaining will be needed before fire can be used effectively.

Limitations of the effects of fire on brush are compromised even more when corners are cut to further reduce the costs of burning. Many people will refuse to use preburned blacklines or will defer grazing for a shorter time than originally planned. This usually results in a less than satisfactory fire effect. In summary, greater realization of the limitations of fire will hopefully result in more realistic goals when incorporating fire as part of an overall management plan.

Increased Use of Fire to Manage Seeds and Seedlings

Research on control and management of woody plant seeds has been virtually ignored, yet the seed is the true source of the brush problem. Wright et al. (1976) found that honey mesquite less than 1.5 years of age were more easily killed by winter burns than were trees 3–5 years old. Seedling and young redberry juniper are also killed by fire (Wright and Bailey 1982). Future research will focus on strategic use of fire and other treatments to limit brush seed production and germination. This may involve building enough flexibility into a management plan to burn in fall or winter after a large seed crop has been produced.

Political Aspects

It is our opinion that the future of prescribed fire in Texas depends partly on politicians becoming educated on the the appropriate application of fire (i.e., it is a characteristic of civilization that the future of any technology will be influenced and directed by the political, social, and economic norms of the time—prescribed fire is no exception). Also, we believe that individuals who want to either support or use prescribed fire need to organize burning associations with clear objectives, and focus their efforts towards the safe and efficient application of fire. These organizations need to offer strong support for their membership as well as promote the benefits of prescribed fire to the general public.

The role of fire in Texas has been and still remains controversial from both an ecological and a management perspective. Negative experiences in Texas, largely with wildfires, gave rise to a collective notion that fire suppression was wise conservation (Scifres and Hamilton 1993). Furthermore, fire was purposely used as a tool of destruction within the state, which did not foster the beneficial aspects of fire. For example, in the early 1880s, grass was burned in retaliation for alleged grievances held against ranchers who were fencing the range. Under these conditions, fire was viewed as a destructive force to be prevented at all costs. Due to many negative experiences with fire, much of the ranching industry implemented fire suppression techniques rather than promoting the use of prescribed fire. For example, the use of fire guards were implemented on most large ranches. The XIT Ranch began plowing guards in 1885, the first year cattle were placed on its range (Haley 1929). Within a year over a thousand miles of guards, one hundred feet wide, had been plowed across the ranch.

Even today, the negative effects of fire receive much more press coverage than the positive effects. Examples include the catastrophic wildfires in Yellowstone National Park in 1988 and the Los Alamos fire in 2000, both of which were sensationalized by the media. These type of fires, along with the press coverage, create a negative feeling toward fire by the general public. However, there may be a shift occurring in public attitudes regarding prescribed fire, if burning is accomplished at the appropriate time and place, and in a safe manner (Scifres and Hamilton 1993).

Because of its political nature, the continued use of prescribed fire in Texas requires a core of range and forestry professionals who are proactively engaged in the development, administration, and interpretation of laws, regulations, training, etc., regarding prescribed fire. This kind of activity is absolutely necessary because there is still a general attitude among the public that range/forest fires are negative in most respects. Also, as the state's population continues to grow with more agricultural land being transferred into the rural/urban interface, fire and smoke management will certainly remain a hot-button issue.

In an attempt to become more politically active, recently, range and forestry professionals throughout the state decided to make prescribed fire a

statewide priority. As a result of their concern, an effort was initiated to so-
lidify the status of prescribed burning in the state. This effort grew out of a
concern that if the professionals did not take the lead and get something positive going, prescribed fire might be overly regulated or even lost as an effective vegetative management tool.

The Texas Case for Prescribed Burning

Since several other states had recently had experience in obtaining special
legislation allowing prescribed burning, it was felt that Texas should follow
in their steps and develop a strategy to insure that the practice of prescribed
fire was not banned. In April, 1998, a meeting of interested parties was held
in Kerrville, Texas to determine interest, gain information from other states,
and generally inform attendees on the status of prescribed burning in Texas.
This meeting was attended by approximately fifty individuals from approximately twenty-five organizations representing universities, state and federal
agencies, private landowners, foundations, conservation organizations, and
others. From this meeting, a mailing list of approximately sixty organizations and individuals was developed.

Subsequent to the Kerrville meeting, an organizational meeting was held
at the Welder Wildlife Refuge in Sinton on October 13, 1998. Approximately
thirty-five individuals attended this meeting, which created the loosely affili-
ated Texas Prescribed Burning Coalition (TPBC). The goals of the organization are to influence positive legislation concerning prescribed burning in
the state, to foster and support training in the art and science of prescribed
burning in Texas, and to disperse accurate information to the public on the
subject of prescribed burning. Three committees were named: legislative,
education and training, and public information.

The legislative committee formulated a burning bill for submission to the
legislature. The bill (HB-2599) passed both chambers, was signed by Governor Bush, and became law in September, 1999. TPBC's education and training committee formulated a curriculum with input from individuals in all
ecological regions of the state. The curriculum is based on the same one used
on several occasions by Texas Parks and Wildlife (TPWD). The public information committee is in charge of dispersal of information regarding the
training curriculum.

House Bill 2599

The burning bill does several things that are positive for prescribed burning
in Texas. It guarantees the right of all landowners in the state to burn on their
own property. It places no additional restrictions on the landowner's right to
burn. HB 2599 will be administered through the Texas Department of Agriculture (TDA). It establishes a prescribed burn manager certification system
and a prescribed burning board and citizen's advisory committee.

The prescribed burning board consists of representatives of TPWD,
Texas Agricultural Experiment Station (TAES), TDA, Texas Natural Re-
source Conservation Commission (TNRCC), Texas Forest Service (TFS),
Texas Agricultural Extension Service (TAEX), Texas State Soil and Water
Conservation Districts (TSSWCD), Texas Tech University-Range, Wildlife,

and Fisheries Department, Texas Christian University-Ranch Management Program, and five private landowners. The prescribed burning board is responsible for setting up the citizens advisory committee, establishing prescribed burning standards, certification, recertification, and training standards for prescribed burn managers, and establishing educational and professional requirements for burn instructors.

The Prescribed Burning Board expects to complete its charge under HB-2599 and make the certification and training process available by mid-2001. This activity is an ongoing process and will require constant vigilance from the state's prescribed fire professionals if fire is to remain a viable management option in the future.

Forming Cooperatives and Associations

Agricultural cooperatives or associations are certainly not new. The Texas Sheep and Goat Raisers' Association and Texas and Southwestern Cattle Raisers Association are examples of producer organizations that were established early in the twentieth century and have served their membership well. The founders of these organizations realized that organizing people with like-minded goals and objectives would be more effective than operating as individuals.

This same principle works for any group who is trying to succeed, especially in an environment where society is increasingly more involved with concern for activities on the state's private lands. In the future, it will take sophisticated professionals who are well organized to reconcile social demands with the realities of prescribed fire. If ranchers or other land managers want to use prescribed fire on a routine basis, they will have to organize at the local level to enhance their influence within the local community.

The Edwards Plateau Prescribed Burning Association: A Case Study

The Edwards Plateau Prescribed Burning Association, Inc., was established in the fall of 1997 on the Texas A&M University Research Station located between Sonora and Rocksprings. Local landowners attended a field tour that highlighted prescribed burning treatments on the research station. After the field tour, landowners were asked if they were interested in forming a burning association that would offer training in the use of prescribed fire, increase participation (provide a critical mass of people) on prescribed burns, pool equipment, and in general, foster a better understanding and appreciation for what prescribed fire could do.

The response to the idea of forming a burning association was very positive. A president was elected along with four board members and the association was off and running. Guidelines for the association were quickly established. Some of the important ones include (1) a $25.00 annual membership fee, (2) officers must be landowners (no agency personnel), (3) all members that are able are encouraged to attend fire training schools, (4) each fire will have its own burn plan that is prepared by the rancher, (5) each rancher will be liable for each fire on their property and proof of liability insurance is required, (6) each landowner is responsible for preparation of their own firelines, and (7) members are encouraged to actively participate on as many burns as possible. Participation is very important because it provides each member with experience on the fireline, helps members become acquainted with other members with the same goals and objectives, and fulfills one of the main reasons for the existence of the association (an experienced and trained labor force). Member participation is recorded for each burn and the level of participation is important when members request a burn on their own property.

Success of the Association Approach as a Future Vehicle

Even though the association is a new organization, it has been a great success. Currently, there are eighty-four members who represent approximately 500,000 acres of rangeland across six counties (Fig. 16.1). During the summer of 1999, fourteen summer burns were safely conducted by members of the association, most of which were conduced under burn bans. If a landowner was a member of the burning association and wanted to conduct a burn during the burn ban, County Commissioners would approve of an exemption due to the landowner's participation in the association.

The burning association has received much support from other organizations. For example, the Sonora Fire Department sold the Soil and Water Conservation District a pumper truck for $1.00 for use by the burning association. The Texas Forest Service lends the use of a large 6-wheel-drive tanker. Both pieces of equipment have been very useful. Both the Texas Co-

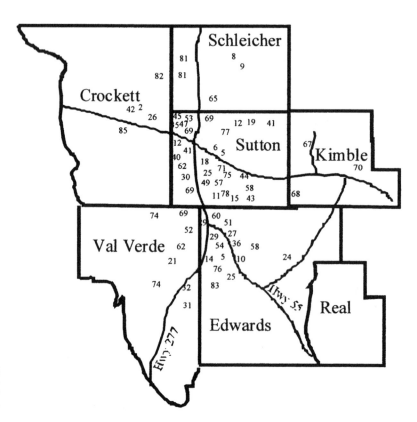

Figure 16.1.
Edwards Plateau Prescribed Burning Association, Inc. Location of Membership.

operative Extension and Natural Resource Conservation Service have been instrumental in the success of the association. Recently, the association gained nonprofit status and became incorporated. This has advantages in terms of receiving gifts, grants, and contributions of money.

The Edwards Plateau Prescribed Burning Association continues to grow in size and concept. It is providing landowners with a tool (fire) that is very cost effective. The association has empowered landowners at the local level and its organizational framework is being implemented across the state. It is having a positive, statewide effect on the application of prescribed fire.

Summary

We have attempted to present a vision of the future regarding prescribed fire. Based on our view, prescribed fire has a bright future, but only if we continue to develop and adapt new technology to improve the safety of fire as well as its effectiveness. Also, educators and researchers must become an active part of the political agenda. A brief overview of two approaches to securing a future for prescribed fire in Texas has been presented. In both instances it involves forming organizations of like-minded people with similar goals and objectives. To be effective and remain relevant, these organizations must also educate and inform the public of the vital role that prescribed fire can play in ensuring a sustainable source of natural food and fiber, wildlife habitat, and open space; conserving water, soil, and air; and maintaining a viable cultural heritage.

Literature Cited

Ansley, R. J., and P. W. Jacoby. 1998. Manipulation of fire intensity to achieve mesquite management goals in North Texas. Tall Timbers Fire Ecology Conference Proceedings 20:195–204.

———, D. L. Jones, T. R. Tunnell, B. A. Kramp, and P. W. Jacoby. 1998. Honey mesquite canopy responses to single winter fires: relation to fine fuel, weather and fire temperature. International Journal of Wildland Fire 8:241–52.

———, W. R. Teague, and W. E. Pinchak. 1999a. The cost of burning medium-sized pastures for mesquite control: data from the Kite Camp study. Page 21 *in* W. R. Teague, editor. Rolling Plains Ranching Systems Report, Technical Report 99-10, Texas Agricultural Experiment Station, Vernon.

———, ———, and ———. 1999b. Prescribed burning on the Kite Camp project: summary of progress 1995–1999. Pages 26–27 *in* W. R. Teague, editor. Rolling Plains Ranching Systems Report, Technical Report 99-10, Texas Agricultural Experiment Station, Vernon.

Blydenstein, J. 1957. The survival of velvet mesquite after fire. Journal of Range Management 10:221–23.

Britton, C. M., and H. A. Wright. 1971. Correlation of weather and fuel, variables to mesquite damage by fire. Journal of Range Management 24:136–41.

Greenlee, J. M., editor. 1997. Proceedings: fire effects on threatened and endangered species and habitats conference. International Association of Wildland Fire, Fairfield, Wash.

Haley, J. F. 1929. Grass fires of the southern plains. Pages 24–42 *in* Aston, B. W., editor. West Texas Historical Association Year Book, Abilene, Tex.

Hester, J. W., T. L. Thurow, and C. A. Taylor, Jr. 1997. Hydrologic characteristics of vegetation types as affected by prescribed burning. Journal of Range Management 50:199–204.

Hobbs, N. T., D. S. Schimel, C. E. Owensby, and D. S. Ojima. 1991. Fire and grazing in the tallgrass prairie: contingent effects on nitrogen budgets. Ecology 72:1374–82.

Humphrey, R. R. 1949. Fire as a means of controlling velvet mesquite, burroweed, and cholla on southern Arizona ranges. Journal of Range Management 2:175–82.

McNeill, A. 2000. Burn, baby, burn. The Cattleman 86:56–64.

Scifres, C. J., and W. T. Hamilton. 1993. Prescribed burning for brushland management: the South Texas example. Texas A&M University Press, College Station.

———, ———, J. R. Conner, J. W. Stuth, J. M. Inglis, T. G. Welch, G. A. Rasmussen, and R. P. Smith. 1985. Integrated brush management systems for South Texas: development and implementation. Texas Agricultural Experiment Station Bulletin 1493.

Sharrow, S. H., and H. A. Wright. 1977. Proper burning intervals for tobosagrass in West Texas based on nitrogen dynamics. Journal of Range Management 30:343–46.

Stanley, C. R. 1997. Effects of summer burning on Texas high plains vegetation. Thesis, Texas Tech University, Lubbock.

Teague, W. R., R. Borchart, J. Ansley, B. Pinchak, J. Cox, J. Foy, and J. McGrann. 1997. Sustainable management strategies for mesquite rangeland: the Waggoner Kite project. Rangelands 19:4–8.

Wright, H. A., and A. W. Bailey. 1982. Fire ecology—United States and southern Canada. John Wiley & Sons, New York.

———, S. C. Bunting, and L. F. Neuenschwander. 1976. Effect of fire on honey mesquite. Journal of Range Management 29:467–71.

Issues in Brush Management

17 Brush Management
Economic and Financial Considerations

J. Richard Conner

During the twentieth century, woody plants, particularly mesquite (*Prosopis* 213
spp.) and juniper (*Juniperus* spp.), have come to dominate much of Texas
that was previously covered by grassland or open savanna (Smeins et al.
1997).

Replacement of grasslands and savannas with woodlands is a trend that
coincides with European settlement and is attributed to a variety of factors,
including reduced fire frequency and overgrazing (Scholes and Archer
1997). When woody species increase in abundance and change grasslands
and savannas into shrublands and woodlands, the ability of the land to provide valuable ecological services is altered. The altered ecological services
include the provision of forage for grazing livestock, habitat for wildlife,
sources of surface and ground water, and carbon and nitrogen sequestration
and cycling potential.

While brush management has long been an important practice on Texas
rangelands, it was, here-to-fore, used primarily to enhance livestock production. Recently, there has been an increased interest in manipulation and
management of woody vegetation on rangelands to (1) enhance their suitability and/or productivity as wildlife habitat, (2) provide sources of surface
water and/or groundwater recharge, and (3) serve as possible sinks for atmospheric carbon. In the first section of this chapter we will examine these
potential ecological services and some of their associated economic aspects
in more detail.

Regardless of the reason for using it, brush manipulation and management are almost always costly, and often require very large investments.
Whether the purpose is to enhance wildlife habitat, water yield, livestock
production, or all of these, there are several economic and financial concepts
and analytical techniques that managers may use to help insure that the
brush management practices employed are as efficient and effective as possible. In the second section of this chapter we will delineate, describe, and explain the possible uses of a few of the most important of these concepts and
techniques.

Ecological Services and Brush Management
Livestock Forage

Benefits from brush control are based on the present value of increased net returns made available to the ranching operation through increases or expansions of the typical livestock (cattle, sheep, or goats) enterprise that would be reasonably expected to result from implementing the brush control program. For this land use, increased net returns would result from increased amounts of usable forage (grazing capacity) being produced by removing the brush and eliminating much of the competition for light, water, and nutrients within the plant communities. Thus, with more grazeable forage produced per unit area per year, stocking rates that are higher than pre-brush control levels can usually be maintained after brush is removed.

If livestock grazing were the only land use of interest, then the landowner would logically want to minimize brush canopy in order to allow the land to produce as much grazeable forage as possible. In the early years of brush control, this concept led many ranchers to clear brush from as much of their land as was practical and to pursue other grazing enhancement practices such as re-seeding rangelands with introduced pasture grasses. Obviously, such practices were not conducive to other land uses such as providing wildlife habitat. For this, and other reasons, complete clearing of management units is practiced much less frequently in recent years.

Wildlife Habitat

One characteristic of rangelands is vegetative diversity and this characteristic is especially prominent in brush-infested rangelands. Due to the differences in dietary requirements, feeding habits, etc. of different kinds of animals, increased vegetative diversity facilitates the utilization of a rangeland ecosystem by a larger variety of different kinds of animals. This characteristic allows for the complementary joint use of many rangeland ecosystems for different enterprises. For example, beef cattle production and deer and/or quail lease hunting enterprises are commonly found simultaneously on many Texas ranches.

Intermittent disturbance of rangelands that are dominated by woody plants can result in a landscape mosaic that supports greater species richness, provides increased forage for livestock, and enhances habitat for many wildlife species. A problem with such rangeland management practices is that it requires continuing inputs to maintain the selected landscape architecture (Fulbright 1996). In a study of Edwards Plateau—where ranchers had both livestock grazing and deer-hunting enterprises—the estimated economically optimal brush cover was 30%, but the survey respondents reported an average current brush cover of 41% on their land and the average preferred brush cover was reported to be 27% (Garriga 1998).

Another problem with brush management for wildlife enhancement is that landscapes deemed ideal for northern bobwhite quail (*Colinus virginianus*) are usually not the best habitat for white-tailed deer (*Odocoileus virginianus*). Likewise, habitat ideally suited for golden-cheeked warblers (*Dendroica chrysoparia*) is not the best black-capped vireo (*Vireo atricapilla*) habitat. Yet, on many properties in this state, with brush sculpting we can create habitat that favors any one of these animal species. In so doing, however, we may make the landscape much less habitable to other species of interest. Thus, we are faced with the need to assess the trade-offs associated with sculpting the brush to enhance habitat for a particular kind of animal in terms of what we will forego because the sculpting decreases the landscapes habitability for other kinds of animals. These trade-offs often have real and direct economic and financial consequences, particularly as they impact hunting lessees and/or nature tourists' perceptions of the suitability of the landscape for their purposes or as they impinge on the productivity of the livestock enterprises concurrently utilizing the land.

Water Supply

Present day shrublands and woodlands have hydrologic characteristics much different from those of the original grasslands. Compared to plants in grasslands, tree and shrub species in shrublands and woodlands are more deeply rooted and have more root biomass and density than grasslands (Boutton et al. 1999). Thus, water that would infiltrate beyond the reach of grass roots and contribute to local groundwater recharge or other hydrologic fluxes would likely be captured and transpired by shrubland or woodland plant communities. Several studies indicate that an increase in brush cover frequently results in depleted water yield because woody plants tend to intercept precipitation and use more water than herbaceous plants (Hibbert 1979, Thurow and Hester 1997).

Research on brush control and water balance began in the 1920s, but the idea of brush control as a possible means of alleviating water scarcity in drought-prone western states started to take hold in the 1970s (Gifford 1975). Although not applicable everywhere, recent research results give compelling evidence of gains in off-site water because of brush control in the Edwards Plateau (Thurow and Hester 1997, Redeker 1998). Actual water yield, however, is dependent upon rainfall variations and many other landscape variables. An exponential increase in water yield has been reported when brush cover declines from 15% to 0% brush cover (Thurow et al. 2001), but few ranchers are likely to control and maintain brush to such low densities without public funding.

The Texas Legislature cited the relationship between brush removal and increasing water yield as a rationale for passing the Texas Brush Control Act to encourage brush control on private ranches (Texas State Legislature 1985). However, no funds were initially appropriated to implement the act because it was unclear which Texas rangelands would likely yield significant amounts of water following brush control (Griffin and McCarl 1989).

Early research, combined with successful demonstration projects on Rocky Creek of the Middle Concho River (Moseley 1987) and Seco Creek in the Medina River Basin (Newman 1992), led to a 1998 feasibility study of brush control for water yield on the North Concho River near San Angelo, Texas. The study was undertaken as a joint project of the Texas Water Development Board, Texas State Soil and Water Conservation Board (TSSWCB), Upper Colorado River Authority, Texas Agricultural Experiment Station, and Texas Agricultural Extension Service. Results indicated that with publicly funded cost-share of 70 to 80%, significant numbers of landowners would participate in a brush control program. State costs for the program were estimated at $49.75 per acre-foot of added water averaged over the entire North Concho Basin (Bach and Conner 1998).

In response to this study, the 1999 Texas Legislature appropriated approximately $6 million to begin implementing the brush control program on the North Concho Watershed. A companion bill authorized feasibility studies on eight additional watersheds across Texas. Subsequently, the 2001 Texas Legislature appropriated additional funds to continue implementation of the program on the North Concho and to begin implementation on several other watersheds across the state.

Carbon Sequestration

The rangelands of today's world were formed during earlier times when atmospheric carbon concentrations were 25 to 50% less than the concentrations today. Transpiration from plants generally declines with an increase in CO_2 concentration, while in many plants photosynthesis and growth increase (Polley 1997). In response to increased CO_2 most C3 plants (woody and cool-season grass species) exhibit increased growth as compared to most C4 plants (warm-season grasses). Some studies have indicated that this phenomenon may partially explain the tremendous increases in shrub and woody plants in formerly open grasslands and savannas (Mayeux et al. 1991).

According to Hibbard et al. (2000) a result of shifting from grass to woody plant dominated land cover in subtropical savanna ecosystems in South Texas is that soils in the first 10 cm of the profile have higher soil organic carbon (SOC) concentrations and mass when associated with woody groves and patches relative to the surface soils of remnant grass-dominated patches. Their studies also show that monthly root biomass fluctuations were greater than annual foliar litter fall in both upland and lowland woody patches. These findings suggest that below ground inputs of organic matter may cause soil physical and chemical properties to change after woody plant establishment. The data show that as the amount of woody plant growth increases in grasslands, SOC accumulation could be rapid and substantial.

Another study in the Rio Grande Plains of Texas indicates that woody patches are sequestering atmospheric carbon derived from both the previous C4 grassland and the present C3 woody vegetation (Boutton et al. 1999). In the same area, models, historical aerial photos, and ground measurements indicate that with succession from presettlement savanna grasslands to the current savanna woodland over the last 100 years, soil and plant carbon mass has increased 10% and 10-fold, respectively (Archer et al. 2001). These scientists expect ecosystem carbon storage to continue to increase as woody vegetation communities mature and continue to expand into the remaining herbaceous areas.

In another report, Follett et al. (2001) estimate that reconverting cropland back to grassland can result in SOC sequestration rates ranging from 400 to 1,200 kg C/ha/yr. They further estimate that this rate could be maintained for approximately 25 years before the reconverted grasslands would reach a steady state where the annual soil output of carbon to the atmosphere would equal its input.

General concern over the rapid rate of increase in CO_2 in the atmosphere has heightened during the past two decades. Recent international climate change agreements and proposed changes in U.S. Agricultural Policy could result in incentives to landowners to adapt carbon sequestering management practices (SWCS 2000). These incentives might be in the form of marketable carbon credits or annual payments for participation. Regardless, one likely result of such a policy would be the reconversion of additional acreage from cropland back to grassland or wood/shrub lands.

Economic Concepts and Analyses Applied to Brush Management Planning

Planning is the primary function of management. Any brush management practices employed should be the result of a thorough, holistic, and strategic planning process like the Integrated Brush Management Systems (IBMS) process (Hanselka et al. 1996). The planning process is generally expected to consist of five steps:

1. *Establish and prioritize goals.* Delineate milestones by which to measure progress. Establish and communicate order of importance of goals and resolve conflicting objectives.

2. *Inventory and assess resources.* The combination and capabilities of the land, animals, finances, facilities, and human resources will be different for each and every ranch and must, therefore, be assessed as to their availability and capability.

3. *Identify and analyze alternative courses of action.* The resources available on a ranch may be used in a variety of different enterprises to achieve a wide array of goals. For each alternative, or combination of alternative courses of action, the planner should determine if there are adequate resources available to support the alternative and assess the expected impact of the alternative on all the goals of the manager/owner(s).

4. *Alternative selection.* Select and implement the alternative(s) that most nearly achieve all goals and objectives.

5. *Monitor results and alter plan.* After selection, the implemented alternative should be monitored and the performance information used to reassess and modify the courses of action to better achieve goals.

Use of the planning process will insure that the (expected) impacts of all courses of action (like brush management) on all of the resource manager's goals will have been considered prior to being implemented.

Opportunity Costs

Opportunity cost refers to the fact that using ones resources—like land, capital, etc.—for a particular purpose means that the same resources cannot be simultaneously used for an alternative purpose. In addition, the foregone alternative purpose will not be achieved because the opportunity to achieve it will be lost. The implication is that if we are to use our resources efficiently, we should devote them to achieving a purpose that is at least as important as the next best alternative that we could expect to achieve with the same resources.

Opportunity cost is an important concept in making decisions about capital investments in that if the objective is to maximize the annual earnings (annual rate of return) from investments, then one should choose investment alternatives for which the expected pay-off is at least as high as the next best alternative. In many cases, land managers/owners will be faced with several alternative investment opportunities, including brush sculpting, water development, food plot establishment, etc. for which there will be limited capital available. In such cases, the opportunity cost concept may be quite helpful when deciding which of the available alternatives to choose.

Cost Effectiveness

There are several approaches (treatment options) available to the land manager desiring to manipulate brush and/or modify landscapes; e.g., mechanical, chemical, fire, hand cutting, etc. Many land manager/owners will find the decision as to which treatment or combination of treatments to use difficult. The difficulty stems from a variety of sources. However, uncertainty about the outcome (efficacy, impact on vegetative competition and wildlife populations, etc.) when applied to their specific landscape and differences in cost of, and time required for, implementation of the different treatments are two of the most important reasons that treatment selection is difficult. Since uncertainty will be discussed later in this section let us now consider treatment costs. There are three important aspects to the consideration of treatment cost. The most obvious is the direct cost of implementation. This is usually the easiest to estimate in that there are few uncertainties involved. That is, the prices and estimates of quantities required of materials and services (herbicides, fuel, equipment rental, and wage rates, etc.) are easily obtained from suppliers.

Indirect costs, associated with implementing specific treatments, however, may be more troublesome. For example, implementing a prescribed burn usually requires that a pasture be deferred from grazing for 6 to 12 months prior to and 2 to 6 months after burning. This is important, because while the direct costs of prescribed burning are usually low the value of the forage used for fuel may be as valuable, or more so, than the value of the direct costs associated with burning. The value of the fuel depends on the amount of total forage available on the ranch, livestock production practices, livestock prices, or the cost of furnishing alternative feeds.

The third aspect of costs that can be troublesome is the timing in which either costs are incurred or benefits (results) are forthcoming. The important consideration here is that costs incurred in one year (e.g., the current year) should not be compared directly to either benefits or costs expected to be accrued or incurred in a later year. This is because the costs or benefits expected in the later year(s) do not have the same "present value" as the current year costs. To appropriately compare costs incurred in one year with costs or benefits expected to incur or accrue in another, the costs or benefits expected in the later years should be reduced to their present value by applying an appropriate discount factor. That is, they should be discounted to reflect the fact that funds used today are no longer available to earn a return that could be obtained from an alternative investment (e.g., a savings account). However, funds not required until later years are, in the interim, free to earn returns in these alternative investments. An example of this cost, is that funds invested in a CD cannot be used (without incurring a substantial penalty) until the CD matures. However, at maturity, interest earnings represent the "value of time." The actual value of the time that the CD is maturing depends upon the original interest rate specified for the CD. The higher the interest rate the more valuable the time period in question. Thus, an investment in brush control requires a certain time period for maturity, just as a CD requires a certain time for maturity. The higher the individual's opportunity cost of money, or interest rate, the greater cost must be paid for the time involved for brush control to mature.

Risk, Uncertainty, and Irreversibility

Selection of a brush management program or system to aid in achievement of livestock, water yield, wildlife and/or recreational enterprise goals has generally been problematic for rangeland managers, primarily because of the difficulty associated with estimating the impacts of a practice or system on their enterprise goals. The difficulty stems largely from uncertainty about how implementation of a practice or system will actually effect the enterprise productivity of a site in the years following implementation. For example, if the enterprise of interest is livestock production, a specific brush management practice (like an herbicide application) would be expected to initially result in a large reduction in the percent composition made up of the brush species, and correspondingly, a significant increase in the production of herbaceous plants. This change in plant composition on the site should then result in increased carrying capacity for cattle and, hopefully, increased net returns per acre.

To date, the accepted methodology for estimating the impacts of a brush management practice or system on livestock and/or wildlife enterprises is through use of estimated response curves. The response curve represents the expected change in carrying capacity over a specified planning period (usually 5–15 years) of a specific site resulting from implementation of a specific practice or system. Estimation of the response curve requires significant previous experience with the practice or system being considered in a variety of cases to allow understanding of differences in impact related to different growth forms of target brush species, pre-practice utilization, soils, etc. In addition to carrying capacity changes, other impacts of implementing the practice or system on enterprise goals (like changes in annual operating cost or individual animal performance) must also be estimated.

Several critical assumptions underlie development of response curves, one of which is that precipitation is normal (based on the long-term average) throughout the planning period. In actuality, however, due to the effects of large year-to-year variation in annual precipitation on practice efficacy and forage production, the extent of changes in carrying capacity and/ or other enterprise impacts can vary significantly from one application of a practice to the next, even when the soils, original species compositions, climates, etc. are similar. Recently, an alternative methodology which allows incorporation of the risk associated with annual variation in forage production, livestock production costs, and prices into the assessment process for brush management practices/systems has been developed (Schuman et al. 2001). The methodology, however, requires the use of sophisticated biophysical and econometric simulation models and is, therefore, quite costly to parameterize and operate.

Another problematic aspect of implementing brush management practices is that once implemented, they are, from a practical point of view, irreversible. While it is true that we may not be able to project the result or outcome of a practice with certainty, it is, nonetheless, also true that the landscape will be forever changed significantly by the implementation of the practice(s). This irreversibility further underscores the need for adequate planning before implementing any brush management or landscape manipulation practice.

One potential impact of brush management that should not be overlooked in the planning process is the likely effect of the proposed action on the market value of a property. Whether the market price is enhanced, or reduced, by the presence, or absence, of brush depends on the interests and intended land use of the buyers dominating the rural land market for an area. In many areas—particularly those where land uses like wildlife habitat, recreation, exurban residences, etc. are important sources of demand—a significant reduction in brush canopy on a property will likely result in a significant reduction in its market value. Alternatively, in areas where buyers primarily interested in livestock production dominate the market, land that is relatively brush free would likely fetch a better price than similar land with a large percent brush canopy cover. It should also be noted that the type of woody plants involved can be significant. For example, landowners in the Edwards Plateau considering participating in a state cost-share program of brush removal to enhance off-site water yield indicated that they would only participate by removing juniper. They indicated they would not control live oak (*Quercus virginiana*) because it would significantly lower the market price of their land. Given its irreversibility, landowners would be well advised to consider the potential impacts of any contemplated brush control on future land sale prices before proceeding.

Conclusion

Rangelands offer a large variety of potential ecological services and alternative land use enterprises, each of which can be enhanced or constrained through manipulation of brush cover. Many of these services and land uses can coexist on a property, and some are even complementary. Significantly, however, many of the ecological services and land uses are competitive and force the land manager into selecting some and excluding others. For example, carbon sequestration and off-site water yield cannot be optimized simultaneously since water yield is enhanced with little or no brush and carbon sequestration increases with brush.

In conclusion, economic and financial considerations of brush management are important aspects of the decision making process. The concepts of opportunity costs and goals or objectives are not the same for any two individuals. Thus, it is not possible to perform a single economic analysis that meets every individual's situation. Individuals must establish their own unique combination of willingness to take risks, identify their individual opportunity costs, and develop acceptable alternatives. After these factors have been identified, the tools of economic analysis can be consistently applied and a specific decision can be made using the results of the economic analysis. What is right for one individual may be unacceptable for another. However, it is extremely important to understand the role and mechanics of the economic tools that are available to assist the individual in making the right decision for their specific question. Just as all carpenters use the same tools to build a house, not all houses end up looking the same. People are encouraged to learn how to use the broad range of economic tools available today. Budgeting, capital budgeting, partial budgeting, cash flow, as well as many other analytical techniques, have been around a long time. New computer software is available to make the tools more operational but the basic concepts of their use do not change over time. These techniques are demonstrated in the following Case Study (Appendix).

Literature Cited

Archer, S., T. W. Boutton, and K. A. Hibbard. 2001. Trees in grasslands: biogeochemical consequences of woody plant expansion. Pages 115–37 *in* E. D. Schultze, S. P. Harrison, M. Heinmann, E. A. Holland, J. Lloyd, I. C. Prentice, D. Schimel, editors. Global biogeochemical cycles in the climate system. Academic Press, San Diego, California.

Bach, J. P., and J. R. Conner. 1998. Economic analysis of brush control practices for increased water yield: the North Concho River example. Pages 209–17 *in* R. Jensen, editor. Proceedings of the 25th Water for Texas Conference—Water Planning Strategies for Senate Bill 1. Texas Water Resources Institute Conference, December 1–2, 1988, Austin.

Boutton, T. W., S. R. Archer, and A. J. Midwood. 1999. Stable isotopes in ecosystem science: structure, function, and dynamics of a subtropical savanna. Rapid Communications in Mass Spectrometry 13:1–15.

Conner, J. R., and J. P. Bach. 2000. Assessing the economic feasibility of brush control to enhance off-site water yeild. Pages 2.1–2.10 *in* Brush management: water yeild feasibility studies for eight watersheds in Texas. Final Report to the Texas State Soil and Water Conservation Board, TWRI TR-182. Texas Water Resources Institute, College Station, Tex.

Follett, R. F., J. M. Kimble, and R. Lal. 2001. The potential of U.S. grazing lands to sequester carbon. Pages 401–30 in R. F. Follett, J. M. Kimble, and R. Lal, editors. The potential of U.S. grazing lands to sequester carbon and mitigate the greenhouse effect. Lewis Publishers, New York.

Fulbright, T. E. 1996. Viewpoint: a theoretical basis for planning woody plant control to maintain species diversity. Journal of Range Management 49:554–59.

Garriga, M. D. 1998. Tradeoffs associated with increasing water yield from the Edwards Plateau, Texas: balancing private costs and public benefits. Thesis, Texas A&M University, College Station.

Gifford, G. F. 1975. Approximate annual water budgets of two chained pinyon-juniper sites. Journal of Range Management 28:73–74.

Griffin, R. C., and B. A. McCarl. 1989. Brushland management for increased water yield in Texas. Water Resources Bulletin 25:175–86.

Hanselka, C. W., W. T. Hamilton, and J. R. Conner. 1996. Integrated brush management systems (IBMS): strategies and economics. Texas Agricultural Extension Service B-6041.

Hibbard, K. A., S. Archer, D. S. Schimel, D. V. Valentine. 2001. Biogeochemical changes accompanying woody plant encroachment in subtropical savanna. Ecology 82:1999–2011.

Hibbert, A. R. 1979. Managing vegetation to increase flow in the Colorado River Basin. U.S. Forest Service General Technical Report RM-66.

Mayeux, H. S., Jr., H. B. Johnson, and H. W. Polly. 1991. Global change and vegetation dynamics. Pages 62–74 *in* J. F. James, J. O. Evans, M. H. Ralphs, and R. D. Childs, editors. Noxious range weeds. Westview Press, Boulder, Colorado.

Moseley, M. 1987. The creek that slumbered 40 years. Pages 158–60 *in* W. White, editor. USDA yearbook of agriculture 1987: our American land. Washington, D.C.

Newman, W. 1992. Seco Creek project: demonstration and research. Pages 8–13 *in* Water for South Texas. CPR 5043-6, Texas Agricultural Experiment Station, Uvalde.

Polley, H. W. 1997. Invited synthesis paper: implications of rising atmospheric carbon dioxide concentration for rangelands. Journal of Range Management 50:561–77.

Redeker, E. J. 1998. The effects of vegetation on the water balance of an Edwards Plateau watershed: a GIS modeling approach. Thesis, Texas A&M University, College Station.

Scholes, R. J., and S. R. Archer. 1997. Tree-grass interactions in savannas. Annual Review of Ecology and Systematics 28:517–44.

Shumann, K. D., J. R. Conner, J. W. Richardson, J. W. Stuth, W. T. Hamilton, and L. Drawe. 2001. The use of biophysical and expected payoff probability simulation modeling in the economic assessment of brush management alternatives. Journal of Agricultural and Applied Economics 3:539–549.

Smeins, F., S. Fuhlendorf, and C. Taylor, Jr. 1997. Environmental and land use changes: a long-term perspective. Pages 1.3–1.21 *in* C. A. Taylor. Proceedings 1997 Juniper Symposium. Technical Report 97-1, Texas Agricultural Experiment Station, San Angelo.

Soil and Water Conservation Society (SWCS). 2000. Growing carbon: a new crop that helps agricultural producers and the climate too. Soil and Water Conservation Society. http://www.swcs.org/f_pubs_education.htm

Texas State Legislature. 1985. Sixty-ninth legislature: session logs. Chapter 6555. Pages 2409–13. Austin.

Thurow, A. P., J. R. Conner, T. L. Thurow, and M. D. Garriga. 2001. A preliminary analysis of Texas ranchers' willingness to participate in a brush control cost sharing program to improve off-site water yields. Ecological Economics 37:137–50.

Thurow T. L., and J. W. Hester. 1997. How an increase or reduction in juniper cover alters rangeland hydrology. Pages 4.9–4.22 *in* C. A. Taylor, editor. Proceedings 1997 Juniper Symposium. Technical Report 97-1, Texas Agricultural Experiment Station, San Angelo.

Appendix: CASE STUDY
Upper Colorado Watershed

The State of Texas has funded several studies to estimate the economic feasibility of programs that encourage rangeland owners to manage brush in order to increase the availability of downstream water. This case study of the Upper Colorado Watershed (Adapted from Bach and Conner 1998, Conner and Bach 2000) details the costs and benefits of brush management for different brush types and densities and illustrates their use in determining cost-share amounts for participating landowners.

Rancher participation in any brush management program primarily depends on its economic consequences for the rancher. Any difference between the total cost of the brush management practices and the amount the participating landowner is willing to pay would have to be contributed by the state in order to encourage landowner participation. Thus, the public must determine whether the benefits of additional water for public use are equal to or greater than the state's share of the costs of the brush management program.

In this case study, the appropriate brush management practices, or treatments, for each brush category and their estimated costs were obtained from focus groups of landowners and NRCS and Texas Cooperative Extension personnel in each watershed. Brush management practices included the initial and follow-up treatments required to reduce all categories of brush types and densities to 3–8 percent canopy cover and to maintain the reduced level for at least 10 years. These treatments varied among watersheds due to differences in terrain, soils, amount and proximity of cropland to the rangeland, etc. An example of the management practices, the year of application, and the costs for the Upper Colorado Watershed are outlined in Table 17.1. Year 0 is the year that the initial practice is applied while years 1–9 refer to follow-up treatments in subsequent years.

Yearly costs for the brush management treatments and the present value of those costs (assuming an 8% discount rate as opportunity cost for rancher investment capital) are also displayed in Table 17.1. Present values of different management programs are used for comparison and occur at different times within the planning horizon (10 years). Present values of total per acre management costs range from $44.89 for moderate cedar that can be initially controlled with mechanical treatments to $94.89 for heavy mesquite that cannot be controlled with herbicides but must be initially controlled with mechanical practices.

Rancher benefits from brush management (and, thus, the rancher cost share) were estimated as those benefits expected to accrue to any rancher participating in the program over a 10-year period. These benefits were based on the present value of increased net returns to the ranching operation through expansions of the typical livestock (cattle, sheep, or goats) and wildlife enterprises that could be reasonably expected to result from implementation of the brush management program.

Most wildlife operations were simple hunting leases with deer, turkeys, and quail being the most commonly hunted species. For control of heavy

Table 17.1. Cost of water yield brush management programs by type, Upper Colorado Watershed.

Heavy Mesquite (Mechanical choice: tree doze, rake & burn; shears, spray, burn; extricate, burn)

Year	Treatment	Treatment cost($)/acre	Present value($)/acre
0	Mech. choice	85.00	85.00
5	IPT or burn	15.00	9.89
		Total	94.89

Heavy Mesquite (Herbicide)

Year	Treatment	Treatment cost($)/acre	Present value($)/acre
0	Aerial herbicide	26.00	26.00
5	Aerial herbicide	26.00	17.70
8	IPT or burn	15.00	7.65
		Total	51.35

Moderate Cedar (Mechanical choice: tree doze, rake & burn; shears, spray, burn; extricate, burn)

Year	Treatment	Treatment cost($)/acre	Present value($)/acre
0	Mech. choice	35.00	35.00
5	IPT or burn	15.00	9.89
		Total	44.89

mesquite, mixed brush, and cedar, wildlife revenues were expected to increase from $0.50 to $1.50 per acre, due principally to the resulting improvement in quail habitat and hunter access to quail. Increased wildlife revenues were included only for the heavy brush categories because no changes in wildlife revenues were expected with moderate brush categories.

Estimates of grazing capacities used in the study were also obtained from landowner focus groups, Texas Agricultural Experiment Station and Texas Cooperative Extension scientists, and USDA-NRCS range specialists with brush management experience in the respective watersheds. The estimates were collected for both pre- and post-control states of the brush categories. The carrying capacities ranged from 52 acres per animal unit year (Ac/AUY) for land infested with moderate cedar to about 25 Ac/AUY for land on which mesquite was controlled to levels of brush less than 8% canopy cover (Table 17.2).

Livestock production practices, revenues, and costs representative of the watersheds were also obtained from focus groups of local landowners. Estimates of the variable costs and returns associated with the livestock and wildlife enterprises typical of each area were then used to develop production-based investment analysis budgets. A partial budget for a cow/calf enterprise typical of the Upper Colorado Watershed is shown in Table 17.3.

In this study, it was assumed that ranchers would adjust livestock numbers to match grazing capacity changes on an annual basis. Annual benefits that resulted from brush management were measured as the net differences in annual revenue (added annual revenues minus added annualized costs) that would be expected with brush management compared to no brush management.

The analysis of rancher benefits was done assuming a hypothetical 1000-acre management unit for facilitating calculations. The investment analysis budget information, carrying capacity information, and brush management methods and costs comprised the data sets that were entered into the investment analysis model ECON (Conner). The ECON model yields net present values for rancher benefits accruing over the 10-year life of the projects being considered in the feasibility study. An example of this process is shown in Table 17.4 for the management of moderate cedar in the Upper Colorado Watershed.

To get per acre benefits, the net present value of $11,895 shown in Table 17.4 must be divided by 1,000, which results in $11.90 estimated present value per acre net benefit to a rancher. The resulting net benefit estimates

Table 17.2. Grazing capacity (Acres/AUY) with and without brush management, by type, Upper Colorado Watershed.

	Year									
	0	1	2	3	4	5	6	7	8	9
Heavy mesquite										
Controlled	38	33	28	25	25	25	25	25	25	25
Not controlled	38	38	38.1	38.1	38.2	38.2	38.3	38.3	38.4	38.4
Moderate cedar										
Controlled	52	43	35	35	35	35	35	35	35	35
Not controlled	52	52.3	52.7	53	53.4	53.8	54.1	54.4	54.7	54.9

Table 17.3. Investment analysis budget for cow/calf production in the Upper Colorado Watershed.

Partial Revenues

Revenue item description	Quantity	Unit	$/Unit	Cost
Calves	382.5	Pound	0.80	306.00
Cows	111.1	Pound	0.40	0.00
Bulls	250.0	Pound	0.50	0.00
Total				**306.00**

Partial Variable Costs

Variable cost item description	Quantity	Unit	$/Unit	Cost
Supplemental feed	480.0	Pound	0.10	48.00
Salt and minerals	27.0	Pound	0.20	5.40
Marketing	1.0	Head	6.32	6.32
Veterinary medicine	1.0	Head	15.00	15.00
Miscellaneous	1.0	Head	12.00	12.00
Net replacement cows	1.0	Head	35.28	35.28
Net replacement bulls	1.0	Head	3.09	6.09
Total				**128.09**

Table 17.4. Net present value to landowner of management of moderate cedar, Upper Colorado Watershed.

Year	Animal units	Total increase in sales	Total added investment	Increased variable costs	Additional revenues	Cash flow	Annual NPV	Accumulated NPV
0	0.0	0	0	0	0	0	0	—
1	4.2	1423	2800	520	0	−1897	−1757	−1757
2	9.8	3557	3500	1171	0	−1113	−955	−2711
3	10.1	3557	0	1171	0	2387	1895	−817
4	10.3	3557	0	1171	0	2387	1754	937
5	10.6	3557	0	1171	0	2387	1624	2562
6	10.8	3913	0	1171	0	2742	1728	4290
7	11.1	3913	0	1171	0	2742	1600	5890
8	11.4	3913	0	1171	0	2742	1482	7371
9	11.6	3913	0	1171	0	2742	1372	8743
					Salvage value:	6300	3152	11895

Table 17.5. Landowner/state cost-shares of brush management by type, Upper Colorado Watershed.

Brush type/ density	PV of total cost ($/acre)	Rancher share ($/acre)	Rancher %	State share ($/acre)	State %
Heavy mesquite (mechanical)	94.89	15.89	16.7	79.00	83.3
Heavy mesquite (herbicidal)	51.35	15.89	37.8	35.46	69.1
Moderate cedar	44.89	11.90	26.5	32.99	73.5

for all of the brush categories for this case study are shown in Table 17.5. Present values of landowner benefits differ by location within and across watersheds. In this example, they range from a low of $11.90 per acre for management of moderate cedar to $15.89 per acre for management of heavy mesquite.

18 Runoff from Rangelands
The Role of Shrubs

Bradford P. Wilcox

Over the last 50–100 years, extensive areas of grasslands and savannas have converted to shrublands as a result of several factors (Archer 1994, Van Auken 2000). A logical question is, "Are increases in shrub cover modifying the hydrologic cycle, and if so, in what way and to what extent?" Of particular interest is whether or not shrubs may modify the amount of water in streams, or streamflow—and if so, how? Research examining the linkages between shrub cover and runoff on rangelands has been limited, particularly at larger scales. But we may use our understanding of hydrologic processes to make some educated guesses about where and under what conditions these linkages might be strongest—and, therefore, about which regions are the most promising for augmentation of water yields through shrub control.

When considering runoff, and in particular the influence of shrub cover on runoff, it is important to be clear both about terminology and the role of scale. "Runoff" is that portion of the water budget that is laterally transported out of a defined area of interest, be it a few square yards, a hillslope, or a 39-mile watershed. The rainfall that does not run off will either evaporate or be stored (in the soil or as groundwater). Runoff is therefore a scale-dependent process. For example, the amount of runoff, on a unit-area basis, from semiarid landscapes generally decreases dramatically as scale increases, because of either channel transmission losses or uneven distribution of precipitation (Goodrich et al. 1997).

In this chapter, the term "hillslope runoff" is used to refer to runoff processes at the hillslope scale; and "streamflow" is used for runoff occurring at larger scales. I examine the interactions between shrubs and runoff on semiarid or subhumid rangelands at three scales: (1) the local scale (the shrub canopy and intercanopy zones), (2) the hillslope scale, and (3) the watershed scale, at which channel as well as hillslope processes influence runoff.

Shrub and Runoff Interactions at the Local Scale

Shrubs modify surface or subsurface soil properties in ways that may affect runoff. The properties that may be modified include (1) soil infiltration capacity, (2) microtopography, and (3) amount of soil water (this last through changes in evapotranspiration processes: interception, transpiration, and evaporation via the soil).

Soil Infiltration Capacity

In general, the accumulation of litter and dust (wind-blown sediments) beneath shrubs increases the porosity, organic matter content, and the infiltration capacity of the soils directly under the shrub (Dunkerley 2000a). Higher infiltration rates beneath shrub canopies than in adjacent intercanopy areas have been broadly demonstrated for many vegetation types (Lyford and Qashu 1969, Seyfried 1991, Joffre and Rambal 1993, Pierson et al. 1994, Bergkamp 1998, Schlesinger et al. 1999). Alternatively, soil differences between canopy and intercanopy may be very slight as demonstrated by Davenport et al. (1996), at least in the case of piñon (*Pinus edulis*)-juniper (*Juniperus* spp.) rangelands in New Mexico. In addition, there are some situations in which the infiltration capacity of canopy soils may be reduced, at least in the short term, as a result of water-repellency (hydrophobicity) caused by the chemical composition of the litter (Doerr et al. 2000). Hydrophobicity can be aggravated following burning (Hester et al. 1997, Cammeraat and Imeson 1999).

Soil infiltration capacity may be modified by the physical activity of shrubs as well. For example, shrub roots may directly modify soil porosity by serving as conduits for the rapid movement of water into the soil profile, vertically or laterally (Joffre and Rambal 1993, Martinez-Meza and Whitford 1996, Cerda et al. 1998, Jackson et al. 2000). Macropore flow along root channels, for example, has been shown to be important in semiarid ponderosa pine (*Pinus ponderosa*) forests of New Mexico (Wilcox et al. 1997, Newman et al. 1998).

Microtopography

Runoff processes are potentially affected by topographic changes resulting from shrub encroachment, and these changes may be at the individual shrub scale or at a larger patch scale. At the shrub scale, mounding is typical: individual shrub plants create soil mounds as they grow, either through the accumulation of sediments from wind or rainsplash, litter accumulation, or as a result of erosion of the surrounding intercanopy (Hennessy et al. 1985, Heede 1987, Parsons et al. 1992, Reynolds et al. 1999, Bochet et al. 2000). The soil surface beneath shrubs becomes somewhat elevated with respect to the intercanopy areas, so that water may bypass them as it travels downslope. Intercanopy areas tend to be connected and act as conduits, efficiently transporting surface runoff.

Amount of Soil Water

The amount of water in the soil, or soil moisture, is governed by processes of evapotranspiration: (1) interception, or the loss of water through evaporation from plant or litter surfaces, (2) transpiration from the plant, and/or (3) evaporation from the soil. Shrubs have the potential to modify each of these. But whereas changes in soil moisture resulting from interception and/or transpiration may significantly affect runoff, those resulting from evaporation via the soil probably do not; for this reason, soil evaporation is omitted from this discussion.

Interception

The interception process has been examined to a much lesser extent in drier landscapes than in more humid ones (Dunkerley 2000*b*). In drylands, water losses through interception by shrub canopies depend on the characteristics of the shrub canopy as well as on precipitation characteristics, and estimates vary widely from as little as 4% to as much as 50% of the water budget (Clark 1940, Skau 1964, Pressland 1973, West and Gifford 1976, Tromble 1983, Young et al. 1984, Nulsen et al. 1986, Thurow et al. 1987, Tromble 1988, Liu 1997, Navar et al. 1999). Evergreen shrubs, such as juniper, have a particularly large capacity for capturing precipitation, both because they are evergreen and because of the large surface area of their leaves. Interception loss from the underlying litter layer may be considerable as well. Thurow and Hester (1997) estimated that interception losses via juniper canopies and underlying litter layers approached 70 to 80%. For some plant communities, however, particularly those capable of producing lush stands of grasses, interception under shrub canopies is no greater than that in the grass-dominated open spaces (Dunkerley and Booth 1999). For example, it is doubtful that interception in mesquite (*Prosopis glandulosa*) communities (canopy and litter) is appreciably greater than interception by the herbaceous component subsequent to mesquite control (Desai 1992).

Transpiration

Shrubs may also influence the amount of soil moisture through their ability to transpire soil water—which, in general, is greater than that of herbaceous vegetation because of their greater leaf area and the fact that shrubs can extract water from deeper within the soil profile (Jackson et al. 1999, Jackson et al. 2000). Evergreen shrubs, such as juniper, have the additional ability to transpire water throughout the year. However, transpiration by shrubs can have an effect on runoff only under conditions of excess soil water (levels above the climate-driven evaporation potential). In semiarid landscapes, where this condition is rarely met, most of the available soil water is evapotranspired regardless of the overstory vegetation and does not affect runoff. The exception would be in the case of phreatophytic plants, which access groundwater directly—such as salt cedar (*Tamarix* sp.) and, on occasion, mesquite.

Shrub and Runoff Interactions at the Hillslope Scale

At the hillslope scale, the response of runoff to shrub cover depends partly on the interplay of the local-scale changes discussed above and partly on the mechanisms of runoff generation at this scale.

Runoff from rangeland hillslopes may be generated via four fundamentally different mechanisms. Horton overland flow occurs when precipitation intensity exceeds soil infiltration capacity. This type is assumed to be the dominant mechanism of streamflow generation for most rangelands, particularly semiarid ones (Dunne 1978). Saturation overland flow occurs when soils become saturated—either because groundwater is reaching the surface or because a shallow impermeable horizon is preventing water from percolating down through the upper soil layer. Saturation overland flow has been documented on some rangelands (Lopes and Ffolliott 1993) and probably occurs on many others. Shallow subsurface flow, sometimes referred to as interflow, is that portion of runoff that travels laterally through the soil, generally because of some impeding soil horizon. Shallow subsurface flow is more common in humid environments, but it can be important in semiarid environments and can be very rapid, especially when macropores are present in the soil (Wilcox et al. 1997). Groundwater flow is streamflow derived from a groundwater aquifer. A perennially flowing stream is an indication that groundwater flow is important, whereas one characterized by ephemeral or "flashy" flow suggests that either Horton overland flow or shallow subsurface runoff is the dominant source.

In summary, at the hillslope scale runoff may occur either as a surface or subsurface process, paralleling the fact that shrubs may modify either surface or subsurface conditions. These relationships are important to keep in mind when considering the influence of shrubs on runoff processes.

Surface Interactions

As discussed earlier, shrubs may modify surface properties (soil infiltration capacity and microtopography). These modifications are likely to have the greatest effect on runoff in regions where runoff occurs as a surface process, such as Horton overland flow. Although few studies have examined changes in Horton overland flow as a result of changing shrub cover, we can make some educated guesses about the link between these processes.

It was pointed out above that increases in shrub cover often lead to higher infiltration capacity directly under the shrub canopy, as the addition of organic matter and the activity of roots increase soil porosity. In contrast, the infiltration capacity of adjacent intercanopy areas may be appreciably lowered, and runoff thereby increased, after shrub encroachment. With the loss of grass patches, the capture of runoff is less efficient; water is routed off the hillslope in reticular fashion, via the interconnected intercanopy zones of relatively sparse vegetation cover. This mechanism has been well documented in creosote (*Larrea tridentata*) shrublands (former grasslands) in Arizona (Abrahams et al. 1995) and southern New Mexico (Schlesinger et al. 1999, Wainwright et al. 2000) and in sagebrush (*Artemesia* spp.) rangelands in Idaho (Seyfried 1991). Increased Horton overland runoff has been documented following conversion of desert grasslands to shrublands in the Chihuahuan Desert (Abrahams et al. 1995) and in piñon-juniper woodlands in New Mexico (Wilcox et al. 1996*a*, Wilcox et al. 1996*b*). The increased runoff favors the maintenance of shrubland conditions (Schlesinger et al. 1990), and over time, the intercanopy areas become progressively depleted of soil through erosion (both wind and water), infiltration capacity is reduced, and an increasingly harsh microclimate is created (Schlesinger et al. 1990, Schlesinger et al. 1996).

In other words, decreased infiltration capacity in intercanopy areas may more than offset higher infiltration capacity under the shrub canopies, with the net result that hillslope runoff from these shrub-dominated landscapes is many times greater than when they were dominated by grassland.

Further examples come from mesquite rangelands of Texas, where overland flow is lower in grassland-dominated sites than in mesquite-dominated ones (Carlson et al. 1990, Weltz and Blackburn 1995); and from juniper rangelands of Texas, where overland flow was lowered by juniper control, owing to a flush of herbaceous growth in combination with increased surface roughness from the woody debris (Richardson et al. 1979, Dugas et al. 1998). In general, we can expect that overland flow runoff will be greater from rangelands covered by shrubs than from rangelands covered by grasses.

In some dryland environments, a different pattern of shrub encroachment follows land degradation. In these systems, shrubs and associated vegetation grow in bands along topographic contours, efficiently capturing water and nutrients generated from upslope runoff (Ludwig and Tongway 1995, Anderson and Hodgkinson 1997, Valentin et al. 1999). In these banded vegetation systems, common in Australia and northern Africa, net runoff from hillslopes is close to zero (Bergkamp 1998).

Subsurface Interactions

Runoff that occurs as a subsurface process can also be dramatically influenced by the presence of shrubs. Although subsurface flow on semiarid or subhumid rangelands is not the norm—because potential evapotranspiration exceeds precipitation many fold—subsurface flow is "short circuited" when soil storage capacity is limited and underlying parent material allows for rapid subsurface flow. For example, there are extensive areas of juniper rangeland in which subsurface flow is important. Preliminary results from studies in these regions indicate that runoff is significantly reduced as shrub cover increases, and that shrub removal increases runoff. Dugas et al. (1998) measured lower evapotranspiration for 2 years following juniper removal. Similarly, Thurow and Hester (1997) reported significantly higher groundwater recharge following complete removal of juniper. In both cases, the difference was attributed to the very high interception capacity of juniper. Increases in spring flow following removal of juniper and piñon-juniper have been reported as well (Wright 1996, McCarthy et al. 1999). Similarly, where soils are very sandy, water is able to move rapidly through the root zone.

Shrub and Runoff Interactions at the Watershed Scale

As the scale (land area) of interest increases, the connection between shrub cover and runoff becomes increasingly difficult to quantify, especially for rangelands where runoff is a relatively small component of the water budget. With increases in scale, an increasing number of factors influence runoff. In general, the connection between vegetation cover and runoff diminishes as scale increases, particularly in the case of large precipitation events (Ward 1978, Dunne 1988, Leopold 1997). Few rangeland studies have evaluated the influence of shrub control at such large scales, simply because of the impracticality of doing so. Work on the Corduroy Creek in Arizona is one such large-scale study (Collings and Myrick 1966).

In some humid environments, changes in runoff at the watershed scale as a result of changing cover of woody plants have been documented. For example, in humid areas of Australia the widespread replacement of *Eucalyptus* and other deep-rooted woody species by pasture and crop species has raised the water table and led to serious salinization problems (Greenwood 1992, Walker et al. 1993). A similar positive relationship between timber harvesting and streamflow is well documented in many other forest types (Stednick 1996)—as is the converse: declines in streamflow as a result of afforestation (Trimble et al. 1987, Calder 1990). For semiarid and subhumid rangelands, however, the correlation between nonriparian woody plants and streamflow is weaker. Hibbert (1983) estimated that only about 1% of rangelands were candidate areas for increasing water yield through brush control. Chaparral woodlands of Arizona and California exhibit conditions conductive for streamflow augmentation via woody plant control. Runoff occurs as subsurface flow and the chaparral shrubs, by virtue of being evergreen and deep rooted, intercept and transpire large quantities of water. Increases in streamflow in chaparral woodlands at the small-watershed scale (10 to 200 acres) have been reported (Hibbert 1983). There have been no other documented cases of significant increases in streamflow (at the watershed scale) following nonriparian brush removal on rangelands, although there are numerous anecdotal reports (Kelton 1975).

In most cases, it is unlikely that changes in runoff observed at the hillslope or small-catchment scale will be expressed (or measurable in any case) at larger scale streamflow because water is captured as it moves down slope. For example, in the Chihuahuan Desert, where increases in hillslope runoff with increasing shrub cover are clearly documented, there is likely to be little if any increase in streamflow at larger scales because water is captured within the landscape before it can become large-scale runoff (Goodrich et al. 1997). For the same reason, the increases in spring flow or small-catchment runoff observed in some woodlands following a reduction in shrub cover may not translate to larger scales.

The greatest potential for increasing runoff through shrub control at large scales probably lies in the control of salt cedar in stream channels and floodplains. Phreatophytic vegetation such as salt cedar, because it has direct access to groundwater, consume a tremendous amount of water. Our understanding of the ecological and hydrological functioning of salt cedar has increased greatly in the last decade (Busch and Smith 1995, Birkeland 1996, Sala et al. 1996, Cleverly et al. 1997, Devitt et al. 1997, Devitt et al. 1998, Ditomaso 1998, Glenn et al. 1998, Stromberg 1998, Xu et al. 1998, Shafroth et al. 2000). On the basis of this and previous work, Zavaleta (2000) demonstrated that investing in salt cedar control provides significant economic returns, not only by increasing water yield but also by reducing cost of flood and sediment control.

Conclusions

The linkage between runoff and shrub cover on rangelands is a complex one. Depending on local conditions, increases in shrub cover may cause runoff to increase, stay the same, or decrease. For semiarid landscapes characterized by Horton overland flow, we can expect that shrub encroachment will result in a "net" decrease in landscape infiltration capacity of the soil and increased interconnectedness of intercanopy patches, which in turn will lead to increased runoff—at least at the hillslope scale. The exceptions are semiarid landscapes in which shrubs occur in bands parallel to the contour of the hillslope, allowing them to efficiently capture runoff. As scale increases, runoff will likely be captured at different points in the landscape. In other, wetter landscapes, the response of runoff to changes in shrub cover will differ depending upon how runoff is generated. For example, on mesquite rangelands where runoff occurs as Horton overland flow and where soils are deep and herbaceous growth is potentially high, changes in shrub cover have a minor effect on runoff. This is because a very high percentage of soil water will be evapotranspired regardless of what the vegetation cover is. Where subsurface flow occurs, increasing shrub cover can reduce runoff because of the dual effect of interception and transpiration loss by shrubs. These conditions exist for some chaparral rangelands in the southwestern United States and some juniper rangelands in Texas.

The literature on the topic linking shrub cover and runoff provides few examples from rangelands where shrub control will likely result in increased streamflow. Two vegetation communities with the greatest potential for increasing runoff through shrub control are the chaparral woodland in the southwestern United States and portions of juniper woodlands in Central Texas. Both have high density evergreen shrubs that intercept and transpire large amounts of water and are in regions where runoff occurs as subsurface flow. These conclusions are on the basis of relatively small-scale studies. Success has been demonstrated on small watersheds (up to 225 acres) for chaparral rangelands. As of yet, increased streamflow has not been documented from juniper rangelands, but smaller scale studies have been encouraging. Runoff processes are scale-dependent. As the scale increases from the hillslope and small catchment to the watershed level, the linkage between shrub cover and runoff diminishes, but little work has been done to explicitly document watershed runoff dynamics at larger scales. I believe that the greatest potential for large-scale augmentation of streamflow from brush control lies in control of undesirable and invasive riparian and phreatophytic vegetation, especially salt cedar. In addition to increasing streamflow, control of salt cedar will result in substantial and economically significant improvement in flood and sediment control.

Literature Cited

Abrahams, A. D., J. P. Anthony, and J. Wainwright. 1995*a*. Effects of vegetation change on interrill runoff and erosion, Walnut Gulch, southern Arizona. Geomorphology 13:37–48.

Anderson, V. J., and K. C. Hodgkinson. 1997. Grass-mediated capture of resource flows and the maintenance of banded mulga in a semi-arid woodland. Australian Journal of Botany 45:331–42.

Archer, S. 1994. Woody plant encroachment into southwestern grasslands and savannas: rates, patterns and proximate causes. Pages 13–68 *in* M. Vavra, W. A. Laycock, and R. D. Pieper, editors. Ecological implications of livestock herbivory in the West. Society for Range Management, Denver, Colorado.

Bergkamp, G. 1998. A hierarchical view of the interactions of runoff and infiltration with vegetation and microtopography in semiarid shrublands. Catena 33:201–20.

Birkeland, G. H. 1996. Riparian vegetation and sandbar morphology along the lower little Colorado River, Arizona. Physical Geography 17:534–53.

Bochet, E., J. Poesen, and J. L. Rubio. 2000. Mound development as an interaction of individual plants with soil, water erosion and sedimentation processes on slopes. Earth Surface Processes & Landforms 25:847–67.

Busch, D. E., and S. D. Smith. 1995. Mechanisms associated with decline of woody species in riparian ecosystems of the southwestern U.S. Ecological Monographs 65:347–70.

Calder, I. R. 1990. Evaporation in the uplands. John Wiley & Sons, New York.

Cammeraat, L. H., and A. C. Imeson. 1999. The evolution and significance of soil-vegetation patterns following land abandonment and fire in Spain. Catena 37:107–27.

Carlson, D. H., T. L. Thurow, R. W. Knight, and R. K. Heitschmidt. 1990. Effect of honey mesquite on the water balance of Texas Rolling Plains rangeland. Journal of Range Management 43:491–96.

Cerda, A., S. Schnabel, A. Ceballos, and D. Gomezamelia. 1998. Soil hydrological response under simulated rainfall in the Dehesa land system (Extremadura, Sw Spain) under drought conditions. Earth Surface Processes & Landforms 23:195–209.

Clark, O. R. 1940. Interception of rainfall by prairie grasses, weeds and certain crop plants. Ecological Monographs 10:243–77.

Cleverly, J. R., S. D. Smith, A. Sala, and D. A. Devitt. 1997. Invasive capacity of *Tamarix ramosissima* in a Mojave Desert floodplain—the role of drought. Oecologia 111:12–18.

Collings, M. R., and R. M. Myrick. 1966. Effects of juniper and pinyon eradication on streamflow from Corduroy Creek Basin, Arizona. Professional Paper 491-B, U.S. Geological Survey.

Davenport, D. W., B. P. Wilcox, and D. D. Breshears. 1996. Soil morphology of canopy and intercanopy sites in a piñon-juniper woodland. Soil Science Society of America Journal 60:1881–87.

Desai, A. N. 1992. Interception of precipitation by mesquite dominated rangelands in the rolling plains of Texas. Thesis, Texas A&M University, College Station.

Devitt, D. A., A. Sala, K. A. Mace, and S. D. Smith. 1997. The effect of applied water on the water use of saltcedar in a desert riparian environment. Journal of Hydrology 192:233–46.

———, ———, S. D. Smith, J. Cleverly, L. K. Shaulis, and R. Hammett. 1998. Bowen ratio estimates of evapotranspiration for *Tamarix ramosissima* stands on the Virgin River in southern Nevada. Water Resources Research 34:2407–14.

DiTomaso, J. M. 1998. Impact, biology, and ecology of saltcedar (*Tamarix* spp.) in the southwestern United States. Weed Technology 12:326–36.

Doerr, S. H., R. A. Shakesby, and R. P. D. Walsh. 2000. Soil water repellency: its causes, characteristics and hydro-geomorphological significance. Earth Science Review 51:33–65.

Dugas, W. A., R. A. Hicks, and P. Wright. 1998. Effect of removal of *Juniperus ashei* on evapotranspiration and runoff in the Seco Creek watershed. Water Resources Research 34:1499–1506.

Dunkerley, D. 2000*a*. Hydrologic effects of dryland shrubs: defining the spatial extent of modified soil water uptake rates at an Australian desert site. Journal of Arid Environments 45:159–72.

———. 2000*b*. Measuring interception loss and canopy storage in dryland vegetation: a brief review and evaluation of available research strategies. Hydrological Processes 14:669–78.

Dunkerley, D. L., and T. L. Booth. 1999. Plant canopy interception of rainfall and its significance in a banded landscape, arid western New South Wales, Australia. Water Resources Research 35:1581–86.

Dunne, T. 1978. Field studies of hillslope flow processes. Pages 227–93 *in* M. J. Kirkby, editor. Hillslope hydrology. John Wiley & Sons, New York.

———. 1988. Geomorphological contributions to flood control planning. Pages 421–38 *in* V. R. Baker, R. C. Kochel, and P. C. Patton, editors. Flood geomorphology. John Wiley & Sons, New York.

Glenn, E., R. Tanner, S. Mendez, T. Kehret, D. Moore, J. Garcia, and C. Valdes. 1998. Growth rates, salt tolerance and water use characteristics of native and invasive riparian plants from the delta of the Colorado River, Mexico. Journal of Arid Environments 40:281–94.

Goodrich, D. C., L. J. Lane, R. M. Shillito, S. N. Miller, K. H. Syed, and D. A. Woolhiser. 1997. Linearity of basin response as a function of scale in a semiarid watershed. Water Resources Research 33:2951–65.

Greenwood, E. A. N. 1992. Deforestation, revegetation, water balance, and climate: an optimistic path through the plausible, impracticable, and controversial. Advances in Bioclimatology 1:89–154.

Heede, B. H. 1987. The influence of pinyon-juniper on microtopography and sediment delivery of an Arizona watershed. Pages 195–98 *in* I. G. Poppoff, C. R. Goldman, S. L. Loeb, and L. B. Leopold, editors. International mountain watershed symposium—subalpine processes and water quality. Tahoe Resource Conservation District, South Lake Tahoe, California.

Hennessy, J. T., R. P. Gibbens, J. M. Tromble, and M. Cardenas. 1985. Mesquite (*Prosopis glandulosa* Torr.) dunes and interdunes in southern New Mexico: a study of soil properties and soil water relations. Journal of Arid Environments 9:27–69.

Hester, J. W., T. L. Thurow, and C. A. Taylor. 1997. Hydrologic characteristics of vegetation types as affected by prescribed burning. Journal of Range Management 50:199–204.

Hibbert, A. R. 1983. Water yield improvement potential by vegetation management on western rangelands. Water Resources Bulletin 19:375–81.

Jackson, R. B., L. A. Moore, W. A. Hoffmann, W. T. Pockman, and C. R. Linder. 1999. Ecosystem rooting depth determined with caves and DNA. Proceedings of the National Academy of Sciences of the United States of America 96:11387–92.

———, H. J. Schenk, E. G. Jobbagy, J. Canadell, G. D. Colello, R. E. Dickinson, C. B. Field, P. Friedlingstein, M. Heimann, K. Hibbard, D. W. Kicklighter, A. Kleidon, R. P. Neilson, W. J. Parton, O. E. Sala, and M. T. Sykes. 2000. Belowground consequences of vegetation change and their treatment in models. Ecological Applications 10:470–83.

Joffre, R., and S. Rambal. 1993. How tree cover influences the water balance of Mediterranean rangelands. Ecology 74:570–82.

Kelton, E. 1975. The story of Rocky Creek. The Practicing Nutritionist 9:1–5.

Leopold, L. B. 1997. Water, rivers and creeks. University Science Books, Sausalito, California.

Liu, S. G. 1997. A new model for the prediction of rainfall interception in forest canopies. Ecological Modelling 99:151–59.

Lopes, V. L., and P. F. Ffolliott. 1993. Sediment rating curves for a clearcut ponderosa pine watershed in northern Arizona. Water Resources Bulletin 29:369–82.

Ludwig, J. A., and D. J. Tongway. 1995. Spatial organization of landscapes and its function in semi-arid woodlands, Australia. Landscape Ecology 10:51–63.

Lyford, F., and H. K. Qashu. 1969. Infiltration rates as affected by desert vegetation. Water Resources Research 5:1373–77.

Martinez-Meza, E., and W. G. Whitford. 1996. Stemflow, throughfall and channelization of stemflow by roots in three Chihuahuan Desert shrubs. Journal of Arid Environments 32:271–87.

McCarthy, F. J., J. P. Dobrowolski, and P. Figures. 1999. Ground water source areas and flow paths to springs rejuvenated by juniper removal at Johnson Pass, Utah. Page 5 in D. S. Olsen and J. P. Potyondy, editors. Wildland Hydrology Proceedings. American Water Resources Association, Middleburg, Virginia.

Navar, J., F. Charles, and E. Jurado. 1999. Spatial variations of interception loss components by Tamaulipan thornscrub in northeastern Mexico. Forest Ecology and Management 124:231–39.

Newman, B. D., A. R. Campbell, and B. P. Wilcox. 1998. Lateral subsurface flow pathways in a semiarid ponderosa pine hillslope. Water Resources Research 34:3485–96.

Nulsen, R. A., K. J. Bligh, I. N. Baxter, E. J. Solin, and D. H. Imrie. 1986. The fate of rainfall in a malle and heath vegetated catchment in southern Western Australia. Australian Journal of Ecology 11:361–71.

Parsons, A. J., A. D. Abrahams, and J. R. Simanton. 1992. Microtopography and soil-surface materials on semi-arid piedmont hillslopes, southern Arizona. Journal of Arid Environments 22:107–15.

Pierson, F. B., W. H. Blackburn, S. S. V. Vactor, and J. C. Wood. 1994. Partitioning small scale spatial variability of runoff and erosion on sagebrush rangeland. Water Resources Bulletin 30:1081–89.

Pressland, A. J. 1973. Rainfall partitioning by an arid woodland (*Acacia aneura* F. Muell.) in south-western Queensland. Australian Journal of Botany 21:235–45.

Reynolds, J. F., R. A. Virginia, P. R. Kemp, A. G. de Soyza, and D. C. Tremmel. 1999. Impact of drought on desert shrubs: effects of seasonality and degree of resource island development [Review]. Ecological Monographs 69:69–106.

Richardson, C. W., E. Burnett, and R. W. Bovey. 1979. Hydrologic effects of brush control on Texas rangelands. Transactions American Society Agricultural Engineers 22:315–19.

Sala, A., S. D. Smith, and D. A. Devitt. 1996. Water use by *Tamarix ramosissima* and associated phreatophytes in a Mojave Desert floodplain. Ecological Applications 6:888–98.

Schlesinger, W. H., A. D. Abrahams, A. J. Parsons, and J. Wainwright. 1999. Nutrient losses in runoff from grassland and shrubland habitats in southern New Mexico: I. rainfall simulation experiments. Biogeochemistry 45:21–34.

———, J. A. Raikes, A. E. Hartley, and A. E. Cross. 1996. On the spatial pattern of soil nutrients in desert ecosystems. Ecology 77:364–374.

————, J. F. Reynolds, G. L. Cunningham, L. F. Huenneke, W. M. Jarrell, R. A. Virginia, and W. G. Whitford. 1990. Biological feedbacks in global desertification. Science 247:1043–48.

Seyfried, M. S. 1991. Infiltration patterns from simulated rainfall on a semiarid rangeland soil. Soil Science Society of America Journal 55:1726–34.

Shafroth, P. B., J. C. Stromberg, and D. T. Patten. 2000. Woody riparian vegetation response to different alluvial water table regimes. Western North American Naturalist 60:66–76.

Skau, C. M. 1964. Interception, throughfall, and stemflow in Utah and Alligator juniper cover types of northern Arizona. Forest Science 10:283–87.

Stednick, J. D. 1996. Monitoring the effects of timber harvest on annual water yield. Journal of Hydrology 176:79–95.

Stromberg, J. C. 1998. Functional equivalency of saltcedar (*Tamarix chinensis*) and Fremont cottonwood (*Populus fremontii*) along a free-flowing river. Wetlands 18:675–86.

Thurow, T. L., W. H. Blackburn, and C. A. Taylor. 1987. Rainfall interception losses by midgrass, shortgrass, and live oak mottes. Journal of Range Management 40:455–60.

————, and J. W. Hester. 1997. How an increase or a reduction in juniper cover alters rangeland hydrology. Pages 9–22 *in* C. A. Taylor, Jr., editor. Proceedings 1977 Juniper Symposium. Technical Report 97-1, Texas Agricultural Experiment Station, San Angelo.

Trimble, S. W., F. H. Weirich, and B. L. Hoag. 1987. Reforestation and the reduction of water yield on the southern Piedmont since circa 1940. Water Resources Research 23:425–37.

Tromble, J. M. 1983. Interception of rainfall by tarbrush. Journal of Range Management 36:525–26.

————. 1988. Water interception by two arid land shrubs. Journal of Arid Environments 15:65–70.

Valentin, C., J. M. d'Herbes, and J. Poesen. 1999. Soil and water components of banded vegetation patterns. Catena 37:1–24.

Van Auken, O. W. 2000. Shrub invasions of North American semiarid grasslands. Annual Review of Ecology and Systematics 31:197–215.

Wainwright, J., A. J. Parsons, and A. D. Abrahams. 2000. Plot-scale studies of vegetation, overland flow and erosion interactions: case studies from Arizona and New Mexico. Hydrological Processes 14:2921–43.

Walker, J., F. Bullen, and B. G. Williams. 1993. Ecohydrological changes in the Murray-Darling basin. I. The number of trees cleared over two centuries. Journal of Applied Ecology 30:265–73.

Ward, R. C. 1978. Floods, a geographical perspective. John Wiley & Sons, New York.

Weltz, M. A., and W. H. Blackburn. 1995. Water budget for South Texas rangelands. Journal of Range Management 48:45–52.

West, N. E., and G. F. Gifford. 1976. Rainfall interception by cool-desert shrubs. Journal of Range Management 29:171–72.

Wilcox, B. P., B. D. Newman, C. D. Allen, K. D. Reid, D. Brandes, J. Pitlick, and D. W. Davenport. 1996a. Runoff and erosion on the Pajarito Plateau: observations from the field. Pages 433–39 *in* Goff, F., B. S. Kues, M. A. Rogers, L. S. McFadden, and J. N. Gardner, editors. Geology of the Los Alamos-Jemez Mountains region. New Mexico Geological Society and New Mexico Bureau of Geology and Mineral Resources, Socorro, New Mexico.

———, ———, D. Brandes, D. W. Davenport, and K. Reid. 1997. Runoff from a semiarid ponderosa pine hillslope in New Mexico. Water Resources Research 33:2301–14.

———, J. Pitlick, C. D. Allen, and D. W. Davenport. 1996*b*. Runoff and erosion from a rapidly eroding pinyon-juniper hillslope. Pages 61–71 *in* M. G. Anderson and S. M. Brooks, editors. Advances in hillslope processes. John Wiley & Sons, New York.

Wright, P. N. 1996. Spring enhancement in the Seco Creek water quality demonstration project. Annual Project Report, Seco Creek Water Quality Demonstration Project, Hondo, Texas.

Xu, X. Y., R. D. Zhang, X. Z. Xue, and M. Zhao. 1998. Determination of evapotranspiration in the desert area using lysimeters. Communications in Soil Sciences and Plant Analysis 29:1–13.

Young, J. A., R. A. Evans, and D. A. Eash. 1984. Stem flow on western juniper (*Juniperus occidentalis*) trees. Weed Science 32:320–27.

Zavaleta, E. 2000. The economic value of controlling an invasive shrub. Ambio 29:462–67.

19 Integrating Wildlife Concerns into Brush Management

Dale Rollins
and
Ken Cearley

And what is a weed but a plant whose virtues have yet to be discovered?
—Ralph Waldo Emerson

The increasing economic and aesthetic importance of wildlife-based recreation in Texas has fostered a paradigm shift regarding landowner attitudes toward brush. Over the last 50 years, this prevailing paradigm has evolved from brush eradication in the 1940s to brush control in the 1960s to brush management in the 1980s. Brush management connotes the idea of managing brush-infested rangeland for multiple uses, including forage, watershed, wildlife habitat, and recreation (Scifres 1980). The "Brush Busters" program (McGinty and Ueckert 1995), which promoted individual plant treatments, continued the evolution from large-scale broadcast treatments to a more strategic effort based upon individual plant treatments. During 1997, the Texas Agricultural Extension Service developed the "Brush Sculptors" program which heralds the continued evolution of brush management (Rollins et al. 1997*a*). Brush Sculptors promotes the planned, selective control of brush as a means of enhancing wildlife habitat.

In some areas of Texas, rural land values are tied more closely to recreational enterprises such as hunting, than to traditional ranching enterprises such as livestock grazing. This trend of the "(wildlife) tail wagging the (livestock) dog" is poised to persist for some time. As it does, wildlife considerations will become increasingly important in determining land management strategies, especially relative to brush control.

Brush is not necessarily a "four letter word." Indeed, the same brush that complicates livestock handling, competes with grass, and vies for underground water, also dictates the habitability of most Texas rangelands as wildlife habitat. But, vast, dense stands of brush are not conducive to livestock, watersheds, or most species of wildlife (Rollins and Armstrong 1997).

As despicable as mesquite (*Prosopis glandulosa*) may be when viewed with a "cowboy hat" on (i.e., livestock perspective), it must be acknowledged for its contributions as a food and cover species for bobwhites (*Colinus virginianus*), deer (*Odocoileus* spp.), and other wildlife (Nelle 1997). Similarly, while pricklypear (*Opuntia* spp.) is a hindrance to livestock grazing, it enhances nest survival for bobwhites on sites that lack sufficient grass cover

(Slater et al. 2001, Carter et al. 2002), and also provides a key forage for white-tailed deer (*O. virginianus*) during dry years (Hanselka et al. 1995).

Brush control can be positive, negative, or neutral for wildlife habitat, depending on several factors. Previous reports (Hailey 1979, Guthery 1986, Rollins et al. 1988, Fulbright and Guthery 1996, Koerth 1996, Guthery and Rollins 1997) have addressed the role of brush management in deer and quail management in Texas. The Brush Sculptor symposia proceedings (Rollins et al. 1997; also available online at http://texnat.tamu.edu) addresses many of the concerns of managing Texas rangelands for wildlife.

This chapter addresses concerns over brush management as it has been applied in traditional ranching contexts, that is, with the primary objective to enhance forage availability. We discuss the implications of such strategies for game species, i.e., deer, quail, and wild turkey (*Meleagris gallopavo*), and the various brush management alternatives available for consideration.

Brush Management and Wildlife

Leopold (1933:xxxi) said, "The central thesis of game management is this: game can be restored by the creative use of the same tools which have heretofore destroyed it—axe, plow, cow, fire, and gun. A favorable alignment of these forces sometimes came about in pioneer days by accident. The result was a temporary wealth of game far greater than the red man ever saw. Management is their purposeful and continuing alignment."

From a rangeland perspective, Leopold's axe consists of brush control. The planned, selective removal of brush can be one of the best tools for managing wildlife habitat; the unplanned, broadcast control of brush is perhaps the worst. Some key points to ponder relative to brush control and wildlife include the following:

1. Brush is a key wildlife habitat component.
2. Vast, dense stands of brush are not conducive to water, wildlife, or livestock.
3. Brush control can be an effective habitat management technique.
4. Clearing intensity is the pivot point around which management conflicts operate.
5. Several factors affect wildlife response to clearing (e.g., site, treatment method).
6. Post-treatment grazing management impacts wildlife response.
7. Different and competing rangeland products cannot be maximized simultaneously.
8. Trade-offs should be quantified and compromises sought based on landowner's goals.

Probably the two most contentious issues for wildlife managers focus on (1) clearing intensity, i.e., how much of the site's brush will be cleared, and (2) the scale of implementation (e.g., 40 acres or 40 square miles). What are the minimum thresholds of brush necessary to maintain wildlife on the site? Are these compatible with clearing intensities sought by livestock operators and water managers?

Confusion sometimes arises over the use, and measurement, of the habitat component satisfied by brush cover. Brush (i.e., woody plants) serves important functions for many wildlife species, including escape cover, browse, nesting, and roosting (Nelle 1997). Brush cover can be quantified at two spatial scales (Fulbright 1997). The first scale is the percent canopy cover of brush at a particular site. Percent canopy cover at the site scale is measured by estimating the amount of ground surface beneath the canopy of shrubs. In other words, how much of the ground would be shaded on a clear day at noon. In a mesquite or juniper community, a canopy >40% is considered thick brush. The second scale is the landscape scale or the percent of the landscape that supports a cover of woody plants somewhat irrespective of the canopy cover at the site. The percent of the landscape that supports a cover of woody plants is measured by determining the percentage of a given area occupied by woody plants versus the amount occupied by grasses and forbs, or the amount of woodland versus grassland.

Further confusion arises when these two spatial scales are considered to be synonymous. A 50% canopy cover of brush over a ranch is not the same as having a brush problem on 50% of the ranch. Similarly, when one suggests that they have "cleared 80% of the ranch," do they mean they have removed 80% of the 50% canopy (10% of canopy remains) or have they applied an herbicide to 80% of their property, which means as much as 50% of canopy cover remains (a ranch-wide canopy cover of 20%)?

The use of the term "clearing intensity" is suggested to describe the amount of the pasture to which a specific treatment is applied. In terms of mechanical control (e.g., chaining), clearing 80% of the pasture would be referred to as a clearing intensity of 80%. The 20% of the acreage left uncleared might contain those pockets of heaviest brush on the site to maximize usable space (Guthery 1997) by our wildlife species of interest. Fulbright (1997) suggested that pockets of brush where a deer feels secure, consist of dense brush (>85% canopy cover).

The concept of "cover thresholds" suggests that animals have a minimum amount of brush that is required on the landscape to make that site habitable (Fig. 19.1). Rollins et al. (1988) studied the short-term (3–24 months post-clearing) response of white-tailed deer to 4 clearing intensities (30, 50, 70 and 80%) of mechanical brush removal (i.e., chaining) in Ashe juniper (*Juniperus ashei*) habitat. They suggested that 50 to 70% of the brush could be cleared while enhancing habitat for deer given the conditions of their study, in which the scale of treatment was about 400 acres. Beasom and Scifres (1977) compared short-term (up to 2 years post-treatment) response of white-tailed deer between bottomland sites in South Texas where 80% of the brush was sprayed in strips, to another site where no spraying was conducted. They observed that deer populations declined initially but rebounded about 22 months post-treatment, presumably as forb populations recovered from the spraying.

Clearing thresholds are not absolute (Guthery 1999). Some of the factors that affect wildlife response to a given level of clearing include (1) species of wildlife concerned, (2) topography, (3) brush community before and after clearing, (4) method of brush control implemented, (5) hunting pressure, and (6) scale of treatment. Whether Rollins et al. (1988) would have

Figure 19.1.
Habitability of a particular site for wildlife is often dictated by the kinds and amounts of brush present.
Courtesy Dale Rollins

observed the same results in flatter country at larger scales of treatment (e.g., 10,000 acres) is unknown. Clearing thresholds relative to deer and quail for aerial spraying are not available other than Beasom and Scifres' (1977) study comparing 0 vs. 80% brush removal via broadcast spraying with herbicides. The lower efficacy of most aerially applied herbicides (e.g., 40–60% root kill) and standing dead brush that remains after treatment may partially ameliorate cover concerns post-treatment relative to mechanical brush control methods.

Landowner Goals

Landowners in Texas can be identified somewhere along a continuum of goals depicted in Fig. 19.2. Landowners in "Class I" are interested exclusively in livestock, with no compensation in management decisions made for wildlife. At the right end of the scale are the "Class V" ranchers, a new breed of landowners in Texas, whose motivation for land ownership is based strictly on wildlife interests. To them livestock may be considered a nuisance. Those ranchers in between the endpoints have varying interests in livestock and wildlife. "Class II" ranchers have livestock as their primary motivation, but are also interested in wildlife. "Class IV" is the converse to Class II, with wildlife being the primary motive for ownership and livestock secondary. While the Brush Sculptor's philosophy can benefit landowners along the continuum, those in Classes III and IV are probably most likely to use these technologies.

Other stakeholders are also part of the landowner/wildlife equation. The growing demand for water from Texas' rangelands by these stakeholders will likely impact landowner decisions relative to brush control. Thus, landowners must analyze the actions and reactions of brush management as they affect not only their needs, but also the needs of society.

Landowners' attitudes towards wildlife (either from commercial or personal motivations) is likely to influence their willingness to (1) participate in government cost-share programs aimed at watershed enhancement, and (2) clear brush at the levels conducive to enhancing water yields (i.e., >90%) (Rollins 2003, unpublished data).

Appreciating Brush

As complex brush management decisions are evaluated, landowners are encouraged to develop an appreciation for brush. We refer to two connotations

Figure 19.2. Landowner attitudes towards brush vary along a continuum that ranges from livestock only to wildlife only. *Courtesy Dale Rollins*

of the word appreciate: first, the idea of "judging with heightened awareness" and second, "being critically or sensitively aware of." An appreciation for brush may require a new way of thinking.

Historically in Texas, the trade-offs at the landowner's level were to balance adequate brush for wildlife habitat needs with clearing brush for livestock grazing needs. More recently, water yield from semiarid rangelands has become increasingly important. Incorporating water concerns into the management equation means managers must strive to clear brush to the extent possible while maintaining adequate brush cover to meet wildlife goals. Thurow et al. (1997) suggested that clearing intensities over 85% would be necessary in order "to achieve sustainable, significant increases in water yield" from (mostly juniper-dominated) West Texas rangelands. Clearing an entire sub-basin or watershed at 90% intensity, however, would likely be detrimental to most wildlife. In order to assess how such intensities of brush clearing affect wildlife, one must understand how and why brush is important for the species of interest (defined in this paper as deer, quail, and turkey).

One of the axioms for wildlife managers is that the two key skills for range managers are (1) knowing your plants, and (2) knowing how to manipulate them. These underpinnings work for cows or quail, lambs or larks, steers or deer. Do not judge a plant's contribution to wildlife by its food value alone; a point well worth remembering for aspiring Brush Sculptors. Land managers should learn to recognize the specific values of various plant species (or individual plants within a species) for their target wildlife species.

Shelter

The term shelter (or cover) may connote any of the following habitat needs: thermal, escape, nesting, loafing, and screening. Each of these will be discussed in more of a qualitative than a quantitative manner.

Thermal cover allows animals to cope with temperature extremes. To this end, junipers are more valuable for thermal cover in winter than in summer and in colder climates than in warmer ones (Leckenby 1978). The popularity of junipers, for example eastern red cedar (*J. virginiana*), as windbreak plantings is suggestive of their value for winter cover. For summer thermal relief, deciduous trees probably are more effective than junipers, allowing more air flow and shade (Johnson and Guthery 1988).

Escape cover is rather generic and can probably be satisfied by any species of brush of sufficient density that may allow an animal to avoid a predator. Cedar (*Juniperus* spp.) breaks and mesquite thickets certainly qualify as dense cover suitable for escape purposes for deer and other wildlife. The need for and value of escape cover varies with factors like topography, human disturbance (e.g., hunting), brush density, and the wildlife species in question. Rollins et al. (1988) attempted to quantify cover thresholds for white-tailed deer on Ashe juniper range in Kerr County. A series of 20-acre clearings was established with progressively smaller strips of brush in-between to identify how much escape cover was necessary for deer. Their findings suggested that as much as 70% of the range could be cleared mechanically by chaining, for example, without adversely affecting deer use of habitats or deer populations within 2 years of treatment.

Loafing cover is especially important for game birds, e.g., bobwhite and scaled quail (*Callipepla squamata*). Quail spend most of their daylight hours under such cover to minimize exposure to various predators, especially raptors. Suitable loafing coverts may include thickets of sandplum (*Prunus angustifolia*), skunkbush (*Rhus trilobata*), littleleaf sumac (*R. microphylla*), lotebush (*Zizyphus obtusifolia*), elbowbush (*Forestiera pubescens*), and other similarly shaped shrubs.

Food Value

Browse, or leaves and tender twigs of woody plants, are a staple in the diet of game species such as white-tailed deer, mule deer (*O. hemionus crookii*), and many exotic livestock in Texas (Nelle 1997). The fruits and/or seeds of woody plants are extremely important to many species of wildlife. Fleshy fruits (often called berries or soft mast) are used heavily by ungulates (e.g., deer, hogs); carnivores (e.g., coyotes [*Canis latrans*], gray fox [*Urocyon cinereoargenteus*]); songbirds (e.g., bluebirds [*Sialia* spp.], robins [*Turdus migratorius*]); and game birds (quail, turkey). Nonfleshy fruits (i.e., nuts or hard mast) are also important to many of the same species of wildlife. A listing of shrubs and trees of Central and South Texas, and their value as browse and fruit, is summarized in Table 19.1 (Nelle 1997).

Brush management, especially via mechanical means or fire, usually enhances nutrition for white-tailed deer, at least for a short period of time (Waid et al. 1984). The regrowth of plants like shinoak (*Quercus* spp.) and elbowbush are more palatable after top removal. Similarly, deer use of relatively unpalatable shrubs such as lotebush increases after a fire.

Effects of Brush Management on Wildlife

Vast, dense stands of brush are not conducive to wildlife, watershed, or livestock management. Ideally, enough brush should be cleared to increase forage production, and provide sufficient access for ease in handling livestock, but maintain adequate cover for wildlife. As mentioned earlier, such cover thresholds are species and habitat specific. The impacts of brush control on wildlife depend upon how much brush is cleared (intensity and acreage), how it is cleared (e.g., mechanically, goats), and the subsequent management on the cleared land (i.e., grazing management). Impacts to wildlife may be both acute (e.g., forage response) and chronic (e.g., habitat fragmentation).

Obviously, clearing too much brush (or too large an area) could negatively impact deer, but the other extreme (clearing too little) can also be problematic. Small, isolated clearings (e.g., 2 acres) are subjected to intensive grazing pressure by wild and domestic herbivores. Repeated browsing on plants like sumacs (*Rhus* spp.) and oaks will eventually kill these species. Regardless of the intensity and scale of clearing, herd and grazing management are important for maintaining healthy plant populations.

Table 19.1. Important browse plants for white-tailed deer in 2 regions of Texas.

Common name	Scientific name	Performance value High	Medium	Low
Brasil	*Condalia hookeri*	X		
Elms	*Ulmus* spp.	X		
Granjeno	*Celtis pallida*	X		
Guayacan	*Guaiacum angustifolium*	X		
Hackberry	*Celtis reticulata*	X		
Kidneywood	*Eysenhardtia texana*	X		
Spanish oak	*Quercus texana*	X		
Texas sophora	*Sophora affinis*	X		
Western white honeysuckle	*Lonicera albiflora*	X		
Acacias	*Acacia* spp.		X	
Catclaw mimosa	*Mimosa biunciferae*		X	
Cenizo	*Leucophyllum frutescens*		X	
Chittam	*Bumelia lanuginosa*		X	
Elbowbush	*Forestiera pubescens*		X	
Guajillo	*Acacia berlandieri*		X	
Hogplum	*Colubrina texensis*		X	
Oaks	*Quercus* spp.		X	
Pricklyash	*Xanthoxylum* spp.		X	
Prickly pear	*Opuntia* spp.		X	
Sumacs	*Rhus* spp.		X	
Western soapberry	*Sapindus drummondii*		X	
Agarito	*Mahonia trifoliolata*			X
Blackbrush	*Acacia rigidula*			X
Cedar	*Juniperus* spp.			X
Lotebush	*Ziziphus obtusifolia*			X
Mesquite	*Prosopis glandulosa*			X
Mountain laurel	*Sophora secundiflora*			X
Persimmon	*Diospyros texana*			X
Whitebrush	*Aloysia gratissima*			X
Wolfberry	*Lycium berlandieri*			X

Source: Adapted from Nelle (1997).

Clearing Methods

Brush is generally managed by mechanical, chemical, biological, or pyric means, either singly or in combination. Specifics relative to various treatment options are covered by other authors in this book, and have been summarized by Koerth (1996) and Fulbright and Guthery (1996). Only some important considerations specific to game species are mentioned here.

Mechanical. Mechanical treatments such as grubbing or chaining are generally the technique of choice for sculpting rangelands for wildlife because they (1) afford a high degree of selectivity, and (2) create soil disturbance (Fig. 19.3). Popular mechanical techniques often used in brush sculpting include grubbing, chaining, disking, tree-shears, and roller choppers (including aerators). Such techniques increase forage production (Rollins and

Figure 19.3. (*facing page, left, and above*) Mechanical options of brush removal are generally the method of choice where wildlife habitat is a concern. *Courtesy Dale Rollins*

Bryant 1986) and nutritional quality (Waid et al. 1984, Soper et al. 1993), at least temporarily. Annual forbs respond positively to the ground disturbance caused by mechanical treatments. Further, browse availability generally increases by top-killing such species as shinoak and liveoak (*Q. virginiana*). Rootplowing, however, is generally discouraged because it has long-term, negative impacts on the species diversity of brush that remains (Fulbright and Guthery 1996).

Chemical. Herbicides are usually less expensive to apply than mechanical means, and have been especially popular on mesquite-dominated rangelands. Broadcast herbicide applications are generally less desirable than mechanical means because they are less selective. Applications of herbicide by individual plant treatment (IPT), however, can provide a level of selectivity akin to that achieved by mechanical methods. By choosing the appropriate herbicide and application rate, herbicides can be used as an effective tool for sculpting rangelands. Care should be taken when the spray mixture includes herbicides such as picloram, that result in more broad spectrum control of woody plants. Including picloram in a mesquite spraying mixture will likely kill desirable shrubs like netleaf hackberry (*Celtis reticulata*) and sandplum.

Broadcast applications of herbicides from fixed-wing aircraft preclude the ability to sculpt anything but a coarse scale, for example strips. The incorporation of variable rate patterning (Koerth 1996) can produce checkerboard arrangements of sprayed and nonsprayed habitats. Finally, the increasing popularity of individual plant treatments such as Brush Busters provides a tool for using chemicals in a manner that is very beneficial for wildlife. Creative use of boomless nozzles for liquid herbicide formulations and Solo backpack blowers for pelleted herbicides (e.g., tebuthiuron) offer options for applying herbicides with minimal impact on nontarget sites or species.

One advantage of treating with herbicides is that the standing dead brush continues to serve as screening cover (Leslie et al. 1996). Dense screening cover that inhibits travel, such as whitebrush (*Aloysia gratissima*) thickets, may receive little use by deer (Bozzo et al. 1992). Disadvantages of broadcast herbicides in particular are that forbs preferred by deer suffer forb shock for up to 2 years after application, depending on the herbicide and rates used, and related site factors, such as soil type. Two to 4 years may be required for forbs to grow back in abundance similar to what existed before herbicide application. Deer may make very little use of treated areas until forbs return to their original abundance (Beasom and Scifres 1977). Forb shock is more acute with herbicides that have residual soil activity, such as picloram. Herbicides also vary with respect to their spectrum of control on woody plants. Picloram, which is often broadcast to control pricklypear in Texas may not kill species like mesquite or lotebush, but it does kill netleaf hackberry.

Fire. Fire can be used as the primary method of brush control in some plant communities (e.g., *Juniperus* spp.), or used as a secondary method to provide maintenance control in mesquite-grassland communities (Ansley and Taylor 2000). Fire has many advantages for wildlife because it (1) improves browse availability, (2) improves browse palatability, and (3) promotes de-sirable perennial forbs (especially legumes). The plant response to burning varies with the intensity of the fire involved, the season of burning, and the post-burn grazing management. Generally cooler fires produce a more mo-saic result which is desired for species like bobwhites, while hotter fires may be more appropriate for reclamation of dense brush (Ansley and Taylor 2000). Generally fall/winter burns promote more cool-season grasses and forbs whereas winter/spring burns promote more warm-season grasses. Attention to livestock grazing management following a prescribed burn is important.

Biological. From the wildlife perspective, biological control connotes mainly the use of goats to suppress brush regrowth. As goats and deer have consid-erable overlap in diets, the potential for competition between the two spe-cies can be an important management consideration. Flash grazing of goats following a burn, or during the dormant season, may be an effective way to utilize goats while minimizing competition with deer.

Species Guidelines
Deer

Rangelands dominated by brush can be tailored to enhance habitat for white-tailed deer by designing brush manipulation to achieve the appropri-ate structure, spatial arrangement, and dispersion of brush (Fulbright 1997). One approach involves clearing small (about 20 acres), irregularly shaped patches scattered throughout the landscape. Fulbright (1997) recommended such clearings should total 40% of the landscape in South Texas, with rela-tively wide remnant corridors of brush between patches that total 60% of the landscape. Areas of tall, dense, diverse brush with canopy cover over 40% should be interspersed throughout the landscape. Brush in and along natu-ral drainage areas and large, single-stemmed mesquites should not be disturbed.

The biggest concern for deer, relative to mechanical treatments, is the scale of the clearing operation. Ideally, brush should be cleared to promote forage availability up to the point that cover (rather than food) becomes the limiting factor. As clearing size exceeds some threshold value (e.g., 50 acres), wildlife use of some portions (i.e., the center) of the clearing decreases. Smaller clearings have proportionately more edge, thus less habitat is lost. For optimum use by white-tailed deer, clearing size should be <20 acres (Fig. 19.4).

The optimum percent canopy cover of woody plants for deer habitat varies among regions. In West Texas, woody plant canopy cover averaged 43% in areas with low deer densities compared to 63% in areas with high deer densities (Wiggers and Beasom 1986). In South Texas, deer densities were greatest in areas with 43 to 60% canopy cover of brush (Steuter and Wright 1980). Greatest deer use during summer occurred on areas with 60 to 97% canopy cover of brush.

In South Texas, mature bucks preferred areas with canopy cover 85% and with dense screening cover (Pollock et al. 1994). Brush management planning should focus on having areas with 85% brush canopy cover interspersed within the landscape. Brush management is not recommended for white-tailed deer habitat improvement on areas with <60% canopy cover of woody plants in South Texas (Fulbright 1997).

Gee et al. (1991) suggested that the optimum percentage of wooded area for deer in the Cross Timbers of Oklahoma and Texas is 40–60% of the landscape, with patchy, irregularly shaped openings <200 yards wide composing the remainder of the landscape.

An important function of woody plants in deer habitat is providing screening cover for concealment. Brush must be >3 feet tall to serve as screening cover. Mature bucks prefer areas with taller screening cover. Mature bucks in South Texas heavily used areas where average seasonal canopy height was 16 feet and did not use areas with brush <15 feet tall (Pollock et al. 1994). Mature bucks select taller screening cover regardless of the amount of herbaceous vegetation present. Creating travel corridors (senderos) via shredding, dozing, or with herbicides within these thickets may increase use by deer (Fulbright 1997).

Drainages, where deer densities are often greatest, are especially important wildlife habitats on most landscapes. Brush management is strongly discouraged within and along creeks and draws. In west-central Texas, bottomland habitat contained higher deer densities than all other habitat types (Darr and Klebenow 1975). Deer densities were almost 6-fold greater in bottomland habitats than in upland savannas. Chaining bottomland habitats reduced deer densities by >50%, with densities decreasing as the amount of area chained increased. The taller vegetation along drainage areas is of major importance for deer because it provides preferred loafing and bedding sites (Inglis et al. 1986).

The Brush Sculptor's goal should always be to maintain, if not increase, plant species diversity. Species like chittam (*Bumelia lanuginosa*), hackberry (*Celtis* spp.), and granjeno (*Celtis pallida*) should be spared in most situations. Steuter and Wright (1980) reported that sites with <50% woody

Figure 19.4.
A series of smaller clearings is better for wildlife than a few large clearings. These clearings are approximately 20 acres in size, and the clearing intensity is about 70%. Desirable trees (e.g., liveoaks) were spared from clearing, and promote better use of clearings by all species of wildlife.
Courtesy Dale Rollins

canopy cover were used more heavily by deer if brush composition was more diverse.

Management plans for using brush control to improve habitat for white-tailed deer should address these general concepts (adapted from Fulbright 1997):

1.   Clear small (about 20 acres) irregularly shaped patches across the landscape. These clearings should total 40 to 60% of the landscape. Stringers of brush should connect clearings and suffice as travel corridors across the landscape. Generally the bottomlands may be thinned but should not be cleared.
2.   Areas of older, taller, denser, and more diverse brush species composition should be interspersed throughout the landscape. Such areas may range in size from 5 to 50 acres.
3.   Avoid disturbing brush in and along natural drainage areas.
4.   Use the brush control method best suited to the habitat. Rootplowing is generally not recommended because of its long-term effects on brush species diversity.
5.   Do not plant exotic grasses such as old world bluestems and buffelgrass.
6.   Use wildlife-friendly retreatment options (e.g., individual plant treatments, prescribed fire).

Quail

Populations of game birds can attain their density potential when individuals can use any part of a pasture at any time. Although intended for bobwhites, this recommendation undoubtedly holds well for any species that is a target of management. Lehmann (1984) believed each and every square inch should be usable each and every day of the year. This philosophy has been called maximization of space-time (Guthery 1997); the philosophy serves as the basis for the patterns applied in brush management.

The habitat component that usually dictates quail use of the available habitat tends to be the availability of suitable loafing and escape cover. G. Huggins of the Noble Foundation (personal communication) refers to the proper threshold for quail as the 50:50 rule, i.e., there should be a covert offering 50 square feet of brush cover spaced every 50 yards. A similar rule of thumb that involves a softball should be used. Usable space for quail will be met if a softball can be thrown (in the air, roll doesn't count!) from one quail covert to the next (Fig. 19.5a). Suitable quail houses, or coverts, include lotebush, sandplum, littleleaf sumac, algerita (*Mahonia trifoliolata*), elbowbush, and other plants with similar growth forms (Table 19.2, Fig. 19.5b).

Guthery and Rollins (1997) developed the following guidelines for brush control to benefit bobwhites: (1) no point in the pasture is further than 25 yards from woody cover, (2) no more than 90% of the pasture is treated, and (3) no woody cover object is less than 75 square feet in area.

Actually, the above prescription probably is conservative for bobwhites. We might be able to accept distances from woody cover up to 75 yards, but such a configuration would be more sensitive to grazing. The above recommendations are subject to "slack;" in other words, the prescription is quite arbitrary (Guthery 1999).

There are some other guidelines in managing brush for game birds.

1.   Preserve mottes instead of solitary plants. Wild turkeys, quail, and deer are more likely to occur in areas with mottes.

2.   Save patches of taller, mature brush. Taller brush is important on semiarid rangelands because of the cooler temperatures it provides during hot days and seasons (Johnson and Guthery 1988).

Figure 19.5a.
This pasture was sculpted mechanically to benefit bobwhites. Loafing coverts ("quail houses") were left about a softball's throw apart.
Courtesy Dale Rollins

Figure 19.5b.
Loafing coverts used by quail should be about the size of a pickup truck. They should be dense above, yet open at ground level to provide quail maximum protection from predators.
Courtesy Dale Rollins

Table 19.2. Woody plants that provide good quail coverts (i.e., "quail houses") in Texas.

Common name	Scientific name	Ecoregion			
		Rolling plains	Rio Grande plains	Edwards Plateau	Trans-Pecos
Sandplum	*Prunus angustifolia*	X			
Lotebush	*Ziziphus obtusifolia*	X	X	X	X
Skunkbush	*Rhus trilobata*	X			
Littleleaf sumac	*Rhus microphylla*	X		X	X
Elbowbush	*Foresteira pubescens*	X	X	X	
Shinnery oak	*Quercus* spp.	X		X	
Agarito	*Mahonia trifoliolata*			X	
Catclaw	*Mimosa* spp., *Acacia* spp.	X	X	X	X
Fourwing saltbush	*Atriplex canescens*			X	X
Prickly pear*	*Opuntia* spp.	X	X	X	X
Mesquite**	*Prosopis glandulosa*	X	X	X	X

*Taller growing forms.
**Sprawling growth forms more desirable than upright growth.

3. Preserve wild turkey roosts and travel corridors (strips of woody cover) radiating from the roosts (Scott and Boeker 1977).

4. Identify and preserve the integrity of special sites like sandplum or chittam thickets.

5. To the degree possible, leave individual trees (e.g., sprawling mesquites rather than upright ones) or species (e.g., lotebush, sumacs) that provide good quail houses.

6. Areas subjected to heavier grazing pressure, which can result in less grass available to serve as screening cover, require more brush than areas with more luxuriant grass cover.

7. Be cognizant of potential forb shock or damage to desirable brush (e.g., hackberry) when using some herbicides (e.g., picloram).

Special Habitats

Some species of wildlife require woody plants for other habitat requisites. For example, wild turkeys require suitable roost sites, and such sites can be the limiting factor in some portions of the Rio Grande turkeys' range (Haucke 1975). Turkeys prefer to roost in the tallest trees available, which often include pecan (*Carya illinoiensis*), liveoak, cottonwood (*Populus deltoides*) and elms (*Ulmus* spp.). Such species usually occur in riparian areas, which should always be spared during clearing operations. However, sometimes chemical drift from adjacent areas can kill sensitive species.

Pricklypear can provide an important nesting substrate for bobwhite and scaled quail, especially when traditional nesting sites (e.g., little bluestem) are limited (<300 per acre) (Slater et al. 2001). Treatment alternatives might include (1) using fire only as a tool for thinning pricklypear, (2) using a reduced rate of picloram following the burn, or (3) applying picloram with a boomless nozzle in a mosaic pattern so that approximately 30% of the pricklypear remains untreated.

The presence of threatened or endangered species can impact brush management decisions. For example, the presence of golden-cheeked warblers

(*Dendroica chrysoparia*) or black-capped vireos (*Vireo atricapilla*) may restrict, or at least modify, brush clearing plans. Always check with the local state wildlife agency, or the U.S. Fish and Wildlife Service, if you suspect that rare species occur on your property.

Applied Landscaping

The same principles practiced by a landscape architect to accentuate one's home, for example attention to natural beauty, aesthetics, and shading can also be applied to rangelands. Indeed, the application of applied landscaping serves to protect the biological diversity of a site while maintaining or enhancing its natural beauty and functionality for the wildlife species of interest.

Applied landscaping is the basis of any brush sculpting plan. It can be conducted at different spatial levels, including the (1) landscape level, (2) individual clearing level, (3) plant community level, (4) plant species level, and (5) individual plant level. Examples of the various levels of brush sculpting are presented in Fig. 19.6. Rollins (1997*a*) provides more detail relative to the various scales.

The animal's perspective must also be addressed. Deer presumably need more and denser escape cover in an area that receives heavier hunting pressure (Swenson 1982). Clearing shapes and sizes are more critical for species with low mobility (e.g., bobwhites) than for more mobile species (e.g., wild turkey).

Applied landscaping is a mix of art and science, and the end product is limited only by the creativity of the sculptor, the ability of the contractor to implement the design, and perhaps the pocketbook of the landowner.

Integrated Approach

During recent years, an integrated approach for sculpting brush has been developed that involves both chemical and mechanical means. For mesquite-dominated habitats, the areas desired to be cleared are first delineated. If quail are a management objective, selected multi-stemmed mesquites are marked for half-cutting (Rollins 1997*b*), usually at a density of about 5 to 10 trees/acre. Generally the clearing is initiated by using the Brush Busters individual plant treatments (foliar spray; see http://texnat.tamu.edu for additional details) targeting all mesquites <6 feet tall. Once these trees are controlled, mechanical means (e.g., grubbing) are employed to remove the larger trees designated for removal. Removal may be done in clearings or simply thinned (i.e., leave every fifth mesquite). Generally only mesquite and junipers are removed, depending on the site. Hackberry, chittam, and other preferred species are not cleared. Follow-up treatments with either Brush Busters or prescribed burning will be needed every 5 to 7 years depending on the site.

Regardless of the method selected, communication with the contractor before and during the clearing operation is imperative (Rollins 1997*a*) (Fig. 19.7). Good aerial imagery and computer applications are now available to facilitate planning efforts (Burroughs and Gibbs 2000). Misunderstandings, such as clearing more brush than what the landowner had in-

Figure 19.6.
Brush sculpting can be conducted at various spatial scales. Going from a coarse to a fine scale, these include landscape, individual clearing, plant community, plant species, and individual plant levels.
Courtesy Dale Rollins

Figure 19.7.
Detailed communication between the planner and the contractor is critical to the success of a brush sculpting effort. New technologies like Global Positioning Systems promise to be increasingly important in such planning.
Courtesy Dale Rollins

tended, may limit habitability of a site for some time. The traditional method of using flagging tape for marking intended boundaries between cleared and non-cleared areas is satisfactory, but new technologies such as GPS-mapping can greatly enhance marking efficiency, effectiveness and accuracy of communications between planners and contractors, and facilitate the implementation of the resulting plan.

Lamentations in Brush Management

Brush management can be one of the best things for wildlife habitat, but historically it has been one of the worst. In order to have a positive affect, wildlife habitat needs must be considered a priori, well before the spray plane is in the air, or the bulldozer is started. Mistakes in planning brush management can have long-term negative impacts on the wildlife diversity and density on a particular site. As the carpenter says, "measure twice, and saw once."

Once the management plan is formulated, ensure that all parties involved clearly understand just what and how various areas are to be cleared. Do not assume that a bulldozer operator appreciates or understands the significance of brush for wildlife. Further, do not specify in a plan to leave all skunkbush and lotebush if the operator does not know how to identify such plants. The land manager should plan on providing close supervision of the operators, at least initially, to ensure they have a grasp of the objectives and what the resulting landscape is supposed to look like.

Research Needs

There are many gray areas relative to the recommendations presented here. Accordingly, additional research is needed to clarify and refine some of the generalizations. Specific items that need to be addressed include: (1) deer and quail response to various intensities and scales of clearing, especially in watersheds targeted for extensive brush control; such efforts should monitor population responses beyond just the initial treatment period, (2) define cover thresholds for various situations, clearing methods, and grazing regimes, (3) develop and validate models for predicting wildlife responses that can be integrated with existing watershed models, (4) evaluate high yield water and wildlife sites in a spatial sense (i.e., are the deer cover sites high or low yield sites for water?), and (5) develop Geographic Information Systems to facilitate implementation of brush clearing plans.

Literature Cited

Ansley, R. J., and C. A. Taylor, Jr. 2000. The future of fire as a tool for managing brush. Pages 159–69 *in* Proceedings rangeland weed and brush management. Texas A&M University, San Angelo.

Beasom, S. L., and C. J. Scifres. 1977. Vegetation and white-tailed deer response to herbicide treatment of a mesquite drainage habitat type. Journal of Range Management 35:790–95.

Bozzo, J. A., S. L. Beasom, and T. E. Fulbright. 1992. White-tailed deer use of rangeland following browse rejuvenation. Journal of Range Management 45:496–99.

Burroughs, R., and M. Gibbs. 2000. The Land Enhancement Services' philosophy for sculpting brush. Pages 64–66 *in* J. Cearley and D. Rollins, editors. Brush, water, and wildlife: a compendium of our knowledge. Texas Agricultural Experiment Station, San Angelo.

Carter, P. S., D. Rollins, and C. B. Scott. 2002. Initial effects of prescribed burning on survival and nesting success of northern bobwhite in west-central Texas. Pages 114–19 *in* S. J. DeMaso, W. F. Kuvlesky, Jr., F. Hernandez, and M. E. Berger, editors. Quail V: Proceedings of the Fifth National Quail Symposium. Texas Parks and Wildlife Department, Austin.

Darr, G. W., and D. A. Klebenow. 1975. Deer, brush control, and livestock on the Texas Rolling Plains. Journal of Range Management 28:115–19.

Fulbright, T. E. 1997. Designing shrubland landscapes to optimize habitat for white-tailed deer. Pages 61–67 *in* D. Rollins, D. N. Ueckert, and C. G.

Brown, editors. Proceedings brush sculptors symposium. Texas Agricultural Extension Service, San Angelo.

———, and F. S. Guthery. 1996. Mechanical manipulation of plants. Pages 339–54 *in* P. R. Krausman, editor. Rangeland wildlife. Society for Range Management, Denver, Colorado.

Gee, K. L., M. D. Porter, S. Demarais, F. C. Bryant, and G. Van Vreede. 1991. White-tailed deer: their foods and management in the Cross Timbers. Samuel Roberts Noble Foundation, Ardmore, Oklahoma.

Guthery, F. S. 1986. Beef, brush and bobwhites. Caesar Kleberg Wildlife Research Institute Press, Kingsville, Texas.

———. 1997. A philosophy of habitat management for northern bobwhites. Journal of Wildlife Management 61:291–301.

———. 1999. Slack in the configuration of habitat patches for northern bobwhites. Journal of Wildlife Management 63:245–50.

———, and D. Rollins. 1997. Sculpting brush for upland game birds. Pages 68–72 *in* D. Rollins, D. N. Ueckert, and C. G. Brown, editors. Proceedings brush sculptors symposium. Texas Agricultural Extension Service, San Angelo.

Hailey, T. L. 1979. Basics of brush management for white-tailed deer production. Texas Parks and Wildlife Department Booklet 7000-35.

Hanselka, C. W., R. Q. Landers, Jr., and J. C. Paschal. 1995. Pricklypear: friend and foe. Texas Agricultural Extension Service Publication B5046.

Haucke, H. H. 1975. Winter roost characteristics of the Rio Grande turkey in South Texas. Proceedings of the National Wild Turkey Symposium 3:164–69.

Inglis, J. M., B. A. Brown, C. A. McMahan, and R. E. Hood. 1986. Deerbrush relationships on the Rio Grande Plain, Texas. Texas Agricultural Experiment Station Publication RM14/KS6.

Johnson, D. B., and F. S. Guthery. 1988. Loafing coverts used by northern bobwhites in subtropical environments. Journal of Wildlife Management 52:464–69.

Koerth, B. H. 1996. Chemical manipulation of plants. Pages 321–37 *in* P. R. Krausman, editor. Rangeland wildlife. Society for Range Management, Denver, Colorado.

Leckenby, D. A. 1978. Western juniper management for mule deer. Pages 137–61 *in* R. E. Martin, J. E. Dealy, and D. L. Caraher, editors. Proceedings western juniper ecology and management workshop. U.S. Forest Service General Technical Report PNW-74.

Lehmann, V. W. 1984. Bobwhites in the Rio Grande Plain of Texas. Texas A&M University Press, College Station.

Leopold, A. S. 1933. Game management. Charles Scribner's Sons, New York.

Leslie, D. M., Jr., R. B. Soper, R. L. Lochmiller, and D. M. Engle. 1996. Habitat use by white-tailed deer on Cross Timbers rangeland following brush management. Journal of Range Management 49:401–405.

McGinty, A. W., and D. N. Ueckert. 1995. Brush Busters—how to beat mesquite. Texas Agricultural Extension Service Publication L-5144.

Nelle, S. A. 1997. Brush as an integral component of wildlife habitat. Pages 3–8 *in* D. Rollins, D. N. Ueckert, and C. G. Brown, editors. Proceedings brush sculptors symposium. Texas Agricultural Extension Service, San Angelo.

Pollock, M. T., D. G. Whittaker, S. Demarais, and R. E. Zaiglin. 1994. Vegetation characteristics influencing site selection by male white-tailed deer in Texas. Journal of Range Management 47:235–39.

Rollins, D. 1997*a*. Applied landscaping: a primer for brush sculptors. Pages 127–32 *in* D. Rollins, D. N. Ueckert, and C. G. Brown, editors. Proceedings brush sculptors symposium. Texas Agricultural Extension Service, San Angelo.

———. 1997*b*. Half-cutting mesquite trees to enhance loafing cover for quail. Page 149 *in* D. Rollins, D. N. Ueckert, and C. G. Brown, editors. Proceedings brush sculptors symposium. Texas Agricultural Extension Service, San Angelo.

———, and W. E. Armstrong. 1997. Cedar through the eyes of wildlife. Pages 4.23–4.31 *in* C. A. Taylor, Jr., editor. Proceedings 1997 Juniper Symposium. Technical Report 97-1, Texas Agricultural Experiment Station, San Angelo.

———, and F. C. Bryant. 1986. Floral changes following mechanical brush removal in Central Texas. Journal of Range Management 39:237–40.

———, ———, D. D. Waid, and L. C. Bradley. 1988. Deer response to brush management in Central Texas. Wildlife Society Bulletin 16:277–84.

———, D. N. Ueckert, and C. G. Brown. 1997. Proceedings brush sculptors symposium. Texas Agricultural Extension Service, San Angelo.

Scifres, C. J. 1980. Brush management: principles and practices for Texas and the Southwest. Texas A&M University Press, College Station.

Scott, V. E., and E. L. Boeker. 1977. Responses of Merriam's turkey to pinyon-juniper control. Journal of Range Management 30:220–23.

Slater, S. C., D. Rollins, R. C. Dowler, and C. B. Scott. 2001. *Opuntia:* a "prickly paradigm" for quail management in West Texas. Wildlife Society Bulletin 29:713–19.

Soper, R. B., R. L. Lochmiller, D. M. Leslie, Jr., and D. M. Engle. 1993. Nutritional quality of browse after brush management on Cross Timbers rangeland. Journal of Range Management 46:399–410.

Steuter, A. A., and H. A. Wright. 1980. White-tailed deer densities and brush cover on the Rio Grande Plain. Journal of Range Management 33:328–31.

Swenson, J. E. 1982. Effects of hunting on habitat use by mule deer on mixed prairie grass in Montana. Wildlife Society Bulletin 10:115–20.

Thurow, T. L., A. P. Thurow, C. Taylor, Jr., R. Conner, and M. Garriga. 1997. Environmental and economic tradeoffs associated with vegetation management on the Edwards Plateau. Pages 2-3 through 2-10 *in* C. A. Taylor, Jr. editor. Proceedings 1997 Juniper Symposium, Technical Report 97-1, Texas Agricultural Experiment Station, San Angelo.

Waid, D. D., R. J. Warren, and D. Rollins. 1984. Seasonal deer diets in Central Texas and their response to brush control. Southwestern Naturalist 29:301–307.

Wiggers, E. P., and S. L. Beasom. 1986. Characterization of sympatric or adjacent habitats of two deer species in West Texas. Journal of Wildlife Management 50:129–34.

20 Conclusion
Developing and Implementing Brush and Weed Management Strategies

Darrell N. Ueckert
and
Wayne T. Hamilton

Significant technological advances have been made in biological, mechanical, chemical, and prescribed burning strategies for managing rangeland brush and weed problems. Effective implementation of these brush and weed management strategies, when coupled with good planning, effective monitoring, and close attention to feedback from monitoring activities, can improve the multiple use value of rangelands for livestock production, wildlife habitat, watershed, recreation, and aesthetic amenities. Ill-advised or poorly planned implementation of brush and weed management practices, or failure to monitor the biological and economic consequences of the practices may diminish the value of rangelands for production of these same services and products, may not be profitable, or may not achieve the desired management objective. Brush (or weed) management plans should be long term and based on sound ecological principles.

Generalized guidelines are presented in this chapter to aid rangeland resource managers in planning and implementing a sustainable, long-term brush or weed management program. As the various steps in this process are discussed, some critical points should be kept in mind. First, simply controlling the existing population of brush or weeds will not provide a long-term solution to the problems on rangeland or pastures. Initial treatments must be followed up with carefully selected and properly applied maintenance treatments. Second, brush and weed management efforts cannot be expected to result in recovery of the desirable vegetation and the expected economic responses unless proper grazing management is implemented. Third, achieving a satisfactory, long-term, sustainable solution to a weed or brush problem hinges upon our ability to accurately assess the root cause of the problem and restore the normal ecological processes of energy flow, nutrient cycling, and the hydrological cycle.

Basic Principles of Brush or Weed Management

The term "brush (or weed) management" means the management and manipulation of brush (or weeds) to achieve a specific management objective and recognizes the potential value of certain quantities of woody plants and

259

forbs in rangeland management (Scifres et al. 1985). Woody plants and forbs were present in limited amounts on our rangelands prior to development of the livestock industry by Europeans, and they are natural components of rangeland vegetation. Some of these plants are seasonally important in the diets of livestock, and many are essential for maintaining healthy ecological processes in our rangeland ecosystems (Scifres 1980). Many woody plants, forbs, and pricklypear (*Opuntia* sp.) cactus are important for providing food and cover for the array of game and nongame wildlife species which are currently very important sources of ranch income (Inglis 1985, Nelle 1997, Rollins 1997).

Brush and weed management strategies should be long term and based on sound ecological principles, and not simply focused on controlling the current stand of brush and/or weeds. Furthermore, they should involve the sequential application of combinations of mechanical, chemical, biological, and fire treatments rather than repeated application of a single treatment. The sequencing of treatments should be orderly, properly timed, and complimentary or synergistic, so that the inherent strengths of one treatment offset the characteristic weaknesses of the other.

There is no single "best" brush or weed management strategy for everyone. Management strategies may vary among pastures or range sites within a pasture because of inherent differences in the soils, species composition, canopy cover, or density of the brush component among pastures and among range sites. Strategies may also vary among ranchers with similar brush problems because their management objectives, goals, and capital or labor resources differ.

Rangeland resource managers should not expect to ever be finished with their brush or weed management program because it is not likely that the problem will be solved within one person's lifetime. Seeds of many weedy species are long-lived in the soil, and they can easily be disseminated over substantial distances by wind, water, mammals, birds, and human activities. In reality, brush and weed management is a never-ending necessity and should be viewed as part of the cost of managing rangeland for livestock and wildlife production and for maintaining or increasing the value of the land. Long-term monitoring is essential to determine if the biological and cost/return consequences of brush management practices are on track relative to achieving the management objective. The decision maker must periodically evaluate feedback from monitoring activities and make adjustments in stocking rate, the timing or method of maintenance treatment or, sometimes, even in the management objective.

Planning and Implementing Brush or Weed Management Strategies

The development and implementation of brush/weed management strategies for rangelands has received much attention over the last 20 years (Scifres 1980, Scifres et al. 1983, Scifres et al. 1985, DiTomaso 2000). The popular terminology for this endeavor has been integrated brush (or weed) management systems (IBMS), indicating that a plan or procedure is followed in which the application of a variety of weed or brush control practices is co-ordinated by the manager in an orderly fashion (Scifres 1980). The steps or processes in designing and implementing a brush or weed management system or strategy (Scifres et al. 1985, Hanselka et al. 1996*b*) include (1) establishing the management objective for the rangeland or ranch resource, (2) assessing or inventorying the resources, (3) selection of treatment alternatives, (4) conducting economic analysis of the alternative treatments, (5) implementation of the plan, and (6) monitoring the results of the plan and feedback.

Establish the Management Objective

The first step is to clearly identify the objective or goal for the rangeland being considered in the planning process (Fig. 20.1) (Hamilton 1985*a*). This is done by the landowner, the managing partner, executor(s), executive, or administrator, depending upon the ownership status of the land. The objective should be carefully matched to the managerial capabilities and capital resources of the one who will be managing the land. Landowners who will be turning over their ranches to heirs should consider the heirs' future interests. For example, a rancher whose personal interest is in growing grass and producing cattle might tend to develop and implement brush manage-

The Planning Process

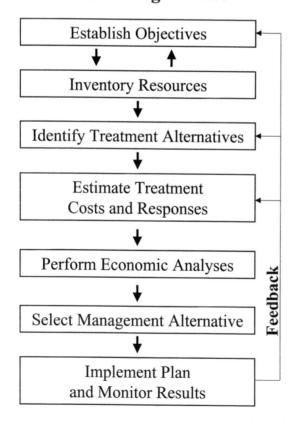

Figure 20.1.
The Planning Process.

ment strategies that would not be conducive to the interest of an heir whose primary interest in the land is wildlife production, aesthetics, or real estate development.

Establishing a specific management objective for the land gives direction to the planning process. For example, the generalized objective might be to develop a profitable stocker yearling operation in coordination with a hunting lease enterprise. However, during the initial planning phase the objective should be somewhat flexible to allow for refinement after the resource inventory and evaluation are completed and to allow consideration of a variety of treatment alternatives.

The people deciding upon the management objective for the land must be willing to implement changes. For example, individuals who initially set a hunting lease enterprise as their sole objective might ultimately switch to a combination of hunting and a commercial cow-calf operation if the resource inventory indicated that the resource lacked the ability to produce deer, turkey, and/or quail at levels required to meet the initial objective. The original management objective might also be subject to change depending upon the development or recognition of new technology or a substantial change in the economic picture.

Inventory the Resources

A thorough inventory of the resources is the next step in the planning process (Fig. 20.1). The inventory provides necessary information to determine if brush or weed control is necessary to achieve the management objective, where control should be applied, the brush species that should be targeted, and critical information for selection of applicable treatment alternatives (Hamilton 1985a). The inventory should include aerial photographs and all available information on soils, topography, roads, fences, water developments, and range site descriptions of the Natural Resources Conservation Service (NRCS). Aerial photographs can usually be obtained from the local NRCS office or the Texas Natural Resources Information Service. Assistance in conducting resource inventories can be obtained through the NRCS or private consultants.

Information on the location of existing fences and watering facilities is essential for decisions relative to changes in grazing management strategies that may be necessary in conjunction with certain brush management alternatives, such as deferments that are necessary for prescribed burning or revegetation. The inventory should include an assessment of the current wildlife populations. For example, for white-tailed deer (*Odocoileus virginianus*), information should be gathered on the current deer density, buck:doe ratio, fawn crop, age class distribution of bucks, etc.

Range condition and trend should be determined on all range sites to assess the current health of the sites and to establish initial stocking levels for each site and management unit (White and McGinty 1992, McGinty and White 1994). This information will be used as the pre-treatment or baseline record for the enterprise. The species of woody plants and data on their canopy cover, density, height, etc. on each range site should be recorded for assessing their impact on herbaceous forage production, the potential of the site for wildlife habitat, and for baseline information to use for selecting the most appropriate treatment alternatives.

By determining the current condition of range sites, stocking rate data can be combined with projected vegetation changes after treatment imple-
mentation to provide a basis for projecting the economic outcome of treatment. For example, low-energy grubbing of redberry juniper (*Juniperus pinchotii*) followed by a prescribed fire on a low stony hill range site in low fair condition (initial carrying capacity 1 animal unit (AU)/45 acres) might be projected to result in a change to good range condition within 10 years (carrying capacity 1 AU/20 acres). This type of change, coupled with any other improvement in animal performance (e.g., conception rates and weaning weights) or a decrease in variable costs, will be the basis for evaluating treatment effect and for selection of a set of treatment alternatives that will optimize production and achieve the management objective.

Selection of Treatment Alternatives

After the management objective has been formulated and the resources have been inventoried and assessed, the next step is to select the initial (reclamation) and follow-up (maintenance) brush management treatments that will be considered as potential alternatives (Fig. 20.1). Excellent overviews of the arsenal of mechanical, chemical, biological, and prescribed burning methods have been presented by the authors of this book and by Valentine (1971), Scifres (1980), Welch et al. (1985), Welch (1991), McGinty and Welch (1995), Ansley et al. (1997), Koerth (1997), Taylor (1997), Wiedemann (1997), and McGinty et al. (2000). The resource manager should objectively evaluate all potential treatments based upon (1) biological effectiveness, (2) characteristic weaknesses, (3) expected treatment life and forage response, (4) application requirements and practicality for the particular situation, (5) the density, age, and size of the specific brush problem being considered, (6) the resprouting ability of the target brush species, (7) the degree of selectivity needed, (8) secondary effects that could create new problems, and (9) their maintenance requirements (Welch et al. 1985, Whisenant 1997).

The process of selecting treatment alternatives is facilitated by the Expert System for Brush and Weed Control Technology (EXSEL) (Hamilton et al. 1993), which is available for use free of charge on the internet at http://cnrit .tamu.edu/rsg/exsel/. This science-based program is user friendly and is updated regularly as new technology develops. EXSEL allows the user to pick a target brush or weed species, then asks the user for specific information which would be available in a resource inventory, such as (1) soil type and depth, (2) the density, stem diameter, and average height of target species, and (3) current soil moisture status. The next steps allow the user to consider (1) individual plant treatments only, (2) broadcast treatments only, or (3) if the user wants the expert system to select the best method. The user is then asked to choose (1) mechanical treatments only, (2) chemical treatments only, or (3) if the system should select the treatments. EXSEL then asks (1) if topographical features will restrict the use of mechanical treatments, (2) if reseeding will be considered, and (3) if the size or location of the brush problem and the proximity to herbicide-sensitive crops will allow aerial spraying to be a viable option. The next four questions relate to whether prescribed fire is a viable treatment option. EXSEL queries the user on the level of root-kill of the target species necessary to meet management objectives (76–100%, 56–75%, 36–55%, or 0–35% root-kill). Then, with a click on the "submit" button, a list of treatment alternatives is available, complete with information on expected response in brush regrowth, forage production, treatment life, and strengths and weaknesses of the treatments. Instructions are given on herbicide rates (for broadcast sprays) or concentrations (for individual plant treatment sprays), timing of spray applications, etc. The system will indicate whether prescribed burning is a viable option based on fuel load, continuity, and distribution. EXSEL's "Ranch Checklist for Prescribed Burning," which will help the user plan, organize, and control a prescribed fire and control grazing on the burned area, can be printed. After EXSEL has been used to select the possible initial (reclamation) treatments for the target species, the user can simply go back through the procedure and ask for the treatment alternatives for maintenance control to be used over time following the initial treatment. EXSEL is highly recommended to anyone planning to manage brush and weeds, and especially those who lack experience in brush and weed management. Very useful decision-aid flow charts have also been developed for mesquite (*Prosopis glandulosa* var. *glandulosa*), twisted acacia (*Acacia schaffneri* var. *bravoensis*), huisache (*Acacia smallii*), Macartney rose (*Rosa bracteata*), pricklypear (*Opuntia* spp.), and juniper (cedar) (*Juniperus* spp.) by Hanselka et al. (1996a).

Grazing Management Considerations

Alternative brush and weed management practices should also be critically evaluated relative to the current or future livestock grazing management program. Grazing management must always be combined with brush management for best results. Brush management efforts cannot be expected to result in recovery of the desirable vegetation if that vegetation is grazed too heavily or at the wrong season (Scifres 1980). Optimum response from many brush management procedures requires closely timed deferments from grazing, which may require the development of a planned grazing system, combining livestock herds, and/or the short-term leasing of grazing off the ranch (Stuth and Scifres 1985). Brush management treatments such as prescribed fire usually require a pre-fire deferment of 4 to 6 months or longer to allow the accumulation of sufficient fine fuel (mulch and standing vegetation) to support an intense fire. A post-fire deferment of 2 to 4 months is usually required following dormant-season fires to allow for recovery of the key forage plants. Considerably longer deferment, possibly 1 to 2 years, may be necessary following intense, summer fires.

If a major investment and management commitment has already been made in a planned grazing system, brush management strategies can likely be incorporated into the existing grazing system. If livestock grazing management is loosely structured, with graze/rest decisions made on a short-term basis or based on forage utilization, then grazing strategies can likely be planned around the necessary deferments to enhance the effectiveness of brush management. Another alternative is to plan brush management and grazing management simultaneously. Excellent overviews on integrating grazing and brush management strategies have been presented by Heitschmidt and Pieper (1983) and Stuth and Scifres (1985). Helpful information on grazing systems is available in papers by Hanselka et al. (1990) and Heitschmidt and Taylor (1991).

Wildlife Habitat Considerations

On rangeland with quality wildlife habitat, and with sufficient planning and marketing, income from hunting leases can be substantial and even exceed that from livestock enterprises (Inglis 1985, Baen 1997, Rhyne 1998). The lease value or potential lease value of ranch land for hunting and recreation is also an important component of its market value. Data from the 1996 Texas Farm and Ranch Hunting Survey, conducted by the Texas Comptroller of Public Accounts, suggested that about 28% of the market value of farm and ranch land in 115 of the 254 counties within the state was associated with the lease value for hunting and recreation (Baen 1997). Consequently, if a ranch firm plans to derive income from hunting leases and recreation and to conserve or increase the market value of its rangeland resource, wildlife habitat concerns must be addressed during the planning and implementation of brush management strategies (Holechek 1981). Economically important game animals, such as white-tailed deer and upland game birds require certain amounts of brush for escape, screening, or thermal cover. However, excessive brush cover suppresses production of forbs, browse, and grass for game and livestock. Anyone planning brush management should learn to identify plants that are important habitat components and utilize selective brush control treatments to the maximum extent possible on sites where these plants occur in limited abundance (Nelle 1997). Dale Rollins and Ken Cearley have done an excellent job explaining how to integrate wildlife concerns into brush management in Chapter 19 (*this book*).

An important habitat requirement for white-tailed deer is a mosaic of cover screen—brush distributed and structured so deer can break visual contact with perceived danger within a few seconds. Ideal cover screen has a thinned quality compared with most brush that would likely be targeted for treatment (Inglis 1985). Areas retained for cover screen should have grass and forb ground cover and browse at deer height so food supplies for deer are relatively abundant within the screen. Brush density and canopy cover in areas retained for cover screen should be sufficient to allow the deer to disappear within the screen at about 50 to 75 yards. Ideal habitat will have about ⅓ cover screen designed in a mosaic so that no point is more than 200 yards from screen, thus treated areas could potentially be 400 yards wide.

Some broadcast mechanical treatments, such as rootplowing, totally remove cover screen, but the soil disturbance promotes growth of forbs. Other mechanical practices, such as shredding, stimulate regrowth of palatable browse for deer. Chemical brush treatments can be more extensive (i.e., wider strips) because the standing dead (or partially killed) brush canopies serve as cover screen. Herbicides temporarily suppress forbs, but this is often followed shortly by a flush of low browse and forbs. Major drainages, which support taller woody plants and good diversity of grasses and forbs, should be dealt with carefully, because these sites are preferred by deer for midday loafing and bedding. Brush treatments such as selective thinning or segmented clearings should be considered for these areas. One or two brush thickets per square mile should be retained for escape cover for mature bucks. Grazing management which promotes improved range condition and increased plant diversity reduces the potential for competition between deer and livestock and favors the stability of deer forage. Information on integrating deer habitat concerns into brush management strategies has been presented by Inglis (1985), Richardson (1990), and Fulbright (1997).

Guidelines presented by Guthrey and Rollins (1997) for planning brush management for bobwhite quail included (1) no point in the pasture should be more than 25 yards from woody cover (50 yard spacing between woody cover), (2) no more than 90% of a pasture should be treated, and (3) brush areas retained for quail should be about 75 square feet in area. Inglis (1985) felt that woody cover retained for escape and loafing cover for quail could be spaced 200 yards apart because the birds would never be more than their flight distance (100 yards) from escape cover. Other guidelines for managing brush for upland game birds include: (1) retain mottes of brush, rather than isolated single plants, (2) retain patches of taller, mature brush for animals to use to escape the heat, (3) preserve wild turkey roosts, such as tall oaks (*Quercus* spp.) and pecan (*Carya illinoinensis*) trees and travel corridors (strips of woody cover) radiating from the roosts, (4) identify and preserve "honey holes," such as sand plum (*Prunus gracilis*) and chittam (bumelia) (*Bumelia lanuginosa*) thickets (Guthery and Rollins 1997).

Economic Analysis of Alternative Treatments

In many cases, two or more alternative treatments or treatment combinations will be considered technically feasible and likely to achieve the same management objective. The next step (Fig. 20.1) is to select the one which is most profitable, poses the least risk, or best matches the landowner's desire for the post-treatment appearance of the landscape. As a contingency, the next best treatment, i.e., one that could be used in the event weather or some other factor prevents use of the first choice treatment(s), should be selected. Estimates of costs (labor, equipment rental, contractor charges, herbicide, equipment, etc.) required to implement the management strategies will be fairly easy to obtain, while post-treatment benefits are more difficult. Increased revenue will be based upon the expected forage production response to the treatments as this affects livestock carrying capacity, reproductive efficiency, the number of game animals that can be harvested, the price that can be charged for lease hunting, etc. Reduced costs for labor and supplemental feed that might occur after brush control should also be estimated. These benefit response curves can be constructed to show the differences between treated and untreated areas over the planning period. Landowners will usually need assistance from qualified state or federal agency personnel or consultants to develop these curves for the economic analysis.

That productivity of the rangeland will likely decline without treatment should be considered during the economic analysis. Partial budgeting can be used to compare the net changes in revenue and costs for each alternative treatment. Since additional revenue and additional costs associated with brush management occur over several years, several criteria may be used, including accumulated net present value, internal rate of return, benefit-cost ratio, and number of years to capital recovery (Whitson et al. 1979). Although many assumptions and estimations must be used in these procedures, they will provide indicators of the relative economic feasibility and risk of the different alternatives. Additional information on economic analysis of brush management strategies is available in Chapter 17 (*this book*) and in papers by Scifres et al. (1983), Conner (1985), Conner and Whitson (1997), and Johnson et al. (1999).

Some conservative estimates of the forage response resulting from controlling various infestation levels of mesquite and redberry juniper in the southeastern part of the North Concho River Watershed area are shown in Table 20.1 (Bach and Conner 1998). Table 20.1 also shows the estimated net present value to a rancher for controlling each type of mesquite and juniper infestation for a 10-year planning horizon, assuming an 8% discount rate, as well as the estimated costs. This study assumed that both initial and follow-up treatments would be required during the 10-year period to reduce the brush cover to a target range of 3 to 8%. This particular economic analysis indicated that controlling heavy mesquite and heavy cedar (>25% canopy cover) would not be profitable if the rancher's costs exceeded $16.06/acre and $19.40/acre, respectively. The break-even costs for controlling moderate mesquite and moderate cedar (10 to 25% canopy cover) were estimated at

Table 20.1. Expected increases in forage production (%), treatment cost ($/acre), and the present value of costs ($/acre) to the rancher for brush control over a 10-year planning horizon in the southeastern part of the North Concho River watershed. Heavy, moderate, and light brush infestations are equal to >25% canopy cover, 10 to 25% canopy cover, and <10% canopy cover, respectively.

Brush type and density	Forage increase (%)	Treatment cost ($/acre)	Present value ($/acre)
Heavy mesquite[1]	25	59.60	16.06
Heavy juniper[2]	50	78.60	19.40
Heavy juniper[3]	50	32.20	19.40
Moderate mesquite[4]	5	23.60	8.35
Moderate juniper[5]	10	28.60	10.06
Light mesquite[6]	0	16.10	5.62
Light juniper[7]	0	18.60	5.87

Source: Adapted from Bach and Conner (1998).

[1]Initial treatment: aerial spraying, first follow-up treatment: chemical individual plant treatment (IPT), second follow-up treatment: chemical IPT or prescribed burn.

[2]Initial treatment: tree doze & burn, follow-up treatment: chemical IPT or prescribed burn.

[3]Initial treatment: two-way chain, first follow-up treatment: prescribed burn for slash reduction, second follow-up treatment: chemical IPT or prescribed burn.

[4]Initial treatment: chemical IPT, follow-up treatment: chemical IPT or prescribed burn.

[5]Initial treatment: chemical or mechanical IPT, follow-up treatment: chemical IPT or prescribed burn.

[6]Initial treatment: chemical IPT, follow-up treatment: chemical IPT or prescribed burn.

[7]Initial treatment: chemical or mechanical IPT, follow-up treatment: chemical or mechanical IPT or prescribed burn.

$8.35/acre and $10.06/acre, respectively. Similar figures for controlling light mesquite and light cedar (<10% canopy cover) were $5.62/acre and $5.87/acre, respectively (Table 20.1). This analysis assumed that no changes in current grazing management would accompany the brush control. It is pertinent to point out that the break even prices shown in Table 20.1 would fall woefully short of the actual costs for all brush densities.

An underlying assumption in most of the discussion above is that most rangeland resource managers are interested in managing brush and weeds to maximize profit. However, this is increasingly not the case. Many who are acquiring rangeland today, either through inheritance or purchase, are not solely interested in either livestock or commercial hunting enterprises or necessarily in making a profit from their rangeland resources. Some are interested in managing brush and weeds simply to improve the aesthetics of their land for their own enjoyment or so they can see more wildlife. Others are interested in managing brush and weeds as a capital investment to improve the terminal value of their land for sale to others. With careful planning, the brush on a property can be managed to optimize the potential for profit from both current returns and long-term returns (Bierschwale 1997, SoRelle 2000).

Implementation of the Plan

A brush or weed management plan can only be successful if it is properly executed. Implementation must be a coordinated process that puts into existence the treatment sets deemed appropriate by the ranch decision makers to achieve their management objectives (Fig. 20.1) (Hamilton 1985b). Specifications for all treatments must be clearly expressed, and those responsible for applying the treatments must understand that the ultimate success depends upon following the plan. Specific areas to be treated must be accurately marked in the pastures as indicated on aerial photographs and plan maps. Equipment that will be used must be mechanically sound, adequately powered, properly equipped, and capable of installing treatments according to specifications.

Timing is very critical for many brush management practices, such as aerial spraying and prescribed burning, so arrangements must be made well in advance with ranch personnel and contractors to assure that the work will be performed as scheduled. Managerial personnel must be responsive to the results from treatment application. For example, they must make the necessary livestock movements to allow scheduled pasture deferments. Management personnel must take advantage of additional forage production by purchasing additional livestock so the enterprise can profit.

Accurate records of expenses should be kept, as well as dates when treatments were applied, and factors which might help explain treatment responses. Contingency plans should be developed to use in the event that uncontrollable factors, such as weather, prevent the scheduled application of a treatment. For example, if a planned prescribed burn for maintenance control of scattered pricklypear plants could not be applied during the planned year due to drought, then there should be an alternative plan of action, such as hand spraying the scattered pricklypear with 1% picloram sprays.

Monitoring

Monitoring is the process of making observations, gathering data, and keeping accurate records after implementation of the brush or weed management treatments has been initiated (Fig. 20.1) (Hamilton 1985*b*). Monitoring provides feedback that allows the manager or decision maker to evaluate progress and assess the effectiveness of applied treatments. Such feedback provides management with the basis for adjustments to the original plan of action, or, in some cases, may influence modification of the original objective. In the final analysis, monitoring activities should feed both biological and cost/income data into an economic assessment to calculate actual versus projected returns from the brush/weed management plan.

Records on livestock responses (calf or lamb weaning weights, calf or lamb crops, cow or ewe conception rates, wool production, steer gains, etc.), supplemental feed and other variable costs, sales, etc. will be used to assess the performance of treatments relative to pre-treatment records or to untreated management units. Wildlife surveys should be conducted and records should be kept on the numbers of animals harvested, their sizes, or other measures of quality for comparison with similar data collected prior to treatment or on similar untreated areas. Vegetation surveys should be conducted to record the effect of treatments on brush cover and density and on the herbaceous vegetation. Permanent photo points may be very helpful in recording vegetation changes that occur after treatment (McGinty and White 1998). The vegetation data provide important feedback that allows management to make appropriate changes in stocking rates or in the timing or sequencing of maintenance brush control treatments. This feedback (Fig. 20.1) also allows management to assess whether the treatments are meeting the objective relative to wildlife habitat qualities, and to make changes in the original plan if they are not. Records on labor and management requirements will show if the brush or weed management program reduced or increased these cost items. Finally, the records mentioned above can be used in a final economic analysis at the end of the planning horizon to determine if the brush or weed management plan and strategies have met the expected economic outcome.

Summary

With some exceptions, most of the plant species present on rangelands, even those viewed as weeds or brush, have potential value. However, many species of forbs, woody plants, and succulents are exceedingly aggressive and interfere with the goals and objectives of rangeland resource managers. Many attempts to control or manage brush and weeds on rangelands have been considered failures for a variety of reasons, but often because the user did not understand the cause of the problem and assumed a single treatment would be the solution. Many technological advances have been made in the arsenal of brush and weed management strategies, but that being said, this technology must be used following an organized plan or procedure in which a variety of brush or weed control strategies are coordinated by the user in an orderly fashion to result in a long-term, sustainable solution to the problem. Rangeland resource managers must be knowledgeable of the biology and ecology of their problem species, base their plant management strategies on ecologically sound principles, and recognize that proper livestock grazing management is critical to the long-term success of brush and weed control treatments.

A planning procedure has been presented to aid rangeland resource managers in developing successful, long-term brush or weed management systems or strategies. The first step in this planning process is to clearly identify the overall goal or objective for the ranch or management unit being considered. Flexibility, relative to this objective, should be maintained because the economic picture may change or it may be realized later in the planning or monitoring process that the original objective is not feasible because of inherent characteristics of the resources.

The second step in the planning process is to conduct a thorough inventory of the resources present on the ranch or management unit. This procedure documents the nature and characteristics of the brush and weed problems, the current health and carrying capacity of the rangeland, and the location of improvements such as fences, water, etc. If the inventory reveals that the original objective is feasible and that brush or weed management is needed to achieve that objective, then the next phase of the planning process is to select alternative initial (reclamation) and maintenance (follow-up) treatments for managing the brush or weed infestations identified as target species during the resource inventory. The habitat needs of important wildlife species should be carefully considered during this step in the planning process. Grazing management must be planned concomitant with the selection of alternative brush/weed management strategies in order to provide required pre-treatment and/or post-treatment grazing deferments. All treatments must be followed by proper grazing management in order to realize their maximum potential relative to improving the health of the rangeland, livestock performance, and wildlife production.

Economic criteria, such as partial budgeting, net present value, internal rate of return, etc. are then utilized to select treatments which would be most profitable and least risky, and those that are next best that could be used in a contingency plan. After this planning exercise is completed, the brush or weed management and grazing management plan must be properly executed or implemented according to the specifications, to the delineated target areas, and according to the planned schedule.

The final phase is to monitor the results so that the rangeland resource manager can evaluate progress and assess the effectiveness of the strategies and the overall integrated brush or weed management system. Monitoring provides feedback that may be the basis for making adjustments in the original plan of action, and in some cases in the original objective. The records compiled during the monitoring process can be used in an economic analysis at the end of the planning horizon to assess whether the management plan has met the expected economic outcome.

Literature Cited

Ansley, R. J., B. A. Kramp, J. A. Huddle, and T. R. Tunnell. 1997. Using fire for sculpting brush. Pages 99–108 *in* D. Rollins, D. N. Ueckert, and C. G. Brown, editors. Proceedings brush sculptors symposium. Texas Agricultural Extension Service, San Angelo.

Bach, J. P., and J. R. Conner. 1998. Economic analysis of brush control for increased water yield: the North Concho River example. Pages 209–17 *in* R. Jensen, editor. Proceedings 25th Water for Texas Conference "Water Planning Strategies for Senate Bill 1." Dec. 1–2, 1998, Austin. Texas Water Resources Institute, Texas A&M University System, College Station.

Baen, J. S. 1997. The growing importance and value implications of recreational hunting leases to agricultural land investors. Journal of Real Estate Research 14:399–414.

Bierschwale, P. 1997. Brush management and its effect on land value. Pages 118–19 *in* D. Rollins, D. N. Ueckert, and C. G. Brown, editors. Proceedings brush sculptors symposium. Texas Agricultural Extension Service, San Angelo.

Conner, J. R. 1985. Technology selection based on economic criteria. Pages 47–54 *in* C. J. Scifres, W. T. Hamilton, J. R. Conner, J. M. Inglis, G. A. Rasmussen, R. P. Smith, J. W. Stuth, and T. G. Welch, editors. Integrated brush management systems for South Texas: development and implementation. Texas Agricultural Experiment Station Bulletin B-1493.

———, and R. E. Whitson. 1997. Sculpting brush to enhance wildlife habitat: economic and financial considerations. Pages 120–23 *in* D. Rollins, D. N. Ueckert, and C. G. Brown, editors. Proceedings brush sculptors symposium. Texas Agricultural Extension Service, San Angelo.

DiTomaso, J. M. 2000. Invasive weeds in rangelands: species, impacts, and management. Weed Science 48:255–65.

Fulbright, T. E. 1997. Designing shrubland landscapes to optimize habitat for white-tailed deer. Pages 61–67 *in* D. Rollins, D. N. Ueckert, and C. G. Brown, editors. Proceedings brush sculptors symposium. Texas Agricultural Extension Service, San Angelo.

Guthrey, F. S., and D. Rollins. 1997. Sculpting brush for upland game birds. Pages 68–72 *in* D. Rollins, D. N. Ueckert, and C. G. Brown, editors. Proceedings brush sculptors symposium. Texas Agricultural Extension Service, San Angelo.

Hamilton, W. T. 1985*a*. Initiating IBMS. Pages 9–14 *in* C. J. Scifres, W. T. Hamilton, J. R. Conner, J. M. Inglis, G. A. Rasmussen, R. P. Smith, J. W. Stuth, and T. G. Welch, editors. Integrated brush management systems for South Texas: development and implementation. Texas Agricultural Experiment Station Bulletin B-1493.

———. 1985*b*. Applying and evaluating IBMS. Pages 55–58 *in* C. J. Scifres, W. T. Hamilton, J. R. Conner, J. M. Inglis, G. A. Rasmussen, R. P. Smith, J. W. Stuth, and T. G. Welch, editors. Integrated brush management systems for South Texas: development and implementation. Texas Agricultural Experiment Station Bulletin B-1493.

———, T. G. Welch, B. R. Myrick, B. G. Lyons, J. W. Stuth, and J. R. Conner. 1993. EXSEL: expert system for brush and weed control technology selection. Pages 391–98 *in* C. D. Heatwole, editor. Application of advanced information technologies: effective management of natural resources. American Society of Agricultural Engineers. St. Joseph, Michigan.

Hanselka, C. W., W. T. Hamilton, and J. R. Conner. 1996*a*. Integrated brush management systems (IBMS): strategies and economics. Texas Agricultural Extension Service Bulletin B-6041.

———, ———, and B. S. Rector. 1996*b*. Integrated brush management systems for Texas. Texas Agricultural Extension Service Leaflet L-5164.

———, B. J. Ragsdale, and B. Rector. 1990. Grazing systems for profitable ranching. Texas Agricultural Extension Service Leaflet L-2211.

Heitschmidt, R. K., and R. D. Pieper. 1983. Integrated brush control and grazing management. Pages 89–95 *in* K. C. McDaniel, editor. Proceedings brush management symposium. Society for Range Management, Denver, Colorado.

———, and C. A. Taylor, Jr. 1991. Livestock production. Pages 161–77 *in* R. K. Heitschmidt and J. W. Stuth, editors. Grazing management: an ecological perspective. Timber Press, Portland, Oregon.

Holechek, J. L. 1981. Brush control impacts on rangeland wildlife. Journal of Soil and Water Conservation 36:265–69.

Inglis, J. M. 1985. Wildlife management and IBMS. Pages 35–40 *in* C. J. Scifres, W. T. Hamilton, J. R. Conner, J. M. Inglis, G. A. Rasmussen, R. P. Smith, J. W. Stuth, and T. G. Welch, editors. Integrated brush management systems for South Texas: development and implementation. Texas Agricultural Experiment Station Bulletin B-1493.

Johnson, P., A. Gerbolini, D. Ethridge, C. Britton, and D. Ueckert. 1999. Economics of redberry juniper control in the Rolling Plains. Journal of Range Management 52:569–74.

Koerth, B. H. 1997. Factors to consider when sculpting brush: chemical methods. Pages 96–98 *in* D. Rollins, D. N. Ueckert, and C. G. Brown, editors. Proceedings brush sculptors symposium. Texas Agricultural Extension Service, San Angelo.

McGinty, A., J. F. Cadenhead, W. Hamilton, W. C. Hanselka, D. N. Ueckert, and S. G. Whisenant. 2000. Chemical weed and brush control suggestions for rangeland. Texas Agricultural Extension Service Bulletin B-1466.

———, and T. G. Welch. 1995. Brush control for small acreages. Texas Agricultural Extension Service Leaflet L-2227.

———, and L. D. White. 1994. Range condition: key to sustained ranch productivity. Texas Agricultural Extension Service Leaflet L-5024.

———, and ———. 1998. Range monitoring with photo points. Texas Agricultural Extension Service Leaflet L-5216.

Nelle, S. 1997. Brush as an integral component of wildlife habitat. Pages 3–7 *in* D. Rollins, D. N. Ueckert, and C. G. Brown, editors. Proceedings brush sculptors symposium. Texas Agricultural Extension Service, San Angelo.

Rhyne, M. Z. 1998. Optimization of wildlife and recreation earnings for private landowners. Thesis, Texas A&M University, Kingsville.

Richardson, C. L. 1990. Brush management effects on deer habitat. Texas Agricultural Extension Service Leaflet L-2347.

Rollins, D. 1997. Brush sculptors: an appreciation for brush. Pages 1–2 *in* D. Rollins, D. N. Ueckert, and C. G. Brown, editors. Proceedings brush sculptors symposium. Texas Agricultural Extension Service, San Angelo.

Scifres, C. J. 1980. Brush management principles and practices for Texas and the Southwest. Texas A&M University Press, College Station.

Scifres, C. J., W. T. Hamilton, J. R. Conner, J. M. Inglis, G. A. Rasmussen, R. P. Smith, J. W. Stuth, and T. G. Welch. 1985. Integrated brush management systems for South Texas: development and implementation. Texas Agricultural Experiment Station Bulletin B-1493.

———, ———, J. M. Inglis, and J. R. Conner. 1983. Development of integrated brush management systems (IBMS): decision-making processes. Pages 97–

104 *in* K. C. McDaniel, editor. Proceedings brush management symposium. Society for Range Management, Denver, Colorado.

SoRelle, J. A. 2000. Economic feasibility of redberry juniper control using individual plant treatments. Thesis. Texas Tech University, Lubbock.

Stuth, J. W., and C. J. Scifres. 1985. Integrating grazing management and brush management strategies. Pages 41–46 *in* C. J. Scifres, W. T. Hamilton, J. R. Conner, J. M. Inglis, G. A. Rasmussen, R. P. Smith, J. W. Stuth, and T. G. Welch, editors. Integrated brush management systems for South Texas: development and implementation. Texas Agricultural Experiment Station Bulletin B-1493.

Taylor, C. A., Jr. 1997. Biological management of brush. Pages 109–14 *in* D. Rollins, D. N. Ueckert, and C. G. Brown, editors. Proceedings brush sculptors symposium. Texas Agricultural Extension Service, San Angelo.

Valentine, J. F. 1971. Range developments and improvements. Brigham Young University Press, Provo, Utah.

Welch, T. G. 1991. Brush management methods. Texas Agricultural Extension Service Bulletin B-5004.

———, R. P. Smith, and G. A. Rasmussen. 1985. Brush management technologies. Pages 15–24 *in* C. J. Scifres, W. T. Hamilton, J. R. Conner, J. M. Inglis, G. A. Rasmussen, R. P. Smith, J. W. Stuth, and T. G. Welch, editors. Integrated brush management systems for South Texas: development and implementation. Texas Agricultural Experiment Station Bulletin B-1493.

Whisenant, S. G. 1997. An overview of brush sculpting principles. Pages 84–87 *in* D. Rollins, D. N. Ueckert, and C. G. Brown, editors. Proceedings brush sculptors symposium. Texas Agricultural Extension Service, San Angelo.

White, L. D., and A. McGinty. 1992. Stocking rate decisions—key to successful ranch management. Texas Agricultural Extension Service Bulletin B-5036.

Whitson, R. E., W. T. Hamilton, and C. J. Scifres. 1979. Techniques and considerations for improving honey mesquite-infested rangeland. Texas Agricultural Experiment Station Technical Report 79-1.

Wiedemann, H. T. 1997. Factors to consider when sculpting brush: mechanical treatment options. Pages 88–92 *in* D. Rollins, D. N. Ueckert, and C. G. Brown, editors. Proceedings brush sculptors symposium. Texas Agricultural Extension Service, San Angelo.

Index

Number Seven:
Texas A&M University
Agriculture Series
C. Allan Jones,
General Editor